Dr. George W. Anderson

Sams **Teach Yourself**

SAP

in **24** **Hours**

SAMS   800 East 96th Street, Indianapolis, Indiana, 46240 USA

Sams Teach Yourself SAP in 24 Hours

ISBN-13: 978-0-672-33542-6

ISBN-10: 0-672-33542-5

Library of Congress Cataloging-in-Publication Data is on file.

Printed in the United States of America

Second Printing November 2011

Trademarks

Warning and Disclaimer

Bulk Sales

Sams Publishing offers excellent discounts on this book when ordered in quantity for bulk purchases or special sales. For more information, please contact

U.S. Corporate and Government Sales
1-800-382-3419
corpsales@pearsontechgroup.com

For sales outside of the U.S., please contact

International Sales
international@pearsoned.com

Editor-in-Chief
Mark Taub

Signing Editor
Trina MacDonald

Development Editor
Sheri Cain

Managing Editor
Sandra Schroeder

Project Editor
Mandie Frank

Copy Editor
Keith Cline

Indexer
Lisa Stumpf

Proofreader
Christal White, Language Logistics, LLC

Technical Editor
A.J. Whalen

Publishing Coordinator
Olivia Basegio

Cover Designer
Gary Adair

Composition
Mark Shirar

Contents at a Glance

Table of Contents

About the Author

Dr. George W. Anderson and his family reside in Houston, Texas. An SAP consultant for 13 years and IT professional for 25, he has had the privilege of working on countless SAP implementations, upgrades, migrations, and other enterprise projects. George is a certified SAP Technical Consultant, SAP NetWeaver '04 OS/DB Migration Consultant, PMI PMP, MCSE, MBA, and recent PhD. He loves to write and share with others through books, journal articles, conference sessions, and more. At Microsoft, he provides thought leadership and strategic direction around next-generation platforms and architectures for SAP and other Line of Business (LOB) applications. He also holds a seat as one of several technical editors for the SAP Professional Journal. When not spending time with his family, friends, and extended church family, he enjoys blogging on Microsoft's TechNet site (http://www.blogs.technet.com/b/lobapps/), playing guitar, studying the Bible, trying new steakhouses, and hearing from his readers. Catch him at his best after midnight at george.anderson@microsoft.com.

Dedication

To my beautiful and encouraging wife Michelle, my three amazing kids, my friend Fazil Osman who worked with and inspired me to write my first SAP book, my friend Raymond Smith who helped me with this most recent book, and finally to all my little helpers (you know who you are!), this book is dedicated to you.

Acknowledgments

When I started my SAP career in 1997, I never would have dreamed I'd be where I am today. I've always been a hard worker, sure. But this book and everything else I've achieved really have little to do with me at all. My favorite book says I can do nothing worthwhile apart from God. On the other hand, I can do everything through the One who gives me strength. When I put my faith in these words a decade ago, my life changed. My successes multiplied, but they are His. My family grew larger and closer; they are a blessing from Him. And my work and hobbies evolved and converged in a way I never could have foreseen; they are an awesome gift from Him. So as I sit here thinking about who to acknowledge for making this book possible, I can't help but point to Jesus and say, "Thank You."

We Want to Hear from You!

As the reader of this book, you are our most important critic and commentator. We value your opinion and want to know what we're doing right, what we could do better, what areas you'd like to see us publish in, and any other words of wisdom you're willing to pass our way.

You can email or write me directly to let me know what you did or didn't like about this book—as well as what we can do to make our books stronger.

Please note that I cannot help you with technical problems related to the topic of this book, and that due to the high volume of mail I receive, I might not be able to reply to every message.

When you write, please be sure to include this book's title and author as well as your name and phone or email address. I will carefully review your comments and share them with the author and editors who worked on the book.

Email: mark.taub@pearson.com

Mail: Mark Taub
         Editor-In-Chief
         1330 Avenue of the Americas
         New York, NY 10019

Reader Services

Visit our website and register this book at www.informit.com/title/9780672335426 for convenient access to any updates, downloads, or errata that might be available for this book.

Introduction

When I was asked to update *Sams Teach Yourself SAP in 24 Hours*, I was completely thrilled. Seriously! The world of SAP and our world in general have gone through major upheavals in the last few years, and I was excited to share with SAPlings and veterans alike just how much had changed. In the same way, I was anxious to realign and simplify this book in the way that Danielle Larocca, the original Teach Yourself SAP author, had done. She did a magnificent job targeting business users and technical readers at the exclusion of everyone else you tend to find on an SAP project. I've tried to reapply some of that same focus here, which should also (not coincidentally) tackle some of the concerns my readers expressed. And, I wanted to address additional concerns vocalized by my readers related to consistency, eliminating repetition, providing better figures, and more. So thank you for picking up the latest and yes, best ever, edition of *Sams Teach Yourself SAP in 24 Hours*. I am confident you'll find it well worth your investment.

In the name of simplification, I have reorganized and revamped the material into five easy-to-consume sections. Part I naturally kicks off with an introduction to all the basics, followed by Part II, which covers SAP's business applications and components. In this way, the stage is set for us to explore SAP from a business user perspective (Part III) and then from an IT professional's perspective (Part IV). With all your newfound knowledge and focus, and in response to comments from many readers over the last five years, Part V concludes with an extensive section devoted to helping you develop a career in SAP.

Along the way, I cover what matters most to SAP newcomers. For the business users, I go beyond simply setting up access to SAP and customizing your user interface, and I walk you through actual business transactions. Together, we explore what it means to create sales orders, update employee personnel records, and more. I ground you in how SAP users are assigned roles and provided authorization to execute transactions related to those roles. We explore mega business processes like "Order to Cash" and how that breaks down into specific SAP business transactions. And we go into detailed reporting and query processes executed not only from SAP itself but through other commonly used business productivity tools like Microsoft SharePoint, Adobe Forms, and more. In this way, prospective SAP business users can really get a taste of a day-in-the-life-of an SAP end user.

For my technical readers, I've done something new and completely overdue. In the last five years, I've received no less than a hundred emails from newbies interested in installing a "demo" version of SAP. So yes, in this latest Teach Yourself SAP we briefly walk through not only a real technical installation together, step-by-step, but also locate and install SAP's very own freeware. In the past, SAP called this MiniSAP. Today it's simply called the Trial version of SAP. And it will significantly change how you apply what we learn together in these 400+ pages. For example, you should be able to walk away with the hands-on ability to fundamentally administer, tune, maintain, and monitor an SAP system just like SAP IT professionals do in the real world. Together we will also look at what it means to prepare for technical upgrades and manage an SAP project. And by covering SAP technology from several different perspectives including cutting edge insight related to SAP and cloud computing, more experienced technical readers will be even better positioned to make a difference at work.

In the end, you have only invested 24 hours inside the pages of this book, reading and walking through exercises. But armed with new insight and awareness, I bet you'll never look at SAP the same way again. You'll be that rare person who embodies a bit of business know-how as well as technical proficiency. You'll understand the basics of what it means to implement and run SAP. And you'll be on your way to transforming your part of the world.

Thank you again for adding this latest book to your library,

SAP?

SAP has come a long way since the first edition of this book was published in the 1990s. From a one-product company to a global software powerhouse creating a suite of applications and technologies used by the majority of big companies around the world, SAP's stable of contemporary business solutions is unparalleled. Even in the wake of economic meltdowns and global shifts in how technology is procured and deployed, the company and its products remain models of both evolution and revolution.

But what is SAP? Unlike familiar office desktop applications like Microsoft Word and Excel used by individuals to perform individual work, SAP's applications are business applications. These are used by individuals to run an entire firm's financial systems, manage warehouse and distribution facilities, figure out how to sell products faster, process payroll for the company, and more. It is this *company-wide* scope of SAP systems that makes them not only complex but critical today to businesses around the world. But these software systems cost millions of dollars and thousands of hours to implement and maintain, and they require knowledgeable technical teams and well-trained business users to get the most out of such an incredibly high investment. That's where this 4th edition of *Teach Yourself SAP in 24 Hours* will be useful, providing the fundamental knowledge needed by IT professionals and business users alike to understand, support, and begin to use SAP.

What's Covered

This book covers everything you need to become well acquainted with the core SAP products and components that are often collectively referred to simply as SAP. Though this is a beginner's book, it's provides the most well-rounded and current outlook on SAP today. As a career SAP professional, I've made sure this book reflects the real-world. I share what you *need* to know, understand, and do. This latest edition is more focused than earlier editions and targets the two largest audiences of those interested in learning about SAP: business users and IT professionals. Readers will appreciate how the book is arranged around these two very different types of skill sets and interests. And by providing an overview to each area coupled with actionable steps or guidance, this is the most useful and "teachable" *Teach Yourself SAP in 24 Hours* yet.

The book begins with the basics and by introducing terminology regarding SAP and its business applications, technology underpinnings, and project implementation considerations. From there begins the process of carefully building on your newfound knowledge to piece together the complex world of SAP. The pace of the book is designed to provide a solid foundation up front so you can grasp the more advanced topics covered in later hours. In this way, even a novice will quickly understand what it means to plan for, deploy, and use SAP. With this understanding, you'll also begin to appreciate the roles that so many people play with regard to an implementation project—how executive leadership, project management, business applications, technical deployment, and the application's business users all come together to create and use SAP end-to-end.

The first several chapters establish a better foundation than past editions, bringing readers up to speed before breaking matters down into areas targeted at business users or IT professionals. The book is also organized more clearly by chapter or "hour," making it even easier for readers interested in a particular subject area to quickly locate material most interesting to them. And like the previous edition, each chapter concludes with a real-world case study enabling readers to put their new-found knowledge to the test.

What's Really New

Beyond important structural changes and a clear focus on business users and IT professional, this latest edition of *Teach Yourself SAP in 24 Hours* includes much new content such as:

▶ Updates related to new products, capabilities, and terminology

▶ Coverage of hot technologies like Infrastructure as a Service (IaaS), Platform as a Service (PaaS), and Software as a Service (SaaS)

▶ An hour dedicated to cloud computing both from SAP's point of view and from the view of many SAP infrastructure partners and hosting providers

▶ An hour dedicated to SAP security fundamentals like roles and authorizations

▶ Coverage of easy access methods using SharePoint and Adobe

▶ Improved real-world SAP project implementation guidance

▶ Streamlined content related to systems management, monitoring, and tuning performed by thousands of SAP Basis professionals day in and day out

▶ Better and broader treatment related to career guidance

▶ An appendix containing SAP-specific acronyms and common terms

To give you a sense of how SAP businesses work with SAP at their desks every day, the book also includes real-world step-by-step instructions for running many common SAP business transactions. These are the same transactions or business processes tens of thousands of users around the world execute in the name of "running the business." Finally, I have also taken the liberty of pointing you not only to readily accessible resources on the Web but also back to previous editions of this book. My coauthors and I in the 2nd and 3rd editions, for example, provided some deep dives into areas that in hindsight were overkill for many but still hold much value even today for those of you interested in more detail. This has allowed me to eliminate some of the too-technical material in favor of greater and broader coverage aimed at true beginners.

Who Should Read This Book

This book is for people new to SAP as well as people interested in filling in some of their own SAP knowledge gaps. For example, reading SAP's perspectives on cloud computing outlined in Hour 19 or looking through some of the new underlying technologies mentioned throughout Hour 3, would probably be beneficial to even an experienced SAP professional. However, I have really focused this latest edition on new business users and technology professionals. Sure, if you're an executive or a Project Manager tasked with implementing or upgrading SAP, there's some good and easy-to-find guidance in these pages. Worst case, such a reader might go through Hours 1, 4, 5, and 15 and pass the book on to a novice business user or technical support professional. But the bulk of the material is geared toward business users and technology professionals with little to no knowledge of SAP and a desire to go beyond the introductory fluff floating across the Web.

All told, this latest edition of *Sams Teach Yourself SAP in 24 Hours* serves as an excellent way to jumpstart into SAP. From all of us at Sams, we hope you enjoy this read. More importantly, we hope this material helps gives you an opportunity to put what you've learned in the fourth edition of *Sams Teach Yourself SAP in 24 Hours* into action!

Conventions Used in This Book

Each hour starts with "What You'll Learn in This Hour," which includes a brief list of bulleted points highlighting the hour's contents. A summary concluding each hour provides a brief bit of insight reflecting what you as the reader should have learned along the way.

In each hour, any text that you type will appear as `bold monospace`, whereas text that appears on your screen is presented in `monospace` type.

`It will look like this to mimic the way text looks on your screen.`

Finally, the following icons introduce other pertinent information used in the book:

| By the Way presents interesting pieces of information related to the surrounding discussion. | **By the Way** |

| Did You Know? offers advice or teaches an easier way to do something. | **Did you Know?** |

| Watch Out! advises you about potential problems and helps you steer clear of disaster. | **Watch Out!** |

HOUR 1

SAP Explained

What You'll Learn in This Hour:

▶ An overview of the software company SAP

▶ SAP's business applications and industry solutions

▶ Components, modules, and transactions

▶ The SAP client concept

▶ What it means to run SAP

In this first hour, we set the stage by introducing the software company SAP and reviewing its history. Then we explore SAP's application legacy and unique collection of acronyms. In this way, we can begin to speak the same language. We wrap up the hour outlining SAP's current technologies and applications.

Overview of SAP: The Company

A beginner's guide to SAP is incomplete without a quick look at how the company evolved to its dominant leadership position today. Headquartered in Walldorf, Germany, SAP is the largest enterprise applications provider and one of the largest software companies worldwide. Although SAP and its enterprise competitors are all distinctly different from one another, they are markedly similar as well. Most provide enterprise-class business software, business intelligence and data warehousing solutions, software for small and medium-sized businesses, platforms for web and application development, integration software to tie computer systems together, various cloud computing offerings, and so on. Each competitor helps sustain SAP, too; SAP counts Oracle as its largest database vendor, for example, and Microsoft provides SAP's most popular operating systems in both the data center and in the office. IBM is SAP's largest consulting partner, and both Microsoft and IBM provide business intelligence solutions used by SAP's applications.

SAP was founded nearly 40 years ago in Mannheim, Germany, by a group of former IBM engineers with a singular vision: to develop a software package that married a company's diverse business functions together. The idea was to help companies replace 10 or 15 different business applications—such as financial systems (running accounts payables and receivables), warehousing applications, production planning solutions, plant maintenance systems, and so on—with a single integrated system. Even better, these former IBMers wanted to create a system that embodied all the best practices that various types of businesses and industries had to offer. In the process, it was envisioned that this new software package would minimize a great deal of complexity and provide businesses with more real-time computing capabilities. This vision became real when *Systems, Applications, and Products in Data Processing* (SAP), or in German *Systemanalyse und Programmentwicklung*, opened its doors in 1972. Those of us working in the SAP ecosystem have long referred to the company and its products interchangeably using a single word best spelled out as *S-A-P (ess aye pea)*, not *sap*.

SAP's goal from day one was to change the world, and the company continues to deliver on that goal today. Beyond their initial vision, the company's leaders created a multilingual and multinational platform capable of easily changing to accommodate new business process standards and techniques. Today, SAP is used by more than a million business users working for more than 100,000 customers across 120 countries. Its 50,000 employees and 2,000 SAP implementation and support partners are busy building and implementing software in 40 different languages and 50 currencies. Finally, all of these SAP business solutions are running on more than 20 different kinds of computing platforms.

To this last point, SAP revolutionized the technology foundation for enterprise applications. They purposefully broke away from the monolithic mainframe-based technology models prevalent in business applications in the 1960s and 1970s. Instead, SAP architected its software solutions to run on a variety of different hardware platforms, operating systems, and database releases. Through this flexibility and openness, SAP in turn gave its customers flexibility and choice. Such a revolutionary departure from the norm created a tipping point in enterprise business software development and delivery that helped propel SAP to the forefront of IT and business circles by the early 1990s. In less than 20 years after they opened their doors, SAP was not only Europe's top software vendor but was giving IBM and others a serious challenge in the enterprise marketplace.

New entrants to the enterprise software field also grew popular during the 1990s, including Baan, Oracle Corporation, PeopleSoft, and JD Edwards. Soon afterward, smaller players began gaining ground, as well, including Great Plains and Navision. Although still widespread, mainframe applications had simply grown too burdensome and expensive for many firms, and the enterprise software industry jumped at the chance to replace those aging legacy systems. IT organizations in companies around the world were just as anxious, finding it easier and cheaper to support a growing number of standardized hardware platforms.

In the same way that new enterprise software companies were gaining traction, new databases from vendors such as Oracle, Sybase, and Informix offered attractive alternatives to the old mainframe IMS and DB2 offerings. And new operating systems helped create low-cost mission-critical computing platforms for these new databases and applications. By the mid-1990s, when SAP began supporting the Microsoft Windows operating system and SQL Server databases, followed soon afterward by the Linux operating system, SAP's place in the enterprise software market was firmly planted—the company's founders had completely delivered on their vision of a multinational, multilingual business solution capable of running on diverse platforms operated and maintained by equally diverse IT organizations. SAP had not only grown into a multi-billion-dollar company by that time, but had indeed succeeded in changing the world.

SAP Business Applications or Components

From a business applications software perspective, SAP is nearly all things to nearly all businesses. SAP's application software foundation is built on the concepts of specialization and integration. Each software component or application within the SAP family of products and services meets a particular need, facilitating day-to-day financial and resource management (SAP *Enterprise Resource Planning*, or ERP), addressing product lifecycle planning requirements (SAP *Product Lifecycle Management*, or PLM), supporting internal company procurement (SAP *Supplier Relationship Management*, or SRM), interconnecting different systems to ease integration headaches (SAP NetWeaver *Process Integration*, or SAP NetWeaver PI), enabling customer relationship management (SAP *Customer Relationship Management*, or CRM), and so on. Divided by SAP into the SAP Business Suite (comprising all the business applications) and SAP NetWeaver (components of which essentially enable the SAP Business Suite, like a portal product, development tools, and business intelligence tools), all of these products and more are explained in subsequent hours of this book; suffice it to say here that there are many SAP applications or components, many products, and therefore many potential SAP solutions that can be assembled and customized for most any business.

SAP Components, Modules, and Transactions

Before we get too far along, it's important to understand the differences between SAP components, modules, and transactions. SAP uses the term *components* interchangeably with the term *business application*, and most of the time this latter term is shortened to *application*. On the other hand, SAP *modules* provide specific functionality within a component. The Finance module, Production Planning module, and the Materials Management module are good self-explanatory examples. These individual SAP modules combine to create the SAP ERP component. It is within a particular module that a company's business processes are configured and put together.

Business processes are also called *business scenarios*. A good example is order-to-cash. It comprises many different *transactions*, from writing up sales orders in the system to managing purchase requisitions and purchase orders, "picking" inventory to be sold, creating a delivery, and invoicing the customer for the order. Each transaction is like a step in a process (step one, step two, and so on). When all these transactions are executed in the right order, a business process like order-to-cash is completed. Many times, these transactions are all part of the same module. In other cases, a business process might require transactions to be run in several different modules, maybe even from several different components (see Figure 1.1).

FIGURE 1.1
SAP components are made up of modules, which in turn comprise transactions used to execute business processes.

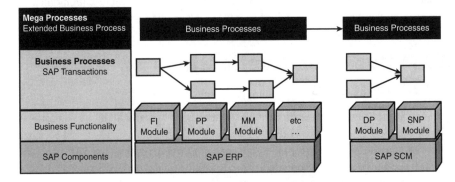

Cross-Application Business Processes

The fact that SAP's transactions can be combined helps create broad and capable platforms for conducting business. In this way, SAP allows companies to obtain greater visibility into their sales, supply chain, and manufacturing trends, or to allow new methods of entering or tracking such trends (to maximize revenue and profit) by extending business processes in several different directions. A good example again is order-to-cash, which is essentially a "back office" accounting process. By combining multiple SAP applications, a company can create a more capable extended version of this business process, something called a *cross-application process*, *mega process*, or *extended business process*.

Our simple order-to-cash process can become much more powerful in this way. For example, we might initiate our process through SAP's Enterprise Portal, which allows a broad base of a company's users or even its partners and suppliers to access the company's SAP system using a simple browser. Once in the system, the user might "punch through" to SAP ERP to actually place an order. Through the business logic enabled at the business process level, control might be passed to the SAP CRM application to determine a particular customer's buying preferences or history. CRM's business logic might then direct or influence the business process in a particular way, perhaps to help the salesperson increase the customer's order size or affect the order's gross margin.

Next, SAP's *Supply Chain Management* (SCM) system might be accessed to revise a supply chain planning process for a set of potential orders, looking to optimize profitability as the system seeks to balance the needs of many different customers with the organization's access to materials, people, and other resources. SAP NetWeaver Business Warehouse might next be queried to pull historical data related to the customer's credit history, financial terms, and sales patterns within a particular geography or during a particular season. After these details are analyzed, the extended business process might turn control over to SAP's Crystal Solutions to create company-internal reports. Simultaneously, SAP ERP or SAP NetWeaver Portal might be used to drive and track the pick-list process, order fulfillment and shipping process, and finally the accounts receivables processes to conclude the overall business process.

SAP Industry Solutions

Beyond enabling broad-based business processes, SAP is also well known for reflecting industry best practices in their software. By adopting SAP best practices rather than inventing their own, companies can more efficiently and effectively serve their customers, constituents, and other stakeholders. This is a big reason why SAP has been so successful: SAP stays abreast of many different industries, making it easy for companies in those industries to not only adopt SAP's software but that industry's best practices as well.

SAP's industry solutions were historically (and today are still loosely) divided into three areas: Manufacturing, Service Industries, and Financial/Public Services. There are actually 24 different groups of industries, such as Aerospace & Defense, Automotive, Banking, Chemicals, Consumer Products, Engineering, Construction, & Operations, Healthcare, Higher Education & Research, High Tech, Insurance, Media, Mill Products, Mining, Public Sector, Retail, Telecommunications, Utilities, and more. These groups in turn are represented by 40 specific industries. For the complete list, point your browser to www.sap.com/usa/sme/whysap/industries/index.epx or just search "SAP industry solutions" from your favorite search engine. One of the nice things about these industry solutions is that they are simply "installed" atop SAP's other products; the Oil & Gas industry solution, for example, is installed on top of SAP ERP.

Connecting the Dots

As touched on earlier, applications such as SAP ERP can be broken down into many different modules. A module's discrete functionality addresses a specific business function (which again is composed of many specific business transactions). Individually, each module is used to manage a business area or functional area for which a particular department may be responsible. Prior to extending a line of credit, for instance, a company's Accounts Receivables group may run a business transaction using the Finance module of SAP ERP to check a customer's credit and on-time payment history.

Likewise, the Shipping department will regularly run a business transaction in the Materials Management module to check inventories at a particular warehouse. Other departments may be responsible for managing payables, real estate, sales estimates, budgeting, and so on. Together, all the various departments in the company work together to do the business of the company, using SAP across the board. In this way, the company benefits from a great amount of consistency between departments while giving the company's management the high-level visibility it needs to make all the strategic decisions necessary to keep the business in good shape.

Do you see a common thread? SAP's products are used to satisfy the needs of enterprises, big and small, enabling them to tend to the business of running the business. SAP's software products are all about the "big picture"—about conducting business by connecting people, resources, and processes around the globe. SAP and its enterprise application competitors—Oracle, Microsoft, NetSuite, and several others—enable this capability on a grand scale, integrating many otherwise discrete functions under a single umbrella.

The SAP Client Concept

We need to look at one more concept before we think about what it means to actually run SAP. In the world of SAP, the term *client* has special meaning. Clients are essentially self-contained business entities or units within each SAP system; using a web browser or one of SAP's special user interfaces, you log in to a client in SAP to actually access and use the system. Each system—SAP ERP, CRM, SCM, and so on—has a unique system-specific client you log in to. Contemporary organizations thus have multiple production clients (one production client per SAP component). And each component contains several nonproduction clients, as well. These are used to develop and test the business functionality that will one day be put into the production client and handed over to the company's end users.

A client has its own separate master records and own set of "tables" (which we cover in detail in Hour 3, "SAP Technology Basics"). The best way to grasp this might be to think about a really large company like ExxonMobil, General Motors, or Honeywell. Within each of these large multinational organizations, for example, you might have three or more other companies or business units. Each SAP client might be tied to a different business unit; really big companies might have two or even three production clients for a single SAP component like ERP. For example, the company might structure its clients around discrete business groups (Chevrolet, Cadillac, and GMC) or by geography (Americas, Europe, and Asia). In this way, a Chevrolet business user might log in to the Chevy client to do her work, whereas business users over at Cadillac log in to the Caddy client on the same SAP system and do their work. In the end, the results can be easily rolled up so that the multinational organization as a whole can easily report on its cross-company financial status, inventory levels, and so on.

When you go to log in to SAP, you choose the specific client you want to log in to. Each one is assigned a unique three-digit number, which you are required to know and type in at login time. This makes it easy to distinguish between clients. A programmer developing the SAP system might log in to client 100 to do some programming, client 200 in another system to review and test new business logic, and client 500 in yet another system to check out the new training system where his code is being used to teach others how to use SAP. In the same way, an end user might log in to client 300 in the production system to do his day-to-day work and occasionally client 200 in a test system to check on the status of new functionality he requested be developed for production.

So just remember this: In the SAP world, the term *client* can mean several things, including an individual PC or workstation. For our purposes here, however, we try to use client in the manner used by SAP—to describe a logically discrete or separate business entity within an SAP system—and try to avoid using this term to describe PCs or workstations.

Running SAP

What does it mean to "run SAP?" Historically, to run SAP meant that the SAP application R/3 was installed and used by business users. For years, the SAP R/3 application was synonymous with SAP. They were one and the same, and to say you ran SAP was the same thing as saying you ran R/3. R/3 was SAP's first true client/server-based *online transaction processing* (OLTP) system—a system that by its very nature satisfied day-to-day transactional needs like you've read about this hour. Like its mainframe predecessor R/2, within R/3 was a number of business modules, such as Finance, Logistics, Human Resource Management, Warehouse Management, and more. SAP ERP is the successor to R/3.

So today when you hear people say they are running SAP, be sure to ask them what that really means in their specific case—with so many different products and solutions out there bearing the SAP label, it's not a good idea to assume anything. Sure, SAP's most popular product remains ERP. However, a lot of older SAP R/3 systems are still running, and even more SAP SCM, CRM, PLM, and SRM systems are out there.

Summary

This hour introduced you to the world of SAP. You gained an understanding of SAP's history and some of the specific business application and technology terms used in the world of SAP. (Until you become more comfortable with SAP's vernacular, feel free to turn to Appendix B, "SAP Acronyms and Common Terms," for quick reminders). When all is said and done, remember that the real work done by SAP is done by its components or applications; this has little to do with technology, but rather involves business processes that have been specifically configured for a company. Business processes are often industry-unique. Fortunately, SAP's large number of industry solutions helps companies implement industry best practices. Also keep in mind that business processes are nothing more than individual SAP business transactions strung together to get the actual work done of running a business. Transactions are associated with specific modules, but business processes may consist of transactions from different modules. Cross-application or mega business processes consist of transactions spanning multiple modules and even multiple SAP components. We are now ready to turn our attention in Hour 2, "SAP Business Basics," to the core business fundamentals behind SAP. First, though, let's take a look at the following case study.

Case Study: Hour 1

This case study winds its way through each hour and is designed to help you review and synthesize what you have learned and to help you to think ahead as you seek to put your knowledge into practice. You can find the answers posed by the questions related to this case study in Appendix A, "Case Study Answers."

Situation

MNC Inc., or simply MNC, is a large multinational mining and manufacturing company with operations in 20 countries. Its customers are located around the world. Although MNC is a fictional amalgamation of many real-world companies that use SAP, the challenges it faces are relevant to those faced by contemporary organizations today. Ongoing financial transparency issues, lack of supply chain visibility, and recent concerns with falling worldwide sales and lost market opportunities have re-emphasized to the MNC executive board its need to replace its collection of old business systems with a single well-integrated business application. The board is particularly concerned with the firm's requirement to address multiple languages and currencies; with 100,000 Microsoft Windows-based users spread out across 500 different offices and other sites, the board is also concerned with how it can possibly connect its diverse user community to a single application. By walking the board through the following questions, your task is to help the MNC leadership team understand SAP's capabilities and how the firm should proceed.

Questions

1. Outside of SAP, which enterprise software companies should MNC also consider investigating?

2. Which SAP components or products would the board be most interested in first learning about?

3. Does SAP offer an industry solution that might prove especially useful to MNC? Explain.

4. Given the great number of employees (and therefore potential SAP end users) that MNC employs, what are some key technology infrastructure considerations the board should address early on?

5. Will language and currency support issues be a problem for SAP?

HOUR 2

SAP Business Basics

What You'll Learn in This Hour:

- ▶ The business roadmap
- ▶ Business architecture and blueprinting
- ▶ Mapping business needs to SAP applications
- ▶ Four perspectives to addressing business needs
- ▶ How SAP technologies support business needs

Though SAP provides a number of applications and underlying technologies to meet a company's business needs, those needs or business requirements must first be understood and then mapped to software applications. Discovering, defining, and mapping needs back to a company's business vision and forward to an application strategy is the subject of business architecture. A roadmap may then be created to help the organization navigate this process. In this hour, we explore the basics of business architecture and developing a business roadmap. You'll see firsthand how business requirements connect an organization's vision and its people to the business applications they ultimately use to run and transform the business.

Business Architecture and the Business Roadmap

Before we can talk about SAP's applications and technologies, we need to understand the purpose and role of business architecture in general and the business roadmap in particular. Business architecture represents the highest level of abstraction, where the company's business vision is deconstructed into required business functions. When these business requirements are understood, they can be translated into a set of fundamental business processes (or *workstreams*), which in turn are married to more specific business functionality (like creating purchase orders or managing the new-hire process) that SAP and other applications provide.

Sometimes business architecture is described as addressing the high-level who, what, where, and when questions. The business roadmap, on the other hand, is the tool used to bring all this together into a logical process. It maps the people who will eventually use SAP itself or SAP's data and reports to the business applications that provide the data and reports. During a new implementation, the business roadmap helps an organization stay on course. Later, after SAP has been installed and is being used, tools and process-es similar to the business roadmap help the organization navigate necessary changes to how they conduct business.

Like building a house without plans, a company can never achieve its long-term vision or effectively take care of its day-to-day business needs without a good business roadmap. The business roadmap takes the outputs of strategic vision and business archi-tecture to describe the company's business requirements, business functions, and appli-cations that provide that functionality. Another way to look at this is that the roadmap shows how specific business functionality is ultimately delivered to meet a company's business requirements and fulfill its vision (see Figure 2.1). In doing so, the business roadmap takes the first steps in making technology relevant to business operations; it synthesizes business matters into what eventually becomes an SAP-derived technology-enabled *business solution*. In this way, SAP's applications and underlying technologies simply represent the tools used by the business arrive at the roadmap's destination.

FIGURE 2.1
The business roadmap con-nects vision and strategy with SAP appli-cations used to run the busi-ness.

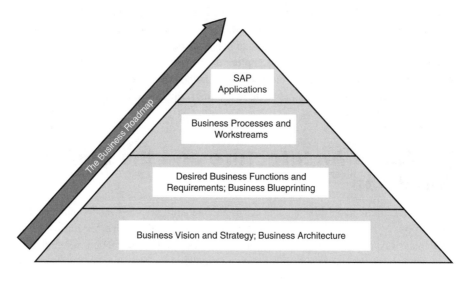

Traditional Business Concerns

Businesses provide goods or services. Many of these businesses exist to create value on behalf of the company and its owners in the form of profit, stockholder value, and the like. Other types of firms like nonprofits and charitable organizations are in business to serve a socially desirable purpose such as feeding hungry children or taking care of the needy. Regardless of their purpose, however, if a business cannot recoup its costs, it fails.

At the core of business architecture, and indeed business, is what the business does (what it sells or provides). Auto companies sell cars, oil companies sell oil, and charitable organizations provide good and services to those who want them. How *well* a company performs its service is another matter entirely, though. Many different dimensions come into play, from financial aspects to matters of sales, marketing, supply chain/logistics, product lifecycle management, payroll, and so on. All these dimensions boil down to two simple tenets: maximizing revenue (or sales) and minimizing expenses (or costs), as explored next.

SAP's Real Purpose and Impact

At the end of the day, SAP applications are used to run the business. But a closer look reveals how SAP also affects financial fundamentals; a well-implemented SAP business solution helps organizations increase their top-line revenue and shave their bottom-line expenses. For example, from a revenue perspective, SAP helps

- ▶ Identify and manage new markets (via SAP Customer Relationship Management, Business Warehouse, and Business Intelligence)

- ▶ Innovate in terms of products and services to address new markets (via SAP Composite Applications, Product Lifecycle Management, and Customer Relationship Management)

- ▶ Improve a company's relationship with its existing customers to sell more goods per customer, establish a deeper sales relationship, or gain a "greater share of wallet" (via SAP Customer Relationship Management, Business Intelligence, and Enterprise Resource Planning)

In the same way, SAP enables cost reductions as it helps

- ▶ Increase business operations efficiency by streamlining business processes, maximizing asset productivity, minimizing unproductive time, and so on (via SAP Enterprise Resource Planning)

- ▶ Reduce a company's cost of raw materials through vertical consolidation (via SAP Supply Chain Management)

- ▶ Reduce a company's cost of goods, materials, labor, and more through increased visibility and business process transparency (via SAP Supply Chain Management and Enterprise Resource Planning)

- ▶ Reduce costs of internal operations (via SAP Supplier Relationship Management)

- ▶ Maximize inventory and supplier discounts (via SAP Enterprise Resource Planning)

- ▶ Reengineer a company's service delivery processes (via SAP Enterprise Resource Planning)

- ▶ Reduce the company's "cost of change" by more quickly identifying opportunities to improve its cost model and optimize inefficient processes (via SAP Business Warehouse and Business Intelligence)

- ▶ Enhance how the company manages, delivers, optimizes, tracks, and improves on its products and services—or the processes used to drive its products and services (via SAP Enterprise Resource Planning)

Companies that increase sales while reducing costs realize greater business success than their industry counterparts, but companies that can better manage the risks of change have any even better shot at beating the competition.

Managing and Mitigating Risk

With every change introduced into the business comes the opportunity to make minor missteps and major blunders. To counter the negative impact inherent to such errors (in judgment, leadership, product marketing, sales strategies, partnerships, alliances, and more), a smart organization proactively identifies, manages, and mitigates risks. This applies to efforts aimed at increasing revenue *or* decreasing costs.

Contingency plans are especially important. An SAP implementation is so far-reaching and subsequently so complex that falling back to Plan B, Plan C, (and maybe D and more!) are to be expected. Knowing and preparing for changes to Plan A makes the difference between a successful business solution and a business solution that simply cannot deliver the transformation promised by SAP in the first place. Successfully developing and executing against this kind of deployment mindset brings up another dimension of business architecture and the SAP business roadmap in particular: business agility (covered next).

Business Agility: Keeping the Future in Mind

Business agility speaks to a firm's ability to transform its products, services, supply chain, sales strategy, IT underpinnings, and so on in such a way as to more nimbly meet customer demand. Agility isn't so much about the present than as about the unknown future; an agile organization beats its less agile competition because it can more quickly close the gap between present-day capabilities and needs and desired capabilities and needs. A good business roadmap, therefore, must reflect matters of business agility that enable an organization to work more efficiently, more quickly, more nimbly, and more effectively. These in turn need to be mapped to enabling SAP applications and technologies.

Increasing business agility is easier said than done. *To change* means to fight the inertia behind "the way things have always been done." *Fighting inertia* means changing how people and organizations work and how business processes are handled; the status quo might be markedly affected. As too many firms find out the hard way, maintaining the status quo is no way to run a business. Indeed, implementing SAP is often seen as a way of disrupting the status quo and reinventing how the work of running the business is optimized, divided, and addressed. Optimization is probably the key because in the end decision making is streamlined, resulting in

- ▶ Better and faster customer relationship management

- ▶ More-effective and less-expensive supply chain management

- ▶ Increased transparency and compliance with regulations

- ▶ Improved cost versus risk metrics and outcomes

- ▶ Measurable business-enabling *return on investment* (ROI)

Only a well-developed business-enabling roadmap has a chance of transforming the business through increased revenue or decreased costs. But it's the next step that's most crucial. If business architecture and strategy is our house's foundation, the actual SAP business process development process, described by SAP as "business blueprinting," is our house's framing.

ASAP and Business Blueprinting

Business blueprinting entails defining a firm's to-be business processes, identifying gaps between the current state and this to-be state, determining how well SAP's templates can be applied, identifying and prioritizing the need for customizations to these templates, and then locking down the scope of work necessary to make all this happen. Organizational matters come into play, as do the organization's original goals (and making revisions to those goals as business realities dictate). In short, business blueprinting serves as the culmination of the initial roadmap development work.

SAP calls out this process of blueprinting in its *Accelerated SAP* (ASAP) project implementation methodology. Blueprinting follows a number of tasks related to project preparation. When blueprinting is completed, each SAP application is specifically configured to turn the envisioned business processes into real-life usable workstreams made up of strings of customized customer-unique business transactions. This phase of ASAP, called *realization*, consumes most of the project's time and budget. (Several iterations of functional, integration, and other types of testing consume a whole lot of time, people, and other resources.) Once realization is completed, final preparation, go-live support, and running SAP post go-live round out the ASAP project lifecycle methodology. ASAP and other matters of project management methodology are covered in more detail in Hour 4, "SAP Project Basics," and Hour 15, "A Project Manager's Perspective on Implementing SAP."

The Business Perspective

As already noted, developing a sound business perspective is a critical first step in solving a business problem or tending to a business need. The business perspective articulates *why* a particular problem needs to be solved or an opportunity explored. Developing a firm's unique business perspective mandates addressing the following:

- The identification of business-relevant stakeholders

- Long-term strategy enablement

- Short-term business objectives

- Core competencies

- Competencies other than the core competencies (and thus opportunities for partnering, developing alliances, or contracting out specific services)

- Procurement and other sourcing strategies (and how those strategies and relationships might change over time)

- SAP globalization and localization realities (where the emphasis tends to shift back and forth between enabling global consistency and roll-up financial reporting, for example, along with addressing the currency and language requirements for local user communities)

The most relevant stakeholders at this level are those involved in strategically aligning and executing the actual business processes or workstreams necessary for survival. Therefore, business executives and other officers of the board, along with functional managers and team leads, business analysts, and any other line-of-business leaders must be included in developing and communicating the business view.

How SAP Technologies Support Business Needs

With the business perspective behind us, the next several tasks of business blueprinting can be addressed. Matters such as developing the underlying architecture and designing the IT platform need to be considered and completed. In this way, the business roadmap will actually align to business goals predicated on responding in an agile manner to changing markets, new business needs, increased governance, and so on—all of which requires an agile technology platform. Technology basics are detailed in Hour 3, "SAP Technology Basics," which in turn sets the stage for developing the technology roadmap detailed in Hour 16, "A Basis Professional's Perspective on SAP."

Working with Stakeholders

Building a business roadmap is impossible without understanding the various stakeholders and their particular perspectives. Therefore, a quick look at stakeholders is warranted. In general, stakeholders are those who are most affected by the problems or concerns of an organization and therefore have significant interest in some aspects of a proposed solution. They can represent the entire company (such as the board of directors) or a just a few people within a particular team or specific function (such as IT, the finance group, or the sales and marketing team).

By directly engaging stakeholders and extracting their priorities and concerns *initially as well as over the course of an implementation*, the SAP Project Sponsor along with the SAP Project Manager may together effectively plan and execute a successful project. In this way, because the right people are involved from the onset and given a "voice" throughout, the project will more likely solve the problems outlined in the first place.

There is no one best way to engage stakeholders. Common methods include kick-off and regularly scheduled follow-up meetings, function-specific workshops, and executive milestone or status meetings. Regular email updates reflecting changes in the project plan, scope, resources, and so on might be appropriate, as well. Frequency of communication tends to be more important than the actual length of time spent providing updates.

It's also important to give stakeholders access at some level to the repositories of data used to track and maintain all the business, functional, project management, and technical decisions made, problems resolved, contact information, and similar such details. By being completely transparent and ensuring stakeholders feel recognized and "in the know," a project team has a much better chance of building and *maintaining* the critical buy-in necessary to successfully pursue and complete a complex implementation such as SAP.

As we conclude our discussion about business blueprinting, you've no doubt noticed how business blueprinting views SAP strictly from a business perspective. This is only one of four dimensions of an SAP implementation, however. The three remaining dimensions are functional, technical, and project implementation. Each of these perspectives is detailed in the next few pages.

Other Perspectives: Mapping Business Needs to SAP Applications

Because of the variety of stakeholders involved in implementing, using, and supporting SAP, a single perspective can never resonate completely with everyone. Few people have the breadth of experience necessary to grasp all the complexities of implementing SAP or other complex business solutions. Therefore, other views into how these business solutions are developed, managed, and enhanced over time can prove helpful. Functional, technical, and project implementation perspectives are all effective views in this regard. For IT stakeholders, a perspective into a business solution's business dimensions, functional requirements, and project perspectives will help fill in their knowledge gaps. In the same way, a functional perspective followed by a more technical view, both of which are supported by an end-to-end project implementation perspective, allows nearly any stakeholder to envision a business solution in its entirety, as discussed next.

The Functional Perspective

The functional perspective is the easiest to grasp for individuals familiar with how to run a business. It is the most difficult to grasp for nonfunctional experts, however. This perspective addresses the *what* surrounding a solution. Not how, or when, or with what, but simply what. It answers the question "What will a particular business process do?" In this way, the functional perspective or view addresses the following:

▶ It describes or communicates the flow of work (business process workflows or workstreams) in a stepwise fashion. The functional perspective asks what steps are necessary to execute a business process and thereby achieve a particular end state.

▶ It describes the properties or qualities to be exhibited by the business process. Thus, the functional perspective seeks to identify the characteristics and properties that each business process must reflect and to what degree these are reflected.

▶ It addresses these matters of workflows and characteristics from technology-independent and SAP-independent perspectives; a good functional perspective doesn't even mention SAP because it's simply not dependent on a particular application vendor's solutions.

As you can imagine, the key stakeholders for such a view are the end users who will ultimately execute the business process as part of their daily work. Business process designers, line-of-business leaders, and others involved with the functionality to be embodied by the solution are important stakeholders, too.

The Technical Perspective

The technical perspective or view addresses the *how* part of the solution equation. It gives legs to the functional view in that the technical perspective describes how the business solution will be enabled through technology. Important considerations include the following:

▶ Focusing on the key dimensions of the system; identifying and then establishing how the system will deliver the performance, availability, scalability, security, agility, systems manageability, and so on required by the business.

▶ Describing the solution's overall components in terms of business applications and other SAP components, data and relevant dependencies, interface requirements, underlying technical infrastructure, and all the underlying relationships and integration points necessary to enable the functional perspective described earlier.

▶ Providing to the extent possible a technology-independent perspective as to how technology helps enable the functional perspective.

Primary technical perspective stakeholders include enterprise and technical architects, solution developers and programmers, infrastructure and other technology specialists, and other technology-focused suppliers, vendors, and partners. Business architects also typically find this view useful.

The Project Implementation Perspective

The project implementation perspective is simple to comprehend. It answers the questions *with what* shall the solution be built, over what time period, leveraging what resources. This implementation-specific view accomplishes the following:

▶ Describes and details the deployment plan, which in turn encompasses organizational and third-party resources, timelines, constraints (business, functional, technical, and other), and so on.

▶ Describes the SAP products and components to be used to fulfill the company's strategic vision and tactical functional needs, including to the extent these needs are fully developed and delivered.

Common implementation view stakeholders are project managers and coordinators, technical specialists, developers/programmers, testers, business process owners, executives, business leaders, power users, and more.

There's often a strong temptation to align specific views with certain disciplines or areas of expertise. Perhaps most obviously, the business and functional views might be lumped into business concerns, whereas the technical view might be seen as an "IT" thing and the implementation view as a "project management" thing. Avoid creating these silos and instead remember that a successful SAP implementation depends on the company and its partners working well together. Break down the walls, build teams that cross boundaries, and give all teams a distinct voice in the overall implementation. The results should speak for themselves.

Combining the Four Perspectives

The four perspectives described this hour work to marry together a business solution's purpose (why), its functions (what), its technical underpinnings (how), and its implementation details (with what). Breaking a solution down into these perspectives allows a firm to communicate across business and technology boundaries.

You probably noticed, however, that references to specific SAP products and components were lacking in this hour. There's good reason for this: A solid business roadmap should be developed well before a specific ERP solution is decided on. Like putting the cart before the horse, planning a roadmap based on the business solutions offered by a particular software vendor (SAP included) makes no sense at all. Figure out what the business needs to accomplish first and then determine how SAP and other vendors in the application solution space might best address those needs. In the succeeding hours, we cover the SAP-specific details necessary to move from conceptual roadmaps to firm implementation plans, technology platforms, and functional business solutions.

Summary

The concepts outlined in this hour prepared you to develop a high-level business roadmap. When you better understand SAP's applications and technologies, you'll be positioned to actually marry a company's business vision and needs with SAP's applications and thus create the underpinnings of an SAP-derived business solution. Before such a marriage is possible, however, the business's strategic and more-immediate business needs must be identified, prioritized, and communicated. This includes goals and requirements related to increasing revenue, decreasing costs, and managing the risk of change. We also discussed the importance of facilitating business agility, the company's ability to nimbly transform itself in response to changing business drivers and operational realities. Finally, we investigated the four high-level perspectives or dimensions by which a business problem may be viewed: business, functional, technical, and project implementation.

Case Study: Hour 2

Consider the following case study and questions related to developing a business roadmap for SAP. You can find the answers posed by the questions related to this case study in Appendix A, "Case Study Answers."

Situation

In a benchmark of its competitors, MNC has found it seriously lags behind in several areas. MNC's customer base does less repeat buying, tends to exhibit less product loyalty, and costs more to service than similar customer-competitor relationships. Further, the business landscape is clearly evolving to one favoring a more direct sales model for MNC's commodity goods. Opportunities for growth capable of outpacing the competition seem reasonable, so MNC's board of directors is encouraged more than ever to pursue its tentative *enterprise resource planning* (ERP) implementation plans. To that end, you have been selected to join a task force to identify important startup concerns. Using the knowledge you gained this hour, answer the following questions.

Questions

1. *Given the early and tentative nature of this ERP project, is it safe to assume SAP will be selected?*

2. *To help the team align, you have suggested reviewing MNC's partially completed business roadmap. What four high-level areas do you expect to find called out in this roadmap?*

3. *Which primary tenet of business aligns best with MNC's problem of a lack of repeat buyers?*

4. *What four perspectives or views should the task force explore?*

5. *Which perspective addresses the "what" surrounding a business solution?*

6. *What does the technical perspective specifically address?*

HOUR 3

SAP Technology Basics

What You'll Learn in This Hour:

- ▶ Technology architecture
- ▶ SAP Basis
- ▶ Hardware server and disk basics
- ▶ Operating system considerations
- ▶ Database considerations
- ▶ Traditional and contemporary infrastructure providers

Now that we've covered the basics of SAP and what it means to run a business using SAP, we need to spend some time discussing the basic technologies "under the covers." In this hour, we investigate several commonly used infrastructure-related technical terms and take an introductory look at the three core technologies necessary to support any SAP application: hardware, operating systems, and databases. We conclude the hour with a discussion about how these technologies are appropriated. Even if you have a strong technology background, this hour is probably worth your time.

SAP Technology 101: SAP Basis

In Hour 2, "SAP Business Basics," we covered the concept of business architecture. Now let's turn our attention to technology architecture. Whereas business architecture covers logical business processes and workstreams, technology architecture is about the technologies under the covers used to support business processes. It describes in a vendor-independent way the technologies that need to come together to do something useful. In our case, hardware, operating systems, databases, and application-specific technologies come together to create a foundation for a business application. When the application atop this foundation is SAP, we call this layered combination of technologies *SAP Basis*.

More generically, we often refer to this "stack" of technologies as the *SAP computing platform*, *solution stack*, or *technology stack*. These interchangeable terms speak to the layers of technology that combine to create the *basis* of an SAP system. Similar to building a house, the technology underneath SAP is like the foundation to the house. An improperly built foundation weakens the ability of your SAP system to weather storms, survive changing business needs, and meet the expectations of its occupants (the SAP end-user community).

We can extend the concept of technology architecture to include more than just SAP's foundation. Client devices like laptops, tablets, smartphones, and traditional PCs and printers play a key role in technology architecture. So does all the network infrastructure tying everything together—the wireless hot spots and routers and even old-school modems used to connect all our "front-end" client devices with the "back-end" SAP application. These front-end technology specifics are covered in later hours. For now, let's focus on the core foundation underneath SAP, starting with server and disk hardware.

SAP Hardware Basics

Hardware is the most basic component of an SAP system. Hardware comprises the servers (big and powerful computers), disk storage systems (ranging from storage area networks or network-attached storage to cloud-based virtualized storage space), and network gear (such as routers, network switches, and security firewalls). All this hardware must work together to create an effective infrastructure for SAP. Improperly addressing technology architecture or simply skimping on a piece of hardware might create a weak link or potential point of failure that in turn might cause problems down the road. For this reason, proper hardware architecture and design (what SAP terms *sizing*) is absolutely critical.

All the major hardware vendors sell systems that fit all types of SAP application needs, big and small. Choosing a hardware partner simply based on name recognition is a good place to start. HP, IBM, and to a lesser extent Oracle are well-known providers of physical hardware you can unbox, rack, and set up yourself in your datacenter. However, things are changing, and the way you procure a hardware platform today can be much different from only a few years ago. For example, well-known names such as Amazon, Microsoft, and Cisco can sell you virtualized server platforms for SAP. Sure, hardware is still under the covers, but it's sitting out in someone else's datacenter. This virtualized hardware, called *Infrastructure as a Service* (IaaS) or *cloud infrastructure*, represents an interesting and cost-effective method of providing the technical foundation for SAP. Many other IaaS cloud providers are jumping on this bandwagon, as well, adding to an already complicated ecosystem of technology architecture methods and practices.

We cover IaaS and other cloud delivery methods later in Hour 19, "SAP and the Cloud." For now, keep in mind that any proposed hardware solutions, regardless of source, need to be vetted against one another, against a SAP shop's risk profile, and ultimately against the kinds of workloads reflected by SAP. After all, not all clouds are mature enough or even capable of supporting mission critical SAP workloads, and not all SAP workloads are actually critical to business operations.

Servers

Whether your SAP server hardware is physically installed and running in your own datacenter or hosted by a traditional outsourcing provider or more contemporary cloud provider, servers are still often classified by cost and performance categories. Interestingly, these categories overlap a whole lot nowadays. The industry continues to refer to servers as small, medium, and large (see Figure 3.1), both in terms of physical size and in terms of "horsepower" (measured in SAPS, as discussed in the section "SAPS Benchmark"). Blurring the lines between small, medium, and large, typical small servers today can host SAP workloads that were considered quite large just a few years ago.

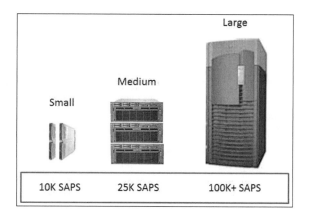

FIGURE 3.1
Servers for SAP come in a variety of sizes, configurations, and horsepower.

Depending on size and configuration, if you go online and purchase an HP server, the one-time cost could range from a few thousand dollars to several million (not including follow-on annual maintenance, which also adds up). The same server computing power hosted in the cloud, on the other hand, can cost pennies to several hundred dollars an hour depending on the cloud vendor. And the costs become a pay-as-you-go proposition, changing one-time *capital expenditures* (CAPEX) into recurring *operational expenditures* (OPEX). This can be an attractive change to the bean counters.

Server and other SAP infrastructure costs can vary significantly, but companies have at their disposal various financial methods to calculate which approach is best for them. But how can you compare the kind of workload different servers running different operating systems and databases can support (for example, the computing platform's horsepower)? For servers, horsepower equates to the combination of many factors. Beyond the myriad operating system and database differences, the number and speed of CPUs and underlying processor cores, the amount of memory in each server, the server's system bus characteristics, and a host of other internal server architecture specifics come into play. A simple comparison is nearly impossible. Fortunately, SAP gave us a standard unit of measurement for workloads: the SAPS benchmark.

SAPS Benchmark

The *SAP Application Performance Standard* (SAPS) compares SAP-benchmarked computing platforms with one another. A standard unit of measurement similar to the more generic tpmC performance ratings provided by the *Transaction Processing Council* (TPC), the SAPS unit of measurement is based on the *Sales and Distribution* (SD) module of SAP *Enterprise Resource Processing* (ERP) and is the most popular SAP benchmark. One hundred SAPS is defined as 2,000 fully processed end-to-end orders per hour (with each order consisting of five line items being sold). The SD business process driving this benchmark is made up of six different SD transactions. In the end, those 2,000 orders equate to 6,000 screen changes (ranging from creating the order to displaying it, creating an invoice, and more)!

Think for a moment about the value of SAPS. With a standard unit of measurement, you can compare vastly different computing platforms against one another in an apples-to-apples kind of way. Assuming all the hardware vendors benchmark their different servers running various operating systems and databases, you can rest assured that a particular platform's horsepower is comparable to another. For example, you can compare the SAPS supported by an HP server running Windows and SQL Server against a similarly configured HP server running Linux and Oracle, in turn against an IBM p-series running AIX and DB2. By leveling the playing field, you can mitigate the risks associated with SAP performance and focus instead on availability strategies, total cost of ownership, and strategic partnering or consolidation initiatives. And for servers that might have not been benchmarked, you can work with the hardware vendor's SAP Competency Center to calculate the rough number of SAPS that platform would support.

To see how useful all this information can be, point your browser to www.sap.com/solutions/benchmark/sd2tier.epx. The two-tiered benchmark is most common (as it's not as cost prohibitive to the hardware vendors to run this benchmark). By way of example, click the *SAPS* column to sort all the results (there are literally hundreds and hundreds). Page down until you get to the point where you can compare all the various server models and configurations capable of hosting 50,000 SAPS. You'll quickly find that although not all hardware, operating system, and database combinations are represented, there are quite a few results to review from many different vendors. Of particular interest, note how well the latest 4P/32C (four processors, eight cores per processor) Intel platforms compare against behemoth 32P and larger servers from only a few years ago!

Server Hardware Vendors

Regardless of whether your servers are virtualized, hosted by a third party like Computer Sciences Corp or my personal favorite, Freudenberg IT, or installed in your own datacenter, the physical servers themselves are manufactured by relatively few hardware vendors. The best-known vendors Fujitsu, HP, IBM, Oracle, and Unisys sell servers based on Intel, AMD, and often their own proprietary CPUs. IBM is a good example. They have a strong line of industry standard servers (x-series) that compete alongside their proprietary PowerPC-based servers (p-series) and even older legacy platforms (i-series and z-series). HP and Oracle offer similar variety.

Low-cost CPUs from Intel and AMD (often referred to generically as *commodity* or *x86* or *x64* platforms) make up the biggest chunk in this market. Commodity server sizes continue to provide IT departments with choice—from dense blade servers to slim-line "pizza box" designs to more traditional rack-mount and standalone big-box designs. And they grow faster and faster every year. Even as these commodity servers continue to improve in price/performance, the hardware providers continue to develop new high-availability, virtualization, and other technology solutions that help put these servers on more of an equal footing with their proprietary, historically more capable, and certainly more expensive counterparts.

Server Availability Features

When purchasing servers and associated hardware for SAP, consider investing in the high-availability features offered for the platform, even if an additional charge is involved. Most servers offer redundant power supplies, redundant memory, disk controllers capable of spanning data across multiple disk drives, and support for multiple *network interfaces cards* (NICs) to get around the failure of a network segment, network switch, or single card. Leveraging these technologies can certainly increase the overall uptime of your SAP solution (although one can argue that the incremental costs become significant as you purchase more and more of these servers).

Server networks should be configured in a redundant fashion, as well. In many IT datacenters, the network represents a major—and avoidable—single point of failure. Dual switches and the use of the aforementioned redundant NICs can eliminate or mitigate what otherwise could be a major outage. Of course, these NICs and switches must be properly and professionally installed, cabled, and configured to actually provide high availability.

Disk Storage Systems

Many of the familiar server hardware vendors also sell disk storage systems (basically enclosures for multiple disk drives). Just as with virtualized server computing power, you can also purchase virtualized cloud-based storage. Either way, this storage is needed by SAP to store its database, the SAP installation binaries or executables, and all the files associated with the installed operating system. The two critical needs for all this storage are speed and availability.

Storage Area Networks

The most robust and well-performing disk subsystems today are called *storage area networks* (SANs), and they are comprised of one or more cabinets housing tens to hundreds of physical disks, all of which are connected to the SAP database server via specialized SAN I/O cards called *host bus adapters* (HBAs). SANs are fast and can be shared by multiple applications. In fact, SANs are often referred to as *shared storage*. Most SAP systems today use SANs as their primary disk storage.

Network-Attached Storage

SAP systems may also use *network-attached storage* (NAS) systems, which are less expensive and generally less powerful than SANs. Like SANs, NAS devices are connected to the database by way of a card installed in the database server. NAS devices use standard NICs rather than HBAs. These NICs may be the same NICs and networks shared by the SAP application servers and other applications. Because these networks are already pretty busy, NAS devices connected to these networks are subject to slowdowns not seen in SAN environments.

Direct-Attached Storage

Direct-attached storage systems are still occasionally used for SAP systems. These disk solutions might simply consist of a few disk drives enclosed in the database server. In other cases, a small cabinet housing several to perhaps 24 disks might be directly connected to each SAP database server. Small IT departments find this approach useful in that direct-attached storage devices are generally pretty fast and individually inexpensive. Of course, the costs mount quickly as more and more SAP components (*Enterprise Resource Planning* [ERP], *Customer Relationship Management* [CRM], *Product Lifecycle Management* [PLM], and so on) and landscapes (production, test, development, staging, training, sandboxes, and so on) are added.

Cloud Storage

The most contemporary method of providing storage to SAP is via cloud-based disk space. Providers such as Amazon, Microsoft, and Rackspace sell virtualized storage at pennies per gigabyte. Although cheap by any standard, the biggest challenge with cloud storage is performance: Active SAP databases need to process thousands and thousands of I/O operations every second, and (with several exceptions) cloud storage is accessed over network links (which might be very slow or very fast). So that you purchase virtualized storage that can keep up with your SAP database's needs, consult with SAP experts so that you can learn and then explain your system's requirements to your storage provider. Realistically, it's pretty easy to use virtualized storage for any sandbox and demonstration systems (or hosting the entire system in the cloud, especially those that don't play a part in the promote-to-production process explained in Hour 21, "SAP Enhancements, Upgrades, and More"). It's the other systems, especially the production SAP system, where you need to spend the most time analyzing requirements and designing a capable storage solution. In the end, you might use cloud storage for a subset of nonproduction systems and use traditional on-premises SANs or NAS storage devices for production and production support environments.

Storage System Performance

Regardless of how your disk space is sourced, vendors tend to market and sell low-tier, mid-tier, and high-end disk storage. The most important metrics to remember are the number of I/O operations per second that the storage configuration can support and the megabytes per second throughput that can be pushed through the device. Among other factors, key metrics include the speed and number of disk spindles, cache (memory used to store recently or frequently accessed data so that relatively slow disk I/O operations can be avoided). Disk space itself is a nonissue when it comes to performance but is obviously important to address SAP's startup and monthly disk-growth requirements. Many SAP systems grow at 10GB to 20GB per month, and growth of 500GB a month and more is not unheard of!

Storage System Availability

Although performance is critical, the disk subsystem's uptime or availability is most important. High levels of availability are traditionally achieved through hardware redundancy and various software solutions. The idea is to eliminate or at least minimize *single points of failure* (SPOFs). At a minimum, your SAP storage should support redundant connections to the database servers connected to it—redundant HBAs (for SANs), NICs (for NAS or cloud storage), or disk controllers (for direct-attached storage). Next, your disks need to be configured to protect against individual disk failures. *Redundant arrays of inexpensive (or independent) disks*, or RAID configurations, eliminate disk-related SPOFs. There are quite a few RAID types, as depicted in Table 3.1, each with specific cost, availability, and performance tradeoffs.

TABLE 3.1   RAID Types and Tradeoffs

RAID Level	Method of Availability	Advantages and Disadvantages
RAID 0	Disk striping	Provides no disk redundancy or protection, so this option is not viable for production systems. Spans multiple disks, all of which are available for storage. Provides the most disk space and excellent performance, however.
RAID 1	Disk mirroring	Every disk is mirrored to another disk. Provides best-in-class performance and redundancy at a high cost, as 2x the amount of necessary disk space is required to be configured.
RAID 5	Disk striping with parity	All data and parity are striped across all drives, providing strong read performance with a low to moderate write penalty (which is minimized further as more drives are added to the RAID 5 group); excellent redundancy balanced by low cost.
RAID 10 (1+0, or 0+1)	Disk mirroring and striping	Data is both striped and mirrored; RAID 10 generally provides the best performance and redundancy at a similarly high cost to RAID 1.

Software solutions can be used to increase your disk storage availability, too. High-end SANs typically support advanced long-distance replication technologies, which can also be useful for disaster recovery purposes. Be sure to look into such capabilities: The ability to copy data between remotely connected SANs or to create "snapshots" of SAP databases on-the-fly is useful in many different ways, from enabling rapid system backups, to allowing systems to be cloned for offline testing and training, to supporting disaster and business continuity requirements in the wake of a disaster.

SAP-Supported Operating Systems

For our purposes, an *operating system* (OS) is software that allows applications like a database or SAP to use a computer's processing, memory, disks, files, network connections, and other resources. The OS is the middleman between the hardware and the application. Operating systems such as Microsoft Windows Server, Red Hat and SUSE Linux, and several UNIX variants (HP-UX, IBM AIX, and Oracle Solaris) are common in today's SAP environments. Less frequently, you'll still find older versions (typically) of SAP running on the OS/400 and z/OS operating systems hosted by IBM i-series and z-series mainframe computers, respectively. Interestingly, SAP develops new components on the Windows and Linux platforms first, an important consideration for early adopters.

Static for many years, the OS playing field is today undergoing significant changes. Robust 64-bit technology in the commodity server market has led many traditional UNIX-based SAP shops to rethink their strategy and migrate to Windows and Linux. Even more interesting, newer cloud offerings like Microsoft's Azure and VMware's vSphere 4 provide new capabilities, resiliency, pricing models, and choice. When choosing an OS, consider the OS's ability to support a flexible and agile SAP computing platform. Then look to the strategic relationship the vendor shares with SAP, the relationship your company or IT department has with the OS vendor, and your own in-house IT skill sets, biases, and the IT department's efficacy and ability to adopt new technology.

Important OS Features

Not all OSs are created equal. Key OS features include computing platform or server support, how much physical and virtual memory is supported, crash recovery, patch management, and security and virus protection. Advanced clustering features can also be important. Consider the OS's built-in management and configuration tools and the extent to which third-party tools might be needed, too. Third-party utilities such as monitoring applications, virus-scanning packages, and backup software are often deemed necessary investments, but you must validate these early to ensure not only that they are needed but that they work well with SAP, the underlying database and file systems, and the overall computing platform.

SAP File Systems

From the OS's perspective, SAP is just a set of executables and libraries that connect users with data and application logic. To make all this happen, SAP runs multiple services and processes on top of the OS. UNIX and Linux OSs store their SAP binaries, log files, profiles, and libraries in a directory named /usr/sap. Windows stores its SAP files in x:\usr\sap. In UNIX and Linux systems, /sapmnt is mounted as an NFS (*network file system*) mount, and the /usr/sap/<SID> is a local file system. In Windows, the x:\usr\sap directory is shared as SAPMNT and is accessible as \\servername\sapmnt. For Windows servers hosting multiple instances of SAP on a single OS installation, all SAP instances must be installed to the same SAPMNT directory; there can be only one SAPMNT share.

An optional but highly recommended service called SAPOSCOL runs the OS collector and allows SAP to gather OS-related performance and other statistics such as CPU utilization, memory utilization, disk I/O activity, and more. Another Windows service called SAPService<SID> (where <SID> is the system identifier of the SAP instance) exists for each instance of SAP on the OS. This service is started with the sapstartsrv.exe executable. It calls the SAP start profile, which tells the system how to start SAP.

It is at the OS level that the term *SAP system* makes sense. An SAP system refers to a single system or collection of systems hosted by a single SAP database supporting a single *system identifier* (SID). For example, an SAP *Enterprise Resource Planning* (ERP) production system named PRD consists of one database, one set of central services (the binaries or executables), and anywhere from 1 to perhaps 100 application server instances (with 2 to 10 most common, depending on the workload that needs to be supported and each physical server's capabilities). An SAP instance (or *installation*) is synonymous with *one* of these installed components. Combined, all these instances make up a single SAP ERP production system. Similarly, you might configure another set of SAP instances to create a single SAP CRM production system.

SAP OS-Based Work Processes

SAP uses the OS to run eight different kinds of work processes, as detailed in Table 3.2. You will sometimes see them collectively referred to as *DVEBMSG*. The *D* equates to dialog work processes, *V* is for update work processes (differentiated by V1 and V2 priority types, designating version), *E* is for enqueue, *B* is for background/batch jobs, *M* is the message service, *S* is used for print spooling, and *G* represents the SAP gateway. The instance profile for each SAP instance describes how many of each type of process will start at system startup time. (The instance profile is a simple text file sitting atop the OS and is discussed in the section "SAP OS-Level Profiles.") You can see which work processes your OS is running by executing a special OS-specific utility or by using SAP's own transactions SM50 and SM66. Although we are getting ahead of ourselves, this ability to see the status of SAP work processes is important: Beyond providing a view into the system's workload, it also reveals in real time the status of the instance and the overall system in terms of what each work process is doing. SM50 shows you only the work processes of a single application server, whereas SM66 is your global window into what is happening with every active work process running across an entire SAP system.

TABLE 3.2   SAP Work Processes

Work Process Type	Description
Dialog	D: Processes real-time information in the foreground
Background	B: Background processing for long-running processes, reports, and batch jobs
Synchronous update	V1: Processes immediate updates to the database
Asynchronous update	V2: Processes updates to the database on a lower priority than V1 (that is, when time permits)
Enqueue	E: Manages database locks
Message	M: Manages communication between application servers
Spool	S: Manages print jobs (the print spool)
Gateway	G: Communicates with other SAP and non-SAP systems

SAP OS-Level Profiles

Each SAP instance comprises three profiles: the default profile, start profile, and instance profile. Profiles are text files that are imported into and maintained by the SAP database and used to start and run the instance. The default profile contains information common to all SAP instances of a particular SAP system. For example, the production system might include a database, central instance, and six application servers; all of these instances use the same default profile. The start profile calls the executables to start SAP, and this would be pretty similar for each instance. Finally, the instance profile contains detailed instance-specific information. In the instance profiles of two of your application servers, you might define a bunch of batch work processes, (for example, to create batch servers). Other instance-specific detailed information might include specific memory configuration parameters, buffer settings, and more. Use SAP transaction RZ10 to change and maintain all these profiles and to access a handy list of all available profile parameters.

Database Basics for SAP

With hardware and operating system details behind us, it is now time to turn our attention to the role of the database underneath an SAP business application. The same care that goes into choosing a hardware platform and OS should be used when choosing a database. Depending on your platform and SAP version, you might be restricted to only one or a few database choices (which underscores the importance of viewing your SAP infrastructure as a holistic computing platform). SAP supports most mainstream databases, including Microsoft SQL Server (and ultimately its cloud counterpart SQL Azure), IBM DB2, and several Oracle database products. SAP also supports its own database, called MaxDB, which has an interesting history and is generally relegated to small systems. And with SAP's acquisition of Sybase in 2010, SAP has told its Sybase customers that it will provide limited support for the SAP-on-Sybase database platform sometime in the future.

Microsoft SQL Server runs only on Windows-based operating systems. Oracle is supported by SAP on Windows, Linux, and all the major UNIX operating systems. DB2 is supported even more broadly because it runs on IBM's legacy mainframe systems.

Most IT departments deploying SAP choose a database vendor and version based on platforms they currently support and their particular level of familiarity and experience. This can be an expensive mistake because much of the traditional work performed by a *database administrator* (DBA) is just not necessary in the world of SAP. That is, SAP "abstracts" a lot of the complexity out of managing and maintaining the underlying database. For this reason, be sure to consider Oracle, SQL Server, and DB2, especially in light of each database's similar performance and scalability profiles and their significantly different pricing models.

Beyond price, consider each database's high-availability options. Clustering, mirroring, and snapshot or cloning capabilities can be important differentiators. Other options, like log shipping, might help support disaster recoverability.

A Quick Database Primer

Whichever database you choose, enterprise applications such as SAP are essentially made up of programs and data that are both used by and created by those programs. The data is organized in a meaningful way within a database, making it easy for the programs to access and find the data necessary to do something useful, such as run a financial report or create a sales order. In the case of most SAP components, such as ERP, the programs and data reside together in the same database.

Each component generally requires its own database (although exceptions exist). For example, a "production environment" consisting of SAP ERP, SAP NetWeaver *Enterprise Portal* (EP), and SAP CRM consists of three different production databases.

The database plays a key role in each SAP system because it houses all the data used by that particular SAP component or application. In the simplest form, a database is composed of tables, columns (called *fields*), and rows (called *records* or *data*). The basic structure of a database is quite similar to the concept of spreadsheets like Microsoft Excel, where columns (fields) store row after row of records (data). The biggest difference between a database and a spreadsheet is just that databases can contain multiple (and extremely large) tables that are connected to one another through relationships. Therefore, a database can be thought of as a much more complex, and ultimately much more useful, spreadsheet.

Tables, Indexes, and Structure

The SAP database contains literally thousands of tables that store information. Some products, such as ERP, comprise greater than 40,000 tables, whereas less-complex offerings such as SAP NetWeaver *Process Integration* (PI) might have fewer than 10,000. Note that in most SAP systems, 10% of the tables house 90% of the data, so some tables can grow quite large and be subject to constant change, whereas others tend to remain small and relatively static. All these tables are tied to each other through established relationships. It is precisely this series of connected multiple tables that creates what is known as a *relational database management system* (RDBMS).

Beyond housing raw data, databases house indexes, which are used to speed up the retrieval of data. An index might best be described as a table of contents or viewed as a copy of a database table reduced to only the key fields. The data in this reduced copy is sorted according to some predefined criteria that consequently enables rapid access to the data. Not all fields from the copied table exist in the index, and the index contains a pointer to the associated record of the actual table. You might be surprised to know that indexes make up approximately 50% of the overall size of an SAP database!

SAP uses another concept called *transparent tables*, which are SAP database tables that contain data only at runtime. A transparent table is automatically created in the database when a table is activated in the ABAP/4 Data Dictionary. This transparent table contains the same name as your database table in the ABAP/4 Dictionary. Each of its fields also contains the same names as their database counterparts, although the sequence of the fields might change. The varying field sequence makes it possible to insert new fields into the table without having to convert it, all of which allows for more rapid access to data during runtime.

Finally, it's important to know a bit about *database structures*. Just remember that database structures are groups of internal fields that logically belong together. Structures are activated and defined in the SAP ABAP/4 Data Dictionary, and they contain data only temporarily (during the execution of a program). Structures are differentiated from database tables based on the following three criteria:

▶ A structure does not contain or reflect an associated ABAP/4 Data Dictionary table.

▶ A structure does not contain a primary key.

▶ A structure does not have any technical properties such as class, size, category, or buffering specifications.

Summary

This hour covered the key components of SAP infrastructure: hardware, operating systems, and databases. Beyond traditional methods of building the Basis layer or computing platform for SAP, we also looked at newer methods of providing this infrastructure as a service. And we looked at what it means to choose and partner with the vendors that must work together to create a well-performing computing platform for SAP.

Case Study: Hour 3

Using your newly acquired hardware, operating system, and database knowledge, read through this hour's case study and address the questions that follow. You can find the answers posed by the questions related to this case study in Appendix A, "Case Study Answers."

Situation

Your employer, MNC, runs the latest releases of SAP's applications on Microsoft Windows and SQL Server. MNC recently acquired *Archaic Manufacturing Incorporated* (AMI), a large competitor who also runs the latest releases of SAP's applications on a combination of UNIX and mainframe platforms running Oracle and DB2 databases, respectively. MNC wants to consolidate like-for-like systems between the two companies in alignment with its own IT cost-reduction strategies. Although AMI's SAP IT costs are said to be much higher than MNC's, the architecture team is not convinced that simply changing platforms will pull enough costs out of the entire infrastructure for SAP. At the direction of MNC's *chief financial officer* (CFO), the team is especially interested in shaving additional costs from the IT capital expense budget.

As one of the technology architects on the team, you have identified four options. The first is to do nothing and continue to have each IT team support its own systems. Second, the team could consolidate all its hardware and other gear as is into a single common datacenter. Third, the team could standardize computing platforms. And fourth, the team could pursue some kind of strategy with the cloud. Assume you have the necessary means, resources, and time to pursue any of these choices, and then answer the following questions.

Questions

1. *Identify the primary advantage to the team's first choice to doing nothing.*

2. *List several disadvantages or challenges related to doing nothing.*

3. *How might the second option, to consolidate existing assets into a single common datacenter, prove beneficial?*

4. *List some of the advantages of standardizing computing platforms.*

5. *If AMI's production landscape consists of SAP ERP, CRM, and PLM, each consisting of four instances, how many production systems does AMI currently support?*

6. *How might the team address the CFO's request?*

HOUR 4

SAP Project Basics

What You'll Learn in This Hour:

▶ SAP project implementation fundamentals

▶ SAP realization resources and timelines

▶ Accessing an SAP system

▶ Several methods of accessing SAP

▶ Walk through several typical business scenarios

Beyond understanding the business and technology basics behind SAP, if you are new to this world you might still be unclear as to what SAP really is (beyond being a large German software company or the generic description of a bunch of business applications). This hour completes our basic discussion as we move from describing what it means to implement SAP to actually using SAP to execute several common business scenarios.

SAP Project Implementation Basics

If someone tells you his company is busy implementing SAP, be sure to ask what that really means. What exactly is the company deploying? SAP *Enterprise Resource Planning* (ERP)? The SAP *Supply Chain Management* (SCM) or *Customer Relationship Management* (CRM) application? As you might remember from Hour 1, "SAP Explained?" many companies around the world have already implemented SAP ERP but continue to add new SAP applications and features. Meanwhile, other companies are extending SAP to other applications (such as Microsoft Dynamics CRM, Oracle PeopleSoft, or HP Neoview). Still other companies are busy doing their first ERP implementations. It's this *scope* of the implementation that you need to understand. Once you understand the scope, you can turn your thoughts to how the project will be managed. Although the specific software products and their purposes differ, an SAP implementation project always requires a tremendous amount of project management to pull everything off.

Like managing traffic in a busy city, the most important and immediate matter is just getting the various stakeholders moving in the same direction (see Figure 4.1). Executive leaders, business leads, functional and technical specialists, end users involved in the project, the organization's IT department and project management office, a host of external partners, and many others all need to be mobilized to help move the SAP project forward. Without this alignment, the project will never successfully reach the point where SAP is turned over to its end users to be *used*—a very special day known as *go-live*.

FIGURE 4.1
Regardless of ups and downs, an SAP project requires teams and key stake-holders to move in the same direction to be successful.

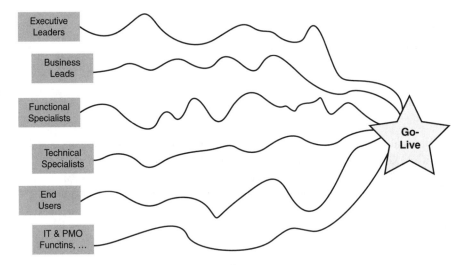

SAP Realization: Resources and Timelines

In Hour 2, "SAP Business Basics," we discussed the basics of SAP's project implementation methodology, called *ASAP*. Remember where most of the time is spent? It's in the realization phase, or phase 3. This is where most of the project's resources are used: time, budgets (money!), and people. At this point, all the project planning tools and processes are in place (phase 1), and the business blueprint has been established and agreed on (phase 2). The next step is to organize the teams responsible for realization.

Although there are several ways to do this, many projects organize the realization phase by function and task, as explored next.

Business and Configuration Teams

Several teams are involved in realization, depending on the scope of the project (that is, the SAP applications being deployed and the specific modules or functionality being implemented). Business teams might be organized by mega process (such as order-to-cash) or by functional modules (such as SAP ERP Sales and Distribution, SAP ERP Materials Management, and so on). During the first part of realization, the business teams work on prototyping each of the business processes or scenarios described in the blueprint. One or more business sandboxes are typically used for each of these efforts. After several weeks to months, after the prototyping has been completed and the business processes modeled well (or well enough), these teams begin *configuration* (that is, actually configuring the SAP business processes in the SAP development environment).

Integration and Development Teams

Other business-oriented teams focus on integrating business functionality across different applications and modules. This process is critical to ensuring that the new SAP system's business processes work well across applications, modules, and technologies that, if overlooked or poorly managed, could act like do-not-cross boundaries. This effort takes place in the *test* or *QA* environments and begins as soon as the configuration teams complete their first round of configuration. Integration testing occurs throughout the rest of the realization phase.

A specialized development team may be employed to fill in the gaps where SAP is lacking. These developers create custom code or specialized integration points to other applications using ABAP, Java, Microsoft .NET, or other programs. Some of this custom configuration will go quickly, but other customizations and systems integration work might take many months to develop, test, and refine.

Test/QA Teams

The QA team is an important team called on to test all this functionality. They either use existing templates or create new "use cases" that reflect each of the to-be business scenarios. As each business scenario is tested, the team discovers areas where things don't work as expected. Perhaps a certain type of customer will be unable to place a particular type of order, or a certain business unit will lack access to key information. The kinds of issues are countless and often complex, making the testing team and the process it employs one of the project's most critical. On a regular basis, the testing team reports their findings back to the development and configuration teams, where the broken configurations, customizations, and integrations are fixed (and retested).

The Data Team

While all this SAP configuration, development, and testing is in progress, another team of people focuses on data. Sometimes referred to as *data architecture* or *information architecture*, this team works to understand how data flows between business processes, systems, and stakeholders. The data specialists figure out how much of the old system's data needs to be kept, where, and for how long. For example, the company might need to retain a large subset of data for legal or regulatory reasons. Other data might need to be staged in a data warehouse to make it possible to view old orders, invoices, or purchase requisitions. Still other data, such as master customer data, might need to be moved into the new SAP system to maintain a certain amount of consistency between the legacy system (which will be retired) and the new SAP system.

The Security Team

A team focused on end-user roles, authorizations, and overall security will work with all the other business teams to help establish and enforce who can see, create, and change data. Similarly, a subset of the technical team works to ensure that the systems are physically secured, protected from viruses, and otherwise safeguarded. Like the business team members, these security specialists get to work as soon as realization commences, and they continue to work throughout the project.

Technical and Other Teams

Finally, a host of technical teams also work throughout the realization phase setting up the necessary servers, operating systems, disk subsystems, and databases required underneath each SAP application. They install and patch both the computing platform infrastructure and the SAP applications, starting with the business and technical sandboxes. Later, they do the same for the development systems, test/QA systems, production systems, and perhaps others, and they carefully move and synchronize configuration updates between these systems. Other technical teams operate the computers and other infrastructure, while still others will manage and maintain all those systems.

Many other teams also play important roles in the realization phase. For example, training teams prepare end users for the day when they will use the new system. Teams focused on *user experience* (UX) might create easy-to-use Microsoft SharePoint-based or Adobe Forms-based front ends. Other UX developers might work toward enabling iPhone, Windows Phone 7, or Android-based smartphones to access SAP. In the end, though, all the work completed throughout the realization phase is for that special single moment in time: go-live. On the day of go-live, after final preparations are completed, the SAP system is ultimately "turned on" so that the system's end users can finally begin to use the new system to do their jobs running the company. How these end users actually access their new SAP system is the topic of the next section.

Accessing Your New SAP Systems

After all the work of designing, configuring, testing, and deploying the new SAP business processes has been completed, an SAP end user is finally allowed (and encouraged) to actually *use* the system. Of course, before an SAP system's end users can get to work, they must be trained to use the new system. How the system is used depends on the role of the end user. In Meagan's daily routine, she might be responsible for moving and tracking inventory and reporting on the status of new toys in each of the company's warehouses. Ashley in the accounting group might need to report on financials and ensure payroll isn't bankrupting the company, while Phillip in the sales team might need to manage his customer orders, track delivery status, invoice his customers, and so on.

Accessing SAP Using the SAPGUI or Fat Client

Assuming every user has been taught how to perform his or her job in the new system, the next step is to access the system. Often, this is accomplished by installing an SAP-specific piece of software that acts as the user interface to the SAP system. The SAP *graphical user interface* (GUI), pronounced *sap goo-ee*, one of the few times it's completely permissible to sound out the otherwise forbidden monosyllabic *sap*) for Microsoft Windows is still one of the most popular user interfaces available for SAP systems today. SAP calls this piece of software the *presentation layer* of an SAP solution. Also called the *WinGUI* or the *fat client*, the Windows interface is the most capable but also eats up a chunky amount of disk space on your PC or laptop and consumes a fair amount of memory to run well. Another user interface, the Java GUI for SAP, is also a fat client. It enables SAP access by non-Microsoft-based front-end clients. See Hour 10, "Logging On and Using SAP's User Interfaces," for more detail.

> **By the Way**
>
> The most common web browser for SAP remains the Microsoft *Internet Explorer* (IE) browser. For Windows-based client devices, IE is highly recommended. IE is tested and used in the real-world more than the others and therefore benefits from greater penetration and, ultimately, reliability. In terms of network bandwidth, it's interesting that none of the web browsers are actually as efficient as their fat-client counterparts. SAP did an amazing job streamlining the SAPGUI's network performance.

Accessing SAP Using a Web Browser

Instead of a fat client, access via a web browser has become much more popular in the past few years. It used to be that the web browser was aimed at users running less-powerful desktops or laptops. Today, though, the idea of performing regular SAPGUI maintenance (which includes patches, upgrades, and all the other little things that must be done to maintain any piece of software) isn't appealing, especially when thousands of individual desktops and laptops are involved. More important, the web browser has become ubiquitous, whether hosted on a personal computer, smartphone, tablet, or something in between. It's just easier, too.

Behind the Scenes: The Access Process

Regardless of the client device, the user interface connects to the SAP *central instance* (where the SAP "executables" or "binaries" run) and then to an SAP application server (which hosts the application logic), which in turn talks to the back-end database holding all the programs, data, and so on. Irrespective of your physical location, if you've got authentic SAP credentials (a logon ID, a password, and a client to log in to) and a network connection to your SAP system, you can access SAP from pretty much anywhere around the world.

SAP User IDs and Sessions

All SAP users are assigned a username or user ID (although you might see the occasional factory, warehouse, or distribution site where several workers share a single SAP user ID—a poor practice indeed). Your SAP security administrator sets your initial password when the ID is created. Upon first signing in, you are forced to change it. In this way, your user ID is secure even from system administrators and others tasked with maintaining security.

Each time you connect to SAP via the SAPGUI, WebGUI, or another user interface, you begin a user *session*. An SAP session simply means you have started the SAPGUI and established a connection with a particular SAP system—and you're now connected, so to speak. You can have multiple sessions open with multiple SAP components (one for SAP ERP, another for CRM, and so on). You may also start multiple sessions with a single system. This can prove useful if you're executing a long-running report, for example, and still want to process open orders in real time, read through a financial report, or simultaneously view the contents of your warehouse storage bins. That is, multiple sessions enable you to multitask. By default, you can open up to six sessions at the same time, although the default can be increased by a system administrator knowledgeable in maintaining SAP from a technical perspective. With six sessions, think about how much more work you can do! Multitasking is indeed alive and well in the world of SAP. With their SAPGUI or WebGUI open and connected to SAP, let's take a closer look at the kind of work a set of typical users might perform on their new SAP systems.

Typical Day-to-Day Business Processes

To give you a sense of why a company spends so much time and money and invests in so many people to introduce SAP, this section covers several common business processes. In each scenario, you'll see how a company's end users use an SAP application in the course of their day-to-day job running the company's business. For even greater detail, see Hour 12, "Using SAP to Do Your Job."

Performing Employee Self-Service Functions

One of the most common business scenarios involves employees viewing and changing their own personnel records. SAP NetWeaver Portal provides special views called *iViews* that enable employees to easily create, display, and change their own personnel records (assuming they've been given these privileges). An employee might change her home address or telephone number, for instance, or update her contact information after a relocation. In other cases, she might be curious about when her paycheck will be deposited or might just want to view the company's updated organization chart in the wake of a management shake-up. These kinds of self-service business transactions used to be completed by dedicated Human Resource representatives; to reduce costs and empower users, these functions are part of SAP's *Employee Self-Service* (ESS) functionality today. A sample ESS process might include the following:

1. Log in to SAP NetWeaver Portal's Welcome page.

2. Choose the Working Time option and then select Record Working Time.

3. Choose Leave Request.

4. Examine the Leave Request's overview.

5. Choose the Personal Information option and select Personal Data.

6. View the home address on record.

7. Choose the Bank Information option.

8. Choose Benefits and Payment and then select "Paycheck Inquiry."

9. Log out of the portal.

These kinds of transactions are not only very typical but also used by the SAP EP-ESS Benchmark.

Balancing the Books

SAP ERP was borne out of the need to marry core manufacturing, distribution, and warehousing functions with a single overarching financial system. Accounts and other financial analysts employed by the company use this functionality to pay the company's bills, balance the books, and so on. One of the most long-lived and useful SAP business scenarios within the finance and accounting function involves displaying, posting, and eventually balancing financial documents. The SAP *Financial Accounting* Benchmark illustrates this process well:

1. Use the SAPGUI to log in to SAP ERP's main screen.

2. Call **Post Document**.

3. Create a customer item.

4. Create a *general ledger* (GL) account item.

5. Choose the **Post** option.

6. Call **Display Document**.

7. Enter the previously posted document's number.

8. Double-click the first line of the document.

9. Call **Customer Line Item Display**.

10. Enter relevant data and then choose **Execute**.

11. Select the first line.

12. Call **Post Incoming Payments**.

13. Enter header data.

14. Choose **Process Open Items**.

15. Select an item in the resulting list.

16. Scroll to the end.

17. Select the last item.

18. Deactivate all selected items.

19. Choose **Post**.

After the documents have been posted, the accountant or financial analyst might execute a similar process for a different general ledger or in support of another of the company's business units. Given SAP's long-time history and understanding of finance and accounting, new SAP finance users are often quite fond of the new-found power and capabilities they have with SAP ERP.

Selling from Stock

Like the other two business scenarios outlined this hour, the sell-from-stock business process is also common. Incidentally, it is the business scenario modeled by the most popular SAP benchmark, the SAP SD Benchmark. This scenario is typically executed by a company's sales team member, such as an inside sales representative. The rep uses SAP ERP either directly via the traditional SAPGUI fat client or by way of a web browser using the SAP NetWeaver Portal or perhaps a Microsoft SharePoint site. The basic sell-from-stock process consists of six transactions:

1. Run VA01 to create an order with five line items.

2. Run VL01N to create a delivery for the previously created order.

3. Use VA03 to display the order.

4. Change the delivery and then "post goods issue" using VL02N.

5. Use VA05 to list the last 40 orders created for one sold-to party.

6. Create the invoice for the order using VF01.

Again, for more examples of how SAP is used in the course of a normal day at work, see Hour 12.

Summary

In this hour, we walked through what it means to run SAP, including some of the basic project resources and timelines related to the realization phase of an SAP implementation project. We also explored SAP system access, user interfaces, and session basics. Finally, by walking through several commonly executed business scenarios, we wrapped some context around what we have studied so far. These fundamentals set the stage for many of the remaining hours in this book.

Case Study: Hour 4

Consider the following case study and questions. You can find the answers posed by the questions related to this case study in Appendix A, "Case Study Answers."

Situation

With your experience implementing SAP at a competitor, your industry experience, and your MNC companywide contacts, you were a shoe in for the new ERP IT project director position at MNC. You are well aware that the executive management team has decided to implement SAP's ERP and supply chain applications, but these decisions haven't been communicated broadly yet, and blueprinting just started. Your first day on the job finds you in a town hall meeting with many of your new team members and direct reports, several of which asked the following questions:

Questions

1. What are we doing with SAP?

2. Once blueprinting is wrapped up, how will you structure the teams for the realization phase?

3. Several business unit VPs are curious if you're going to go with browser access or do some kind of thing with a fat client. What should you tell them?

4. Another member of your team volunteers that the fat client is really slow and that you should obviously put web browser access at the top of your access strategy list. What should you share with him?

5. One of your senior project managers is under the impression that the blueprinting phase will consume most of the project's time and budget. What is your response?

6. After the town hall meeting, an employee runs into you in the elevator. He asks whether his job in finance will be impacted.

HOUR 5

Overview of SAP Applications and Components

What You'll Learn in This Hour:

▶ SAP Business Suite applications

▶ SAP's small and midsize enterprise solutions

▶ The role of SAP NetWeaver components

▶ How to pick the right solution for your business

Through its Business Suite offerings, SAP provides software solutions for some of the largest and most well-known companies around the world. But SAP solutions are aimed at more than just the biggest companies. SAP also boasts more than 30,000 *small and medium enterprise* (SME) customers. And its SAP NetWeaver components play critical roles throughout the SAP ecosystem, as well. In this hour, we identify and compare SAP's offerings big and small and draw distinctions between those used for different types of businesses.

SAP Business Suite Components

Without a doubt, the SAP products sold as components of the SAP Business Suite are some of the company's most well-known. For years, large organizations have been deploying these solutions which today are synonymous with SAP, including

▶ SAP *Enterprise Resource Planning* (ERP)

▶ SAP *Customer Relationship Management* (CRM)

▶ SAP *Product Lifecycle Management* (PLM)

- SAP *Supply Chain Management* (SCM)

- SAP *Supplier Relationship Management* (SRM)

Each of these are explored next. For more details, see Hour 8, "The SAP Business Suite and Other SAP Applications."

SAP Enterprise Resource Planning

Within the broad umbrella of SAP ERP solutions are basic business functions, including the following:

- **SAP ERP Financials**—Includes Financial Accounting, Treasury Accounting, Controlling, Treasury and Corporate Finance Management, Real Estate Management, and more. Built-in compliance for Sarbanes-Oxley and Basel II enable companies to provide transparent financial reporting and corporate governance (necessary hassles thanks to Enron and other such past events).

- **SAP ERP Operations**—Includes Procurement and Logistics Execution, Product Development and Manufacturing, and Sales and Service. These solutions take logistics to the next level, introducing sales, warehousing, procurement, transportation, and distribution into the realm of collaborative business solutions.

- **SAP ERP Human Capital Management (HCM)**—Transforms an HR department into an organization well equipped to manage and retain its people, the core of any successful business. HCM pushes HR business processes out to the Web, enabling ubiquitous access to long-time HR staples like recruiting, e-learning, and employee self-service.

- **SAP ERP Corporate Services**—Bundles many core company services into a neat package ranging from Project and Portfolio Management to *Environment, Health, and Safety* (EH&S) Management, Travel Management, Quality Management, and more.

- **SAP ERP Analytics**—A powerful business analytics function marrying financials, operations, and workforce-based analytics and reporting in one place.

The preceding list comprises SAP ERP's latest business solution offerings. The latest version of SAP ERP also includes numerous functional enhancements for better addressing an organization's finance, HCM, operations, and vital corporate services functions. SAP ERP enables its users to use these enhanced business capabilities more easily because all new functional enhancements through at least the year 2013 will be available as SAP ERP extensions called *enhancement packages* (EPs). EPs are one of the most important innovations to come out of SAP in the past decade; they replace expensive and time-consuming business application upgrades. For more information, check out Hour 7, "SAP ERP: SAP's Core Product."

SAP Customer Relationship Management

SAP CRM brings together a company's sales, services, and marketing functions. In this way, CRM helps a company focus on three related customer-related areas: driving top-line revenue growth, achieving operational excellence, and increasing customer-facing business agility. Key business scenarios include

▶ **Marketing support**—Enhances marketing effectiveness, maximizes resource use, and empowers the sales team to develop and maintain long-term profitable customer relationships. From a user's perspective, this includes marketing resource management, campaign management, trade promotion management, market segment management, lead/prospect management, and marketing analytics.

▶ **Sales support**—Helps remove barriers to productivity by enabling teams to work with their customers in a consistent manner. CRM Sales empowers and provides the team with the tools they need to close deals. For example, territory management, account and contact management, lead and opportunity management, and sales planning and forecasting help sales forces identify and manage prospects. Then, by leveraging quotation and order management, product configuration, contract management, incentive and commission management, time and travel management, and sales analytics, the team has the information it needs to keep customers happy while hopefully increasing sales volume and margins and decreasing the costs of doing all this.

▶ **Service support**—Assists service management teams in maximizing the value obtained from post-sales services. This enables teams to profitably manage a broad range of functions geared toward driving successful customer service and support, including field service, Internet-enabled service offerings, service marketing and sales, and service/contract management. These happier customers benefit from improved warranty and claims management and effective channel service and depot repair services. And the company's service team benefits from insight gleaned from service analytics, which enable the team to maximize profit per customer.

▶ **Web channel**—Increases sales and reduce transaction costs by turning the Internet into a service channel (or sales and marketing channel) geared toward effectively connecting businesses and consumers. This makes it possible to increase profitability of existing accounts while also reaching new markets.

▶ **Interaction Center (IC) management support**—Complements and arms a company's field sales force. This functionality supports marketing, sales, and service activities such as telemarketing, telesales, customer service, e-service, and interaction center analytics.

▶ **Partner channel management**—Improves processes for partner recruitment, partner management, communications, channel marketing, channel forecasting, collaborative selling, partner order management, channel service, and analytics. In this way, a company can attract and retain a more profitable and loyal indirect channel by managing partner relationships and empowering channel partners.

▶ **Business communications management**—Enables inbound and outbound contact management across multiple locations and communications channels. Business communications management integrates multichannel communications with a firm's customer-facing business processes to create a seamless communications experience across several different communications mediums (including voice, text messaging, email, and others).

▶ **Real-time offer management**—Helps manage the complexities of marketing offers in real time, using SAP's advanced analytical real-time decision engine. This functionality also optimizes the decision-making process across different customer interaction channels, enabling a company to quickly and intelligently enhance its customer relationships.

With its focus on customers and improving top-line revenue, SAP CRM gets a lot of attention from companies looking to implement the "next big thing." It has consistently grown in popularity since its introduction and accounts for much of SAP's growth over the past few years.

SAP Product Lifecycle Management

SAP PLM is valuable to organizations tasked with managing the product lifecycle. PLM is focused on helping companies develop new products by helping those organizations embrace and facilitate creativity and innovation. Further, SAP PLM helps companies identify and remove productivity-robbing organizational constraints.

It also serves as the foundation for successful *new product development and introduction* (NPDI). Using NPDI, companies tie together people and information, effectively connecting sales, planning, production, procurement, maintenance, internal service provider, and other organizations to one another. And outside of a firm's own internal organizations, PLM enables companies to easily bring together partners, suppliers, contract manufacturers, external service providers, and even customers under the singular umbrella of developing better products.

SAP Supply Chain Management

SAP SCM is the most mature component within SAP's Business Suite. By transforming a supply chain into a dynamic customer-centric supply chain network, SAP SCM enables companies to plan for and streamline the firm's network of logistics and resources that merge to form a supply chain. Generally speaking, a supply chain comprises three areas: supply, manufacturing, and distribution. The supply portion of a supply chain focuses on the raw materials needed by manufacturing, which in turn converts raw materials into finished products. The distribution aspect of a supply chain focuses on moving the finished products through a network of distributors, warehouses, and outlets. A good SCM product opens the door to increased velocity and improved profitability resulting from cross-company collaboration; enhanced visibility into a company's suppliers, vendors, and customers makes it easier to create a more predictable supply chain capable of capitalizing on circumstances, minimizing costs, and maximizing margins through the following:

▶ Improving responsiveness via real-time insight into the entire supply chain

▶ Improving inventory turns by synchronizing inputs with outputs (that is, balancing supply with demand)

▶ Encouraging collaboration by providing visibility into trends as seen through supply chain monitoring, analysis, and business analytics

This combination of capability and application maturity makes for a true win-win: better service, increased productivity, and improved profitability.

SAP Supplier Relationship Management

SAP SRM is SAP's venerable solution for managing the procurement and support of the very goods and services a company needs to use internally to run day in and day out. Just as SAP CRM manages the relationship between a company and its customers, SAP SRM helps to optimize and manage the relationship between a company and its suppliers. As another one of SAP's more mature offerings, SRM integrates seamlessly with PLM, enabling a high degree of collaboration between product buyers and parts suppliers. Bidding processes are streamlined, as well. All this naturally impacts SAP ERP, too, because financial and logistics data are updated and shared between systems. SRM also ties into SAP SCM, extending and enabling tight integration with a company's supply chain. Much of this native interoperability comes as a result of SAP's NetWeaver platform and components. (The open standards-based SAP NetWeaver platform is discussed next.)

SAP NetWeaver Components

While SAP Business Suite has taken care of hundreds of thousands of users and their day-to-day application needs, SAP NetWeaver and its various products have quietly found their home in enterprises around the world. In principle, SAP NetWeaver provides the foundation for Business Suite. However, many specific products fall under the label of NetWeaver, too. The NetWeaver umbrella has become so crowded in the past few years that SAP has organized this collection of applications, utilities, and tools around six areas or themes:

▶ **Foundation Management**—Includes SAP NetWeaver Application Server (the platform for Business Suite), Identity Management (for user identity and system access), and SAP Solution Manager (to manage SAP's implementation and operations throughout the system lifecycle)

▶ **Middleware**—Comprises SAP NetWeaver Process Integration (used to integrate SAP and non-SAP applications and data sources together), partner adapters (to simplify complex system connections across business networks), and support of various industry-standard protocols (necessary to support business to business connections)

▶ **Information Management**—Includes SAP NetWeaver Master Data Management (for managing and synchronizing companywide data), SAP NetWeaver Business Warehouse and Warehouse Accelerator (SAP's long-time data warehouse and search solutions), and SAP Information Lifecycle Management (to efficiently manage legacy SAP systems in the name of legal compliance)

▶ **Team Productivity**—Includes user experience tools and applications like SAP NetWeaver Portal (which provides role-based web access to SAP's applications), SAP NetWeaver Mobile (access for mobile users), and SAP NetWeaver Enterprise Search (SAP's gateway to the enterprise's information)

▶ **Composition**—Includes tools to develop, monitor, and manage business processes using SAP NetWeaver Composition Environment, SAP NetWeaver Developer Studio (for more complex business applications), and SAP NetWeaver Visual Composer (for rapid model-based business application development, no coding required)

▶ **Business Process Management**—Comprises a subset of the SAP NetWeaver Composition Environment, including SAP NetWeaver Business Process Management (to specially model and run business processes) and SAP NetWeaver Business Rules Management (to create and manage the business rules that describe business processes)

Many of these NetWeaver components, tools, and utilities are outlined further in Hour 6, "SAP NetWeaver: The Foundation for SAP."

Small and Medium Enterprises

As you've seen this hour, SAP offers a whole lot of big-business software solutions and a host of tools that extend, manage, and optimize these solutions. As we all know, however, there's a whole lot more small and medium businesses than large ones. These smaller entities have different business requirements and a smaller financial appetite for the applications and tools they need to take care of business. With these differences in mind, SAP markets three different solutions for the SME market: SAP Business One, SAP Business ByDesign, and SAP Business All-in-One. See Table 5.1 for a brief comparison of these three very different solutions (and refer to www.sap.com/usa/sme/solutions/businessmanagement/comparebm.index.epx for more details).

TABLE 5.1   Comparing SAP's SME Solutions

SAP SME Solution	Business One	Business ByDesign	SAP All-In-One
Simple description	A single, integrated application to manage your entire business	The best of SAP delivered on-demand	Comprehensive, integrated and easily configured as *Software-as-a Service* (SaaS)
Number of company employees/users	Up to 100	100–500	Up to 2,500
Country availability	40 countries	Limited to US, UK, Germany, France, India, and China	50 countries
Implementation type or method	On-premises	On-demand	On-premises or hosted
Implementation timeline	2–8 weeks	4–8 weeks	8–16 weeks
Transaction volume	Low	Moderate	High
Industry solutions	Several	Few	Many

For years, SAP has publicly stated that the SME market is where it expects to achieve much of the growth in its customer base. Back in 2007, SAP had a goal of achieving 100,000 customers by 2010, the key to which was success in the SME space. By 2010, SAP had actually overachieved on this target, hitting 105,000 customers. The SME market played a big role in this success. Next, let's take a closer look at the three business solutions that made this milestone possible.

SAP Business One

The idea behind Business One is to replace isolated, disparate applications with an integrated software system handling CRM, manufacturing, and financial solution requirements—much of what a small business needs in a single system. SAP Business One is designed for small firms, those with typically fewer than 100 employees across five branches or locations and independent subsidiaries. SAP positions Business One as the ideal solution for multinational company *subsidiaries* because the solution is easily linked with SAP's Business Suite solution back at corporate headquarters (which is often employed by such multinational companies).

Business One is designed to be affordable. It is delivered to the customer via SAP's worldwide network of qualified business partners. Another key selling point is the solution's relatively short implementation time. In fact, whereas Business Suite implementations are measured in months (if not years), Business One implementations are typically measured in weeks. With such a small timeframe, it's easier to develop a quick estimate of the implementation cost and the disruption and impact to the business are minimized.

Functionality

Like its more capable big-business counterpart SAP ERP, Business One supports the following key business processes:

- Financial management
- Warehouse management
- Purchasing
- Inventory
- Manufacturing
- Banking
- CRM

Business One also supports the Web. Further, it allows for the implementation of a simple e-commerce solution, which in turn enables the business to market and sell goods and services online while providing integration with financials, inventory, and shipping information.

Features

One of the key features of Business One is that it increases control by providing almost instant access to all the business information in one system. Because Business One is a complete, integrated system, there might be no need to integrate it with other systems (although this is certainly possible). This all-encompassing nature results in savings in both integration costs and the maintenance costs associated with maintaining otherwise multiple systems.

Business One is designed to be easy to use. It includes the Drag & Relate feature, for example, which provides users with end-to-end visibility into operations and enables users to easily create reports. The solution is also integrated with Microsoft Outlook, which supports management by exception alerting and business process workflow. Finally, SAP has designed the application to be easily customized without the need for expensive and time-consuming technical training.

Implementation

Business One is designed to be implemented quickly. It provides for countryspecific localizations. Business One is implemented on a single server; there's no need for the traditional multisystem landscape described in Hour 3, "SAP Technology Basics." System and functionality changes can therefore be introduced quickly because there are no development or quality assurance systems to deal with.

Technically speaking, Business One is implemented on the Windows Server platform. This makes for a straightforward installation and enables IT organizations with only moderate experience running business-critical Windows-based applications to quickly hit the ground running. Leveraging either Microsoft SQL Server or IBM DB2 Universal Database Express edition, Business One is not only simple to administer from a database perspective, but its database licensing costs are less than SAP's enterprise-class offerings.

Development

Business One is not just a scaled-down version of existing SAP software components; in fact, it was developed as a completely separate product. As such, development is different from a traditional SAP ERP environment. Mentioned earlier, most Business One customizations may be implemented without technical training and nearly instantaneously. Business One has its own *software development kit* (SDK). The SDK contains three *application programming interfaces* (APIs): a User Interface API, a Data Interface API, and the Java Connector. In addition, SAP partners have developed more than 430 industry-specific and other solutions handy in extending Business One's usefulness across a growing enterprise.

SAP Business ByDesign

The newest of SAP's SME offerings, SAP *Business ByDesign* (BBD) is SAP's SaaS-based integrated SME business management software. BBD includes preconfigured best practices for managing financials, customer relationships, human resources, projects, procurement, and the supply chain. SAP takes care of system installation, maintenance, and upgrades so that you can focus on your business rather than IT. Said another way, BBD allows customers to focus on their business, leaving SAP to worry about maintaining hardware and software, running database backups, addressing performance and capacity planning, implementing updates and fixes, and so on.

BBD is designed for midsize companies with between 100 and 500 employees supporting multiple locations and independent subsidiaries. It was originally rolled out to a small group of customers in only four countries, where the product was met with ho-hum acceptance. In the past few years, SAP invested a tremendous amount of time and money improving BBD.

BBD customers pay $149 a month to SAP for each user (minimum of 25 users and lower pricing for self-service users). Like all SaaS-based solutions, BBD's fee structure is based on a pay-as-you-go concept. You can easily add users as you grow.

By providing a standardized solution, SAP reduces the complexity, cost, and risk normally associated with introducing business software in an organization. BBD is marketed as a complete, integrated solution designed to provide a low *total cost of ownership* (TCO), especially when compared to compiling and integrating a collection of miscellaneous "point" solutions, which when cobbled together provide the same or similar functionality. SAP does not position ByDesign as a competitor to Business One or Business All-in-One. Rather, it is a solution intended to fill a market of customers seeking to avoid investing in business software and all the necessary infrastructure and support personnel associated with such an investment.

Implementation and Adaptability

One of the primary advantages to BBD is its ease of configuration. Nontechnical users can build business processes using visual modeling tools and web services. The underlying technology includes the NetWeaver *Composition Environment* (CE), Enterprise Services Repository, and Enterprise SOA—tools that make it possible for do-it-yourselfers to quickly model, test, and configure BBD. A company deploying BBD does not necessarily require SAP partners or consultants for implementation. Instead, BBD's users can change their business processes themselves using the provided tools.

Functionality and Features

If there is one drawback to this do-it-yourself approach, it's the degree to which BBD can be customized. The product supports moderately complex business processes. The current functionality is most applicable to companies in the following industry sectors: automotive, consumer products, high tech, industrial machinery and components, manufacturing, mill products, professional services, and wholesale distribution. Service and Support as well as Business Analytics are built in to the BBD. For companies with the need for deep, industry-specific functionality in other industry verticals (or a highly customizable solution), look elsewhere.

One of the common themes among SAP's SME offerings is providing a superior user experience. Business ByDesign includes features such built-in learning, help, and support, all designed to improve the user experience and increase adoption. Another idea taking place at SAP is the idea of communities. In addition to the SAP support center, you can tap into the knowledge and experience of experts and other users all over the world.

Advantages of BBD's Approach to Hosting

SAP hosts your Business ByDesign system in an enterprise class datacenter designed to provide high availability and reliability. In addition to providing the hardware and software underneath BBD, SAP also maintains this solution. For example, SAP takes care of backups, offsite media protection, infrastructure patching, and so on. BBD provides automated support via automated health checks. You also receive automatic updates, so your software is always up-to-date. The net of all these features is that you also don't need a technical staff to maintain or configure Business ByDesign.

BBD and SAP Partner Challenges

Although Business ByDesign has several good things going for it, a few obstacles stand in its way. First, its lukewarm introduction allowed SAP's competitors the chance to attack's its execution ability and ultimately its commitment to SaaS-based solutions. Second, BBD by its very nature doesn't require an army of partners and consultants. Traditionally, SAP's partners have profited by adding value in the form of installation, integration, customization, and support services. Without these extra opportunities to make money, only time will tell to what extent BBD is promoted as a solution by SAP's partner-rich customer base.

In the same way, BBD does not enjoy the same specialized solution development opportunities SAP's partners provide for Business One or Business All-in-One. With little opportunity to bring in extra income, SAP will have to find a way to either convince partners to sell Business ByDesign to SMEs (difficult at best) or become adept at directly selling this solution—a real paradigm shift for SAP and its ecosystem.

A final BBD challenge relates to data and application hosting. SAP needs to convince its customers to house their data and run their systems from SAP's very own datacenters. Customers need to feel confident that their data stores are at least as safe and secure as if the solutions were housed in a customer's own datacenter. SAP has a long and rich history of hosting and co-hosting its solutions, but its start-and-stop history of providing these kinds of services works against it.

SAP All-in-One

SAP All-in-One is designed to meet the needs of midsize companies with between 100 and 2,500 employees, supporting multiple locations/divisions and all types of subsidiaries. All-in-One is a complete business solution, an integrated suite of products designed to provide increased control via real-time information and to allow for more efficient workflows. SAP All-in-One is adaptable, built on the SAP NetWeaver platform, including Enterprise SOA. It is a proven business solution, too, based on SAP ERP, with a custom CRM solution specifically designed and built in to the product to address mid-size company needs. This means that medium-size businesses receive the same benefits of SAP ERP that enterprise customers enjoy, plus the benefits of best practices, including quicker, more predictable and therefore less-costly implementations. Finally, All-in-One provides an intuitive user experience, based in large part on the use of the new SAP NetWeaver Business Client.

SAP All-in-One Functionality

If you turn back and review the goals of SME solutions presented at the beginning of this hour, it should be obvious how well All-in-One meets a small or medium business organization's requirements. The All-in-One solutions include core business processes such as analytics, planning, purchasing, inventory management, production, sales, marketing (CRM), financials and controlling, human resource management, and a host of industry-specific business processes related to fields such as discrete manufacturing, process manufacturing, professional services, wholesale/distribution, retail, and others. These solutions are enabled and delivered via preconfigured best practices from SAP. Further extensibility is made possible via partner solutions. And All-in-One includes great CRM functionality, as well, such as the following:

▶ Account and Contact Management

▶ Activity Management

▶ Pipeline Performance Management

▶ Campaign Management

▶ Segmentation

All-in-One provides enhanced business visibility and reporting, too. Boasting tight integration with Microsoft Excel, SAP makes it possible to access custom analytical reports in Excel—where users can manipulate, display, and analyze their data using Excel's familiar features and tools. This eliminates the need to pull reports from various systems, too, or to integrate disparate systems in order to obtain a complete picture of the entire business. And with All-in-One's support for regulatory compliance (including documentation and reporting by country and industry for select regulations, including Sarbanes Oxley in the United States), business transparency is easily achieved.

All-in-One Partners and Solution Centers

SAP All-in-One benefits from an ecosystem of over 1,000 partners supported by regional SAP-based Solution Centers. SAP Partners build and deliver solutions designed to cover highly specific industry needs (SAP refers to these as *microvertical solutions*). Hundreds of solutions have been developed by partners in 50+ countries. The SAP Solution Centers qualify partners. This makes it apparent which solutions deliver the functions and processes appropriate to your industry. A sampling of All-in-One's solutions includes the following:

▶ **Automotive**—72 partner-developed solutions qualified

▶ **Chemicals**—58 partner-developed solutions qualified

▶ **Consumer products**—83 partner-developed solutions qualified

▶ **Professional services**—47 partner-developed solutions qualified

Again, partners play an important role in All-in-One. In addition to developing solutions, partners provide implementation and support, and customization expertise. The SAP Solution Centers aid partners by providing deployment tools and methodologies; they also provide detailed documentation of business processes to help accelerate implementation.

Features and Functionality

To compete in the midmarket, SAP had to make All-in-One easier to use, configure, and administer when compared to the SAP Business Suite. To this end, SAP also provides a user-friendly interface (the SAP NetWeaver Business Client software) based on predefined roles, making it easy for employees to accomplish their daily tasks. A related feature is Power Lists, which list activities related to the current business process. Role-based reporting is also included, plus the ability to use the SAP Business Explorer tool (smart plug-in for Excel). Put together, these features make it easier for a user to accomplish his or her job (and the roles can be customized if needed).

An important feature of Business All-in-One is the ability to provide a predictable cost of ownership, which starts with a predictable implementation time and cost. This is realized by using SAP best practices during the implementation to simplify configuration of Business All-in-One, thereby making implementation time more predictable. This is because SAP best practices facilitates the creation of industry-specific business processes and operations. The advantage to best practices is that the business processes have been tested—you're not building business processes from the ground up.

SAP has built a best practices library based on more than 35 years of customer implementations in more than 25 industries worldwide. You can take advantage of the lessons they have learned from this experience to implement documented, preconfigured business scenarios (in many cases, specific to your industry). The documentation includes end-user training guides and configuration guides.

One of the selling points of Business All-in-One is the ability to adapt to changing business needs in a rapid fashion—a key requirement for midsize businesses. The primary enabler of this adaptability is the SAP NetWeaver platform. In addition, Business All-in-One is extensible via partner solutions, as you learned earlier this hour. Finally, remember that Business All-in-One is essentially SAP ERP and can be customized in the same manner.

SAP Business All-in-One is built on the SAP NetWeaver platform, the same platform used by the SAP Business Suite. NetWeaver is based on industry-standard protocols, which can be used to integrate Business All-in-One with third-party products. (It also provides the integration platform for SAP solutions.) In addition to supporting the development of enterprise *service-oriented architecture* (SOA)-based applications, NetWeaver provides a Java development environment and supports applications developed in the Microsoft .NET and IBM WebSphere development environments.

All-in-One's Intuitive User Experience

Business All-in-One comes with the latest version of the SAP NetWeaver Business Client designed to provide an intuitive user experience with an easy-to-use interface. SAP is trying to reduce the disruption inevitably caused by the introduction of new business software, which can potentially change existing business processes. SAP has improved usability through role-based navigation, which can be configured to meet your requirements. Examples of predefined roles include Financial Accountant, Sales Person, Purchaser, and Shop Floor Specialist.

As an example of how the focus on roles simplifies usability, a user's role determines the contents of the user's navigation list; the user only sees the tasks relevant to his or her role. The user's role also controls the Power Lists presented to him or her. Power Lists are links to navigation folders and links to business objects, such as all open sales orders—the activities relevant to completing tasks required by the user's role. Access to reports is also based on roles. The end result is that users have access to the business objects relevant to their roles in the organization in an intuitive manner, while administration is made easier.

To improve productivity, SAP has also included guided procedures with embedded contextual help. The guided procedures walk the user through completing a task while providing help on the screen. (This can be turned off when it is no longer needed.) The idea behind all these improvements is to minimize the disruption of a new business application by creating an intuitive user experience.

Selecting the "Best" SAP Solution

The "best" solution depends on many factors, including cost, required functionality, features, preference for onsite versus hosted solutions, size, and complexity of the business processes to be configured. SAP provides a breadth of products, each targeted a bit differently at addressing these factors, as detailed next.

Cost

The cost of any business software is much more than the initial cost of the software licenses. Cost is normally an important factor in the decision-making process, so it is crucial that the true cost be determined. The following should be accounted for when determining the true cost of an SME solution:

▶ Initial costs, including licenses, installation, and configuration (especially true of on-premise rather than hosted solutions), the cost of data migration (from the current systems, if necessary), the cost of customization, and the cost of integration (with other systems that will remain intact, as applicable)

▶ Ongoing "operational" costs, including support (both technical and functional in nature) and software maintenance (an annual fee paid to the software provider)

Despite the initial outlay of cash, it's actually the ongoing costs that add up to represent the greatest expense over the business solution's lifetime.

Functionality

The solutions offered by SAP and their competitors may differ significantly in regards to functionality. The key here is to find a solution that meets the business's requirements—for example, it doesn't make sense to pay for functionality you will never use.

Features

Many of the features involve making the application easier to use. If two competing solutions provide approximately the same functionality, the solution providing the feature set most applicable to your business is probably the best choice.

Hosted Versus On-Premises

One of the primary considerations is whether a business wants to house the solution on its premises or have it hosted by SAP or a partner. Business ByDesign is a hosted solution, whereas Business One and Business All-in-One are normally housed at a SAP customer's own site. Keep in mind that it is possible to have a partner host the on-premises solutions, too—for a fee, of course.

Number of Employees

SAP has established guidelines concerning the size of a business appropriate for each solution. Business One is generally targeted at companies with fewer than 100 employees. Part of this probably has to do with the underlying technology. Business One is designed to run on a single server and is therefore limited to some extent by the underlying computing platform. Business ByDesign is targeted at companies with between 100 and 500 employees; SAP requires that at least 25 users be licensed. At the high end, Business All-in-One is suitable for companies with between 100 and 2,500 employees.

Business Process Complexity

Business process complexity has to do with how customizable the software in question is. SAP Business All-in-One is very customizable. It is based on SAP ERP and runs on the NetWeaver platform. On the other hand, Business One is designed for small companies with relatively straightforward business processes. It is important to keep in mind that SAP partners have built solutions for specific industries and verticals; therefore, a prepackaged solution might already exist for your specific industry or business.

Choosing SAP SME Offerings over Business Suite

Another way to describe SAP's SME offerings is to compare them to SAP's Business Suite. Small and medium enterprises choose *not* to implement the SAP Business Suite for multiple reasons. For example

- ▶ The license costs associated with SAP Business Suite

- ▶ The complexity of SAP Business Suite, which directly drives the cost of consulting and other professional services necessary for implementation

- ▶ A lack of the IT professionals necessary to maintain and support the complexities of SAP Business Suite

- ▶ Little appetite for the long timeframes (oftentimes years) involved in implementing the SAP Business Suite

- ▶ Little appetite for all the risks associated with implementing the more costly, complex, and time-consuming SAP Business Suite

- ▶ Less time and money to invest in training end users on how to use the more comprehensive and feature-rich SAP Business Suite solutions

Summary

In this hour we reviewed the full gamut of SAP's big-company Business Suite offerings: ERP, CRM, PLM, SCM, and SRM. We then briefly explored the six SAP NetWeaver areas spanning Foundation Management to Middleware, Information Management, Team Productivity, Composition, and Business Process Management. We concluded this hour comparing and contrasting SAP's three small and medium business solutions with one another and with SAP Business Suite. In the next hour, we take a closer look at many of the specific SAP NetWeaver applications themselves.

Case Study: Hour 5

Consider this case study and the questions that follow. You can find the answers posed by the questions related to this case study in Appendix A, "Case Study Answers."

Situation

MNC has a number of subsidiaries, many of which are classified as small and medium enterprises. All these subsidiaries roll up their financials to MNC corporate, and some have their own special business requirements. MNC has just acquired a new company that will operate as a subsidiary. This new subsidiary runs several business software packages that may or may not be particularly well suited for interfacing with MNC's corporate SAP ERP and other flagship Business Suite systems. Your job is to answer several questions from MNC corporate IT and try to select the "right" solution from SAP's broad lineup of business applications.

Questions

1. *Which is the best solution from SAP if the subsidiary has fairly complex business processes and comprises more than 1,000 users?*

2. *What solution would be ideal if the subsidiary ran less-complex business processes and needed a fully deployed system in two to three weeks?*

3. *What is the best solution from SAP if the subsidiary consists of about 250 employees and seeks to deploy a system customizable by the subsidiary's own business users?*

4. *What is the best solution from SAP if the subsidiary employs 2,500 employees and intends to double in size over the next year?*

5. *The CEO of the new subsidiary has expressed a reluctance to implement a business solution because the company really does not have the appropriate infrastructure or personnel to maintain it. What solution from SAP might you suggest?*

SAP NetWeaver: The Foundation for SAP

What You'll Learn in This Hour:

▶ History and strategy of SAP NetWeaver

▶ Overview of SAP NetWeaver

▶ Strategic benefits of SAP NetWeaver

▶ Designing a NetWeaver system using building blocks

SAP NetWeaver provides the technology foundation for most of SAP's products and applications. Like the foundation of a building, these components supply the horizontal underpinnings on which SAP business solutions are built. In other cases, SAP NetWeaver components and tools provide the vertical support necessary to tie applications together, extend and push SAP out to the Internet or mobile devices, or facilitate business analytics and reporting. In this hour, we look closer at these SAP's NetWeaver "building blocks," including how they can be used individually and combined to create and support an SAP business application environment.

A Brief History of SAP NetWeaver

Prior to the introduction of SAP NetWeaver in 2004, a large part of the SAP technology stack was synonymous with the SAP computing platform. We often referred to this stack simply as the *SAP Basis layer*. And despite seeming complex at the time, the stack was indeed simple by today's standards. SAP supported a handful of operating systems and databases, all systems were built on *Advanced Business Application Programming* (ABAP), and the systems could be extended a bit (to include tax bolt-ons, faxing systems, printing solutions, and the occasional other system or two) but were generally part of a somewhat isolated SAP-only landscape.

Today, we still use the term *Basis*, and it still conjures up images of a technology stack that needs to be administered, maintained, and monitored. But things are much different. Sure, system administration tasks such as performance monitoring, tuning, and security need to be performed. We need to monitor and support internal and external systems, make sure our email systems are connected, and so on. And we still need to manage the development repository of SAP's ABAP programming language and database objects. However, the relative simplicity of the client/server era that gave birth to SAP R/3 is long gone, and the complexities of the post-client/server era are all around us. Basis has grown up and raised a family, but none of the offspring left for college or struck out on their own. And we're faced with managing and maintaining the whole lot. A quick trip back to the crazy days of the late 1990s is in order.

Back to the Future

With the Internet boom of the 1990s, the demand for applications to adapt to the Web was vital, and SAP was particularly keen to get a jump in this area. As a result, SAP introduced its *Web Application Server* (WebAS). WebAS essentially extended the Basis technology stack to the Web by integrating SAP's *Internet Transaction Server* (ITS), formerly a separate product, into SAP's core technology stack. SAP then introduced SAP Java to provide a platform-independent model for web development, followed by connectivity and support for Microsoft .NET (consistent with the company's vision to adopt open standards while providing customers with a choice of development options).

WebAS was SAP's initial move to offer a standalone technology product that could be installed independently from the SAP business modules as either a traditional ABAP technology stack, as a Java technology stack, or as both. The goal was to separate the technical layer from the business layer so that companies could perform more modular upgrades rather than being forced to upgrade the technical and application stacks at the same time—a process that consumed a lot of time (including hard-to-arrange business application downtime) and money. This more componentized model paved the way for the release of SAP's next wave of innovation: NetWeaver.

Introducing NetWeaver

In 2004, SAP introduced SAP NetWeaver and broadened the technology stack concept into a complete integration platform. Finally conceding to the idea that large-scale businesses ran more than just SAP, the idea was to simplify how SAP connected with other business systems and applications. The earliest NetWeaver foundation included WebAS ABAP and Java components. SAP's mature Business Warehouse and Enterprise Portal products were tucked into NetWeaver, as well; the former enabled underlying reporting and basic business intelligence, whereas the latter extended the SAP user interface in a new way to the Web. A hub-and-spoke integration technology called *Exchange Infrastructure* (the precursor to today's SAP NetWeaver Process Integration) allowed

SAP and non-SAP systems to connect more easily. And SAP worked to develop and share a methodology around people, information, and processes to bring these first NetWeaver components together.

As each Business Suite component was updated, SAP took the opportunity to NetWeaver-enable them, In this way, SAP R/3 Enterprise eventually morphed into SAP *ERP Central Component* (ECC). Applications like SAP SRM soon followed, while brand new components like SAP *Product Lifestyle Management* (PLM) benefited developmentally from a clean slate. Other SAP NetWeaver products followed and through valuable additions to SAP's application portfolio, quickly complicated what was once a fairly crisp vision.

The SAP NetWeaver Umbrella: Six Areas

SAP NetWeaver provides the foundation for Business Suite. But many specific products fall under the label of NetWeaver, too. The NetWeaver umbrella has become so crowded in the past few years that SAP finally organized this portfolio of applications, utilities, and tools around six areas (sometimes called *domains* or *themes*):

- ▶ Foundation management

- ▶ Middleware

- ▶ Information management

- ▶ Team productivity

- ▶ Composition

- ▶ Business process management

The six areas are detailed next.

Foundation Management

The idea of *foundation management* speaks to both NetWeaver's unified platform atop which applications such as SAP CRM and ERP run and to two other products useful in ensuring a successful SAP implementation. These applications and tools include

- ▶ **SAP NetWeaver Application Server**—The base platform for the SAP Business Suite; an open, reliable, extensible, and scalable platform for business transformation.

- ▶ **SAP NetWeaver Identity Management**—Used to manage user identity and cross-system enterprise-wide access.

▶ **SAP Solution Manager (SolMan)**—SAP's ubiquitous tool for managing SAP's implementations and operations. SolMan includes implementation and upgrade guidance, change control management and testing, root cause analysis, real-time solution monitoring, service level management, an avenue for centralized administration, and IT and application support.

Middleware

Middleware is traditionally about connecting different systems so that they can share data and support cross-application business processes. SAP's middleware solution is called SAP NetWeaver *Process Integration* or PI (formerly SAP Exchange Infrastructure). Although not the most capable or efficient middleware on the market, it nonetheless effectively integrates SAP's applications with one another.

Less effectively, SAP NetWeaver PI also ties non-SAP applications and data sources together with your SAP systems. Often this integration also requires a third-party adapter. PI adapters are plentiful, though. They come in several "flavors." Technology and protocol-specific adapters include the following and more:

▶ **IDOC**—Standard SAP interchange document format

▶ **RFC**—Standard SAP function call

▶ **File/FTP**—Local and remote file systems including FTP servers

▶ **HTTP(S)**—Servers using the Web protocol

▶ **SOAP**—Web services

▶ **JMS**—Messaging services

▶ **JDBC**—Relational databases

▶ **SMTP/POP3/IMAP**—Email servers

▶ **EDIFACT/ANSI X.12**—For *electronic data interchange* (EDI)

▶ **IBM 3270/5250**—Screen-based mainframe/midrange system access

Many application-specific adapters have been developed over the years for other enterprise resource planning, customer relationship management, business-to-business, supply chain management, and other systems. A recent review of SAP's supported adapters included Ariba, Baan, BroadVision, IBM's venerable CICS, Clarify, i2, IBM IMS/TM, JD Edwards World and OneWorld, Lawson, Lotus Notes, Manugistics, Microsoft Dynamics CRM, PeopleSoft, Siebel, Vantive, and more.

In addition, SAP NetWeaver PI supports industry-specific *business-to-business* (B2B) adapters, such as the following:

- HL7 (healthcare data exchange standard)

- UCCnet and Transora (consumer products data exchange standard)

- SWIFT (financial transactions)

- CIDX (chemical process integration)

- RosettaNet (high-tech process integration)

- Automotive EDI standards

- Chemical EDI standards

- Consumer products EDI standards

- High-tech EDI standards

- Paper EDI standards

- Pharmaceutical EDI standards

- Retail EDI standards

Finally, SAP's middleware capabilities extend to technology standards. SAP NetWeaver supports several different technologies and standards, including these:

- Java

- Microsoft .NET interoperability

- IBM WebSphere interoperability

- Web services

- Security, including security mechanisms targeted at providing data integrity, protection, and confidentiality

- Globalization, specifically worldwide business and legal requirements

- Accessibility, in that SAP works to make its product portfolio of solutions accessible to people with disabilities

Given that middleware's purpose is to move and share data between source systems, let's take a closer look at how SAP turns data into information.

Information Management

Information management involves speeding up decision making by getting the right information to the right decision maker at the right time. SAP identifies four ways to accomplish this:

▶ SAP NetWeaver Master Data Management, which supports customer data integration, enables global data synchronization and spend analysis, facilitates product content management, and helps companies sort out data needs of those in the midst of mergers and acquisitions.

▶ SAP NetWeaver *Business Warehouse* (BW), SAP's long-time scalable enterprise data warehouse.

▶ SAP NetWeaver Business Warehouse Accelerator, a highly capable, scalable, and efficient appliance used to accelerate the results of BW queries at a lower cost than would be possible using BW's technology model.

▶ SAP Information Lifecycle Management, which enables companies to efficiently comply with legal and regulatory mandates related to managing their legacy SAP data's access, storage, and retention. (Yes, SAP has been around so long now that it falls into the realm of legacy system provider.)

With regard to efficiency, SAP NetWeaver also includes a domain or area dedicated to team productivity, covered next.

Team Productivity

SAP's concept of *team productivity* includes *user experience* (UX) tools and applications intended to help individuals work more smartly and teams collaborate more efficiently:

▶ SAP NetWeaver Portal, with its intuitive web interface and role-based views into an organization's enterprise, enables collaboration and knowledge sharing. Although not the most feature-rich portal, many companies today use SAP's portal nearly exclusively, helping users avoid having to install and maintain the SAP "fat" client on their desktops and laptops. The SAP NetWeaver Portal can also be integrated with Microsoft SharePoint and Citrix, providing end users with a simpler or more consolidated method of working.

▶ SAP NetWeaver Mobile, which arguably belongs with SAP's other development tools, supports building functionality that extends applications to the mobile Web. Mobile users can run their mobile-enabled applications without actually being connected to the network and then later synchronize their data when they have the time or ability to connect back into the corporate network.

▶ SAP NetWeaver *Enterprise Search* (ES) provides a simple and secure gateway to an organization's enterprise information and business processes. By making information easier to find, SAP NetWeaver ES speeds up decision making, helps keep users informed, and makes work simpler.

All these SAP NetWeaver applications and products can be extended and made more powerful through SAP's composition tools, as discussed next.

Composition

SAP NetWeaver *composition* involves tools used to develop, monitor, and manage business processes that span multiple applications and technologies. We've covered several quasi-development tools already that SAP has aligned with other areas. With regard to the composition area, SAP outlines three toolsets used to "compose" (in this case, connect) applications that in turn support various business scenarios:

▶ SAP NetWeaver *Composition Environment* (CE), a Java development environment intended to build and run composite applications rapidly and efficiently. To cover SAP NetWeaver CE would require its own book. Suffice it to say that CE is powerful, necessarily complex, and quite useful when it comes to designing, implementing, and running composite applications.

▶ SAP NetWeaver Developer Studio, an open source Eclipse-based tool used to develop *Java 2 Enterprise Edition* (J2EE)-based, multitiered business applications. Whereas SAP NetWeaver CE is generally used to connect systems, Developer Studio is used to create full-featured systems based on Java and web services.

▶ SAP NetWeaver Visual Composer, used to create ad hoc "freestyle" user interfaces based on drag-and-drop technology. Therefore, there's no coding to do; Visual Composer is model-driven and requires no manual coding. Such ease of use makes this tool a favorite of business owners who seek to quickly create effective (if limited) user interfaces. A favorite development pattern is to create special iViews for SAP NetWeaver Enterprise Portal. Such an iView might bring together a bunch of data on a "page" that can be updated in any direction and used as a dashboard to reflect the status of a particular business process, for example.

A special kind of development pattern involves creating and managing business processes. SAP defines this as the sixth and final SAP NetWeaver area, described next.

Business Process Management

SAP NetWeaver *Business Process Management* (BPM) can be looked at as a subset of the SAP NetWeaver Composition Environment. BPM lets you model, execute, and monitor an organization's business processes based on a common process model. After composing and defining process steps, you set up business rules and exceptions. Then you model process flows using industry-standard business process modeling notation, test and execute your process models, and set up user interfaces or interactive forms as desired. BPM also enables you to monitor these process flows over time to improve their speed and efficiency. All this functionality is made possible through three tools:

▶ Process composer, used by architects and developers to create and test business process models. Like a project plan or flow chart, each business process model walks through a specific set of steps where rules are defined and exceptions are noted.

▶ Process server, which actually executes the process models. This easy-to-use tool is tied into SAP NetWeaver Composition Environment.

▶ Process desk, accessed by process users to perform their specific BP steps.

SAP NetWeaver BPM works hand in hand with other NetWeaver tools to create what SAP describes as a "rich and unified development and deployment environment," including the following:

▶ SAP NetWeaver Composition Environment

▶ SAP NetWeaver Business Rules Management

▶ SAP NetWeaver Process Integration

▶ SAP NetWeaver Portal

▶ SAP NetWeaver Identity Management

There's an upside to all this toolset integration and plain old complexity. SAP NetWeaver BPM makes it possible to create simple, intuitive, and efficient business processes capable of dynamically handling exceptions and dealing with errors. For SAP end users, work goes more quickly, and life is easier.

Strategic Benefits of NetWeaver

Given what we have already covered, you might have surmised by now that SAP implementations based on NetWeaver provide benefits on several fronts:

▶ More rapidly deployed business solutions.

▶ Decreased development and testing costs.

▶ Easily enabled integration, speeding up the time necessary to deploy SAP and shrinking the time necessary to perform system upgrades and so on.

▶ Reduced system lifecycle *total cost of ownership* (TCO), primarily because maintenance and support costs are dramatically reduced in the wake of platform standardization. (Before NetWeaver, each SAP product was installed a little bit differently than its counterparts.)

▶ Through SAP NetWeaver, a company's IT organization needs to spend less time performing low-value maintenance task.

▶ Greater potential for innovation; IT organizations can spend more time figuring out how to meet the changing needs of the business.

When SAP NetWeaver 2004 was released, it made a nice splash. IT organizations, hosting providers, consultants, and others loved the newly simplified SAP technology platform. That was only the beginning, however. Within a short period, SAP NetWeaver 2004s was released, and the original component model was replaced by a newer and bolder concept, including broader support for SAP's most recent applications. In the next section, we discuss these changes.

SAP NetWeaver Building Blocks

After the first few NetWeaver iterations, SAP realized in hindsight that although the NetWeaver component model was an improvement over previous approaches, it did not provide the flexibility and agility required of today's businesses. NetWeaver components such as Business Warehouse and Enterprise Portal provided core reporting and accessibility capabilities to SAP, for example, but these business solutions failed to cleanly map back to specific business requirements necessary to support SAP customers. For this reason, SAP developed the concept of installable software units that today represent the system building blocks of SAP systems. These building blocks are installed as either mandatory or optional components based on the particular IT scenario needed by the business. That is, a financial solution requires one set of building blocks, whereas a human capital management solution requires a decidedly different set of blocks. These blocks or units might be further broken down into three primary areas: systems with usage types, standalone engines, and clients.

By the Way

SAP NetWeaver 2004 was the first release of NetWeaver. Predicated on the WebAS 6.20 platform—the first real production-ready version of WebAS—SAP NetWeaver 2004 was synonymous with mySAP ERP 2004. When SAP upgraded its Business Suite in 2005 and 2006, however, it needed to provide an updated NetWeaver stack along with support for an updated WebAS (6.40). SAP provided this support via what was termed a "minor release" in the form of SAP NetWeaver 2004s, which incidentally also supported mySAP ERP 2005, a new release of SAP BW, and several other new components and xApps (composite applications). More recently, SAP NetWeaver's stacks have been renamed SAP NetWeaver 7.0, 7.1, and so on.

Systems with Usage Types

The systems with usage types listed in this section are part of the core group of what was previously known as the SAP NetWeaver 2004 technology components discussed in the last section, admittedly with a few additions and changes. SAP applied the same concepts used for years in the Central Transport System of the ABAP stack to the Java world.

The SAP NetWeaver Portal consists of two usage types. The Enterprise Portal Core includes the base components formerly installed during the standard portal installation. The Enterprise Portal installation now bundles the former add-on components (Collaboration, Knowledge Management, and others) into one usage type:

Development Infrastructure (DI)	*Business Warehouse Java* (BW Java)
Enterprise Portal (EP)	*Enterprise Portal Core* (EPC)
Business Warehouse (BW)	*Process Integration* (PI)
Application Server Java (AS Java)	*Application Server ABAP* (AS ABAP)

Standalone Engines

Standalone engines are software or services that generally combine with usage types to enhance functionality or extend usability. For instance, the Search and Classification Engine, TREX, works along with SAP NetWeaver Portal and SAP business intelligence applications to improve the performance of search and query functions. Likewise, the SAP Web Dispatcher provides load-balancing capabilities for WebAS ABAP and WebAS Java systems. The six engines install on a separate server or along with other system usage types on the same server:

Content Server	Gateway
SAP Job Scheduler by Redwood	liveCache
Search and Classification (TREX)	Web Dispatcher

Clients

The SAP clients are a combination of front-end components and development tools provided to facilitate or customize the user experience. The traditional SAP *graphical user interface* (GUI) options for Windows, HTML, and Java are still available, as are standard web browsers and the BI Business Explorer. The Developer Workplace (of which

Developer Studio is a subset), the Mobile Infrastructure Client, and Adobe LiveCycle Designer offer rich development environments for Java applications, mobile devices, and SAP forms, respectively:

SAPGUI

Developer Workplace

Adobe LiveCycle Designer

Mobile Infrastructure Client (MI Client)

Business Explorer (for BW)

Developer Studio

Web Browser

Bringing It All Together

So now that we have covered the history and components of SAP NetWeaver, let's work through how this applies to actual SAP implementations. As companies seek to address new business challenges through SAP NetWeaver technologies, they must gather requirements to determine the type of solution needed. SAP provides the SAP NetWeaver Master Guide for system administrators and technology consultants to assist with the implementation of their SAP NetWeaver systems. This guide is available at http://service.sap.com/instguidesNW73 (see Figure 6.1). Note that these documents are available only to those with a valid SAP Service Marketplace user ID.

FIGURE 6.1
The SAP NetWeaver 7.3 Master Guide is available online to SAP Service Marketplace users with a valid user ID.

The Master Guide provides a common reference for the entire SAP NetWeaver implementation cycle and is a valuable resource for those new to NetWeaver.

With your Master Guide handy, consider the following example. A company has decided to use SAP to build a new collaboration portal for its sales force. After gathering requirements, the company has determined that it is operating under the IT scenario "Enabling User Collaboration," so it looks to its SAP technical team to help decide precisely what to implement. The SAP technical group references the SAP NetWeaver 7.3 Master Guide and finds that the following installable units need to be in place to provide the technical foundation for this collaboration portal:

- **Usage types**—BI (also requires AS ABAP) and BI Java (which requires AS Java, EP, and EPC)

- **Standalone engines**—Search and Classification Engine (TREX)

- **Clients**—SAP GUI and BW Business Explorer

The technical team can now take this information and begin to assemble an SAP landscape for the company's collaboration portal using the system-specific installation and configuration guides available from the SAP Service Marketplace. It is important to determine how the Portal's user community will access and use the portal's functionality; usage types, client access methods, and the role of the standalone engine all need to be decided in advance.

By the Way

SAP renamed *Business Warehouse* (BW) to *Business Intelligence* (BI) many years ago and then renamed it again back to Business Warehouse several years later. However, the documentation and product folks at SAP have not completely left the BI moniker behind. Therefore, even in the newest Master Guides and other references, you are likely to see references to BI. Rest assured they're generally interchangeable.

With this example, it is easy to figure out how business requirements can be mapped back to enabling SAP NetWeaver technologies. This approach gives us an easier-to-manage system post-implementation, too, because we need to install and manage only the specific components outlined in the guide.

Summary

From its inception, SAP NetWeaver was established to reduce the amount of time necessary to integrate disparate applications, reduce deployment and development time associated with new implementations, and minimize ongoing support and maintenance associated with in-place solutions. As NetWeaver has evolved, these goals have remained consistent. SAP has added to this strategy to increase business agility across enterprises by building a technical platform with ultimate flexibility. Now that we have laid the groundwork with SAP NetWeaver, we're ready to cover Hour 7, "SAP ERP: SAP's Core Product," and Hour 8, "The SAP Business Suite and Other SAP Applications."

Case Study: Hour 6

Consider this SAP NetWeaver case study and the questions that follow. You can find the answers posed by the questions related to this case study in Appendix A, "Case Study Answers."

Situation

MNC has recently upgraded its SAP Business Warehouse system, and the company now wants to take advantage of some of BW's new features. MNC has a number of financial and purchasing reports currently running in the enterprise that end users access via the BW Business Explorer (a BW add-on). MNC's purchasing department wants these same reports to be available via email, using information broadcasting, and has asked the company's SAP technical team to answer the following questions to assist with the design and implementation of the required new BW functionality. You are a member of the SAP technical team tasked with satisfying the purchasing department's request. Based on the material this hour, answer the following questions.

Questions

1. *What are some of the strategic benefits that MNC may realize by implementing this new NetWeaver functionality?*

2. *Of the six NetWeaver component areas or themes, which two focus on development?*

3. *What sources or guides can be used to assist with the planning and implementation of information broadcasting on the new SAP BW system?*

4. *Are BI scenarios different from BW scenarios?*

5. *Using SAP NetWeaver Process Integration, how might MNC connect SAP BW with its old legacy system that adhered to the Chemical EDI standard?*

HOUR 7

SAP ERP: SAP's Core Product

What You'll Learn in This Hour:

▶ The evolution of SAP ERP

▶ Differentiating between SAP ERP, ECC, and R/3

▶ A closer look at the four core SAP ERP solution offerings

▶ An overview of the modules underpinning SAP ERP's solution offerings

SAP ERP and its predecessors are *online transaction processing* (OLTP) systems—systems that by their very nature are used by a number of company employees and other end users, day in and day out, to do their jobs. Within SAP *Enterprise Resource Planning* (ERP) are a number of modules or subcomponents that provide various kinds of business functionality. Typical functionality includes finance-related tasks, logistics, human resource management, customer service, quality management tasks, and many others we look at this hour.

OLTP systems are nothing new. They are just business applications accessed simultaneously by many online (real-time) users who "use" the system to run the business. An OLTP user might run business transactions to book an order, create a reservation, post a change to a material or warehouse requisition, delete an invalid accounting entry, or change an employee record to indicate someone left the company. By their very nature, these are "small" transactions. Combined across many users, though, OLTP systems often represent some of the most heavily loaded and important business applications used in the course of running a business.

By the Way

The Evolution of SAP ERP

SAP ERP is simply the evolution of SAP's original SAP R/3 OLTP application (which itself evolved from the earlier mainframe-based SAP R/2). SAP ERP comprises SAP ECC; the two are synonymous. Again, ECC stands for *ERP Central Component*, although you will probably see the terms *ERP Core Component* and *Enterprise Core Component* incorrectly used across different websites, blogs, whitepapers, and other literature. Thanks to the SAP NetWeaver foundation discussed in Hour 6, "SAP NetWeaver: The Foundation for SAP," SAP ERP supports open Internet and web services standards alongside Microsoft .NET and J2EE interoperability. It is therefore much more extensible and powerful than its older R/3 and R/3 enterprise siblings. And it is much more nimble, as well; by embracing a services-oriented architecture and leveraging a web-based computing platform, SAP ERP lends itself to enabling greater business agility than its predecessors. You can change business processes on-the-fly, and as an SAP developer you can turn around changes to business solutions and scenarios in days or weeks rather than months or years. The four primary business scenarios hosted by SAP ERP are outlined next.

SAP ERP Business Scenarios and Modules

Several SAP ERP solutions or business scenarios are contained within SAP ERP:

▶ SAP ERP Financials

▶ SAP ERP Operations

▶ SAP ERP Human Capital Management

▶ SAP ERP Corporate Services

Note that the core business modules shared among R/3 and ECC are essentially the same; only the arrangement and specific configuration of each module helps differentiate R/3's somewhat vertically oriented deployment methodology over SAP ERP's more horizontally oriented and much-extended approach. Point your browser to www.sap.com/solutions/business-suite/erp for additional information.

SAP ERP is composed of many different modules, referred to as *business modules*. By combining business modules (and often other SAP components and tools), SAP enables an organization to address specific business scenarios like those outlined in the introductory paragraph. Figure 7.1 illustrates how these modules work and link together to one another to create different business scenarios.

With SAP's architecture, a company deploying SAP ERP need not completely develop each module within its implementation. For example, if a company is bringing in SAP to take care of financial accounting, controlling, and perhaps treasury cash management, there might be no need to develop SAP's logistics offering, human capital management capabilities, and so forth. You might already have another system that takes care of these other needs. In that case, SAP might simply be brought in to interface with (talk to) these pre-existing systems using technologies and tools outlined in Hour 6.

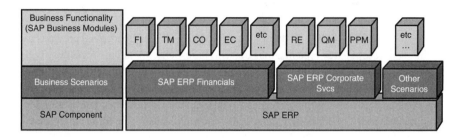

FIGURE 7.1
The SAP ERP component can be used to create several different business scenarios, each comprised of SAP business modules.

Because SAP ERP is so tightly integrated, however, it's nearly impossible to maintain a singular focus on a single SAP ERP module. Why? Because business processes still need occasional access to a certain amount of business rules, master data, and perhaps customer data outside of a single module, and companies might find it easier and less expensive to include that basic information within SAP ERP instead of building and forever maintaining yet another interface to another system.

SAP ERP Financials

SAP touts its SAP ERP Financials package as enabling financial transformation. New general ledger capabilities streamline the financial reconciliation process, reduce the cost of administration and control, and minimize user error. This in turn frees up an organization to focus strategically—another area SAP ERP Financials enables. By offering more effective collaboration with its customers, vendors, and suppliers, SAP ERP Financials enables governance, helps manage risk and compliance, increases inventory turns, frees up cash and working capital, provides greater financial transparency, and simplifies other complex invoicing and payment processes. The ability to drill down into areas such as profitability analysis and take advantage of built-in analytic solutions empower end users as they make better decisions faster across many different financial domains and, therefore, address financial matters such as the following:

- ▶ Governance, risk, and compliance (GRC)
- ▶ Financial and managerial accounting
- ▶ Controlling (financial controls and audit support)
- ▶ Enterprise controlling
- ▶ Treasury management

▶ Global trade services (GTS)

▶ Financial supply chain management (FSCM)

Each of these is discussed in more detail next.

Governance, Risk, and Compliance (GRC)

SAP provides a solution for governance, risk, and compliance called SAP *Governance, Risk, and Compliance* (GRC). With its integrated SAP ERP back end, SAP provides the visibility and transparency organizations demand in response to various regulatory body and internal control requirements. SAP GRC enables a firm to effectively manage risk and increase corporate accountability, thereby improving the firm's ability to make faster, smarter decisions and protect its assets and people. By giving end users a tool to simply recognize critical risks and analyze risk-reward tradeoffs, the time and expense required to implement SAP GRC is quickly recouped in cost savings. SAP GRC's business benefits include the following:

▶ Well-balanced portfolios boasting well-vetted risk/reward analyses. Through GRC's transparency, visibility, and companywide hooks, the solution can enable a firm's decision makers to make smart decisions—decisions based on risk and the probability of return.

▶ Improved stakeholder value, yielding preserved brand reputation, increased market value, reduced cost of capital, easier personnel recruiting, and higher employee retention.

▶ Reduced cost of providing governance, risk, and compliance. GRC is no longer an optional service a firm should provide on behalf of its stakeholders but rather a mandatory part of doing business in a global world tainted by less-than-ethical business practices. Effective GRC is a differentiator today.

▶ Enhanced business performance and financial predictability. SAP GRC provides executive leadership teams the confidence they need in their numbers and methods to quickly rectify issues.

▶ Organizational sustainability despite the risks associated with poorly managed GRC, particularly legal and market ramifications.

All of this amounts to increased business agility, competitive differentiation, and other brand-preserving and company-sustaining benefits.

Financial and Managerial Accounting

The Financial and Managerial Accounting module enables end users to enhance companywide strategic decision-making processes. It allows companies to centrally manage financial accounting data within an international framework of multiple companies, languages, currencies, and charts of accounts. The Financial and Managerial Accounting module complies with international accounting standards, such as *Generally Accepted Accounting Principles* (GAAP) and *International Accounting Standards* (IAS), and helps fulfill the local legal requirements of many countries, reflecting fully the legal and accounting changes resulting from Sarbanes-Oxley legislation, European market and currency unification, and more. The Financial and Managerial Accounting module contains the following components:

▶ **General ledger accounting**—Provides a record of the company's business transactions. It provides a place to record business transactions throughout all facets of the company's business to ensure that the accounting data being processed by SAP is both factual and complete.

▶ **Accounts payable**—Records and administers vendor accounting data.

▶ **Accounts receivable**—Manages the company's sales activities and records and administers customer accounting data through a number of tools specializing in managing open items.

▶ **Asset accounting**—Manages and helps a company supervise its fixed assets and serves as a subsidiary ledger to the general ledger by providing detailed information on transactions specifically involving fixed assets.

▶ **Funds management**—Supports creating budgets by way of a toolset that replicates a company's budget structure for the purpose of planning, monitoring, and managing company funds. Three essential tasks include revenues and expenditures budgeting, funds movement monitoring, and insight into potential budget overruns.

▶ **Special purpose ledger**—Provides summary information from multiple applications at a level of detail specified according to business needs. This function enables companies to collect, combine, summarize, modify, and allocate actual and planned data originating from SAP or other systems.

Accounts payable and accounts receivable subledgers are integrated both with the general ledger and with different components in the Sales and Distribution module. Accounts payable and accounts receivable transactions are performed automatically when related processes are performed in other modules.

Controlling

Cost accounting is facilitated by the Controlling module, which provides functions necessary for effective and accurate internal cost accounting management. Its complete integration allows for value and quantity real-time data flows between SAP Financials and SAP Logistics modules. The Controlling module contains the following:

- **Overhead cost controlling**—Focuses on the monitoring and allocation of your company's overhead costs and provides all the functions your company requires for planning and allocation. The functionality contained within the Controlling module supports multiple cost-controlling methods, giving you the freedom to decide which functions and methods are best applied to your individual areas.

- **Activity-based costing**—Enables you to charge organizational overhead to products, customers, sales channels, and other segments and permits a more realistic profitability analysis of different products and customers because you are able to factor in the resources of overhead.

- **Product cost controlling**—Determines the costs arising from manufacturing a product or providing a service by evoking real-time cost-control mechanisms (capable of managing product, object, and actual costing schemes).

- **Profitability analysis**—Analyzes the profitability of a particular organization or market segment (which may be organized by products, customers, orders, or a combination thereof).

A "sister" module, Enterprise Controlling, extends cost accounting, as explored next.

Enterprise Controlling

SAP's Enterprise Controlling module is divided into a number of components:

- **Business planning and budgeting**—Comprises high-level enterprise plans that allow for the adaptable representation of customerspecific plans and their interrelationships. This also takes into consideration the connections between profit and loss statements, balance sheet, and cash flow strategies.

- **Consolidation**—Enables a company to enter reported financial data online using data-entry formats and to create consolidated reports that meet your company's legal and management reporting mandates.

- **Profit center accounting**—Analyzes the profitability of internal responsibility or profit centers (where a profit center is a management-oriented organizational unit used for internal controlling purposes).

Another key financial module is Treasury Management, which is outlined next.

Treasury Management

The Treasury Management module provides functionality needed to control liquidity management, risk management and assessment, and position management. It includes the following components:

- ▶ **Treasury management**—Supports a company's financial transaction management and positions through back-office processing to the Financial Accounting module. It also provides a versatile reporting platform that your company can use to examine its financial positions and transactions.

- ▶ **Cash management**—Identifies the optimum liquidity needed to satisfy payments as they come due and to supervise cash inflows and outflows.

- ▶ **Market risk management**—Quantifies the impact of potential financial market fluctuations against a firm's financial assets. The Cash Management package, in combination with the Treasury Management package, helps a firm control for market risks, account for interest and currency exposure, conduct portfolio simulations, and perform market-to-market valuations.

- ▶ **Funds management**—Helps create different budget versions, making it possible to work with rolling budget planning. It's tightly integrated with the Employee Self-Services online travel booking function to track estimated and real costs.

Global Trade Services

In reality, the component of SAP GRC known as SAP *Global Trade Services* (or GTS) is also an SAP ERP Financials solution that further qualifies as an SAP Corporate Services solution and global supply chain enabler. GTS makes it possible for international companies to connect and communicate with various government systems using a company-wide trade process. In this way, SAP GRC GTS lets a business do the following:

- ▶ Meet international regulatory requirements

- ▶ Manage global trade by integrating companywide trade compliance across financial, supply chain, and human capital management business processes

- ▶ Facilitate and expedite the import/export process for goods traveling through different country customs organizations

- ▶ Facilitate increased supply chain transparency by sharing cross-border trade-related information with partners (insurers, freight handlers, and so on)

SAP GRC GTS thus enables a firm to mitigate the financial and other risks associated with doing business around the globe. By ensuring compliance with international trade

agreements, SAP GRC GTS customers can optimize their supply chain, reduce production downtime, and eliminate errors that otherwise yield expensive penalties. In a nut-
shell, SAP GRC GTS makes it possible for firms to do business across country borders
and to do so more consistently and profitably.

Financial Supply Chain Management

With all the attention today on driving inefficiencies out of an organization's supply
chain, there's little wonder why SAP continues to optimize functionality geared toward
financially streamlining supply chains. The *Financial Supply Chain Management*
(FSCM) module facilitates

> ▶ Credit limit management and control

> ▶ Credit rules automation and credit decision support

> ▶ Collections, cash, and dispute management

> ▶ Electronic bill presentment and payment

> ▶ Treasury and risk management

As you've probably noticed by now, there is quite a bit of overlap between particular
solutions and modules. Although it can be confusing, this flexibility is one of SAP's
greatest strengths—the ability to customize a business solution in this way makes it possible to create innovative business processes capable of meeting the needs of most any
organization's finance and executive leadership teams.

SAP ERP Human Capital Management

In the 1990s, SAP made the strategic decision to incorporate human resource management, or what it has termed *human capital management* (HCM), into R/3. A dramatic
departure from SAP's roots in manufacturing and financial support systems, HCM really
completed SAP's R/3 and subsequent systems. Why? People are an organization's greatest asset, making a company's human resources management system one of the most
critical systems deployed by the firm. In HCM, SAP has pulled together a robust collection of integrated and self-described "talent management" capabilities.

Today, SAP breaks the SAP ERP HCM solution down into several areas: workforce
process management, workforce deployment, end-user service delivery, talent management, and workforce analytics. HCM has evolved quickly over the years, though, and is
frequently refined by SAP. Point your browser to www.sap.com/solutions/business-suite/
erp/hcm/ for SAP's latest HCM solution offerings.

HCM improves organizational insight into the talents of the firm and provides hiring and
ongoing training support. And because the system reflects the languages, currencies, and

regulatory requirements of so many different countries, HCM can be deployed by global firms seeking to adopt both a comprehensive and a consistent method of managing its people.

By the Way

With SAP *Employee Self-Service* (ESS), employees can be responsible for the preservation of their own employee data and can get access to their information, on their own time, without requiring a PC connected to SAP (and without any SAP training). This saves time for the employees because they no longer need to stop working and visit the Human Resources department, and it saves time for the HR professionals who otherwise need to stop their other important work to assist the employees.

SAP HCM also facilitates a *human resources* (HR) shared services center augmented by reporting and analytics capabilities. In this way, HCM marries what the organization needs to measure internally (related to how well its own HR teams are performing against targets and other metrics such as hiring goals, for example) with the organization's services to its customers—the firm's employees, long-term contractors, and others. This self-service functionality includes or supports a number of roles and company needs, including the following:

▶ A centralized employee interaction mechanism, which is nothing more than a central point of contact for employees that acts as a single source of company, HR, and other related information. As the primary venue for interacting with the employer, this tool becomes a ubiquitous source of "the answers" company-wide. Meanwhile, the company's HR team uses the tool to access and help manage the information needed behind the scenes.

▶ ESS, which is perhaps best known as a tool used to maintain personal data, book travel, and conduct other administrative activities that lend themselves to an "online" support environment. Questions such as "How many dependents am I claiming?" and "Who is named as the beneficiary of my life insurance policy?" used to take up way too much time to address. In response to this problem, SAP developed ESS, an effective means of providing real-time access and data upkeep capabilities to employees.

▶ *Workforce Process Management* (WPM), or the bundling of common country-specific employee master data. This might include time entry, payroll, employee benefits, legal reporting, and organizational reporting—all of which are brought together and standardized to meet local regulations or country codes. The majority of WPM is not done via self-services but rather by an administrator or through a shared services function.

▶ *Manager Self-Service* (MSS), a cockpit of data used by leadership to identify, retain, and reward the firm's top performers; manage budgets, compensation planning, and profit/loss statements; sort and conduct keyword searches of employees' records; conduct the annual employee review process; and address other administrative matters quickly and from a centralized location.

▶ Workforce deployment, geared for project teams rather than individuals. Teams are created based on projects, and individual team member competencies and availabilities may then be tracked along with time, tasks, and so on.

> SAP's MSS is a manager's equivalent to ESS. It enables a manager to do his or her job well and successfully manage the team—grow it, care for it, use it in the smartest way possible given any number of business or personal constraints and other factors, and proactively retain its team members.

Several of these HCM services actually fall into two broad focus areas that SAP still tends to use as labels: *Personnel Administration* (PA) and *Personnel Planning and Development* (PD). Each addresses different aspects of a company's HR functions; the integration of the two creates a well-oiled HR machine that, when integrated with a firm's other business processes, creates a competitive advantage for the business.

SAP Personnel Administration and Talent Management

The PA module of HCM manages functions such as payroll, employee benefits enrollment and administration, and compensation. Beyond personnel administration, SAP's Talent Management enables recruiters and managers visibility into the various phases of employment, from employment advertising and recruitment through onboarding, employee development/training, and retention activities. It also provides a companywide profile of the firm's human capital (people), making it possible to seek out and manage the careers of people holding particular skills, jobs, or roles. Underlying solutions include

▶ Enterprise compensation management is used to implement a company's pay, promotion, salary adjustments, and bonus plan policies. Functions managed by this solution include salary administration, job evaluations, salary reviews, salary survey results, compensation budget planning and administration, and compensation policy administration. Use it to create pay grades and salary structures and make compensation adjustments—an important piece of functionality to help companies retain their top talent. SAP accomplishes this by marrying performance ratings with compensation standards, industry trends, performance-based pay standards, bonus payouts, and more, which not only helps create bulletproof justifications but reduces the time, the effort, and therefore the risk otherwise germane to such time-sensitive matters.

▶ E-Recruiting helps companies manage their employee recruiting process. Recruitment initiates from the creation of a position vacancy through the advertisement and applicant tracking of potentials, concluding with the notification of successful and unsuccessful applicants and the hiring of the best candidate. E-Recruiting also ties all the data associated with attracting, acquiring, educating, and developing talent and future leaders into a single system of record.

> Lean Sigma and Six Sigma speak to increasing the quality of a process. The difference between the two is generally seen as one of improving process flow or speed (Lean Sigma) versus reducing process variation or increasing quality (Six Sigma). Ultimately, Lean Six Sigma will bring these two approaches together in the name of advancing continuous improvement.

By the Way

▶ Time management provides a flexible way of recording and evaluating employee work time and absence management. Companies can represent their time structures to reflect changing conditions, using the calendar as a basis. Flextime, shift work, and normal work schedules can be used to plan work and break schedules and manage exceptions, absences, and holidays.

▶ Payroll efficiently and accurately calculates remuneration for work performed by your employees, regardless of their working schedule, working calendar, language, or currency. Payroll also handles fluctuating reporting needs and the regularly changing compliance requirements of federal, state, and local agencies.

In contrast to these solutions, SAP provides tools to better manage people and traditional HR functions, including organizational management and workforce planning. Some of these include the following:

▶ **Organizational management**—Assists in the strategizing and planning of a comprehensive HR structure. Through the development of proposed scenarios using the flexible tools provided, you can manipulate your company's structure in the present, past, and future. Using the basic organization objects in SAP, units, jobs, positions, tasks, and work centers are all structured as the basic building blocks of your organization.

▶ **SAP enterprise learning**—Helps a company coordinate and administer companywide training and similar events and also contains functionality to plan for, execute, confirm, and manage cost allocations and billing for your company's events. By creating an efficient and personalized learning process and environment, SAP enterprise learning takes into account an employee's job, tasks, qualifications, and objectives to create a custom training regimen that aligns with pre-established career development goals.

▶ **SAP learning solution**—A component of SAP enterprise learning that also falls under the talent management umbrella (discussed previously), the SAP learning solution links employee learning to a firm's business strategy and objectives. To pull this off, the SAP learning solution brings together SAP ERP

HCM with knowledge management and collaboration solutions and provides this in an innovative Learning Portal. Intuitive in form and function, the Learning Portal encompasses not only specialized learning management software, but also tools to author tests and to manage content through a customizable taxonomy and collaborate across an enterprise.

SAP Manufacturing and ERP Operations

SAP ERP provides several solutions that assist firms in achieving operational excellence through process efficiencies, business agility, and streamlined business operations. Essentially logistics, these solutions encompass all processes related to a firm's purchasing, plant maintenance, sales and distribution, manufacturing, materials management, warehousing, engineering, and construction. SAP Manufacturing and SAP ERP Operations (an aging but still useful term) include the following solutions:

▶ Procurement and logistics execution, enabling end users to manage their end-to-end procurement and logistics business processes as well as optimizing the physical flow of materials

▶ Product development and manufacturing, from production planning to manufacturing, shop floor integration, product development, and so on

▶ Sales and service, which range from actual sales to managing the delivery of services and all the processes necessary to pay out commissions and other sales incentives

SAP manufacturing connects a firm's manufacturing processes with the rest of its business functions: logistics, financials, *environmental health and safety* (EHS) requirements, and more. It also allows a firm to manage its manufacturing operations with embedded Lean Sigma and Six Sigma, both of which help create and improve competitive advantage.

SAP manufacturing allows discrete and process manufacturing firms to better plan, schedule, resequence, and monitor manufacturing processes so as to achieve higher yields and greater profitability. This is accomplished through partner and supplier coordination, exception management, embracing Lean and Six Sigma, complying with EHS requirements, and so on—all facilitated by SAP manufacturing. Through continuous improvement, SAP seeks to provide management and shop floor teams alike the ability to view and optimize real-time operations. SAP manufacturing's powerful analytics support the firm's ability to make changes on-the-fly. Thus, SAP manufacturing allows a company to transform itself through enhanced manufacturing capabilities such as the following:

▶ **SAP lean planning and operations**—Accelerate and maintain lean operations (through high throughput, high quality, and low overhead)

▶ **SAP manufacturing integration and intelligence**—Obtain the data that a manufacturing team needs to take the proper action at the proper time

▶ **SAP supply chain management**—Optimize the supply chain hosted by SAP ERP

▶ **SAP solutions for radio frequency identification (RFID)**—Further optimize the supply chain through more efficient asset tracking and management

▶ **SAP ERP Operations**—Enable the manufacturing team to gain greater visibility into its operations and in turn increase control and business insight

The last solution, SAP ERP Operations, has been a mainstay of SAP ERP for many years. In fact, the bulk of the SAP ERP Operations core functionality hails from the days of SAP R/3 and its logistics-related modules, some of which are covered next.

Production Planning and Control

Within SAP ERP Operations, the focus of SAP's *Production Planning and Control* module is to facilitate complete solutions related to production planning, execution, and control. The Production Planning module includes a component called Sales and Operations Planning, which is used for creating realistic and consistent planning figures to forecast future sales. Depending on your method of production, you can use SAP's production order processing, repetitive manufacturing, or KANBAN production control processing. KANBAN is a procedure for controlling production and material flow based on a chain of operations in production and procurement. In the end, Production Planning and Control helps manage the following:

▶ Basic data

▶ Sales and operations planning, master planning, and capacity and materials requirements planning

▶ KANBAN, repetitive manufacturing, assembly orders, and production planning for process industries

▶ Production orders and product cost planning

▶ Plant data collection, production planning, and control information system

The implementation of the Production Planning and Control module makes it possible to eliminate routine tasks for the end users responsible for production scheduling. The related reduction in time allows for additional time to be dedicated to more critical activities within the company.

Materials Management

A firm's inventory and materials management business processes are essential to the success of the company. Streamlined day-to-day management of the company's consumption of materials, including company purchasing, managing warehouses and their inventory, tracking and confirming invoices, and so on, are all part of the *Materials Management* module. Its components include inventory management, warehouse management, purchasing, invoice verification, materials planning, and purchasing information system. In this way, Materials Management saves time and money, conserves resources, and helps optimize the company's supply chain.

Plant Maintenance

The main benefit to SAP's *Plant Maintenance* module is its flexibility to work with different types of companies to meet differing designs, requirements, and workforces. Different management strategies are supported within the application, including risk-based maintenance and total productive maintenance. Some benefits that your company will derive from the implementation of the Plant Maintenance module involve reduced downtime and outages, the optimization of labor and resources, and a reduction in the costs of inspections and repairs. The Plant Maintenance module includes

- ▶ Preventative maintenance
- ▶ Service management
- ▶ Maintenance order management
- ▶ Maintenance projects
- ▶ Equipment and technical objects
- ▶ Plant maintenance information system

On the whole, the integration of the Plant Maintenance module supports a company in designing and executing its maintenance activities with regard to system resource availability, costs, materials, and personnel deployment.

Sales and Distribution

The *Sales and Distribution* (SD) module arms a firm with the necessary instruments to sell and to manage the sales process. SD provides a wealth of information related to a company's sales and marketing trends, capabilities, and so on. An SD end user can access data on products, marketing strategies, sales calls, pricing, and sales leads at any time to facilitate sales and marketing activity. The information is online, up-to-the-minute support to be used to service existing customers and to mine for potential customers and new leads. Also included within the SD module is a diverse set of contracts to meet diverse business needs. Agreements concerning pricing, delivery dates, and delivery quantity are all supported within this module.

SAP ERP Corporate Services

The final SAP ERP business solution, *Corporate Services*, assists companies with stream-lining internal lifecycle processes. Modules of Corporate Services include the following:

- ▶ **Global Trade Services (GTS)**—Manages international trade activity complexities, from regulatory compliance to customs and risk management. (GTS was discussed in much more detail earlier this hour.)

- ▶ **Environment, Health, and Safety (EHS)**—Assists firms with managing how they comply with matters of product safety, hazardous substance management, waste and emissions management, and so on.

- ▶ **Quality Management**—Reflects the controls and gates necessary to proactively manage the product lifecycle.

- ▶ **Real Estate Management**—Manages the real estate portfolio lifecycle, from property acquisition through building operations, reporting, maintenance, and disposal.

- ▶ **Enterprise Asset Management**—Addresses design, build, operations, and disposal phases.

- ▶ **Project and Portfolio Management**—Manages a firm's project portfolio (including tracking and managing budget, scheduling, and other resource-based key performance indicators).

- ▶ **Travel Management**—Process travel requests to managing planning, reservation changes, expense management, and specialized reporting/analytics.

Several of these services and modules are explored in more detail next.

Real Estate Management

SAP's *Real Estate* module integrates real estate processes into your company's overall organizational structure. The Corporate Real Estate Management model is divided into two components: Rental Administration and Settlement; and Controlling, Position Valuation, and Information Management. For a company to successfully use the Real Estate component, special configurations are required in the Materials Management, Plant Maintenance, Project System, and Asset Accounting modules.

Quality Management

The Quality Management module improves product and to some extent process quality. To produce high-quality products, the Quality Management system ensures product integrity, which in turn helps foster good client relations and company reputation. Quality Management services include the following:

- ▶ Quality planning, inspections, and quality control

- ▶ Quality notifications and quality certificates

- ▶ Test equipment management

- ▶ Quality management information system

The Quality Management module enables a company to analyze, document, and improve its processes across several dimensions.

Project and Portfolio Management

Once simply called the Project System module, the *Project and Portfolio Management* module is an important component of SAP ERP corporate services and assists a company in managing its portfolio of projects. Such high-level cross-project insight allows for outstanding planning, execution, and financial oversight, facilitating true project management in the process. As such, it is centered on managing the network of relationships within the system and establishing project management links.

Use project and portfolio management to manage investments and marketing, software and consulting services, research and development, maintenance tasks, shutdown management, plant engineering and construction, and complex made-to-order production. The components of the Project System module include basic data, operational structures, project planning, approvals, project execution and integration, and project system information system.

Like most project management approaches, the system is based on *work breakdown structures* (WBSs). A WBS is a structured model of work organized in a hierarchical format; work or tasks are managed in a stepwise manner during the course of conducting a project, where large tasks are broken down into key elements that represent the individual tasks and activities in the project.

Summary

This hour provided background into SAP R/3 and how it evolved into what is known today as SAP ERP. SAP ERP consists of several high-level solution offerings, including Financials, Operations, Human Capital Management (HCM) and its various solutions, and Corporate Services. An introduction to these core solutions areas was further bolstered by discussions of specific functional solutions and modules underpinning each SAP ERP solution offering.

Case Study: Hour 7

Consider this SAP ERP case study and the questions that follow. You can find the answers posed by the questions related to this case study in Appendix A, "Case Study Answers."

Situation

MNC is implementing SAP HCM and several SAP ERP logistics solutions. As a member of the development team, you have been asked to answer a number of questions posed by several of MNC's business stakeholders.

Questions

1. *What does the acronym SAP ERP HCM stand for, and why is it a compelling solution for organizations today?*

2. *What are the components of Plant Maintenance?*

3. *What kind of business solutions does SAP ERP Operations address?*

4. *Why is there so much overlap among SAP ERP's business solutions, modules, and business processes?*

5. *For the most robust yet targeted set of SAP ERP analytics, what should MNC consider implementing?*

The SAP Business Suite and Other SAP Applications

What You'll Learn in This Hour:

▶ What makes SCM, CRM, SRM, and PLM unique

▶ The purpose of SAP Innovations 2010

▶ SAP CRM business impact

▶ Different venues for using SAP SRM

▶ Gaining business insight through SAP PLM

▶ Insight into SAP Manufacturing and SAP Service and Asset Management

Outside of SAP ERP, SAP offers several additional business applications or components. These components, along with SAP ERP, constitute a family of tightly integrated business solutions under the umbrella of the SAP Business Suite. In Hour 7, "SAP ERP: SAP's Core Product," we looked at *SAP Enterprise Resource Planning* and many of the business scenarios it enables. In this hour, you learn about the other components, how they fit into the big picture, how they are used, and the value they provide. To set the stage, let's take a closer look at what SAP calls Innovations 2010.

SAP Innovations 2010

Although not an application or product, SAP Innovations 2010 highlights SAP's work to enhance how Business Suite, the NetWeaver platform, and various SAP applications impact business agility. This program or initiative was borne out of the need to help companies recover from the global economic crises spanning 2008 to 2010. Innovations 2010 focuses on three areas: facilitating a lean enterprise, growing the business, and improving business decision making.

With regard to assisting companies to manage their way back to economic health, Innovations 2010 marries together precepts of standardization, consolidation, transparency, and simplicity to help companies regain their financial footing. The successful enterprise and the lean enterprise are synonymous; the program outlines practices that help companies conserve cash, manage cash flows, reduce costs, and optimize business processes. In this way, companies can prepare for the next step in the Innovations 2010 initiative: new growth.

Preparing for growth requires attention to several areas. Business networks need to be stabilized and strengthened. Manufacturing processes need to be better integrated. More generally, supply chains need to be further optimized in terms of velocity and productivity. And the whole idea of managing customers to maximize and improve customer loyalty is critical. The new enterprise needs greater flexibility than ever, from staffing models to connectedness to increased visibility and greater in-built sustainability.

Smart organizations must purposefully drive both sustainability and lower costs. To enable smart decision making, SAP Innovations 2010's third area of focus involves deploying business analytics. The name of the game is smarter decision making, and this is accomplished through transparently connecting an organization's people, products, services, customers, and financials. With better insight into supply chains, customer relationships, and so on, organizations can tweak key performance indicators related to the cost of goods, price, profitability, quality, compliance, carbon footprints, incident management, and much more. At the end of the day, the organization capable of innovatively hitting on all three cylinders—removing bulk, growing the business, and making smarter decisions—will enjoy greater effectiveness and longevity than their less innovative counterparts.

SAP Supply Chain Management

It's generally agreed that the greatest opportunities to shave costs and increase profitability come from SAP *Supply Chain Management* (SCM), SAP's oldest and most mature Business Suite component. SCM enables organizations to optimize if not reinvent their supply chains. From SAP's venerable *Advanced Planner and Optimizer* (SAP APO) application to more contemporary supply chain planning functionality and analytics solutions, SAP SCM streamlines many of an organization's most critical and financially impactful business processes.

The Purpose of SAP SCM

Business users employ SAP SCM to model the company's supply chain connecting suppliers with manufacturing and distribution engines. This reflects the three general components of a supply chain: supply, manufacturing, and distribution. Goals and forecasts are created, modeled to reflect changes as new batches of sales orders require the supply chain to be rebalanced, optimized in response to updated schedules and priorities, reoptimized to reflect changes in raw materials, again optimized to reflect last-minute lower-cost transportation and distribution arrangements, and more. As the supply chain changes, SCM planners help companies to model these changes in an effort to maximize return on assets and profitably.

Beyond modeling, SAP SCM enables organizations to put these plans into action and make changes on-the-fly. SCM highlights opportunities to increase efficiency and move goods at the lowest possible cost. SAP SCM's real-time visibility ensures that companies have the whole picture at their disposal. Supply chain analytics provide visibility into the most complex supply chains—those spanning multiple parties inside and outside the organization. Strategic analysis and supply chain collaboration enable SAP-enabled businesses to monitor and optimize the extended supply chain.

SCM Business Benefits and Impact

SCM impacts the company's bottom line like little else. Companies can literally shave millions in cost and drive improved margins in the process by using SCM's planning, execution, and analytics capabilities. The benefits include the following:

▶ Increased responsiveness to changing supply and demand realities, enabling your organization to see and respond to new opportunities

▶ Improved customer satisfaction, given the improved underlying communication and collaboration made possible

▶ Improved regulatory compliance and governance

▶ Better coordination and synchronization between a company and its suppliers, vendors, distributors, warehouses, and other business partners

▶ Improved cash flows in light of the need for lower inventory levels or in conjunction with the improved number of inventory turns made possible

All the aforementioned items enhance profitability through lower costs made possible by timely planning, execution, and supply chain coordination, particularly APO. Typical SAP APO applications are outlined next:

▶ From the Supply Chain Cockpit (SCC), a firm can use APO to launch a query comprising company-specific supply chain elements. This might include products, resources, locations, transportation lanes, and other variables. Query results can be displayed in a map, in lists, or in any number of table-based or graphical formats.

▶ Using APO's Demand Planning application, a firm can also forecast market demand for its products or services and then follow this up through the creation of a demand plan. Different models can be created, too, changing the balance of supply and demand to affect profitability, minimize inventory turns, and so on. In doing so, the firm feeds not only its sales forecast, but also its sales analysis processes.

▶ From APO's Production Planning application, a firm can create a production schedule that balances and reflects a supply plan with its point-in-time manufacturing capacity.

▶ Using APO's Purchasing Planning application, a firm can model and develop various plans for balancing raw materials and other resources against the demand for its products and generate a well-thought-out supply plan.

▶ Leveraging APO's transportation and handling capabilities, a firm can also plan for, optimize, and manage the transportation and handling processes surrounding a particular product group.

▶ Finally, using APO's SNP Planner, a firm can schedule the people, products, and other resources that need access to its internal facilities.

Through these types of scenarios, it's easy to see how SAP SCM maximizes a company's return on assets, increases its profitability, and through improved competitiveness helps the organization thrive in even the harshest economic climates.

SAP Customer Relationship Management

SAP's *Customer Relationship Management* component continues to grow in the CRM marketplace. In its traditional role, SAP CRM supports customer-related processes end to end. It enables a firm to obtain a 360-degree view of its customers and their various touchpoints into the organization. SAP CRM also augments typical back-end functions such as order fulfillment, shipping, invoicing, and accounts receivable. And it folds in and enables enterprise-wide customer intelligence—business intelligence specific to a company's customers and their needs. By bringing a host of sales, marketing, service, contact center, e-commerce, and other functionality together, SAP CRM facilitates better and faster decision making. This increased velocity improves profitability per customer while helping address the business's strategic priorities. Exactly how all this is accomplished is covered next.

Extending ERP with SAP CRM

SAP CRM effectively extends and deepens SAP ERP's functionality. It brings together and integrates industry-specific processes to better support a firm's customers; customer-facing organizations benefit from insight obtained across many different touchpoints, from marketing and sales to service, support, back-end financials, and more. And because SAP CRM is tied to these essential touchpoints, the solution collapses field interactions, Internet-based transactions, and even channel- and partner-based transactions into a single powerful customer-centric view. Within this view lies the true power of SAP CRM—powerful analytics let a firm capitalize on what it knows about its customers so as to not only retain them but maximize profit per transaction and expand revenue in the process.

CRM Industry-Specific Processes

CRM processes are typically very customer-focused, built around the needs of a particular business unit or organizational entity. SAP CRM takes these fundamental capabilities and brings them up a notch, helping firms manage and deliver customer-focused value within their unique industry vertical. And because SAP CRM is easily adapted to different industries, it's uniquely positioned to service multiprovider organizations. Several additional industry-specific features round out SAP CRM. For example, SAP CRM enables trade promotion management, which enables account and trade managers to improve control and visibility into the trade promotion process. Here are some other examples of the power that SAP CRM delivers relative to industry-specific CRM processes:

- ▶ **Professional services industry**—Use SAP CRM to manage prospects, opportunities, client relationships, project resources, and the development of client deliverables.

- ▶ **Automotive industry**—SAP CRM can also manage the automotive sales cycle from start to finish, including vehicle market planning, sales, financials, distribution, and post-sales management.

- ▶ **Leasing entities**—SAP CRM provides end-to-end lease management, ranging from identifying financing opportunities for new leases or loans to remarketing existing leases and terminating leases as appropriate.

- ▶ **Consumer products industry**—Manage customer trade promotions, including brand management, activity planning, demand planning, budgeting, program execution, evaluation, and subsequent analyses of each phase.

- ▶ **Media industry vertical**—SAP CRM can manage *intellectual property* (IP), help you leverage this IP to your financial benefit, and manage any resulting royalties or other payments.

- ▶ **Utilities vertical**—Manage both commercial and industrial customers from a sales perspective, including opportunity and quotation management, cross-system contracts, and key revenue-producing accounts.

▶ **High-tech industry**—From managing and measuring business volume to viewing customer demand, managing channel inventory, and splitting commissions, SAP CRM addresses high-tech partner and channel relationship needs.

▶ **Public sector**—Through constituent services and tax and revenue management, SAP CRM can help a public sector organization manage and address tax administration, service programs, and more.

▶ **Pharmaceutical industry**—Use SAP CRM to manage and support the stages of drug commercialization, from strategy definition through sales planning and execution, on to measuring the success of each drug's respective sales and marketing programs.

▶ **Manufacturing vertical**—Manage orders, the manufacturing process, fulfillment, and more via SAP CRM's lean batch-management capabilities.

SAP CRM's business benefits are as far-reaching as they are diverse. And with visibility into customer data effectively spread across a firm's enterprise (from financial systems to its supply chain, ERP, and HR repositories), CRM expedites decision-making just as much as it enables strategic objectives to be balanced against tactical needs. Like SAP SCM, SAP CRM can provide the kind of measurable and achievable return on investment necessary to justify its implementation and support costs.

SAP PLM: A Platform for Product Management

Product Lifecycle Management (PLM) facilitates rapid development and delivery of the products upon which your business depends for its revenue. PLM's technology platform sets the stage for usefulness but in itself does not solve any business problems. Only by affording a holistic view into the processes and resources that come into play during a product's lifecycle does PLM become a comprehensive problem solver. With it, an organization can come up with new product ideas, work out manufacturing complexities, address a host of change management challenges (from design to engineering, production ramp-up, and so on), post-sales service, and post-sales maintenance needs.

Business Benefits and Impact of SAP PLM

SAP PLM's business benefits are both numerous and diverse. For example, SAP PLM may be deployed to

▶ Quickly develop and deliver innovative products that fulfill existing market demands or help drive new demand.

▶ Reduce the total costs related to planning for and deploying a new product.

- Gain agility versus the competition, and react and take advantage of changing market realities and competitive opportunities faster than ever.

- Optimize the product development process while ensuring compliance to internal quality metrics, industry standards, and regulatory requirements.

- Reduce the waste and inefficiency that surrounds typical product lifecycle management processes; realize a faster time to market as a result of rapid development capabilities.

- Speed up delivery and production by tying together an organization's supply chain and its procurement engine with PLM; in this way, manufacturing operations are streamlined.

- Capitalize on core competencies while outsourcing noncore tasks, thereby minimizing your overall costs.

- Measure and evaluate the progress of discrete product-oriented projects across different product lines.

- Leverage PLM's modular approach to product development and ramp-up, so as to incrementally meet your product's needs as it evolves through the product lifecycle.

- Maximize team productivity through the use of simple and effective role-based enterprise portal access.

- Make better and faster business decisions, taking advantage of powerful analytics across the product lifecycle (portfolio management, quality, occupational health and safety, maintenance management, and others).

Ultimately, the greatest business benefit of PLM is found in the improved business results a firm will enjoy as a result. PLM enables a company to pursue and develop new products; innovate, explore, and analyze new markets; penetrate those new markets; gain a higher market share in existing markets; and increase customer satisfaction throughout the entire product lifecycle.

Using SAP PLM

At the end of the day, SAP's comprehensive solution for product lifecycle management aids a company in its day-to-day execution surrounding product management. Use PLM to enable collaborative product development, engineering, and associated project and quality management. Plug in your partners as you all seek to meet environmental, health, and safety requirements. Gain visibility across your enterprise by extending PLM via the entire SAP Business Suite—from CRM and SCM to SAP ERP and more. In doing so, PLM can tie together various intercompany and partner-led organizations. This enables you to optimize communications, strengthen marketing and sales efforts, and ensure your post-development service and support organizations are tied into the process. In the end, SAP PLM makes it possible to push new products through their development and engineering phases into manufacturing and ultimately into the hands of your customers, faster and more profitably—reaping better margins and faster turn-arounds than possible otherwise.

SAP Supplier Relationship Management

SAP *Supplier Relationship Management* enables a firm to lower its costs through its integration with the other components found in the SAP Business Suite. This is especially so with "operational" systems such as ERP, CRM, computer-aided design, and supply chain systems. Through this integration, SAP SRM positions an organization to improve its product and sourcing strategies, shortens sourcing cycle times, and effectively reduces procurement costs. By reducing the costs of goods sourced and used throughout your company, yet improving supply efficiencies, SRM enables a firm to manage its bottom line. Business benefits revolve around sourcing, contract lifecycle management, and spend performance management:

▶ Sourcing strategy improvements, which include improved access to each supplier's performance, improved management of supply, and therefore decreased supply-related risk.

▶ On-demand sourcing, which encourages or provides sustainable cost savings, 360-degree supplier insight, greater intercompany flexibility, and rapid time-to-value.

▶ Compressed cycle times made possible through faster *request for payment* (RFP)-to-receipt processes, use of online approvals to speed up the procurement cycle, and improved supplier responsiveness.

▶ Accelerated time-to-contract made possible via automated contract creation and collaboration capabilities.

▶ More consistent savings and revenue recognition enabled via contract visibility and awareness.

▶ Reduced legal, financial, and regulatory risks made possible via standardized legal language and reporting.

▶ Greater control and better compliance throughout the contract lifecycle via system integration, alerting, and reporting.

▶ Lower overall unit prices in light of the consolidation made possible, along with reduced costs for carrying inventory and by using competitive bidding.

▶ Reduced process costs facilitated through simplification, process automation, and low-cost integration and connectivity with other systems; elimination of maverick buying.

▶ Rapidly identified savings opportunities, spend visibility and reduced supplier risks as a result of SAP SRM's spend performance management.

SRM-to-PLM Integration Benefits

With its tight integration into the SAP NetWeaver foundation and the SAP Business Suite's other applications (particularly SAP PLM), SRM users benefit from the following:

▶ Improved design collaboration and therefore time to market.

▶ Streamlined access to engineering documentation and other materials useful in optimizing product quality, manufacturing processes, and more.

▶ Better visibility into ERP back-end data, such as materials management processes, financial documents, and *bills of materials* (BOMs).

▶ The capability to mark up and "red line" computer-aided drawings.

▶ By the same token, SAP PLM users benefit from PLM's tight integration with SRM's sourcing capabilities.

A high degree of collaboration is made possible by SAP PLM during the design and engineering phases of a product as workers focus on technical specifications and work together to develop *requests for proposals* (RFPs) and *requests for quotes* (RFQs).

SRM Business Benefits and Impact

SAP SRM also enables strategic purchasing and sourcing by supporting a host of management, development, and analysis functions. For example, use SRM to do the following:

▶ Effectively manage contracts relative to overall compliance with each contract's terms and conditions, and more.

▶ Create, manage, and administer an organization's procurement catalog, using built-in tools to import new product detailed data from external sources, to manage your product hierarchy or schema, and to index your products so that search capabilities are enabled.

▶ Manage the supplier-selection process, thereby creating a base of supply and inherently improving process repeatability. Use electronic auction and bidding tools to analyze each supplier's performance, to collaborate with your suppliers, and to minimize procurement risks.

▶ Develop strategies for supply, again using built-in tools to aggregate the demand for particular materials and services across the enterprise.

▶ In the same way, manage and analyze the company's product portfolio, conduct product management tasks, and more effectively control the purchasing process.

▶ Analyze your spending patterns through global spend visibility; conduct analytics related to your products and suppliers, and then share this data across your enterprise (populate data warehouses, data marts, other procurement systems, as well as electronic catalogs, supply chain management systems, and other internal systems).

Finally, SAP SRM makes it possible to collaborate with suppliers and thus streamline procurement processes, provide better information access to a firm's purchasers, make better sourcing decisions, and more:

▶ **Collaborate with product developers**—Share data between trading partners and your own purchasing team to enable faster product development cycles.

▶ **Collaborate with your suppliers**—Give them access to your inventory and replenishment data so they can help you maintain your minimum required inventory levels.

▶ **Connect and integrate your suppliers with your team**—Use standard *Extensible Markup Language* (XML)-based document exchange technology to gain real-time access into the lowest prices, best volume discounts, and so on.

By using SRM's breadth of capabilities, a firm can truly optimize, integrate, and automate procurement processes into its own day-to-day workflows. This helps the organization never to miss out on supplies essential to conducting business.

SAP Manufacturing

Though the previous SAP Business Suite offerings reflect standalone products, SAP offers several solutions (or applications) that are actually amalgamations of existing products assembled to deliver a particular service or capability. Briefly outlined in Hour 7, SAP Manufacturing is one of these amalgamations. It allows a firm to fully connect the manufacturing process—and insight into the process—with the rest of the business.

SAP Manufacturing integrates manufacturing with other operations, too, all while enabling manufacturing quality control through embedded lean and Six Sigma processes. Through the SAP Manufacturing solution, a firm's management and production departments can gain real-time visibility into key data, enabling them in turn to act quickly.

Managers can document, track, and interpret quality and performance using rich analytics capabilities, as well. Finally, manufacturing capabilities may be extended and augmented with the complete set of solutions for manufacturing, including the following:

▶ **SAP Lean Planning and Operations**—Accelerate lean transformation and sustain lean operations.

▶ **SAP Manufacturing Integration and Intelligence**—Deliver actionable intelligence to production personnel.

▶ **SAP ERP Operations**—Gain control and insight and create value.

▶ **SAP Supply Chain Management**—Connect and empower your organization.

▶ **SAP Solutions for Auto-ID and Item Serialization**—Formerly SAP's *radio frequency identification* (RFID) solution, use this to enable agile supply chain execution, efficient asset management, and adaptive manufacturing.

SAP Service and Asset Management

SAP Service and Asset Management is used to manage service delivery, service parts, and track asset maintenance and performance. As such, it is really an extension or combination of SAP's other applications, particularly SCM, SRM/Procurement, and CRM solutions; the specifics surrounding SAP Service and Asset Management depend on a firm's business scenarios to be implemented. As SAP shares with its customers, though (whether a manufacturer, third-party service provider, utility or telecommunications provider, or involved in an asset-intensive business), SAP Service and Asset Management improves service delivery and asset maintenance. Consider the basic solution's capabilities as outlined by the SAP Service Marketplace:

▶ **Service management**—Manage, optimize, analyze, and continuously improve your entire service operation.

▶ **Service parts management**—Reduce investing in service spare parts while ensuring that you have the right parts in the right place at the right time.

▶ **Enterprise asset management**—Gain real-time visibility into asset performance and maintenance to reduce operating costs, manage capital expenditures, and improve asset productivity.

▶ **IT service and asset management**—Optimize your IT service support and delivery processes and keep track of your IT assets throughout their lifecycle.

This targeted solution provides the tools necessary to increase service revenues all with margins. Service becomes a competitive differentiator as a firm learns to reduce service and maintenance costs, enhance asset reliability and availability, improve productivity, and increase its return on assets. Regulatory compliance is maintained, as well; requirements from agencies such as the Food and Drug Administration (FDA) and Occupation Safety and Health Administration (OSHA) and regulations such as Sarbanes-Oxley are taken care of transparently through SAP Service and Asset Management. In fact, everyone from the firm's employees and partners to its customers may be provided with a well-thought-out, consistent, and integrated view of the firm's service activities, including the following:

- ▶ Handling service sales and marketing

- ▶ Managing service-level agreements

- ▶ Overseeing service call centers

- ▶ Tracking warranties and claims

- ▶ Providing customer self-service over the Web

- ▶ Performing field service, in-house maintenance and repair, and depot repair

- ▶ Addressing service parts management, including execution and planning along with providing mechanisms for managing service performance and conducting financial analysis

Thus, SAP Service and Asset Management provides asset owners and operators a method for managing assets, equipment, and facilities, unlike anything SAP has provided in the past. SAP Service and Asset Management is comprehensive, addressing the complete asset lifecycle—from design specification and procurement, to installation and startup, maintenance and operations, and finally decommissioning and disposal.

Summary

As you can imagine, the complexity of the SAP business solutions discussed in this hour are much greater than reflected here. Indeed, each SAP component within the broader SAP Business Suite umbrella constitutes a complex SAP implementation project in its own right. However, the skills and knowledge you have gained in the past hour have equipped you with a wide-ranging understanding of how each solution provides business benefit.

Case Study: Hour 8

Consider this hour's case study regarding the SAP Business Suite and its associated applications. Read through and respond to the questions that follow. You can find the answers posed by the questions related to this case study in Appendix A, "Case Study Answers."

Situation

In your new role as director of strategic applications at MNC, you have tasked your team with conducting an application portfolio assessment. SAP's Business Suite components and applications are among the company's most critical, but there's concern that the applications are not being used as broadly or effectively as they could be.

Questions

1. *Which features in SAP CRM augment your capability to support new customers?*

2. *What are the three areas targeted by SAP Innovations 2010?*

3. *Can an organization purchase SAP Manufacturing in the same way it can purchase one of the five SAP Business Suite components (like SAP CRM or SRM)?*

4. *How does SAP SRM's tight integration with PLM benefit your SRM users?*

5. *Which of the Business Suite components or products is the most mature?*

6. *What are the three general components of a supply chain?*

A Business User's Perspective on Implementing SAP

What You'll Learn in This Hour:

▶ Business perspective relative to implementing SAP

▶ Business users and teams needed for implementation

▶ The special role of the SAP power user

▶ The seven phases of the SAP project lifecycle

SAP arguably provides the most comprehensive business solutions on the market today. Implementing these solutions requires technical knowledge of these business solutions. But to ensure the necessary business functionality is actually implemented, a cross-section of company-internal business users and external experts must be brought together. Among many other activities covered this hour, they help translate a firm's business requirements into functional specifications, which in turn are used as a guide to configuring SAP's business processes.

The Business User's Role

The job of converting a firm's business requirements to functional specifications that may in turn be used to configure SAP appropriately is the responsibility of a special collection of businesspeople and business-oriented teams. These include row leaders, configuration specialists, power users, and others focused on making SAP's applications usable.

Many of these business people are company-internal. Other business users work with the implementation team to deploy SAP, and some of these team members aren't necessarily employed by the company adopting SAP. Like power users, these "hired guns" are also business domain specialists. In the world of SAP consulting, they're called *functional business area leaders* or *"row" leaders*. Their role is outlined next.

Row Leaders

Rows are equivalent to functional business domains. A typical SAP implementation will involve 5 to as many as 20 rows that together form the core functional team for the SAP implementation. Row leaders, the functional business area experts who work with the company's power users to translate business requirements into functional specifications, are normally divided into two groups: functional rows and master rows.

A particular functional row leader might focus on SAP ERP's Materials Management module, for example. Another functional row leader might be put in charge of the Controlling module and another the Plant Maintenance module. In every case, these row leaders are functional experts—the people whom others look to for guidance and expertise.

Master data row leaders, on the other hand, are primarily responsible for the data to be used in the SAP project implementation. Data includes things such as the firm's unique material or product numbers, stock numbers assigned to products, employee records, customer and vendor records, names assigned to plants and storage locations, and so on. Further differentiation between functional and master data row leaders includes the following:

▶ Functional row leaders are responsible for delivering the overall solution (consisting of work processes brought together to form systems) for their row. As they go about their work, functional row leaders help ensure that end-user site requirements are addressed (such as verifying desktop and laptop configurations meet the SAP *graphical user interface's* (GUI's) minimum requirements and the network connection between the sites is robust enough to carry all the "SAP traffic"). The functional row leaders are also tasked with introducing and leading work process change with site leadership; how well change is introduced into an organization is directly related to how well the organization embraces the changes.

▶ Master data row leaders work with end users and leadership teams as well but from a different perspective. They are responsible for data cleanup and rationalization efforts first and foremost. This means working through the data to remove old data no longer relevant to the business, to consolidate data (such that the same product code or identifying number is assigned to the same part or component regardless of site), and to develop a taxonomy that helps bring all the data together under a single unified umbrella. Master data row leaders also assist in work process development and deployment, helping functional teams understand how a business process changes based on the site, plant, or company code associated with the data being processed (for instance, creating a sales order for a particular site might require special shipping and handling data not needed for sales orders created for other sites). The master data row leader also has a hand in end-user training and creating the documentation needed for both the business processes and data.

Whereas the functional and master data row leaders get the most visibility, another team of specialists tends to do most of the work. These are the functional configuration specialists, many of whom work for the prime integrator and subsequently contract to the firm implementing SAP. Other specialists work for the firm itself, too, as discussed next.

Functional Configuration Specialists

Apart from the aforementioned, other key resources exist who are really customers to the project team but play a role within the project. They are the mirrors to the prime integrator's configuration specialists. These employees and other company-internal representatives help ensure the prime integrator achieves what is described in the *business blueprint*. They are involved in helping define and validate the business blueprint, typically to the point of actually configuring functionality alongside their integration partner counterparts. They also play an important role in user acceptance testing, act as SAP component business liaisons, and provide other expertise from the business (primarily) and IT (occasionally).

The company-internal functional specialists are important, but it is rare for a single person to hold enough knowledge to single-handedly design and implement all the business processes germane to a particular functional area (such as finance, logistics, and human resource/capital management). The company-internal functional specialists therefore lean heavily on one another, their external counterparts, and other key experts in their various roles (namely, power users).

The Role and Perspective of the Power User

Within each functional business area or row are the business's power users. Power users are typically known as the company's internal business experts. Johnny T. in Accounting might be "the man" when it comes to understanding the intricacies of how the firm handles accounts payable, for instance. If he's got the right attitude and network of contacts and company-internal business relationships, Johnny could make a great power user.

In the context of an SAP implementation, the importance of power users can't be underestimated. As senior team members, power users are specialists in their respective business domains. They help define what the SAP system's business processes need to accomplish, what the SAP input screens should look like, and more:

▶ They participate with the technical team in defining and reviewing how the implementation's technical solutions will solve the firm's business problems.

▶ They help define and refine business processes alongside the functional specialists, leading business blueprinting, reviewing and approving identified solution gaps, and prioritizing potential changes.

▶ They are the experts in how the firm leverages and deploys global standards, where and how it maintains documentation, and so on.

▶ They serve as internal consultants to the "real" consultants, coaching the implementation team in terms of how business is currently conducted.

▶ They provide ongoing support to the site's business group or department, often acting as a single point of contact relative to nagging final questions or clarifications around their business areas.

As the experts in a site's or department's work habits and more formal business processes, power users are engaged in the implementation project throughout most if not all of the project lifecycle. They work with their respective teams to build buy-in for SAP, help in testing and validating the system from functional and performance perspectives, assist with training end users, and help ensure documentation is accurate and complete. Power users need not only possess the required business knowledge and expertise to affect authentic change but also must be open-minded as new approaches to addressing the functional area's work are introduced, weighed, and potentially implemented. "Business as usual" has no place in a power user's attitude toward adopting SAP.

At the conclusion of the SAP implementation, you might think that the power users' importance would be diminished as they return back to their old jobs (admittedly using a new system to get their work done). This is far from true. By the end of the implementation, power users have learned so much more about how their functional area fits and integrates into the firm's larger business scope that they're more valuable than ever. Power users become the experts in SAP functionality, as well; with their combination of business and SAP skills, power users will be looked to as the experts long after go-live. Probably the greatest challenge organizations face after go-live is retaining their power users.

The SAP Project Lifecycle

A lifecycle approach to implementing SAP helps us illuminate the broad-brush phases or tasks associated with ASAP's blueprinting phase (introduced in Hour 2, "SAP Business Basics," and detailed later in Hour 15, "A Project Manager's Perspective on Implementing SAP"). An SAP project lifecycle may be divided into seven phases or steps, each of which involves various business users or configuration specialists:

1. Project initiation

2. Matching and prototyping

3. Design and construction

4. System integration testing

5. Business acceptance testing

6. Cut-over preparation

7. Stabilization

In terms of blueprinting, steps 2 through 5 are most useful to dissect. Deliverables or outputs are associated with each step and act as input into the subsequent step. Each step is also associated with particular objectives and goals. A timeline illustrating the SAP project lifecycle is shown in Figure 9.1.

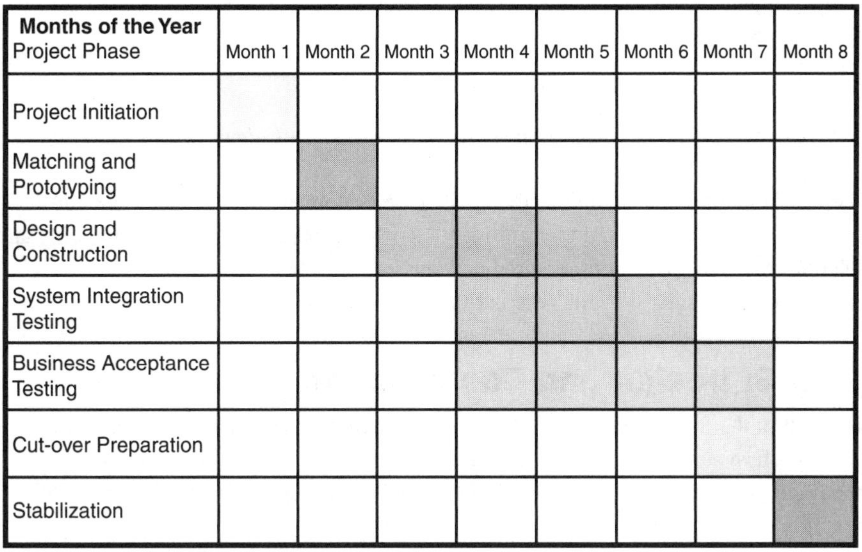

Months of the Year Project Phase	Month 1	Month 2	Month 3	Month 4	Month 5	Month 6	Month 7	Month 8
Project Initiation								
Matching and Prototyping								
Design and Construction								
System Integration Testing								
Business Acceptance Testing								
Cut-over Preparation								
Stabilization								

FIGURE 9.1
The SAP project lifecycle comprises seven sequential steps or phases.

Step 1: Project Initiation

Project initiation commences the SAP project lifecycle in terms of driving the planning and overall strategy of the project—how it will be staffed, executed, managed, and evaluated. This involves several tasks similar to ASAP's phase 1:

▶ Establishing objectives and scope

▶ Designing and staffing the implementation team

▶ Training the team

▶ Establishing controls and other project management processes

▶ Conducting the project's formal kickoff

Outputs include publishing a defined scope of work (project scope), filling out the team's roster of resources, aligning business units and their respective power users, establishing measurable success criteria, and creating the initial business templates to be used for prototyping.

Step 2: Matching and Prototyping

In prototyping, functional experts and other row leaders work with power users and SAP component specialists to review SAP's solutions. Through this exercise, each functional team works to prototype a workable, albeit limited, business-specific SAP solution. Tasks associated with prototyping include the following:

▶ Developing and sharing a complete set of business scenarios

▶ Mapping the firm's unique business processes and workflows to the SAP solution being adopted

▶ Identifying gaps relative to the previous task

▶ Conducting initial integration testing (also called *shakedown testing*)

Outputs from these prototyping activities include a complete list of agreed-upon in-scope business scenarios, a document mapping work processes to SAP functionality and solution sets, a list of gaps in required and desired business functionality, and a set of integration test results showing whether the proposed solution is on track.

Step 3: Design and Construction

In step 3 of the SAP project lifecycle, the new functionality required by SAP's systems to meet a firm's business requirements are outlined from both technical and business perspectives. From a technical point of view, the teams responsible for design and construction do the following:

▶ Conduct reviews focused on the scope and design of all development items

▶ Document and complete all functional configuration and programming work required to meet a firm's business requirements

From a business perspective, the design and construction teams perform many tasks:

▶ Align new or updated business processes with row leader expectations

▶ Train power users in the various SAP workflows and business processes

▶ Publish standard operating procedures for workflows and business processes

Step 3 outputs consist mainly of published documents reflecting technical solution scope and design, standard operating procedures, and the entire process surrounding how to train power users and later the business end-user community in general.

Step 4: System Integration Testing

System integration testing (SIT) demonstrates that the system is capable of supporting the business's requirements. This is a massive undertaking requiring a detailed schedule. Unit and functional testing are followed by testing with all necessary master data.

Once individual functionality is proven, entire business processes are woven together and tested, culminating in a system integration test. Final outputs include the deployment of a "rollout system" capable of supporting the new SAP-derived business processes.

Step 5: Business Acceptance Testing

Business acceptance testing demonstrates that the newly configured SAP system is capable of supporting the company's business requirements. An extension of both SIT and user acceptance testing, business acceptance testing involves the following:

- ▶ User acceptance signoff

- ▶ End-user training signoff

- ▶ Standard operating procedures signoff

There are many different types of business acceptance testing, depending on the scope of a project. However, four types are prevalent throughout most SAP projects:

- ▶ **Unit/functional testing**—Validates each step of a business process or functional transaction to ensure it operates as expected.

> **Watch**
> *Out!*
>
> Be careful to manage the time spent prototyping; without a clear scope of work and meticulously managed marching orders, a team of expensive consultants and a slew of company-internal resources can be quickly consumed by prototyping that might never bear fruit. Carefully align this activity with the scope of work and manage it closely.

- ▶ **System integration testing (SIT)**—Involves walking through all the steps in a business process to verify the entire business process works as expected and then taking the tests up a notch to determine how well they work for a business group or entire site. An example might include testing the sales-to-cash business process from ordering through procurement, shipping, delivery, and final billing.

▶ **User acceptance testing**—This type of testing is more detailed than system integration testing because it includes all real-world as well as what-if test cases. Instead of being performed by the business configurators (as is the case with SIT), row leaders and power users tend to drive the bulk of user-acceptance testing. Such testing might include ordering a mix of products from various sites and with various payment terms and shipping requirements to various distribution centers around the world—just as real users would presumably do one day.

▶ **Load or stress testing**—This form of testing (also called *volume testing*) is required to ensure that business processes run well with other business processes—all under the load placed by hundreds or thousands (whatever is realistic) of users doing their work, just as they will one day do in production. This will validate whether database locking becomes a problem when the system is under load and at what point the system no longer responds well (also called *smoke testing*). As you can imagine, load testing is especially useful to the technical teams tasked with ensuring SAP performs well.

Outputs from business acceptance testing include verification that all users are indeed trained and ready to work on the new system, that the new system and its business processes work as intended (that is, they work as described by the scope of work outlined initially, including the impact that subsequent change orders would have had on the system), and that all business test cases and other real-world scenarios are tested and signed off by the business.

Step 6: Preparation for Production Cut-Over

Production cut-over requires preparation like any other phase. Once all the preceding activities have been signed off on, a series of business-oriented and technology-oriented "checks" should be conducted. Only once all issues have been resolved or deemed non-critical can the system be cut over and go-live achieved. The following constitute several such checkpoints:

▶ Completed "transports" of all configuration and development changes, which are initiated in the development environment, tested in QA/Test, and upon sign-off transported from development directly into the production system

▶ Master data integrity check, to ensure all master data is up to date, consistent, validated by the business, and present (like configuration and development changes, master data is transported across the SAP system landscape, too)

▶ Transaction data migration from legacy and other systems to the SAP system landscape, which gives SAP's end users the ability to look at recent albeit pre-SAP transactions (useful when accounts or shipping status needs to be validated shortly after go-live and the old systems have been retired)

▶ Stress/load testing, to ensure the system scales well under the load of hundreds or thousands of users

▶ SAP EarlyWatch reporting, which entails SAP or a local SAP-approved partner connecting to the SAP system and running through a series of technical checks intended to validate stability, availability, and performance

The SAP support team also needs to develop and publish an SAP production support plan in preparation for production cut-over. This comprehensive plan provides the framework defining how issues are captured, escalated, and managed; how performance is monitored; how business processes are monitored to ensure their performance meets established service level agreements; and so on. The production support plan also includes a contingency plan—the firm's backup plans in case something goes horribly wrong and the system crashes or key functionality failure represents critical business disruption. Outputs are numerous and generally reflect the items listed earlier.

> Just like the development and configuration aspects of developing a new system, transports will also consume a huge amount of time during an SAP implementation. Don't underestimate the manpower required, not to mention the timing and coordination necessary between the functional consultants, row leaders, power users, and others. It's more work than you think. And it only gets worse after go-live!

By the Way

Step 7: Operational Stabilization (Run)

Step 7 is actually post-go-live and is therefore the step or phase of longest duration in the SAP project lifecycle. It maps well to ASAP's phase 6: Run (also called Run SAP). The team is busy on several fronts during this time. Simply initially supporting the end-user community and their respective business groups consumes many resources. Other team members are busy planning for the first several change waves (where new functionality will likely be introduced that didn't make the cutoff in time for go-live). Developers continue doing their work of developing, transporting, and testing changes and bug fixes alike, while the firm's project management office publishes its conclusions and lessons learned, measures and reports against the project's success criteria, obtains final signoffs for all outputs and other deliverables, and closes out the project. Still others focus on refining the tools used for monitoring and maintaining the system—from the lowest levels of the SAP technology stack to the applications, integration points, and bolt-on products necessary to run a business.

Operational stabilization outputs include finalizing and publishing all project documentation, publishing all end-user and technical team training materials, handing off operations support to the appropriate post-go-live teams, and finalizing all project actuals, resource status, and other communications mechanisms, including the project's lessons learned.

Summary

In this hour, we explored the roles of various business users and others tasked with turning an empty SAP shell into a functional business solution. This included row leaders and power users, test specialists, and more. And we walked through the SAP project lifecycle from a business user's perspective. In this way, we covered much of what an SAP implementation entails from a business perspective. In the next hour, we take what we've learned and use it to log in to SAP, customize our user experience, and more.

Case Study: Hour 9

Review the following case study, which reflects a business user's perspective of an in-process SAP deployment. You can find the answers posed by the questions related to this case study in Appendix A, "Case Study Answers."

Situation

As MNC continues to deploy SAP *Enterprise Resource Planning* (ERP), it needs to begin involving its most senior and experienced business users. You have just been tagged responsible for identifying prospective power users across MNC's business teams spread out over 10 different sites. Each site represents a different MNC business group or function. You're also responsible for evaluating risks, and you are unfortunately (and realistically!) behind schedule.

Questions

1. Given your late start in identifying and taking advantage of the knowledge held by the company's power users, what might be some risks related to the actual SAP business solutions currently being developed?

2. Explain how power users help the prime integrator's functional specialists get their jobs done.

3. List the four types of testing that the power users will support in one form or another.

4. With regard to the company's power users, what might be the biggest challenge faced by MNC's management team after go-live?

5. Although power users play an important role in an SAP implementation, who owns the job of converting a firm's business requirements to functional specifications that may in turn be used to configure SAP?

Logging On and Using SAP's User Interface

What You'll Learn in This Hour:

- ▶ Logging on and off
- ▶ Session management and toolbars
- ▶ SAP screen elements and objects
- ▶ Tips for entering data in SAP screens
- ▶ SAP screen objects

In this hour, you learn how to log on to SAP using the SAPGUI and its various SAP screens elements and objects. We cover the fundamental elements of SAP screens, how to manage our SAP session, and then discuss many of the different types of screen controls. Due to either their similarity or ease of use, SAP's web browser user interfaces are not covered.

Logging On to Access SAP

The SAPGUI user interface is also called SAP's presentation layer. It is through the user interface that you gain access to SAP. For example, if you happen to be visiting your company warehouse and realize you forgot to perform an important task back at the office, you can perform it from this site (assuming the computer is connected to SAP via the company network or intranet). By logging on to SAP, the system recognizes who you are and what activities you are allowed to perform.

Configuring the SAP Logon Pad

End users who need to access several different SAP systems (such as SAP *Enterprise Resource Planning* [ERP], SAP *Customer Relationship Management* [CRM], SAP

Product Lifecycle Management [PLM], and so on) should use the SAP Logon Pad. Through this simple utility, you can quickly log on to different systems. Configure the SAP Logon Pad by manually keying in specific data needed for access (see Figure 10.1) or by asking your SAP system administrator to copy a preconfigured list of SAP servers (maintained in a saplogon.ini file) to your laptop, desktop, or other SAP access device.

FIGURE 10.1
Provide a description, SAP application server name or IP address, system number, and SID.

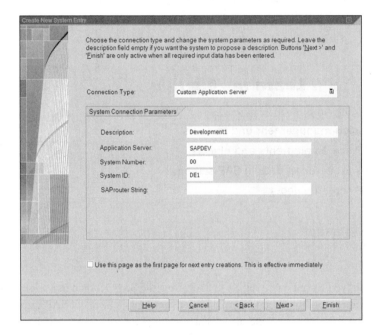

To modify an entry that already exists in the SAP Logon Pad, right-click the SAP system's description and then select **Properties**. Update the SAP application server information necessary for you to connect to the system. This information can also be obtained from your SAP administrator, and it includes the SAP application server computer's hostname or its TCP/IP address, its *system ID* (SID, a unique three-character identifier), and the two-digit system number. The SID and system number are assigned by the SAP administrator. Edit the description to reflect something meaningful (such as SAP ERP production system) and then click the **OK** button when you finish.

The next screen you see when first connecting to SAP is the SAP logon screen. Figure 10.2 shows an example, but keep in mind that the logon screen associated with different SAP products or components might look different. On this screen, you need to provide the client number, your user ID, and the initial password assigned to you. Optionally, you can enter a two-character language identifier. Afterward, click the check mark in the upper-left corner or press the **Enter** key on your keyboard to continue.

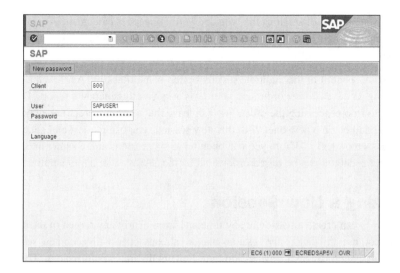

FIGURE 10.2
The next screen you see after starting the logon process is the SAP Logon screen.

SAP Client, User ID, and Language

As discussed in Hour 1, "SAP Explained," a client in the context of SAP is a logical, separate legal business entity defined within the SAP system—typically a company or a major division within a company. To log on to SAP, on the main logon screen type in the three-digit client number associated with the business group (or development team, or technical team) you're assigned to. Then enter your unique SAP user ID. All SAP users are assigned a user ID (although you might hear of factory, distribution site, or warehouse workers sharing a single SAP user ID). An SAP security specialist or system administrator assigns user IDs. When you connect to SAP using your initial password, you are forced to change it immediately upon logging on, thus securing your user ID from system administrators and others tasked with maintaining security.

You might or might not need to provide a two-character logon language on the initial logon screen. Your system will likely be configured to default to a standard language for your organization (such as EN for English). If your organization requires multilingual SAP logon capabilities, and those particular languages have indeed been set up for your system, you can specify a two-digit language code in the language box. Check with your administrator or business lead for the language-specific codes you might need in your case.

Session Basics

Each time you connect to SAP via the SAPGUI user interface, you begin a user session. You can have multiple sessions open with multiple SAP components—such as SAP ERP, CRM, and so on—or you can open one or more sessions with a single system. The number of the current session is displayed in the status bar, which you will see in a few minutes. Because each session uses system resources, your company will normally set limits to the number of sessions that you and your colleagues can create. Alternatively, your company might encourage the SAP user community to limit itself to only one or two sessions.

One obvious benefit of this multiple session option is multitasking. Assume that you are processing a new customer order and your boss asks you to generate a report. There is no need to stop processing the order. You can leave that session (screen) open on your computer and begin a new one. With this new session, you can request and generate your boss's report. By default, you can open up to six sessions at the same time, although the default can be raised or lowered by the SAP system administrator.

Creating a New Session

In SAP, you can create a session at any time and from nearly any screen in the system. You do not lose any data in the sessions that are already open with each new session you create, either. Create a new session by following the menu path **System**, **Create Session**. You will now have two sessions open on your computer. If you want to determine which session you are currently in, check the status bar at the lower right of your screen.

Ending a Session

When you finish using a session, it is a good idea to purposely end it. Each session uses system resources that can affect how fast the SAP system responds to your requests and those of your colleagues. Before you end a session, save any data you want to keep. When you end a session, the system does not prompt you to save your data if you are in the middle of a transaction, for instance. Ending a session is similar to creating a session. You follow the menu path **System**, **End Session** (or enter **/O**, a shortcut). From the Overview of Sessions box, you can selectively close a session by selecting it and then clicking the **End Session** button. Give it a try.

Assuming you've followed along and opened a number of SAPGUI sessions, select number **2** by single-clicking it and then click the **End Session** button. It might not initially appear that anything has happened, but the session was indeed closed. To verify this, return to the Overview of Sessions box by entering the transaction code **/O** in the command field. Transactions 1 and 3 should still be listed, but number 2 is no longer open. Follow the same steps to end session 3, leaving only session 1 open.

Logging Off of SAP

To terminate your SAP session or connection, you can select the **System**, **Logoff** option from the main menu or select the **Windows X** icon in the top-right corner of your SAPGUI window. You may also type in /nex on the SAPGUI command field and press **Enter**. SAP prompts you with a window confirming shutdown of your SAP connection.

SAPGUI Basics

Despite its age, the SAPGUI window remains the most common SAP user interface. At the top of the window is the title bar, which gives the screen (or transaction) description for the window that is displayed. Figure 10.3 shows the standard elements of an SAPGUI window.

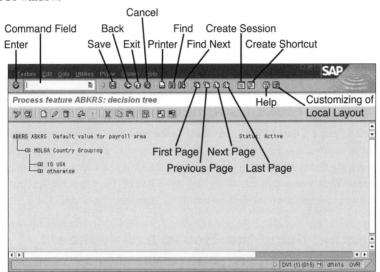

FIGURE 10.3
The standard elements of the SAPGUI title bar.

Below the title bar, the menu bar contains all the menu options available. The menu bar changes from screen to screen to match the SAP transaction or function module that you are currently processing. The last two items on the menu bar, System and Help, remain constant on all SAP screens and contain the same submenu options.

The Standard Toolbar

The standard toolbar is easy to identify because of all the buttons. It varies slightly but generally contains the same basic components on every screen. The main navigational, printing, page viewing, and help functions are all made available here.

The Application Toolbar

The application toolbar is located under the standard toolbar. This toolbar is application-specific and in some cases transaction-specific and varies depending on the screen (or transaction) you are currently processing in. For example, if you are at the Finance module, Create Rental Agreement screen, your application toolbar contains buttons that enable you to copy or retrieve master data from SAP. If you are at the ABAP/4

Workbench Initial Editor screen, however, your application toolbar contains buttons for the Dictionary, Repository Browser, and Screen Painter.

Navigation Basics

To perform the tasks related to your job, you need to understand how to navigate the SAP system. For example, a salesperson needs to know how to enter a sales order and check on the status of an existing order. Menu paths and transaction codes are used to call transactions. The menu bar and toolbars, in conjunction with the mouse and keyboard, complete the transaction and save the data.

Performing Tasks Using Menu Paths

When you first start using SAP, you are likely to use the SAP menus to navigate to the transactions required in your job/role. Your SAP user menu (or Easy Access menu) allows you to navigate through all the functions, areas, and tasks in SAP down to the individual transactions. With menus, you can easily drill down into business-specific application transactions and other functions without having to memorize transaction codes.

Navigation Using the Mouse and Keyboard

After starting a transaction, you will use the SAP menu bar and the standard and application toolbars to navigate through the screens required to complete the task. To select an entry from the SAP menu bar, single-click the menu to display the various options listed beneath that menu. Menu entries that contain an additional list of objects (submenus) include an arrow.

Menu bars can also be selected with the keyboard. To select items from the SAP menu bar using your keyboard, press **F10** (to activate the menu bar) and then use the navigational arrow keys on your keyboard to select and display the menu. You choose a function by highlighting it with the arrow keys and pressing **Enter**.

Stopping a Transaction

Occasionally, you might need to stop a transaction—for example, right after you realize you just accidentally kicked off a long-running batch job. The easiest way to do this is to click the curious little icon in the upper-left corner of the SAPGUI, as shown in Figure 10.4, and select **Stop Transaction**.

Understanding and Using Fields

With your knowledge of what an SAP business transaction looks like, it's time to develop an understanding of how to interact with the SAP screens, to really use an SAP application. Let's start with the concept of an SAP screen itself. The screen is the visual contents you see within the SAPGUI after you have run (or "called") a transaction. Most transactions require only a single screen to enter, display, or manipulate data. Complex transactions may require several screens.

FIGURE 10.4
Use the icon in the upper-left corner of the GUI to stop a long-running transaction or any other inadvertent misstep.

As you enter data into the various data entry fields in an SAP screen and then "save" the data, you are essentially creating a record in the SAP database. For example, from within the SAP ERP 6.0 application, use the command field to navigate to transaction code /nFF7A. This transaction code takes you to the Cash Management and Forecast screen in the Financial Accounting module where many data entry fields await completion, in this case by a finance clerk (see Figure 10.5).

Most screens in the SAP system contain fields used to input data into the SAP system. These types of fields are often called input fields. Input fields vary in length (how many keyboard characters you can type into it). The length of the rectangular box around an input field indicates the length of the longest valid data entry for that field. This simple limitation can be helpful to users unfamiliar with what might be expected in a particular input field.

When you place the cursor anywhere in an empty input field, the cursor appears at the beginning of the field. Because the cursor is located there, that particular field is said to be the active field. This is also helpful to the end user. Remember that the field can only hold data that fits into its rectangular box. After entry, the cursor remains in the input field until you press the Tab key to move the cursor to the next field, press the Enter key to check your entry, or click another input field.

FIGURE 10.5
This SAPGUI screen reveals several data entry or input fields.

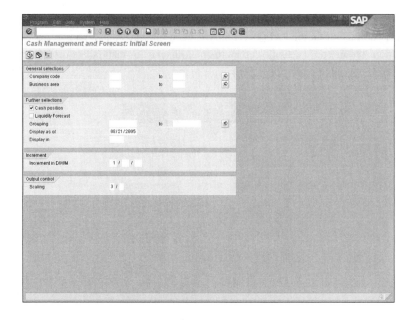

Replace and Insert Modes

Your computer keyboard has a button called Insert in its top-right area above the Delete button. This Insert key toggles your computer setting between two writing modes. The Insert mode enables you to insert data into an existing field without typing over it. The Overwrite mode enables you to type over existing data in a field. The Overwrite mode is the SAP default.

You can tell which setting your SAP system is using by looking at the bottom-right area of your screen. In the box to the left of the system clock, you will see the abbreviation OVR for Overwrite mode or INS for Insert mode. This setting is based on an end user's preference. Keep in mind that with each new session you create, the default Overwrite mode setting is active unless you change it.

Possible Entries for an Input Field

Many fields are quite specific and only accept entries that have already been defined in the database (either by the system's developers or via another transaction) as a valid entry for that field. If you are unsure of a valid entry (that is, the exact name of an entry that already exists in the table), you can click the **Possible Entries** button to select a valid entry from the list (see Figure 10.6).

Any field containing a right arrow on the far-right side has a Possible Entry function. Give one a try. Use the Transaction code /NFK10 to travel to the Vendor: Initial Screen Balances Display screen. This screen contains three input fields. Use your **Tab** key to navigate between the three fields. You will see that as you travel from one field to another, the Possible Entries down arrow appears only when the field is active. You will also see that the Possible Entries down arrow is not present on the Fiscal Year field. Use your **Tab** key to return to the Company Code field. Use your mouse to select the Possible Entries arrow, as displayed in Figure 10.7. (The Possible Entries Help button down arrow disappears when the Possible Entries window opens.) In this example, after selecting the **Possible Entries** down arrow for the Company Code field, you are presented with a list of possible entries that are acceptable and valid for that field.

Input field with Possible Entries help

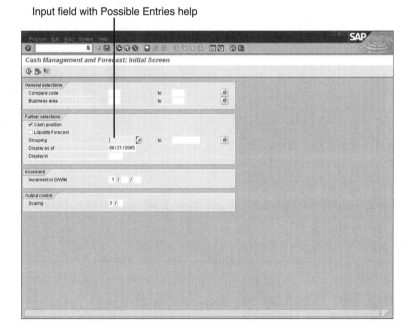

FIGURE 10.6
Many fields in the SAP system contain Possible Entries Help, where you can select an appropriate value from a list rather than typing it in directly.

To select an item from a Possible Entries list, you can double-click it or use your mouse to highlight it once and then choose the green check mark icon. The list disappears, and the value selected is then present in your Company Code field.

See what happens when you enter a value that is not an item listed in the Possible Entries Help. Return your cursor to the Company Code field, type your initials, and press the **Enter** key. A warning or error message appears in the status bar area. This error or warning message prevents you from progressing to additional screens until the issue is corrected.

Not all input fields have lists of possible entries. You cannot determine whether such a list is available for an input field until you place the cursor in the input field. Also, some fields that contain Possible Entries Help do not use a drop-down arrow even if the field is active. In these cases, press your keyboard's **F4** button to retrieve the Possible Entries Help in any SAP field where it is available.

By the Way

FIGURE 10.7
The Possible
Entries Help
window displays
available com-
pany codes.

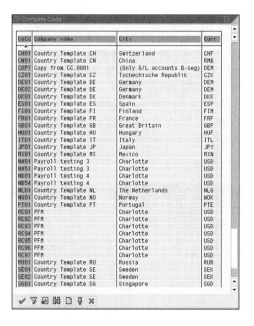

FIGURE 10.7
The Possible
Entries Help
window displays
available com-
pany codes.

By the Way

Sometimes the SAP system saves the last value entered in an input field into "memory." Even when you replace it with a new value, the old value is retained. To clear the SAP memory for an input box, press the exclamation point key (!) and press **Enter**; this clears the memory for that input field.

Editing the Data in an Input Field

Now that you have an invalid entry in your Company Code field, you need to return to that field to correct the input. Place your cursor in the Company Code box and then select the **Possible Entries Help** down arrow for the Company Code field. Select any item from the list of possible entries and click the green check mark. Now your invalid entry is replaced by a valid one. Press **Enter**. SAP checks your entry to confirm that it is acceptable and removes the warning message from the status bar.

Required Input Fields

In the case of certain SAP screens, some fields might require input data before you can proceed. These are called required fields, and in the early days of SAP they contained a question mark (?). Today, these required fields contain a square with a check mark inside it, as shown in Figure 10.8. Required fields include the following:

▶ A purchase order number field on a Create Purchase Order screen in the Financials module

▶ An employee personnel number on a Change Basic Pay screen in the Human Capital Management module

▶ A date of accepted delivery field in an Inventory Management Control screen in the Logistics module

FIGURE 10.8
Required fields require data before you can "save" the screen's contents or proceed to a follow-on screen.

Generally, if a screen does not contain a square with a check mark, you can navigate to the next screen without entering data in any fields. However, some screens that contain required fields are not marked in this way. For example, this situation can occur when you enter data in an optional field that has associated required fields.

If you have not completed all the required fields on a screen and then try to proceed to another screen, the SAP system displays an error message in the status bar at the bottom of the SAPGUI screen. At the same time, it returns the cursor to the first required field that needs data entered so that you can make the necessary changes.

Field Entry Validation

After entering data into input fields on the screen, use the **Enter** key or the green check mark on your SAP toolbar to check the validity of your entries. If your entries are valid, the system advances to the next screen in the task. If the system checks your entries and finds any errors—for example, entries in the wrong format—it displays a message in the status bar and positions the cursor in the field that you need to correct.

Canceling All the Data Entered on a Screen

To cancel all the data you just entered on a screen, use the menu path **Edit**, **Cancel** or use the red X (Cancel) button on the toolbar. In most instances, you are prompted with an SAP window confirming that data will be lost if you proceed to exit the current screen. Click the **Yes** button if you still want to exit.

Saving Your Data on the Screen

The SAP Save button appears on the standard toolbar at the top of the SAPGUI screen, and it looks like an open folder. When you are working through a business transaction that consists of several screens, the system temporarily stores the data you have already entered. After you complete all the necessary screens associated with your business transaction, save your data permanently by clicking the **Save** button. The Save button sends your data (or data changes) to the database where it may then be processed.

Replicating Data

No one really enjoys entering a lot of data. Not only is it boring, but it can quickly become tedious! SAP has several ways to simplify or speed up this data entry process. Quickly holding, setting, and deleting data are covered next.

Hold Data

Let's assume you need to enter 100 new employees into the ERP Human Capital Management module, and all the new employees have the same hire date. Using the Hold Data or Set Data SAP functions, you can set the hire date to automatically default to a particular date, letting you avoid having to rekey data in this field for every employee.

To use the Hold Data function on any SAP screen (except the logon screen), enter the data that you want to hold in an input field. While your cursor is still in the input field, navigate to the menu path **System, User Profile, Hold Data**, as shown in Figure 10.9.

The data will be set in memory for that field for each new record you create until you turn the Hold Data setting off. The Hold Data feature also has another advantage: The input field defaults to the data you have set to hold, yet it also allows you to override the data.

Set Data

The Set Data feature works in the same fashion as the Hold Data setting, but it does not enable the user to override the default in the input field. The advantage to using the Set Data setting is that it lets you skip fields where data has been held; you do not need to tab from field to field during data entry.

To use the Set Data function on any SAP screen (except the logon screen), enter the data in an input field that you want to set. While your cursor is still in the input field, go to the menu path **System, User Profile, Set Data**, as shown in Figure 10.10.

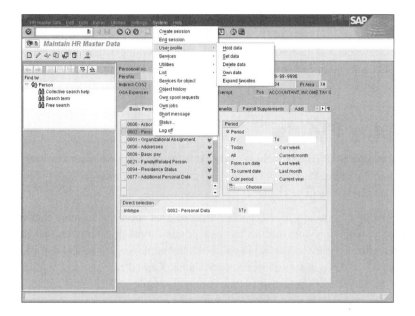

FIGURE 10.9
Hold Data is a useful tool for entering data in SAP.

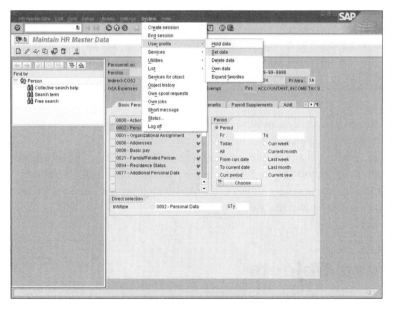

FIGURE 10.10
Using the Set Data option restricts users from changing the set value in the field.

Deleting Data That Is Held or Set on a Screen

You can hold data for as many different screens as you like. The data you enter and hold on a screen is held for that screen until you delete it or until you log off the SAP system. If you want to remove the setting without having to log off the system, place the cursor in the input field that you want to delete and follow the menu path **System**, **User Profile**, **Delete Data**. Once you select Delete Data, the possible data entries associated with that field are removed, and the next time you access the screen the data is not displayed. In case you're worried, the actual data you entered and saved as part of running your SAP business transactions us still safe and sound in the SAP database.

Display Fields

Another type of SAP field is a display field. This type of field is not used to enter data, but only to display it. Display fields are always shaded with a gray background to indicate that the field cannot be changed.

Display fields are typically used for values that were set according to some configuration in the system or by previous steps in business process. What this translates to is that fields are often assigned values based on configuration that occurs behind the scenes. For example, if you add a new employee to your Human Capital Management module, on the new-hire screen will be a display field listing the employee's status as active. This value is assigned and displayed by the system and cannot be changed by the user.

By the Way

> Some fields come preconfigured from SAP as display only, but you can also customize your system to change these additional fields as well to "display only." By doing so, users are unable to make changes to the data (whether by accident or intentionally).

In the same way, when system administrators run processes for maintaining the system, their screens often include date fields storing the current date. These are also display only. The system does not enable you to change the value in these fields because in most cases the values are used by the SAP system for accurate processing. Using the Human Capital Management example, if you hired a new employee and were able to change his hire date, the new employee's vacation time and other benefits would likely be incorrectly calculated.

Screen Objects

This section covers the different types of items you will see on SAP screens. Regardless of the SAP component's module you are processing in, the same types of screen objects generally appear on the different SAP screens.

SAP promotes itself as logically designed and organized; a user can easily navigate through its system. The style of the SAP system is much different from many popular applications available on the market today, such as the Microsoft Office family of products. Often absent in SAP are the friendly pictures, detailed formatted text, and elaborate design. Most screens in SAP are designed in tabbed formats or tree structures through which the user navigates by "drilling down."

SAP Trees

You will soon become accustomed to using SAP trees in navigating through the SAP system (see Figure 10.11). SAP menus are examples of SAP trees. SAP's logically devised environment centers on a basic tree structure. SAP trees appear similar to the Windows structure you see in Windows Explorer. The tree structure is formulated so that you can drill down in the tree to reach deeper levels (branches) until you reach the endpoint (leaf). To use an SAP tree for navigation, you need to select the arrow sign to expand or compress the tree to view more or fewer selections, respectively. Older versions of SAP used plus and minus signs, respectively, to expand and compress the tree.

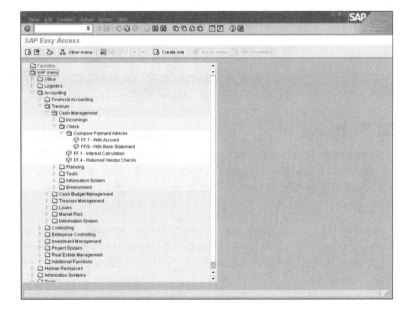

FIGURE 10.11
SAP ERP and similar SAP systems' menus are based on an elementary tree structure.

Check Boxes

When you are working in SAP, entering information sometimes involves selecting options. These options can be in the form of check boxes, like the ones shown in Figure 10.12. A check mark placed in the check box indicates that the box is selected, and an empty box indicates that the box is not selected.

FIGURE 10.12
Check boxes
are used to
respond with a
yes or no to a
selection.

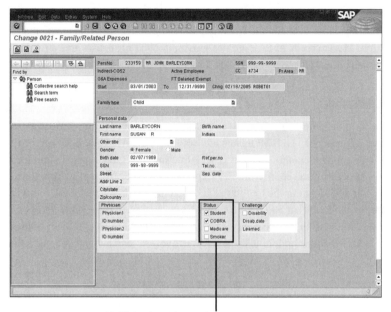

Multiple check boxes in a group can be selected

Check boxes are used when a person has the opportunity to select more than one option. On a single screen, a person can select multiple check boxes.

Radio Buttons

When you are permitted only one option among a selection of many, you will see a group of radio buttons provided rather than check boxes. A group of radio buttons accepts only one selection for the group. That is, you cannot mark more than one radio button in a group.

A mark placed in the circle indicates that the radio button is selected, and an empty circle indicates that the radio button is not selected (see Figure 10.13). An example of a radio button is the designation of an employee in the Human Capital Management module as male or female.

Dialog Boxes

Dialog box is a fancy term for a window that pops up to give you information. These are also sometimes called information windows. Here are two situations in which a dialog box appears on your screen:

▶ The system needs more information from you before it can proceed.

▶ The system needs to give you feedback, such as messages or specific information about your current task.

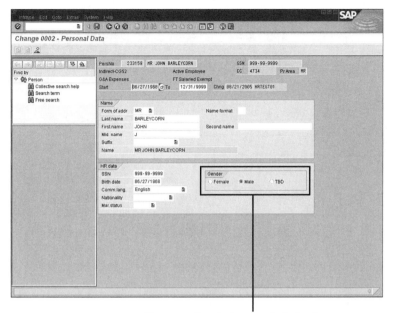

FIGURE 10.13
Radio buttons
are always
shown in a
group of at
least two or
more; choices
are mutually
exclusive.

You can only select one radio button in a group

For example, you might receive a dialog box on your screen when you are logging off
SAP. If you select the **SAP** icon in the top-left corner of your screen and then click the
Close button, you are prompted with a dialog box confirming that you indeed want to
log off the system.

Table Controls

A final object used in SAP screens is the table control (see Figure 10.14). Table controls
display data in a tabular format similar to a Microsoft Excel spreadsheet. Table controls
are popular for displaying or entering single structured lines of data.

Several advanced concepts related to using the Clipboard are addressed next.

Using the Windows Clipboard

You can transfer the contents of SAP fields (and in some cases, the entire contents of an
SAP screen) into your Windows Clipboard. Once in the Clipboard, data may be pasted
into other SAP fields or into applications such as Microsoft Word and Excel.

SAP Table Control

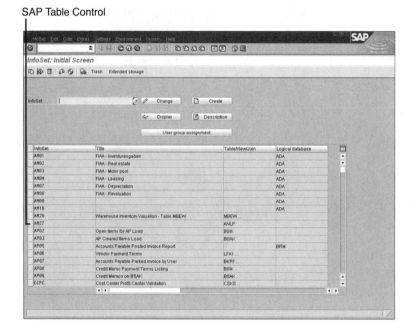

Moving and Copying Data

To move data from a field, highlight the text and press **Ctrl+X**, **Ctrl+V**. The Cut (or Move) command is generally used on input fields. To copy data from a field, highlight the text and press **Ctrl+C**, **Ctrl+V**. The transferred data remains in the Clipboard until you use Cut or Copy again to move or copy new text onto the Clipboard.

Copying Unselectable Data

You are not able to select certain data displayed on SAP screens using your mouse and the methods previously described. To give you an example, return to your main SAP window and use the transaction code /nSE11 to travel to the SAP Data Dictionary Initial screen. Place your cursor in the Object Name field and press the **F1** key to launch the field-specific help. (If you do not have access to transaction code /nSE11, place your cursor in any SAP field and press the **F1** key on your keyboard.) A window will appear giving detailed definitions and technical information for the field you selected.

Try to use the mouse to select the text displayed on this screen. You will see that you are unable to select the data. In cases like these, you need to add one more keyboard combination. Use your mouse to tap once anywhere on the screen. Next use **Ctrl+Y** to change your mouse to a crosshair cursor. Use this cursor to select the desired text and follow the same steps as before: **Ctrl+C** to copy the text and **Ctrl+V** to paste the text.

Summary

At this juncture, as a user, you should feel comfortable working in the SAP system. Many of the once-obscure objects, functions, and concepts should now be familiar. For instance, you should be well equipped to enter data into the SAP system, and you are now quite familiar with the SAP objects that you will encounter on the different screens, including dialog boxes and radio buttons. You also should feel more comfortable with SAP terminology as it applies to screens and controls. You should also understand how to use the Windows Clipboard to store data as you move between screens and applications.

Case Study: Hour 10

Consider this case study regarding the SAPGUI and the questions that follow. You can find the answers posed by the questions related to this case study in Appendix A, "Case Study Answers."

Situation

You have been asked to help familiarize a new SAPGUI user by showing him how to run several different SAP transactions. Assume you have the necessary authority to run the following transactions.

Questions

1. *What information will you need so that you can set up an entry for the new system in your SAP Logon Pad?*

2. *Assuming you have never entered a sales order, what is the easiest way to find the sales order entry transaction?*

3. *Navigate the SAP menu to CCMS (Tools, CCMS). What type of screen object is the SAP menu structure?*

4. *Is the two-character language identifier necessary when logging on to SAP?*

5. *Execute transaction* /nSM04 *(User List). How would you copy your terminal name to the Clipboard?*

SAP User Roles and Authorizations

What You'll Learn in This Hour:

▶ An overview of SAP security
▶ The purpose of the SAP Profile Generator
▶ Single roles versus composite roles
▶ User authorizations
▶ How user authorizations differ based on SAP application server type

In this hour, we look at SAP security. An overview of this broad subject is followed by a closer look at SAP roles and authorizations. In this way, we set the stage for Hour 12, "Using SAP to Do Your Job," which is where an SAP end user can finally focus on getting actual work done in SAP.

What Is SAP Security?

In the same way an SAP implementation is complex, so is the topic of SAP security. SAP security can be confusing, too. To IT infrastructure professionals, security usually means safeguarding the hardware and operating system from unauthorized access. Database administrators usually think of securing sensitive database tables and indexes so that only certain people can see, change, insert, or delete data. And SAP Basis professionals equate SAP security to locking down the SAP Basis layer and application integration points. But SAP security to the largest group of people, SAP's end-user community, refers to something different: establishing the functional roles and authorizations necessary to do your job using SAP. For example:

▶ Each SAP Business Suite and NetWeaver component requires user IDs to be created.

▶ Within each application (such as SAP *Enterprise Resource Planning* [ERP] Financials, Logistics, Warehouse, and so on), functional or "domain-specific" roles need to be defined. You might create a purchasing role, a sales role, an auditor role, an accounts payable clerk role, and so on.

▶ Roles need to be carefully tuned; within the finance functional area, for example, different types of roles must be carefully segregated from one another in the name of "separation of duties."

▶ The user IDs created previously need to be associated with one or more roles. (A/P clerks need to be tied to the A/P clerk role, for example.)

▶ One or more specific authorizations (giving role owners the ability to run specific business transactions) need to be added to every role.

For SAP environments comprised of many different SAP applications and components, all these roles, authorizations, and user IDs need to be synchronized (best case) or managed (at minimum) across nonproduction and production systems. SAP provides identity management tools to helps facilitate this process, but a discussion of those tools is beyond the scope of this discussion. Refer to www.sdn.sap.com/irj/sdn/nw-identitymanagement to learn more about SAP identity management.

Overview of SAP Security

SAP security covers a number of broad domains. Before we focus on SAP security from an end user's perspective, let's set the stage with a review of SAP technical infrastructure security followed by the concept of process security.

SAP Technical Infrastructure Security

The best way to decompose SAP infrastructure security is to subdivide it the same way we divide the SAP technology stack—by layers:

▶ Building and site security, such as physical access to a datacenter or other SAP hosting facility

▶ Network infrastructure, including protecting routers, switches, and network links connecting SAP to its users and providers

▶ Hardware infrastructure, particularly safeguarding the system's physical servers and disk infrastructure from internal and remote attacks

▶ Operating system layer, which most often amounts to hardening the OS from viruses, Trojans, and similar threats

▶ Database layer, hardening from worms and other threats, and protecting data.

▶ SAP Basis (application) layer, including controlling access to SAP's executables or binaries and data

▶ Other applications and their integration points, which play an important role in building end-to-end SAP business scenarios

▶ SAP access layer and methods, such as SAPGUI and WebGUI access and special interfaces

After an SAP organization's SAP infrastructure is locked down and protected, the system may be similarly locked down from an application perspective.

SAP Process Security

Creating a process model or workflow helps SAP security professionals create a secure system. This is done in conjunction with SAP functional specialists, or the experts in specific business processes and scenarios. Let's take the purchasing process as an example. Procurement professionals need to work within the constraints of different approval levels; an expensive purchase should be approved by a more senior manager, whereas a less-expensive purchase might be approved by a junior clerk. Most organizations set up tiers to reflect these approval levels.

Next, the person who creates the purchase should not be the person who approves it. Otherwise, this person could abuse the system (if only for a short while, until someone reviewed the financials associated with such purchases). And the person who receives and signs for the purchase should probably not be the one who places the order (unless we're talking about a carefully controlled self-service scenario).

By looking at business processes from a workflow perspective, we can create process models that reflect the proper controls and balances necessary to keep honest people honest. For instance, we could also institute a general ledger review process intended to identify potential purchasing irregularities. It's these process models that are used to establish workflows and ultimately identify the worker roles to which users are assigned. Through their roles, users complete the work associated with a business scenario, explored in more detail next.

SAP Roles

SAP provides several methods that help us create and manage roles. The idea behind a role is simple: A role is used to assign access to the system. Roles are easier to manage than individual user IDs. For example, if Joe is a procurement professional, he needs the ability to execute several procurement-specific business transactions. All of these necessary business transactions can be brought together in a role specially developed for procurement professionals. Then, when another procurement professional is hired one day, he or she needs to be assigned only to the procurement role to begin working with SAP.

This is much easier than trying to figure out all the transactions Joe is authorized to execute and then duplicate them for the new user, especially if Joe had been granted the authorizations to run *other* transactions related to roles he might have previously held. Let's turn our attention to SAP's tool for creating profiles: the SAP Profile Generator.

SAP Profile Generator

SAP introduced the SAP Profile Generator (sometimes abbreviated as PG) more than a decade ago. The Profile Generator is executed by running transaction /nPFCG. Its purpose is to assist an SAP end-user security organization with implementing an SAP application-layer security model.

Based on the concepts of authorization objects and profiles, the Profile Generator provides an SAP application security professional with a tool and the necessary capabilities to manage how users get their work done across a complex set of SAP applications. End users are assigned to one or more roles (called *activity groups* in the earliest releases of the Profile Generator), and these roles are then assigned authorizations.

As part of the role development process, a security specialist assigns to users the user menu that is displayed after they log on to the SAP system. The security specialist creates the roles reflecting the specific authorizations needed by a subset of end users to access and run their reports, transactions, and web-based applications.

Combined, all the various roles set up in SAP should completely map back to the various business departments and other functional organizations that ultimately comprise the SAP end-user community. Because business is complex, authorizations can naturally become very detailed and complex as well. Certain users might require additional capabilities based on their specific job within a department. Jobs might be consolidated or changed over time, and these changes need to be captured by updating SAP's roles. As roles become too complex, they need to be revisited and possibly reformed.

A good rule of thumb is the Rule of 15: If a role reflects more than 15 discrete business transactions, it's probably too broad. Smart SAP security organizations bring together two or more single roles to create a *composite role*. In this way, single roles act as easily manageable "building blocks," which can be fine-tuned as a company's business needs and the roles people play change over time.

As you can imagine, initially setting up these roles is very time-consuming, and managing and updating them as the company's business needs evolve is even more time-consuming. For more detailed information, refer to SAP's online help (http://help.sap.com) or one of the many excellent texts on security administration and support.

SAP Authorizations

Although a detailed treatise on SAP security is beyond the scope of this book, a brief discussion of SAP authorizations and the role they play in securing data and business processes is in order. The data stored in SAP needs to be secured not only from outside intrusion, but also from within the end-user community. Assume that your company has implemented SAP ERP Materials Management and Human Resources; you would not want individuals from your Materials Management department accessing confidential HR data, nor would you like to see HR employees mucking around in your warehouses. To avoid this, SAP uses the concept of assigning "authorizations" to users based on the jobs or roles the users hold in their organizations.

Authorization Profiles

To simplify the administration of security authorizations, SAP uses the concept of creating authorization profiles. Authorization profiles are assigned to specific SAP user IDs. Your user ID refers exclusively to profiles when designating access privileges in SAP. In turn, these profiles grant (or by their exclusion, deny) a certain level of system access on behalf of an end user. Table 11.1 provides several examples of ERP authorization profiles.

TABLE 11.1 SAP ERP Authorization Profiles

Authorization	Abbreviated Authorization Description Profile Name
SAP_ALL	All SAP system authorizations
S_ABAP_ALL	All authorizations for ABAP/4
S_ADMI_ALL	All administration authorizations
S_A.ADMIN	Operator
S_A.CUSTOMIZ	Customizing (for all system setting activities)
S_A.TMSADM	Authorization for system user TMSADM
S_A.TMSCFG	Authorization to maintain CTS configuration
S_A.SYSTEM	System administrator (superuser)
S_ADDR_ALL	All authorizations for the central address management
S_ADMI_SAP	Administration authorization except spool administration
S_ADMI_SPO_A	All spool administrations

TABLE 11.1   SAP ERP Authorization Profiles

Authorization	Abbreviated Authorization Description Profile Name
S_ADMI_SPO_D	All spool device administration
S_ADMI_SPO_E	All extended spool administration
S_ADMI_SPO_J	All spool job administration for all clients
S_ADMI_SPO_T	All spool device type administration

SAP security professionals need to assign SAP user profiles to the job functions performed by individuals in your organization. For example, Human Resources administrative clerks require access to the basic data entry screens to enter and maintain new
employees' personal data; however, they might not need access to your company's organizational chart and reporting structure.

Your SAP system contains some preinstalled standard authorization profiles.
Although these might seem like a fast solution for security configuration, it is not
a good idea to try to mold your organization into these limited standards. Also
instead of manually creating, changing, and assigning authorization profiles, we
recommend you use the SAP Profile Generator. This tool lets you generate and
assign profiles automatically based on roles. Creating specific roles reflecting
your organization's structure will serve you better in the long run. Be prepared,
though—such work consumes a significant amount of time.

User Authorizations for ABAP Application Servers

User authorizations can vary depending on the type of SAP application server used to
host your SAP application. As you've learned, users may be assigned one or many
authorizations depending on their roles in an organization. User authorizations are stored
in the master record of each user. The master record is a data record containing the prin-
cipal employment and authorization data on a user that usually remains unchanged,
including the user's system authorizations, standard printer settings, and transaction settings. A user master record generally contains the following fields:

- Username

- Assigned client

- User password

- Company address

- User type

- Start menu

- ► Logon language

- ► Personal printer configuration

- ► Time zone

- ► Activity group

- ► Authorizations

- ► Expiration date

- ► Default parameter

Use transaction /nSU56 to review authorizations you, as an end user, are currently assigned. Conversely, if you try to run a transaction and the system tells you that you aren't authorized to run it, use transaction /nSU53 to identify the specific authorizations you are missing. Then you can share this information with your SAP security team to determine whether it can be added to your user profile.

By the Way

These fields are maintained by SAP security professionals. They need to be updated, for example, to reflect changes in employment, job held, or other conditions that reflect a change in job role.

User Authorizations for Java Application Servers

Just like ABAP-based application servers, user access to applications and resources hosted on Java-based application servers need to be controlled. The Java application server supports two types of authorizations: roles and *access control lists* (ACLs). Whereas roles define and assign activities to users, ACLs control the use of objects on the Java-based application server.

Users and authorizations are managed with the User Management Engine (UME). The UME provides centralized user management for all Java applications and lets you access user management data from various data sources, such as LDAP directories, user management of ABAP-based application servers, and more.

Authorizations are assigned to users through UME roles. UME roles reflect a user's function within the company. To create, change, and assign UME roles, SAP security professionals use either the SAP NetWeaver Administrator or the standalone console. When using the SAP NetWeaver Administrator, enter **http://<AS_hostname>:<AS_HTTP_port>/nwa** in your web browser and follow the menu path System Management, Administration, Identity Management. To review a list of all available roles, select **Roles** in the search area, choose **Go**, and review the search results, as shown in Figure 11.1.

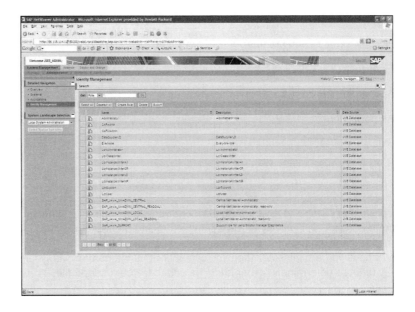

Summary

We briefly reviewed SAP security this hour. As you learned, technical professionals consider security akin to locking down physical assets such as servers and data centers. To application professionals and end users, SAP security is all about users IDs, user roles, and authorizations. After a brief review of the SAP Profile Generator, we worked through what SAP means by user roles and authorizations.

Case Study: Hour 11

Consider this user roles and authorizations case study and the questions that follow. You can find the answers posed by the questions related to this case study in Appendix A, "Case Study Answers."

Situation

You're the new SAP security manager at MNC. Your SAP environment is quite complex given that MNC runs SAP ERP, SAP *Supply Chain Management* (SCM), SAP *Product Lifecycle Management* (PLM), SAP NetWeaver Portal, and several SAP NetWeaver *Business Intelligence* (BI) systems. Your team is responsible for SAP application security, and you have been assigned to work with your peer in the SAP infrastructure security team to help ensure MNC approaches security in a holistic manner. Your first assignment is to help your team understand their roles in safeguarding the company's data and business processes.

Questions

1. *How should the team view or decompose the SAP infrastructure team's view on security?*

2. *What is the purpose of an SAP security process model?*

3. *What is the transaction to run the Profile Generator?*

4. *What is the Rule of 15?*

5. *If an end user calls the team complaining about being unauthorized to run a particular transaction, what should you do?*

Using SAP to Do Your Job

What You'll Learn in This Hour:

▶ Customizing your SAP display

▶ How to select the best version of the SAPGUI

▶ How to customize the SAP front end to your specifications

▶ How to customize colors and fonts

▶ Printing from SAP

▶ Walking through common SAP business scenarios

Regardless of whether you are an SAP end user, a system administrator, or a manager of a team tasked with supporting or using SAP day to day, there will come a time when you want to customize the SAP user interface to your liking. In this hour, you learn how to select and customize the SAP display. We then review printing from SAP and conclude the hour with a review of several SAP business scenarios.

Which SAP User Interface Is Best?

With a number of flavors of the JavaGUI, the WebGUI, the WinGUI, and access methods like Citrix at your disposal, a bit of insight is in order so that you can select the best user interface for your purposes (keeping in mind that often this decision is made by your company's IT management or business teams and, therefore, perhaps out of your hands). Consider the following points when choosing your SAP user interface:

▶ The SAP business functionality you need to execute. (Sometimes the SAPGUI provides the easiest way to navigate complex transactions.)

▶ Your desktop, laptop, or other "front-end" client hardware platform. (If you have a slow CPU, little RAM, or are low on disk space, you might ask for a Citrix-based access method.)

> ▶ Your front-end client operating system platform. (Windows, UNIX, Linux, and Mac OS might best support specific user interfaces.)

> ▶ The network infrastructure connecting your desktop or laptop to SAP. (Slow links can be navigated best via Citrix or the fat client.)

The following section describes some of the benefits and drawbacks of each SAPGUI flavor.

JavaGUI: SAPGUI for Java

For users of UNIX, Linux, and Mac OS, the JavaGUI might well be the only choice for connecting to and working with SAP. The JavaGUI supports Windows, as well, including Windows Vista. The JavaGUI not only be can run as a standalone application but also as an applet in a web browser, providing the same functionality as the standalone solution. Support for Mac OS was less than desirable until SAPGUI 6.10. This and later versions have been working well, though—they install smoothly and offer the basic and advanced functionality seen in the SAPGUI for Windows.

Installation of the JavaGUI requires a *Java Runtime Environment* (JRE), which is simply a utility program that needs to be installed before the JavaGUI. After it's installed, the total desktop footprint (that is, disk space required on the desktop) is relatively small—depending on the platform, about 20MB to 70MB is required for the JRE, and about 40MB is required for the JavaGUI itself. And the product works well. It's as fast as the SAPGUI for Windows and offers most of the functionality.

You can also run the SAPGUI for Java on 64-bit hardware if there is a 32-bit JRE available for that specific hardware platform and operating system combination.

If the best description of your company's desktop environment or your own worksite conditions is "variable," you will do well to consider the JavaGUI. It operates in an identical manner on all supported platforms, despite its platform independence. It supports all SAP *enterprise resource planning* (ERP) transactions, and it boasts an ultra-thin network protocol (very efficient). Other than several limitations such as the Office integration and limited drag-and-drop capabilities, it is comparable to the WinGUI or SAPGUI for Windows.

The JavaGUI files range from 20MB to 40MB—quite reasonable compared to the SAPGUI for Windows, and maybe another reason to consider using it.

WebGUI: SAPGUI for HTML

Today, the SAPGUI for HTML emulates the full features of the traditional SAPGUI with no real difference except for the fact that a web browser is used. The latest SAP

NetWeaver release supports both Microsoft Internet Explorer (IE) and the Firefox browser. It's leaner than previous versions (requiring less network bandwidth than before) and supports virtually all of the native SAPGUI's transactions.

Because the hardware footprint is minimal (no disk space is necessary per se, assuming the web browser is already installed by default), the SAPGUI for HTML makes a lot of sense for many SAP users. Drawbacks exist, though. The WebGUI does not support the same level of Microsoft Office integration as the SAPGUI for Windows, nor can it display interactive business graphics or support drag-and-drop mechanisms supported by the WinGUI.

WinGUI: SAPGUI for Windows

Because it is the most mature user interface offered by SAP, it comes as no surprise that a number of SAPGUI for Windows "flavors" are available. For years, the only option was the plain gray screen displayed called the "classic" SAPGUI for Windows. In typical German fashion, it was very functional. However, it was not known for its good looks. Subsequent versions such as Streamline and Tradeshow offered a more appealing user interface.

The space needed for a local installation is between 110MB up to 510MB, depending on whether Microsoft Office and Microsoft IE need to be updated. Although the SAPGUI for Windows is quite resource-intensive from a desktop footprint perspective, it is efficient when it comes to network resource consumption. Like the SAPGUI for Java, the WinGUI boasts an ultra-thin network protocol, making it run fast on otherwise slow networks. To obtain the latest WinGUI, point your browser to ftp://ftp.sap.com/pub/sapgui/win/. From here, select the version and then select what you want to download. Typically, the latest compilation is available along with add-ons, patches, and scripting tools.

WinGUI Configuration and Tools

The Tweak SAPGUI is a new tool SAP introduced with the latest version of the SAPGUI for Windows. It is a standalone application and has its own icon on the Windows desktop. The tool lets you change the visual appearance of the WinGUI. You can select from several different styles and preview changes you make. Once you start the Tweak SAPGUI tool, you can see in the top-left corner the menu option Visual Design. The Theme Selection item under Visual Design gives you the option to choose from several themes and lets you set the default theme for the WinGUI.

The Customizing of Local Layout Button

In the top-right area of every SAPGUI for Windows screen, there's a multicolored button next to the Help (?) button. This is the Customizing of Local Layout button, and it is informally referred to as the Customizing or Settings button. It gives you access to several menu options, as illustrated in Figure 12.1.

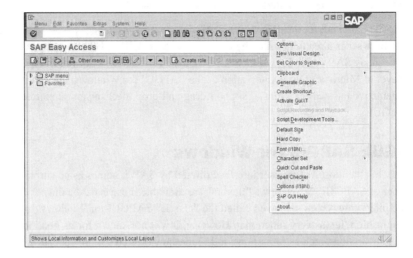

A number of the other menu options are self-explanatory, such as the spell checker, the character set selector, the ubiquitous About option, and so on. The About option is especially useful because it not only displays the version and patch level of the SAPGUI, but it also identifies the version of each loaded *dynamic link library* (DLL), provides system information details, and provides a button useful for saving this detail into a text file for safekeeping.

From the Customizing menu, select **Options**. An Options window appears, similar to the one shown in Figure 12.2. From this Options window, through the use of different tabs, you can perform the following actions:

▶ Define when dialog boxes pop up (with success, warning, and/or error messages) and whether such an action incurs a beep.

▶ Change the cursor width and enable a block cursor (for Overwrite mode).

▶ Specify your default working directory for local data (that is, data that you save from the SAPGUI via %pc or other means, discussed in later hours).

▶ Set trace options.

▶ Set scripting options.

The Options Tab

From the Options tab, you can change how the system notifies you of certain events and how quickly SAP Help is invoked. Be sure to note the default settings for this tab in case you are unhappy with any changes you make; that way, you can easily restore your settings back to the defaults.

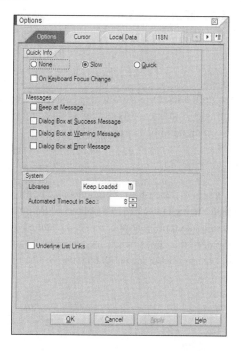

Quick Info

The Quick Info option controls how quickly the help information (simple description) launches whenever you place the pointer or cursor over an item in the button bar. For example, if you hover over the Customizing button for a period of time, you'll note that a description displays with the button's full name and its shortcut (in this case, Alt+F12). The Slow setting is indeed pretty slow; we recommend the Quick option. Users who tend to execute the same transactions daily should go with None.

There is also an option to enable On Keyboard Focus Change. With this option enabled, if you tab between buttons, for example, the help information is displayed as each button is highlighted. This setting is also useful when you are in new SAP territory. For users who tend to repeat many of the same functions over and over, this setting will grow tiresome.

Messages

The options in Messages enable you to configure how the SAP system presents you with information. The default setting is that any messages from the system appear in the status bar in the bottom-left area of your screen. By default, all messages pertaining to system output, warning messages, and error messages appear in the status bar. You can set these messages to appear in a pop-up box as well by selecting the appropriate box. Experienced users tend to keep none of these checked. Users new to a particular module, or with a critical need to ensure they don't miss an error message, should enable the Dialog Box at Error Message option.

System

The System option refers to the location from where SAP retrieves its help files, along with a default timeout. It is best to leave this setting as it is; any changes need to be made and tested by the system administrator.

The Cursor Tab

The Cursor tab enables you to make custom setting changes to the position and appearance of your cursor. The default setting is usually best, as shown in Figure 12.3. In some cases, though, you might want to make modifications. You can change how the cursor is displayed in lists, for example, so that the cursor marks an entire column or simply one character. The default cursor position or cursor width can also be changed, as discussed next.

FIGURE 12.3
Your SAP cursor placement can have a big impact when you are doing a lot of data entry in your SAP system.

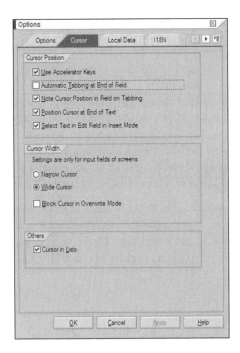

Cursor Position

With the Automatic Tabbing at End of Field option, you can determine whether the system automatically moves the cursor to the next input field when the cursor reaches the end of the current input field.

> For data entry, Automatic Tabbing (AutoTAB) is useful when you must enter data in many fields and you don't want to press the Tab key to move from field to field.

In the SAP system, you can determine where you want the cursor to appear when you click in the blank area of an input field. The place where your cursor appears in an entry field is called the *cursor position*. You can change this setting so that your cursor automatically tabs to the end of a field (when you use the Tab key on your keyboard to navigate between fields). You can also set the cursor to appear exactly where you place it in the field, whether or not there are blank spaces. Options such as these and others are designed to make your SAP environment more user-friendly and enable you to set the screen and placement of the cursor to your liking.

> If you primarily work in tasks that require a great deal of data entry, it is helpful to place the cursor at the end of any text when you click anywhere behind the text. This is the SAP default setting. This way, when the input field is empty, the cursor appears at the beginning, enabling you to freely enter data without worrying about extra spaces in front of the cursor.

Cursor Width

Cursor Width is just what it sounds like: Use it to fatten up or thin down your cursor. And use the check box option in this section to enable Block Cursor in Overwrite mode, which enables you to block out all the text when replacing data in a field. This is handy for users who often must overwrite existing field data—because it saves time compared to pressing the Delete or Backspace keys to clear a field.

If you want to change your SAP system from Overwrite mode to Insert mode, press the **Insert** key on your keyboard. You then see the abbreviation in the bottom-right corner of your SAP window change from OVR to INS. With each new session you create, the system defaults back to Overwrite mode.

The Local Data Tab

As illustrated in Figure 12.4, the Local Data tab lets you configure history and local cache settings, enable front-end security, and specify the default directory for any local data you choose to save in the course of conducting work with the SAPGUI. We find the defaults to be quite useful, although at times we change the local data directory to suit the needs of various SAP customer systems or sites.

FIGURE 12.4
The Local Data tab is useful in configuring history and local cache settings as well as the default directory for saving local data.

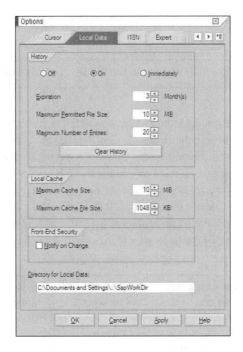

The Trace Tab

Traces can be set to keep a record of errors and warning messages a user receives. In addition, traces monitor where a user has been by keeping a file of each transaction code for each screen visited by the user. The Trace tab has options that enable you to create a file to trace activity in the system (see Figure 12.5). Be sure to turn trace off after using it, as it can measurably impact the entire system's performance when the trace setting is enabled. The settings under the Trace tab are managed by your system administrator.

New Visual Design Selection

Beyond the Options selection, the Customizing button offers users great flexibility in configuring SAPGUI settings through the New Visual Design selection. This is accomplished using two tabs:

▶ General

▶ Color Settings

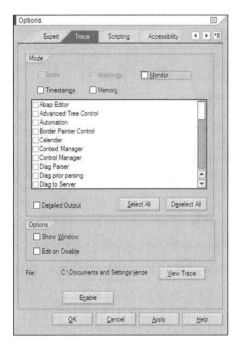

FIGURE 12.5
The Trace tab is ideal for diagnosing user system problems.

The General Tab

Within the General tab, a number of high-level options are available. You can select the active theme or mode used by the SAPGUI, for instance. Selections include Enjoy, High Contrast, Streamline, Tradeshow, and System Dependent. You can easily change the font size from here and enable or disable audio.

The Color Settings Tab

Like the General tab, the Color Settings tab lets you change the theme. The idea here, though, is that the display within this particular window is changed in real time, enabling you to see the impact that different selections and color settings have relative to each theme. Given its maturity, it comes as no surprise that the Enjoy option has the greatest number of color settings available. Use it to quickly walk through different options and then customize your display.

Clipboard Selection

Although rather simplistic, the Clipboard selection from the Customizing button's drop-down menu gives you the ability to cut and paste items, and it includes the following commands:

- ▶ Select (Ctrl+Y)
- ▶ Cut (Ctrl+X)

▶ Copy (Ctrl+C)

▶ Paste (Ctrl+V)

Font Selection

You can make font configuration changes in a number of places. However, this particular selection, from the Customizing button, is the most powerful. Select Font, and from this window you can change the appearance and size of the fonts used in your SAPGUI. This option is most useful when your screen resolution varies from desktop to desktop or monitor to monitor.

To change the font, follow these steps:

1. Under the Font section, select one of the possible entries.

2. Under the Font Style section, choose **Regular**, **Italic**, **Bold**, or **Bold italic**.

3. Under the Size section, choose the font size.

As you make changes, a sample of text in the font and size you have chosen appears in the Preview box display.

Status Field's System Information Icon

At the bottom of the SAPGUI for Windows, you can click the small arrow to display or hide a set of status fields. These fields include the following:

▶ System

▶ Client

▶ User

▶ Program

▶ Transaction

▶ Response Time

▶ Interpretation Time

▶ Round Trips/Flushes

These fields are mutually exclusive in that only one can be displayed at a time. We normally enable the response time tracker, although we occasionally use the transaction option when documenting a system's configuration or performance or when working with an end-user helpdesk (so as to automatically capture the current transaction's T-code, such as MM02, in a screenshot). The status field next to the System Information icon displays the server to which you are connected. Finally, the status field to the right-most of the screen indicates your data entry mode—*Insert* (INS) or *Overwrite* (OVR).

Printing from SAP

Printing enables you to make hard copies of lists, tables, and reports from SAP. The SAP Print button is available on most SAP screens (see Figure 12.6). Let's look at the printing features in SAP. (Even if you are not connected to a printer, you can still follow along.)

Print button

FIGURE 12.6
The SAPGUI Print button is available from most SAP screens.

The SAP Print Screen List

From any SAP screen where the Print button is available, click the **Print** button on the standard toolbar. You are then prompted with the Print Screen List window, which is used to enter the output device (printer) you intend to print to—select or type in the name of your printer, make any other updates to the number of copies or pages, and select the green check box to continue.

If you are not presented with this screen or if you receive a warning message saying your system is not connected to a printer, contact your system administrator for assistance in connecting to a printer.

To see a list of available output devices connected to your SAP system, select the down arrow to the right of this field. The Number of Copies field is where you specify the number of copies of the document you want to print.

Spool Request Attributes

To customize the settings for a spool (print) request, click the **Properties** button in the Print Screen List window. The Spool Request Attributes window appears. The parameters are grouped by function; you just double-click a parameter line to change the parameter's value, as shown in Figure 12.7.

FIGURE 12.7
The Spool
Request
Attributes
screen allows
you to cus-
tomize your
printer settings.

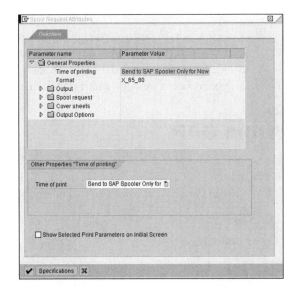

General Properties

We now walk through some of the more commonly changed spool request attributes, starting with General Properties. The Time of Printing parameter determines when the request is sent to the printer. Send to SAP Spooler Only for Now places the request in the SAP spooler without sending it to the printer. You can choose to print it later by choosing System, Own Spool Requests. The Print Out Immediately option sends the spool request to the output device immediately. This setting is usually selected if you are printing small reports. This option will bypass the standard spool routing and send the request directly to the designated printer. Finally, the Print Later option allows you to schedule the time when the job will be sent to the printer. This option is normally used to schedule the printing of large reports when the printer is less busy.

The Format field contains the spool request format for output. The Rows field determines the number of lines per list page. The Columns field contains the current line width of the list; the maximum line width of a list is 255 characters. It is a good idea to accept the default settings for these fields. It is also a good idea to test the different formats listed to find one that is most acceptable for the output you are printing.

Spool Request

The Name field contains the name of the spool request. As you will learn, everything in SAP is assigned a name or an identifier within the SAP system. This name designates the item (in this case, a print request to the system). For example, if you go to your printer and do not find your output, you can search in the SAP system by this spool request name and find out what happened to it. Although you can change the spool request name, it is usually a good idea to accept the name proposed by the system.

You can, however, add a description of your own in the Spool Request Title field. It might consist of any combination of letters, digits, special characters, and blanks. This field can help you to identify your spool request.

Cover Sheets

The SAP Cover Sheet field determines whether to include a cover sheet with your output that is sent to the printer. Information such as recipient name, department name, and format can all be included on your SAP cover sheet. The permitted values for this field are System Administrator: Default Settings, Do Not Print, and Print.

The OS Cover Sheet field determines whether the standard operating system cover sheet is to be sent with the print job and has the same values as the SAP cover sheet.

The Receivers field contains the spool request recipient's name that appears on the cover sheet of hard copy printouts. The default value for the name of the recipient is the current user's name.

The Department field contains the name of the department originating the spool request. On hard copy printouts, the name is displayed on the cover sheet.

Output Options

The Delete Immediately After Printing option determines whether to delete the spool request immediately after it has been sent to the output device or only after the spool retention period has expired. The default setting for this option is that the Delete After Printing box is cleared, indicating that the spool requests are saved for the duration of the spool retention period set in the retention period box. This is helpful in the previous scenario we detailed where a printout was lost. If the spool request was immediately deleted, you would not be able to go back and search for the item.

Most users check the Delete After Printing box in an effort to conserve space by not saving a spool request for every item printed. The box is cleared only when the user feels it is necessary to retain the request for very important spool requests.

Setting Default Values for the Printer

Each time you select the Print button in the SAP system, you are prompted with the SAP Print Screen List. You can set a default value for each field in this screen so that you need not re-enter your settings each time you print. Do this by clicking the **Specifications** button in the Spool Request Attributes windows; this brings up the Maintain Settings dialog box. Next, select the field name and set the field default value and the validity settings—decide whether you want the value to be valid for only this report or all reports, reports generated by batch jobs, dialog processing, or both. After you have entered all the settings to your specifications, click the **Copy Settings** button. Repeat this for each field name you want to set a default for and click the green check box when you are finished.

Using Your SAPGUI

With your SAPGUI customized and ready to be used, it's time to put it to use! We look at several SAP ERP sample business processes and scenarios next. The idea behind this section is to help a novice or aspiring SAP business user understand what a "day in the life of an SAP end user" might look like. These business scenarios and hundreds more are detailed on http://help.sap.com. Keep in mind that the specific steps outlined here could very well differ based on the version of SAP ERP you are using and the degree to which it has been customized.

Changing a Sales Order

Sales orders often need to be changed to reflect new data related to individual items in a sales order. To change a sales order, from the initial SAP screen, follow these steps:

1. Choose **Logistics**, **Sales and Distribution**, **Sales**.

2. Choose **Order**, **Change**.

The system automatically proposes the number of the last order you created during the current work session. You may retain this number or enter the number of a different sales order you want to change.

3. Press **Enter**.

4. Make your changes and save the document.

Managing Accounts

To display SAP customer account balances, from the initial SAP screen, follow these steps:

1. Navigate to the Accounts Receivable or Accounts Payable menu.

2. Choose **Account**, **Display Balances**.

3. Select the account by specifying an account number, a company code, and a fiscal year (if you are unsure of one of these fields, use SAP's search function).

The system then displays the balances by posting period for the specified account in this company code.

Posting Business Transactions in A/P

To enter a business transaction in SAP Accounts Payable using the standard transaction, from the initial SAP screen, follow these steps:

1. Choose **Accounting**, **Financial Accounting**, **Accounts Payable**, **Document Entry**, **Invoice**, **Other**, **Invoice—General**.

2. The Enter Vendor Invoice/Credit Memo: Header data screen appears. Enter the required document header data.

3. Enter the posting key and the vendor account number of the first line item. Save your entries.

4. The Enter Vendor Invoice (or Credit Memo): Add Vendor Item screen appears. Enter the data for the first line item. (The posting key and the account number at the end of each screen determine which fields are displayed on the next screen for entering a line item.)

5. Enter at least one vendor line item and one G/L account line item.

6. If necessary, adjust or complete the line item.

7. Once the debits equal the credits, and the data is complete, post the document.

Displaying a Goods Movement

Displaying a goods movement is quite common, oftentimes a top-ten transaction executed for large manufacturing organizations. From the SAP main menu, follow these steps:

1. Select the order in display or change mode.

2. On the header data screen, choose **Extras**, **Order Documents**, **Goods Movements**.

The system displays a list of the goods movements that have previously taken place for the order.

Posting a Goods Movement for Materials

Moving a material from one location to another requires a post goods movement. From the SAP main menu, follow these steps:

1. Select **Logistics**, **Central Functions**, **Handling Unit Management**, **Goods Movement of Handling Units**, **Posting General Goods Movements (with HU)**.

2. To post goods movements for materials, choose the **Material** tab.

3. Enter the following data on the upper half of the SOURCE material entry tab:

   ▶ The process that you want to post

   ▶ The material that you want to move

   ▶ The plant at which the material is located

   ▶ The storage location at which the material is located

   ▶ The quantity that you want to move

   ▶ Enter any other entries such as batch, valuation type, or cost center (specific to the movement type)

4. If it is necessary to do so for the process, go to the TARGET material entry tab and enter the necessary target data such as destination plant and destination storage location. You may now delete errors (if you entered the wrong material) or create a delivery.

5. Once the delivery is created, you may go directly to delivery processing.

Summary

In this hour, we explored the different SAP user interfaces; how to customize the WinGUI to best suit your needs, likes, or personality; and how to make other GUI changes. Then we reviewed printing from SAP and concluded the hour by putting the SAPGUI to use and walking through several common business transactions/scenarios.

Case Study: Hour 12

Consider this hour's case study regarding SAPGUI navigation and the questions that follow. You can find the answers to the posed questions related to this case study in Appendix A, "Case Study Answers."

Situation

Congratulations! You have just been hired as the newest SAP Basis Administrator for MNC. This is an exciting position in a very dynamic SAP environment because MNC runs nearly the entire SAP Business Suite—from SAP ERP and Enterprise Portal, to SAP Supply Chain Management, and more. After getting settled in, you are asked to define a new SAP background job (using transaction SM36) in all seven SAP production systems. You have logged on to several of these production systems and currently have many different open WinGUI sessions.

Questions

1. *How do you determine which SAP instance and which SAP client you are currently logged on to?*

2. *Working with several different SAP systems and SAP clients at the same time can be confusing. One option is to use different color settings for different WinGUI sessions to better track in which SAP system and SAP client you are working. Where are the color settings for the WinGUI changed?*

3. *When you make changes through the Customizing button, do they apply only for the current WinGUI session?*

4. *Which other feature of the SAPGUI for Windows will help you to keep track of in which SAP system and SAP client you are working?*

Reporting and Query Basics

What You'll Learn in This Hour:

- ▶ Overview of the reporting options in SAP
- ▶ Introduction to variants
- ▶ Creating an SAP Query
- ▶ SAP QuickViewer
- ▶ Using the InfoSet (Ad Hoc) Query

This hour covers reporting concepts and introduces the SAP Information System, which contains the General Report Selection Tree. Other reporting options are also discussed briefly. At the end of this hour, we wrap up with detailed discussion of several SAP reporting tools (SAP Query, InfoSet Query, Ad Hoc Query, and QuickViewer).

Reporting Tools

SAP has the capability to support and manage all a firm's business processes and underlying data. Although this data is stored in the SAP system and can be presented on SAP screens, you might still want to produce printed or custom output from the system. These are called SAP reports. You can use reports to extract and manipulate the data from your SAP database. Several methods are available, including the following:

- ▶ ABAP List Processing (ABAP programming)
- ▶ ABAP Query Reporting
- ▶ Ad Hoc Query Reporting
- ▶ Structural Graphics Reporting
- ▶ Executive Information System
- ▶ SAP Information System (report trees)

ABAP List Processing (ABAP Programming)

Custom reports can be created in SAP by writing ABAP code to generate lists. This method is called List Processing. Using List Processing, ABAP programmers write statements in the ABAP Editor that query the database and generate reports. Writing reports using ABAP List Processing is therefore rather technical in nature and subsequently relegated most often to the post-go-live technical team.

This option becomes viable when you require a report that the canned reports cannot create. This option is also used for creating interface files or files that provide input to (and thus feed) external systems. For example, if you need your SAP system to connect to an external enterprise system such as an outside third-party bolt-on product, you might consider using the ABAP List Processing method to write a report, the output of which is transmitted to the external system.

ABAP Query

You create custom reports in SAP by creating queries using the ABAP Query tool. ABAP queries are based on logical databases, functional areas, and user groups. Creating reports using ABAP Query is covered in more detail later in this hour.

Ad Hoc Query

The Ad Hoc Query is a reporting tool that was borne out of the original SAP *Enterprise Resource Planning* (ERP) Human Resources functionality. Like the ABAP Query tool, it was initially based on logical databases, functional areas, and user groups—as the name implies, an Ad Hoc Query used in an "ad hoc" manner to query your SAP database. The output from the query can then be formatted into a report. Creating reports using the most updated Ad Hoc Query functionality is also covered later in this hour.

Structural Graphics

Structural Graphics is an additional Human Resources tool used in the Organizational Management application component. This method enables you to display and edit the structures and objects in your organizational plan and to select reports directly from the graphical structure for an object.

Executive Information System

The *Executive Information System* (EIS) is just what it sounds like: a reporting tool tailored for high-level decision making. EIS is old but useful for users who require quick access to real-time information found in SAP ERP (and do not require the time and expense necessary to deploy full-fledged data warehousing or analytics and reporting systems such as SAP NetWeaver *Business Intelligence* (BI) and *Strategic Enterprise*

Management (SEM) or SAP BusinessObjects, for example, any of which could easily consume a year's time and a large budget). Using the Executive Information System Report portfolio, you call up a hierarchy graphic defined for access to your own report portfolio. You can also use the Report selection, in which you call up either the general report tree of drill-down reports or your own custom tree. Or you can use the Report Portfolio report, in which you enter the name of an individual report portfolio and then display it.

SAP Information System (Report Trees)

Most of the reports you need are available within each module. That is, each module contains its own Information System that houses reports specific to that module. In earlier hours, you reviewed some of these module-specific Information Systems. One example is the SAP ERP Human Resources Information System. Note that you can access all canned SAP reports via the general SAP Information System.

General Report Selection

SAP has many tools within SAP ERP and other components used to extract and then present data in the form of reports. In the past, basic reporting capabilities were afforded through transaction code SART or by navigating via the menu path **Information Systems**, **General Report Selection**. In newer SAP releases, SART is not available directly; instead, use SARP to access report trees.

Executing Reports

You can execute reports directly from the General Report Selection screen. Depending on the modules currently installed on your SAP system, different reports are available. To execute a common HR report, for example, drill down into the report tree as follows:

1. Expand the **Human Resources** node.

2. Expand the **Payroll** node.

3. Expand the **Americas** node.

4. Expand the **USA** node.

5. Expand the **Payroll** node.

6. Double-click one of the reports, such as the Simulation or Start Payroll report.

Double-clicking the report icon launches the selection screen for the report. Selection screens are used by most SAP reports to enable an end user to clarify the output desired by entering precise input data (such as a payroll period, personnel number, reason for running a particular payroll cycle, and so on).

Once the input data is provided, execute the report by clicking the **Execute** button on the toolbar. The Execute button is equivalent to the F8 function key on the keyboard. The report executes, and output appears on the screen. This output can be viewed, saved electronically in RTF or XLS format by executing %pc in the transaction dialog box, or printed.

Report Attributes

To look at the attributes of a particular report in the General Report Selection Tree, execute SARP. A window appears, which is similar to Figure 13.1. The window provides basic details about the report, including the report type, technical name of the underlying executable program, report description, and variants (if any).

FIGURE 13.1
SAP's Report Attributes window gives you additional information about the selected report.

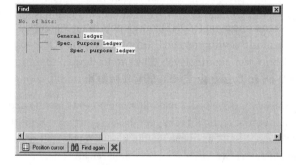

Searching for Reports

The General Selection Tree has a search function in which you can enter search criteria and search for a report based on its name. From any starting point in the tree, use the menu path **Edit**, **Find**, **Nodes**. You are presented with an SAP Find dialog box like the one shown in Figure 13.2. Enter your search criteria (for this example, enter the word **ledger**).

FIGURE 13.2
Use SAP's General Report Selection Tree to search for reports.

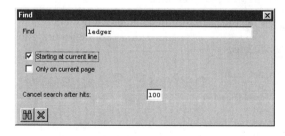

After you type your search criteria in the Find box and click the **Find** button, a new Find window displays the results of your search. The new window includes hot keys (sometimes referred to as *hypertext* in SAP documentation) that link the text to the corresponding reports so that you can jump directly to the report. If no reports matched your search criteria, you receive a message box indicating something to the effect that the search has proven unsuccessful.

Selection Screens

Selection screens are presented when you execute an SAP report. The selection screens are useful in delimiting precisely which output you seek (to avoid huge reports). For example, to generate a list of all open purchase orders, execute a report listing your company's purchase orders and indicate on the selection screen that you only want to display orders with the status of Open. In some cases, though, each time you execute a report, you are looking for the same specific data. In this case, you need to fill in the selection fields on the screen for the data you desire. To assist you in this task, SAP makes use of a concept called variants, discussed next.

Variants

A *variant* is a group of selection criteria values that has been saved to be used again and again. If you want to run a report using the same selection criteria each time, you can create a variant to save the data that you filled in on your selection screen. The next time you execute the report, you need to enter only the variant name, rather than re-enter the individual values in each of the selection criteria fields.

If you use variants, the selection screen for the report does not appear at all. The report can also be preset to execute with the variant automatically so that no data needs to be filled in at all. A report can have several variants, with each variant retrieving different types of information. For example, a purchase order report might have one variant to retrieve all open purchase orders for your company and another variant used to display purchase orders for a specific vendor only. Use SAP's Save As Variant screen to save your selection criteria as a variant.

Variants are largely used for background execution of reports that tend to run a long time and therefore are often scheduled to run behind the scenes. Variants are also used simply for convenience; if you tend to look at the same data day in and day out but require a fresh view into this data, the use of variants can save a considerable amount of time. And with SAP's capability to schedule reports to run at certain times of the day, month, or year, executing a transaction using a variant is simple indeed.

Modifying Variants

From SAP's General Report Selection main screen, select a report that has variants available for it and then follow the menu path **Goto**, **Variants**. This brings you to the ABAP: Variants – Initial screen, similar to the one shown in Figure 13.3.

FIGURE 13.3
Access the
ABAP: Variants–
Initial screen by
selecting a
report in the
report tree and
then following
the menu path
Goto, Variants.

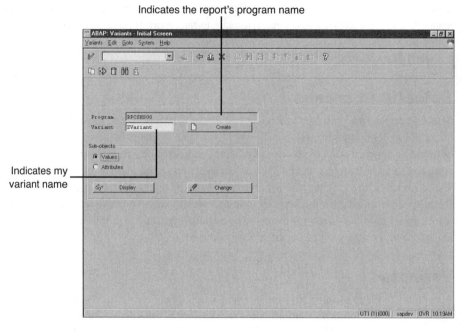

Indicates the report's program name

Indicates my
variant name

From the ABAP: Variants – Initial screen, you can create new variants and modify existing variants. For example, you can enter the name of an existing variant, select the
Values subobject, and then click the **Change** button. This brings you to the selection
screen for the report, which enables you to modify the selection criteria for your variant.
You can also select the **Attributes** subobject and click the **Change** button, which brings
you to the Save As Variant screen for the report. This screen enables you to modify the
name, description, and attributes for your variant. On this screen, you can also specify
additional variant criteria, such as whether the report should be generated (created) in
real time or in the background.

By the
Way

A key advantage of background processing is that the report or job is started in
the background by SAP, and therefore does not impact online users in the same
way it otherwise might—many of the resources used to execute jobs in the background are distinct and different from those used to host online users. Therefore,
the performance of both the batch job or report and the online user response
time wind up being much improved (compared to executing a long-running report
in the foreground).

Lists

After generating a report in SAP, you can save the output as a list. On all report output screens, list options are available that enable you to save the file in Office, a report tree, or to an external file (such as Microsoft Word or Excel). Save the list using the menu path **List**, **Export**, and then choose **Word Processing**, **Spreadsheet**, **Local File**, or **XML**.

Note the distinction between a report and a list. A report generated at any time in the system contains real-time data at the time of generation. A list is saved output from a previously generated list and does not reflect the real-time data in your SAP ERP system. In other words, lists are static, whereas reports are dynamic.

By the Way

SAP Reporting Tools (SAP Query, InfoSet Query, Ad Hoc Query, and QuickViewer)

In the earliest versions of SAP, two tools were delivered for end-user reporting. The ABAP Query was designed for all modules, and the Ad Hoc Query was designed exclusively for the Human Capital Management module.

Today, the ABAP Query is now called the SAP Query, and its features have been enhanced. In addition, the Ad Hoc Query tool can now be used with all modules in SAP under the name the InfoSet Query (although in the Human Capital Management module SAP still refers to it as the Ad Hoc Query). Both reporting tools enable you to create reports within your SAP environment, and neither requires any technical skills. SAP also introduced another tool, the QuickViewer. In this section, you learn how to create custom reports using these reporting tools, including the necessary configuration and administrative decisions to get you on your way.

The Structure of the Query Reporting Tools

The query tools (SAP Query, InfoSet/Ad Hoc Query, and QuickViewer) are built on the foundation of three main components:

- ▶ Query groups (/nSQ03)
- ▶ InfoSets (/nSQ02)
- ▶ Administrative decisions (company specific)

Each component permits a user with no technical programming skills to create custom reports. The query tool's structure is depicted in Figure 13.4.

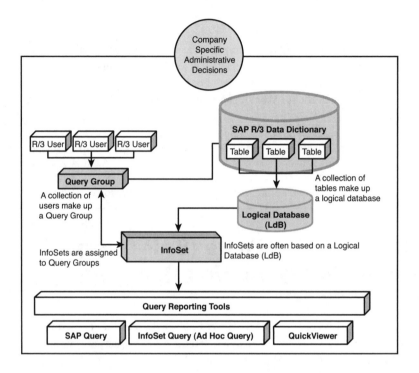

If you think about custom reporting in SAP in layman terms, you picture a programmer sitting down at a terminal and typing lines and lines of ABAP code that go to the core SAP database to collect the information needed for the report. The programmer also has to code to account for security access, output, formatting, and so on. The purpose of the SAP delivered query tools is that all the work is done for you behind the scenes. The use of the three main components holds it all together.

Query Groups

Let's start with the first component, query groups (formerly known as user groups in earlier versions of SAP). The technical definition of *query groups* is a collection of SAP users who are grouped together. A user's assignment to a user group determines which queries he or she can execute or maintain. Additionally, it designates which InfoSets (data sources) the user can access. Basically, query groups permit users to create, modify, and execute reports in a certain area within SAP ERP. For example, you can create a query group for the Finance department that includes your financial users; similarly, you can create a query group for the Human Resources department that contains reports specific to Human Resources. Query groups are an easy way to group and segregate your reports.

Query groups are often maintained by the system administrator and are created on the Maintain Query Groups screen, which you can access running transaction code /nSQ03. Users can belong to multiple query groups and might, under certain circumstances, copy and execute queries from other query groups (only if the permissions are the same). Any user within a user group has authority to execute queries that are assigned to that group, but only users with the appropriate authorization can modify queries or define new ones. Users cannot modify queries from other query groups. Although maintaining query groups is usually a task for your system administrator, we show how to create a sample user group later in this section.

InfoSets

InfoSets (known as *functional areas* in the early days of SAP) are the second component of SAP reporting. InfoSets are created on the Maintain InfoSets screen, which you can access running transaction code /nSQ02. Based on the technical definition, InfoSets are areas that provide special views of logical databases and determine which fields of a logical database or data source can be evaluated in queries. Basically, an InfoSet is the data source; it's where you get your data to use in your reports. InfoSets can be built on a variety of sources, but the most common is the use of what is known as a *logical database* (LdB). Recall that writing reports without query tools requires a programmer to write code that goes into the main SAP ERP database and retrieves the records it needs. This is no easy skill. SAP's answer to this issue is the logical database.

Logical databases are rational prearranged groupings of data from multiple related tables that are indexed. In layman terms, logical databases place all the fields you want to report in an easy container from which you simply select the fields you need to include in your report. Although maintaining InfoSets is usually a task for your system administrator, you learn how to create a sample InfoSet later in this section.

Administrative Decisions

Creating query groups and InfoSets is an easy task. Before you begin, you must first review the following administrative decisions to see which best applies to your organization:

- ▶ What is your client/transport strategy?
- ▶ Will you use the standard or global query area?

With regard to your client transport strategy and custom-coded ABAP reports written by programmers, the traditional methodology for report creation is as follows: A programmer accesses a development environment where the first draft of the custom report is coded. The report is then transported to a testing client where it is tested. Assuming it passes testing, the report then moves on to your production environment for use. This methodology differs from the strategy often used with the query family of reporting tools. The addition of the query tools to SAP enables end users to create reports in real time with no technical skills. It is with this in mind that your organization has to make a decision regarding your transport strategy.

The creation of query objects can be performed in any client. However, you should follow some best practices. For starters, end users who will be using the query tools often only have user IDs in the live production environment. Therefore, many companies maintain query groups live in the production client.

Did you Know?

Depending on your SAP authorization privileges, you might need to request assistance from your system administrator in creating a test query group, functional area, and query. It is also possible, if you are working with a newly installed SAP system, that you will receive a message saying you must convert objects first. If you receive this message, contact your system administrator. He or she will be required to perform a standard administration function to convert the objects before you can proceed.

Similarly, InfoSets can be created in any client; however, best practice dictates that InfoSets be treated inline with normal programming methodology. It's best to create InfoSets in a development environment and then transport them to a testing client, where they are tested and then moved on to production for use. InfoSets are treated differently because a trained user has the capability to add special coding or programs to InfoSets (outside the scope of this book) that can have an impact on system resources or functioning, and testing them is required in those cases. That leaves the reports (queries) themselves. Unlike custom-coded ABAP reports, query reports are designed to be made in real time in an ad hoc fashion, so the best practice is to create your queries live in your production environment.

After determining your client/transport strategy, the second administrative decision you need to make is to choose a Query area. SAP supports two:

▶ Standard query areas—Client-specific, so they are available only within the client in which they were created. For example, if you created a standard query in the production client, it exists only in the production client. You can transport query objects created in the standard area between multiple clients on the same application server via the Transport Truck function on the main InfoSets screen (SQ02). This bypasses the customary Workbench Organizer.

▶ Global query areas—Used throughout the entire system and are client-independent. SAP delivers many of its standard reports in the SAP global query area. These queries are also intended for transport into other systems and are connected to the ABAP Workbench. A common best practice is to allow SAP to continue to deliver reports via the global area and for end users to use the standard query area to create query-related reports. With your administrative decisions completed, you are ready to begin the configuration.

Creating a New User Group

To create a new user group, follow these steps:

1. Navigate to the Maintain User Group screen using transaction code SQ03.

2. Ensure that you are in the standard query area by following the menu path **Environment**, **Query Areas**, and then selecting **Standard Area (client-specific)**.

3. Type the user group name to create, **ZTEST**, and click the **Create** button.

4. Type a name for your user group on the User Group ZTEST: Create or Change screen and then click the **Save** button.

5. A message appears in your SAPGUI status bar stating that the user group ZTEST has been saved.

6. Click the **Assign Users and InfoSets** button. Type the SAP user IDs of any users you want to include in your test group. Be sure to include your own user ID.

7. Save the entry by clicking the **Save** button on the toolbar. A message appears in your SAPGUI status bar stating that user group ZTEST was saved.

Now that you have created a user group, the next step is to create an InfoSet.

For nearly all modules in SAP, field groups are empty; you need to manually move fields to them. The exception is the Human Capital Management module and the InfoSets that support it. The field groups in this module are created for you with a default set of fields, although you might add additional information if required.

By the Way

Creating a New InfoSet

To create a new InfoSet, perform the following steps:

1. Navigate to the Maintain InfoSets screen using the transaction code SQ02.

2. Ensure that you are in the standard query area by following the menu path **Environment**, **Query Areas**, and then selecting **Standard Area (client-specific)**.

3. Type the InfoSet name you will be creating, **ZTEST**, and click the **Create** button.

4. On the InfoSet: Title and Database screen, input a description for your InfoSet. Select the logical database to be used as your data source.

5. After entering a name and selecting the appropriate logical database from the drop-down list, select the green check mark to continue.

6. You are presented with a screen listing the tables stored in the logical database.

7. Assign fields to the field groups (shown at the top-right of your screen) within your InfoSet. These field groups appear in your query tools while reporting. Only the fields that you include in your field groups are available for field selection in your query-reporting tools that use this InfoSet as its data source. By default, these field groups are empty (noted exception follows).

8. Place your cursor on the first field group, Flight Schedule, and then select fields from the left side of the screen from the Flight Schedule table and add them to the Flight Schedule field group. Place your cursor on a field on the left side of the screen and right-click the option **Add Field to Field Group**.

   Your newly added field to the Flight Schedule Field group now appears at the top-right area of the screen.

9. Now add fields to your selected field group following the procedures outlined previously. Select the field group with your cursor and then move fields from the left side of the screen to the right using the procedure outlined previously. Be sure to add fields to the appropriate field group. For example, you can add the fields in the Flight Schedule table to the Flight Schedule field group or add fields from the Flight Booking table to the Flight Booking field group.

Did you Know?

> Note that some of the SAP screens and SAP Help text still use the *functional area* moniker rather than InfoSet or refer to query groups by their old name, user groups. Just be aware of this. You can also assign the InfoSet to a query group by using the Maintain User Groups screen (SQ03) and by clicking the **Assign Users and InfoSets** button on the toolbar and selecting your InfoSet from a list.

10. Click the **Save** button on the toolbar. A message appears in the status bar saying that the InfoSet ZTEST was saved.

11. Generate the InfoSet by clicking the **Generate** button (the red beach ball) on the application toolbar. A message appears in the status bar saying that the InfoSet ZTEST was generated. The process of generating your InfoSet determines whether any errors are present in the logic of the configuration of the InfoSet.

12. Finally, exit the Maintain InfoSet screen by selecting the green back arrow.

Assigning the InfoSet to Your Query Group

You have now accomplished the first two configuration steps: You have created both a query group and a follow-on InfoSet. The last step before you begin creating reports is to assign the InfoSet to your query group. This is an easy two-step task:

1. From the InfoSet: Initial screen (transaction code SQ02), make sure your InfoSet ZTEST is present in the InfoSet text box and click the **User Group Assignment** button.

2. From the InfoSet ZTEST: Assign to Query Groups screen, highlight your query group name by selecting the gray button to the left of it, and then click the **Save** button.

A status bar message appears indicating that the InfoSet ZTEST was saved.

SAP Queries

Create and maintain SAP queries through the Maintain Queries screen, accessible via transaction code SQ01. Unlike query groups and InfoSets, which are often maintained by system administrators, SAP queries are primarily maintained by trained end users (after the configuration steps are complete) and power users.

Only users with the appropriate authorizations can modify queries or create new ones. Security for managing query reporting is available on a couple of different levels. Besides the user group segregation, there are also authorization group specifications. Security configurations are very customer-specific; contact your systems administrator to learn more about your company's security configuration.

Creating an SAP Query

With the one-time configuration completed, the fun can finally begin. Creating an SAP query is a relatively elementary task. To begin creating your first SAP query, follow these steps:

1. Navigate to the Maintain Queries Initial screen using the transaction code SQ01. A graphical version of the SAP Query is available called the Graphical Query Painter. If you have not used the query tool, this will be set as your default. To turn it off and learn to create easy step-by-step reports, follow the menu path **Settings, Settings** and deselect the **Graphical Query Painter** check box.

2. The title bar lists the query group you are currently in. For example, your screen might read Query of User Group ZTEST: Initial Screen. (If you are assigned to multiple user groups, you can see a list of the groups by pressing **Shift+F7**.)

3. It is always a good idea to ensure that you are in the standard query area by following the menu path **Environment, Query Areas** and selecting **Standard Area (client-specific)**.

4. In the Query field, type a name for the query you are creating (in this example, **ZMYQUERY**) and click the **Create** button.

5. The InfoSets of User Group ZTEST window will list all the available InfoSets for your query group. Select the **ZTEST** InfoSet and press the **Enter** key to proceed.

6. The Create Query Title Format screen is shown, which enables you to save the basic formatting specifications for your query, including the name (title) and any notes you want to store for the query. The only required field is the title. Enter a title.

7. After entering a title, click the **Save** button on the toolbar. To navigate to the next screen in the SAP query-creation process, click the next screen (white navigational arrow) button on the application toolbar. You can use these navigational arrows to navigate between the different screens of the SAP Query.

8. A screen will appear listing all the field groups available within your InfoSet (in this example, you can see Flight Schedule [SPFLI], Flight Demo Table [SFLIGHT], and Flight Booking [SBOOK]). Place a check mark next to all field groups from which you want to include fields in your report. Click the next screen (white navigational arrow) button from the application toolbar.

9. A Select Field screen will appear, listing all the available fields within the field groups you selected. Place a check mark next to all fields you want to include in your report. You can use the Page Up and Page Down arrows to navigate between all the fields. Select the next screen (white navigational arrow) button from the application toolbar to continue.

10. You are now presented with the Selections screen, which lists all the fields you have selected. You can now add any of the fields to the selection screen that appears when you execute your report. This enables you to specify your report output when the report is executed. You can add any fields you want to the Selection screen by placing a check mark next to each field. This is the last screen in the basic query sequence. To continue, click the **Basic List** button on the application toolbar.

11. The Basic List screen shows you a list of the selected fields you want to include for your report. For each field, you can specify the Line and Sequence number as you want them to appear on your report. In addition, you can use this screen to indicate sort order, totals, and counts, if needed. Start by entering the Line and Sequence numbers.

12. For this basic SAP Query example, proceed directly to the report. Press the **F8** key to execute the report.

13. You are presented with the report's selection screen. The selection screen gives you an opportunity to specify any criteria for the output of your report. Click the **Execute** button again to display the report. Your report output will now appear.

Advanced SAP Queries

You have created a basic query using the SAP Query tool. Before you start investigating the more advanced options available in ABAP Query, it's a good idea to try creating a few queries using different InfoSets (based on different logical databases). To do this, you need to start from the section "Creating a New InfoSet" earlier this hour, select a different logical database, and then assign it to your query group.

When you become familiar with the SAP Query tool, you will want to try some of its more advanced options. To investigate the advanced options available for processing your queries, follow these steps:

1. Navigate to the Maintain Queries Initial screen using the transaction code SQ01 and select one of your existing queries.

2. Click the **Modify** button followed by the **Basic List** button on the application toolbar from the Basic List screen.

3. You can use the next screen (white navigational arrow) button from the application toolbar to navigate to the additional seven screens that house the more advanced functions of the SAP Query, including the following:

▶ Grouping, sorting, and subtotaling—Group, sort, and subtotal your SAP data onto reports and modify your subtotal texts. For example, you can create a report listing all open purchase orders and their amounts grouped by vendor and location with custom-named subtotals.

▶ Manipulating colors and texts—Manipulate the colors and text styles of the different data presented on reports. For example, your report can contain subtotals in yellow, group totals in green, and individual line items in boldface red text.

▶ Alter the column widths, add colors, hide leading zeros—Manipulate the layout of the report output to be used in interfaces or flat file transfers.

▶ Custom headers and footers—Create custom headers and footers to be shown on each page of your printed reports. Your report can include the name of the report and the date and time it was created at the top of each printed page.

▶ Charts and graphics—Include graphics and create charts of your SAP data on reports. You can create a bar graph displaying the open items currently available in your warehouse in comparison to the items sold.

Understanding the InfoSet (Ad Hoc) Query

> You can also create calculated fields in your queries to be used in your SAP Query reports. Calculated fields can be used to include variables that are not currently stored by SAP. Examples include a calculated field to store an invoice amount multiplied by a discount percentage or a calculated field to change output based on a number you enter on the Reports Selection screen. You can also create advanced calculated fields using "if-then" type logic. This is performed by using the Local Fields function on the Select Fields screen.

Unlike the SAP Query, which is a complete reporting solution tool, the InfoSet Query is designed for basic users to retrieve simple single-use lists of data from your SAP *Enterprise Resource Planning* (ERP) database. Using this tool, all query information (including the selection criteria) is available on a single screen. Since version SAP R/3 4.6, the Human Capital Management module reporting tool, called the Ad Hoc Query, was combined with the technology of the SAP Query and made available for all modules. It's now called the InfoSet Query (although it is still referred to as the Ad Hoc Query when executed for HR reporting). This section refers to it as the InfoSet (Ad Hoc) Query; the functionality is the same regardless of its name.

Unlike the SAP Query (with the seven basic screens and seven advanced screens), all query information—including the selection criteria for InfoSet Query reporting—is available on a single screen.

You can use the InfoSet (Ad Hoc) Query to quickly answer simple questions, such as how many employees received stock options last year, or to create a comprehensive report for printing or downloading to your PC. The InfoSet (Ad Hoc) Query is designed so that users can pose questions to the SAP system and receive real-time answers. Other sample questions you might pose using an Ad Hoc Query include

▶ How many employees are over the age of 45?

▶ Which invoices are charged to cost center 691211?

▶ How many widgets were available for delivery on 07/05/2011?

The InfoSet (Ad Hoc) Query is a helpful tool that your functional users can use to retrieve important, comprehensive information in a quick-and-easy fashion.

Creating an InfoSet (Ad Hoc) Query

When the one-time configuration is completed, creating an InfoSet query is a relatively elementary task. To begin creating your first InfoSet (ad hoc) query, follow these steps:

1. You can access the InfoSet Query in three ways: through an application-specific role using the Easy Access menu, using the SAP Query (transaction SQ01) and then clicking the **InfoSet Query** button, or by using transaction code PQAH.

2. You are prompted to select your query group and InfoSet (data source) from a dialog box and then to press **Enter**.

   The main screen contains three areas: the actual InfoSet from which you select and choose your fields, the sample report display, and the Selection screen values.

3. To start creating your report, simply check the **Output** box next to each field you want to appear in the report.

4. Next, choose fields for the Selection screen by marking each field's **Selection** check box.

   The Selections section works just as a standard Selection screen does, by enabling you to input values to specify your reporting output.

5. After selecting all the fields you want to include, press the **F8** key to execute the report. By default, your report displays in the SAP ALV grid, from which you can easily drag and drop the columns or manipulate the look of the output.

Understanding the QuickViewer

Unlike the SAP Query, which is a complete reporting solution tool, the SAP QuickViewer tool is a "what-you-see-is-what-you-get" utility for quick collection of data from your SAP ERP system. To define a report with the QuickViewer, you simply enter text (titles) and select the fields and options that define your *QuickView*. Just as SAP Query creates queries, QuickViewer creates QuickViews. QuickViews are not as handy as queries, however; they cannot be exchanged among users. The good news is that they can be converted to queries to be used with the SAP Query. Use QuickViewer to quickly answer simple questions. Like SAP queries, InfoSet (ad hoc) queries are built on the foundation of query areas, query groups, and InfoSets.

Creating a QuickView

After the one-time configuration is completed, creating a QuickView is also a relatively elementary task. Like the SAP queries explained earlier, QuickViews can be run in Basis or Layout (Graphical) mode. In Basis mode, the system automatically renders the report from parameters. In Graphical mode, a user can tweak the report's interface via a visual tool. Like SAP queries, QuickViews are easier to work with in Basis mode. To begin creating your first QuickView, follow these steps:

1. Access the SAP ERP QuickViewer in one of three ways: by using transaction SQVI, by using the **QuickViewer** button on the main screen of the SAP Query (transaction SQ01), or by using an application-specific role from the Easy Access menu.

2. On the main screen, enter a name for your QuickView and click the **Create** button. You are then prompted to select a data source.

3. You use three main tabs to specify your QuickView. The first tab is your list of output fields. Just select fields listed in the Available Fields column and select the arrow keys to move them to the output column. The second tab enables you to dictate the sort sequence for your selected fields. The third tab enables you to indicate selection fields for specifying your final output.

4. Note in the middle of the screen that you have different export options for your QuickView. Select one from the drop-down box and then click the **Execute** button to see the Reports Selection screen. You can further specify your selections. Next, click the **Execute** button to see your completed QuickView.

If you created a QuickView and you want to convert it to an SAP Query report, simply follow these quick steps:

1. Navigate to the main screen of the SAP Query (SQ01).

2. Follow the menu path **Queries**, **Convert QuickViews**.

3. Select your QuickView from the drop-down box and press the **Enter** key. You are prompted to type a name for the query.

4. Press the **Enter** key again to convert the QuickView.

The skills you learned in this hour might be the most meaningful end-user takeaway from this book because they empower you to extract data from your own SAP system. Keep in mind that trial and error is usually the best method for getting accustomed to working with queries in SAP. To this end, seek to "test" your queries in nonproduction systems.

Summary

SAP offers a host of reporting capabilities, ranging from dedicated SAP NetWeaver components and SAP BusinessObjects to built-in capabilities found in SAP ERP and other SAP Business Suite components. This hour provided an introduction to the basics of reporting in SAP, including the concepts of variants and background processing. One of the biggest concerns of using a new system is your ability to retrieve output from the system in a manner that is relatively easy to do, in an equally easy-to-use format. Having all the data stored in your SAP system is good, but to be able to output that data into meaningful reports is crucial—SAP reporting makes this possible.

Case Study: Hour 13

Consider this case study and the questions that follow. You can find the answers posed by the questions related to this case study in Appendix A, "Case Study Answers."

Situation

MNC just hired a new director of finance who is also an SAP novice. She has asked for someone on the MNC Enterprise Reporting team to help her review the reporting options within SAP ERP Finance. Lucky you, your Enterprise Reporting Manager assigned you to the job! Help your new director up to speed.

Questions

1. *What reporting mechanism is used to pose "ad hoc" queries to the database?*

2. *What is a variant?*

3. *What is the transaction code to access the Create InfoSets screen?*

4. *What is the transaction code to access the Create SAP Queries screen?*

5. *What does a query area include?*

6. *What are the two different query areas?*

7. *What must you always do after creating or modifying an InfoSet?*

8. *What is the transaction code to access the QuickViewer?*

Extending SAP with Microsoft and Other Products

What You'll Learn in This Hour:

▶ Built-in SAP/Microsoft functionality
▶ Integrating SAP with Microsoft Office
▶ Extending SAP with Microsoft SharePoint
▶ An introduction to Duet Enterprise
▶ How OpenText and Adobe forms extend SAP
▶ Microsoft Active Directory integration

Because most corporate work is still done on "the desktop," integration between SAP, Microsoft, and other vendors' software continues to play an important role in making work easier for SAP application end users. This hour looks at how new products and methods of tying SAP together with other applications makes for a better SAP end-user experience. For starters, let's review the most ubiquitous integration combination: SAP and Microsoft Office.

SAP Integration with Desktop Applications

It has been possible for many years to use Microsoft's Office suite to access and analyze SAP data. Familiar applications such as Microsoft Excel, Word, Access, and so on have had the ability to connect to SAP and download SAP data using a simple technology called *object linking and embedding* (OLE, pronounced "oh el ee" or "oh lay"). And with the latest joint product development between SAP and Microsoft—Duet

Enterprise—this connection or integration continues to grow deeper and more valuable. Microsoft SharePoint, Exchange, Outlook, Visio, various database sources, and more have been added to the list of Microsoft products that can integrate with SAP. Using OLE, you can take data out of the SAP system and place it into another system, all the while maintaining the format and integrity of the data. For example, you can view data residing in any number of SAP database tables as a series of columns and rows in Microsoft Excel—an easy way to view and manipulate data otherwise trapped in the SAP database as a difficult-to-decipher collection of numbers and words. This is accomplished through the SAP Assistant.

SAP Assistant

The SAP Assistant is the OLE interface used for calling SAP functions and transactions from non-SAP applications. The SAP Assistant exposes both ActiveX controls and OLE object classes, for logging in to SAP, managing data and tables, calling functions and transactions, and more. Beyond the Microsoft Office suite of OLE-compatible applications, the SAP Assistant also supports

- Google Docs, Spreadsheets

- Corel Office, including Paradox

- Star Office

- Lotus SmartSuite

- Various web server development environments

In addition, nearly all modern application development languages in use today support OLE. This includes the old-school C++ programming language, the latest and greatest Microsoft .NET Visual Basic offerings, IBM's WebSphere Information Integrator, and SAP's Sybase PowerBuilder. In this way, the developer of most any non-SAP application can create objects capable of accessing information in SAP.

Using %pc to Download Data

Another easy method of pulling data out of SAP involves executing %pc in the SAPGUI's transaction dialog box. Type in the characters %pc in the transaction dialog box (see Figure 14.1) and press **Enter**.

A pop-up menu appears, giving you a choice of several file formats and a Clipboard option (see Figure 14.2). Choose the format most appropriate for your immediate needs, press **Enter**, browse to the desired directory path, type the name of the output file you want to create, and then click **Save** to save the list data to the filename you specified. Let's take a closer look at several of these file formats next.

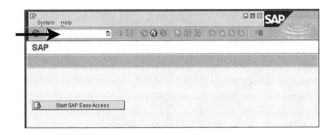

FIGURE 14.1
The box at the top of the SAP display is called the transaction dialog box. This is where you enter commands, like **%pc**.

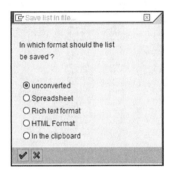

FIGURE 14.2
Use this simple pop-up to select the file format you want to convert your SAP data into.

Exporting SAP Data to Microsoft Excel

Microsoft Excel provides a user-friendly format and helpful tools to assist you in the process of analyzing and presenting data. There are several ways of getting your SAP data into Microsoft Excel. The most basic method involves the System List function, which enables you to save lists displayed on your SAP screen.

You can also use the SAP Query tool to export data to Microsoft Excel, as follows:

1. Execute an SAP Query.

2. The options listed on the selection screen enable you to designate the type of output you want for your report. For a basic transfer to a Microsoft Excel spreadsheet, select the **Display as Table** radio button.

3. From here, select **List**, **Save**, **Local File** to download this table into Microsoft Excel. A Save As box appears, enabling you to select the download file format. Be sure to select the spreadsheet option.

4. After the download is complete, start Microsoft Excel and open the data you have just saved.

5. Return to the SAP Query output screen displaying your table (see Figure 14.3).

You can use the same method detailed later in Hour 13, "Reporting and Query Basics," to download InfoSet or other "ad hoc" queries.

FIGURE 14.3
Your Microsoft
Excel spread-
sheet contain-
ing your SAP
Query data
looks the same
as the data in
your original
query output.

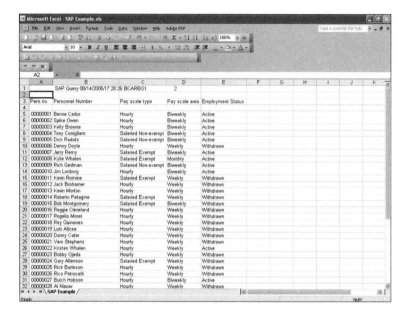

Creating SAP Form Letters in Microsoft Word

SAP features a great interface for creating form letters and other documents using
Microsoft Word. Let's assume you need to output SAP HCM employee data into Word
so that you can create a form letter to all employees. Follow these steps:

1. Select a query to execute.

2. From the selection screen, use the **Display as Table** option and then execute
   your report.

3. When the output appears, rather than saving this file to Microsoft Excel, click
   the **Word Processing** button at the top of your Query Output screen. Doing so
   opens the Word Processor Settings dialog box. Press **Enter** to continue.

4. The dialog box that is displayed presents you with a number of options. You
   can designate whether you want to create a new Word document, use a current
   Word document (one that is currently "open" on your system), or use an existing Word document (one that is saved on your computer). Click the green
   check mark to begin the merge between SAP and Microsoft Word. Upon execution, SAP opens Microsoft Word (see Figure 14.4).

The mail merge toolbar containing
a link to your SAP fields

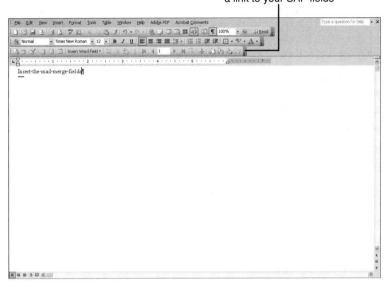

FIGURE 14.4
A Microsoft
Word applica-
tion launches
with a new doc-
ument.

5. Note that your Microsoft Word application now contains a new mail merge toolbar that enables you to insert SAP fields into your Microsoft Word form letter. In Microsoft Word, press the **Enter** key to begin at a new line and then click the **Insert Merge Field** button on the toolbar. In the drop-down list (or the Insert Merge Field pop-up window, in the case of the older Microsoft Office 2003), you see all the SAP fields contained in your original SAP Query.

6. As appropriate for your needs, select one of your SAP fields. It appears in brackets in your Microsoft Word document. Press **Enter** and insert another SAP field. Type into your Microsoft Word document and then insert another SAP field.

7. To preview the output of your form letter, click the **ABC (View Merged Data)** button on the mail merge toolbar.

8. Use the record selector (forward and backward) buttons on the mail merge toolbar to view the various records.

As you have seen, exporting SAP data to Microsoft Excel and Word is useful when it comes to performing further offline manipulation of your data, for creating reports and graphs, or for drafting form letters. Exporting data to a Microsoft Access database is quite useful, too, especially when it comes to general reporting.

Importing SAP into Microsoft Access

When an XLS-based file resides on your local system or an accessible file share, you can import this file into Microsoft Access, as follows:

1. Launch Microsoft Access on your system.

2. From this initial window, select the **Blank Database** option and click **OK**. You are prompted to create a name and to select a location for your database. In this example, the C:\My Documents directory was selected and the database named mySAP.mdb.

3. Click the **Create** button; you then see the main Microsoft Access window.

4. To bring the SAP data into Microsoft Access, use the Microsoft Access menu path **File**, **Get External Data**, **Import**. This is where you have to input the location and filename of the output file you saved earlier. By default, the Files of Type box lists Microsoft Access (*.mdb). You have to change this to **Microsoft Excel (*.xls)**.

5. After changing the Files of Type box and selecting your file, click **Import**. Just as in the Microsoft Excel import, in Access you are presented with an Import Spreadsheet Wizard.

6. On the first screen of the Import Spreadsheet Wizard, click the **Next** button to continue. On the second screen, it asks whether you want to create a new table or add the data to an existing table. To create a new Access database table containing your SAP data, click **Next**. The next window gives you an opportunity to name each of your fields.

By the Way

You can save your Microsoft Word merge document for repeated use. The next time you want to use the same form letter (but with the latest data from SAP), you need to reopen the SAP query that serves as the source of the document, select the **List**, **Word Processing** option from the menu and then select the **Existing Word Document** radio button. You are then prompted to enter the name of your Word document where you saved the file. Microsoft Word will launch, displaying your existing form letter containing the latest data from your SAP system.

7. By selecting each column (use your mouse to do so), you can type a field name for each. After you name all your fields, click **Next**.

8. The following screen enables you to assign a unique identifying number for each of your records; click the **Next** button to continue.

9. The last screen asks you to provide a name for your table. Type **MySAP** and click **Finish**. Microsoft Access then presents you with a confirmation window.

10. Click **OK** in the final Import Spreadsheet Wizard confirmation window; you are returned to the Microsoft Access main window, and your new table is now listed under the Table tab.

11. To look at your table, select it and then click the **Open** button. Your SAP list now appears as a Microsoft Access table; it also includes an additional primary key field.

This process takes longer than exporting SAP data into Microsoft Excel. However, Microsoft Access is a sound reporting tool used by a large number of SAP customers as their primary reporting tool—especially when other applications or tools such as SAP NetWeaver Business Warehouse (BW), SAP Business Objects, SAP Crystal Solutions, Microsoft's business intelligence tools, or IBM's Cognos analytics tool are unavailable.

Microsoft Access Report Wizard

Creating reports in Microsoft Access is easy using a tool called the Microsoft Access Report Wizard. In this case, the Report Wizard simplifies the layout process of your fields by visually stepping you through a series of questions about the type of report you want to create. The wizard walks you through the step-by-step creation of a report, while behind the scenes Access is formatting, grouping, and sorting your report based on the selections you make.

Instead of you having to create a report from scratch, Microsoft Access provides a number of standard report formats. Some of these, such as tabular and columnar reports, mail-merge reports, and mailing label formats, lend themselves to meeting basic reporting requirements. Reports created using the Microsoft Access Report Wizard can also be customized to fit your needs. To use the Report Wizard, perform the following steps:

1. Close any open Access databases by using the menu path **File**, **Close**.

2. In the main Microsoft Access database window, click **Reports**.

3. From here, click the **New** button to launch the Microsoft Access Report Wizard (or choose the option to create a report in Design view).

4. Assuming you are running the Report Wizard, select the **Report Wizard** option in the top box and your table name in the second box. Click **OK** to proceed.

Exporting to Microsoft Access is helpful when you want to compare data among multiple systems. For example, if your company stores your vendor master data in SAP and also stores this vendor master data in a non-SAP application (implying you have not implemented SAP NetWeaver Process Integration with Master Data Management), you can use Microsoft Access as a tool to quickly compare the two sources relative to overall data consistency.

By the Way

5. You are presented with a field selection screen. From this screen, you can select which fields are output to your report. Select a field by highlighting it with your mouse and then use the Next button to include it in the report. In Figure 14.5, the Employment Status field has been selected.

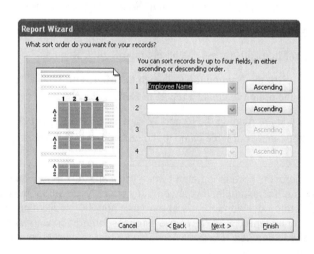

6. After you click **Next**, the Report Wizard asks whether you want to add any grouping levels to your report. This is a helpful step when you are creating a report where you might want to group and subtotal portions of the output. Otherwise, click the **Next** button to continue.

7. Now identify your sort order criteria. In Figure 14.6, we choose to sort by Employee Name.

8. The Report Wizard lets you specify formatting criteria. The orientation of the report (portrait or landscape) and the layout of the report (columnar, tabular, or justified) are designated on this screen. After making a selection, click **Next**.

9. You can choose from a selection of predefined formats for your report. After making a selection, click **Next**.

10. The last step asks you to type a name for your report. Do so and click **Finish** to complete the creation of your report.

For users with minimal skills to create reports, Microsoft Access is a great reporting tool. Using Access, you can also include graphics in your reports, or you can create graphs and charts of your SAP data.

Integrating SAP with Office: Quick References

The following sections provide simple step-by-step instructions for executing many of the reporting processes just discussed. Use the following sections as a quick reference to speed you through each respective reporting process.

By the Way

For advanced users, consider writing a macro that automatically retrieves the latest SAP download file and imports it into your existing Microsoft Access table—replacing the old data and thus automating the Microsoft Access import process. For more information about this function, search the Microsoft Access help for "automate importing." In the same way, advanced ABAP or Java programmers can write a program that automatically generates a file used by the download portion of this process, thus automating the entire SAP-to-Access reporting process.

Exporting Lists to Microsoft Excel

To use the System List function to export SAP lists to Microsoft Excel, do the following:

1. Navigate to the SAP screen containing the list you want to output.

2. Follow the menu path **System, List, Save, Local File**.

3. Use the possible entries help button to change the location and filename of your new file.

4. Click the **Transfer** button.

5. Launch Microsoft Excel and open the file.

Exporting SAP Query Reports to Excel

To output SAP Query reports to Microsoft Excel, do the following:

1. Execute the SAP Query report that contains the data to include in your report.

2. Select the **Display as Table** option and then execute the report.

3. Select the **List**, **Download to File** menu option.

4. Use the possible entries help button to change the location and filename of your new file.

5. Click the **Transfer** button.

6. Launch Microsoft Excel and open the file.

Creating Form Letters with Word

To create SAP form letters using Microsoft Word, do the following:

1. Execute the SAP Query report that contains the data to include in your report.

2. On the selection screen, select the **Display as Table** option, and then execute the report.

3. Select the **List**, **Word Processing** menu option.

4. Click the **Enter** button in the Word Processing Settings dialog box.

5. Select your required options from the MS Word Settings dialog box and then click the **Enter** button.

6. Type your document and insert merge fields using the **Insert Merge Field** button on the Microsoft Word mail merge toolbar.

7. Use the **ABC View Merged Data** button to review your document and the record selection buttons to navigate between records.

Exporting Lists to Access

The following is a recap of the steps required to use the System List function to export SAP lists into Microsoft Access. The initial steps of this process are the same for downloading files to Microsoft Excel:

1. Navigate to the SAP screen containing the list you want to output.

2. Follow the menu path **System**, **List**, **Save**, **Local File**.

3. Use the possible entries help button to change the location and filename of your new file.

4. Click the **Transfer** button.

5. Open your file in Microsoft Excel, and use the menu path **File**, **Save As** to save it as a Microsoft Excel worksheet. Close **Excel**.

6. Launch Microsoft Access and create a new database.

7. Use the menu path **File**, **Get External Data**, **Import** and select your Microsoft Excel file to import the file into Access using the Import Spreadsheet Wizard.

Integrating SAP with Microsoft SharePoint

Microsoft Office SharePoint Server provides many capabilities to companies and their office workers. It is often used to build the company's intranet portal, for example, and is also used to quickly and easily build websites. (SharePoint refers to these as simply *sites*.) SharePoint sites can serve as the repository for a diverse set of business data. When used in conjunction with SharePoint's collaboration and business tools, sites become powerful business tools; they allow organizations the ability to share information, work together on documents, and make smarter decisions.

SharePoint integrates with Microsoft Exchange "out of the box" (that is, without any extra work necessary to tie the two products together). This is important for several reasons, primarily that you do not need to leave SharePoint to "see" Exchange-based workflow approvals and other processes. Because SharePoint itself has evolved significantly over the past several years, let's take a look at the two most recent SharePoint releases and how they make it easier to work with SAP.

SharePoint 2007

There are several methods to integrate SAP data within SharePoint. Though not exhaustive, this list provides a high-level understanding of what is possible:

▶ SAP Business Server Pages and SAP Web Dynpro

▶ SAP Web Services with SharePoint Business Data Connector

▶ SAP Portal iView as a SharePoint Web Part

Each method is outlined next.

SAP Business Server Pages and Web Dynpro

One way SAP data can be consumed and displayed as a web page is through what SAP calls *Business Server Pages* (BSPs). BSPs are designed and developed to be displayed within a web browser. The Web Dynpro serves as the user interface. Combined, you can extract data from SAP and display it through a web browser. And for our purposes, you can use these technologies to extract data from SAP and display it in SharePoint.

The main advantage to this SAP access method is that you can control the look and feel of the data. In other words, you can make the output match the look and feel of your SharePoint site so that it visually appears to be seamless to the consumer of the data, the end user. The look and feel is handled on the SharePoint side and requires the help of a SharePoint developer.

Accessing SAP using BSPs and Web Dynpro requires that *Single Sign-On* (SSO) be established between SAP and SharePoint using a technology called SPNego (which is briefly outlined from a technical perspective in Hour 18, "SAP Technical Installation"). If you have access to transaction SE80, the ABAP Development Workbench, you can browse the available BSP applications and begin working with your SharePoint developer to host these BSPs in SharePoint.

SAP Web Services

SAP can also expose its data through what is called a *web service*. A web service is nothing more than a program that in this case takes SAP data and formats it to be displayed within a web browser. By way of comparison, consider viewing an invoice using the SAPGUI. Using Internet Explorer, Firefox, or another web browser, that same invoice can also be opened as a web page simply because SAP has written a web service to read the data for that SAP transaction. This functionality is nice in that occasional SAPGUI users can conceivably avoiding using the SAPGUI altogether if their data and transactions are properly exposed. To make this easier, SAP has published a list of available services that you can browse and choose from (if your company has set up the SAP Enterprise Services Repository). Check with your SAP Basis or ABAP Development team to determine which services are available to you and then consider exposing the data most frequently accessed by each end user or team. Once exposed, all the information from your various web services can be pulled together into SharePoint 2007 through *Business Data Connector* (BDC). The BDC in SharePoint acts as an information hub where you define data sources that are external to SharePoint and then add those sources to a SharePoint site. Again, work with your SAP ABAP developers and SharePoint administrators to enable this functionality.

SAP NetWeaver Portal iView

Another method of displaying SAP data on a web page involves using the SAP NetWeaver Portal. It displays data on a web page through an iView. When you view an SAP portal page and see a table or something that resembles a spreadsheet, this is actually an iView. The SharePoint equivalent is called a Web Part (discussed earlier this hour); there are specific Web Parts used to display iViews. Like BSPs and Web Dynpro, this functionality also requires that SSO be set up. For SharePoint 2007, use SPNego. One disadvantage to using iViews with SharePoint 2007 is that you cannot change the visual characteristics of this data—how the data looks in SAP NetWeaver Portal is exactly how it is presented in the SharePoint Web Part.

SharePoint 2010

As of this writing, SharePoint 2010 is the latest SharePoint release from Microsoft. While everything already outlined with regard to SharePoint 2007 continues to work in SharePoint 2010, some of the terminology has changed. For instance, Business Data Connector in SharePoint 2007 has been replaced by *Business Connectivity Services* (BCS) in SharePoint 2010. BCS has greater capabilities and extends additional options such as bidirectional communications; not only can you display data from SharePoint, but you can update SAP data from SharePoint, as well. In addition, the iView Web Part has been replaced by the iFrame Web Part. The main difference is that the iFrame provides the ability to make visual changes to the way your SAP information is presented in SharePoint. This can help create a more consistent look and feel of the SharePoint site.

In addition, support for Microsoft Silverlight has been expanded. Silverlight is a highly interactive programming language recently developed by Microsoft. You can use this software to build highly dynamic and intuitive business applications. Such an application might comprise various data sources located in SAP, in SharePoint, or in another database or application entirely. Imagine a sales report that combines data from several different business units and other sources and covers many years. Using Silverlight controls, a SharePoint site can enable SAP end users to intuitively drill down into sales data by quarter, region, product line, business area, and more—all without a lot of back-end technical coding or programming.

Introduction to Microsoft Duet

Still sometimes referred to as its code name, Mendocino, Duet 1.x was a suite of products jointly developed by Microsoft and SAP. The product suite consisted of server components, client components, tools, and applications that presented SAP processes and data to the Microsoft Office suite. The earliest versions of Duet introduced several common business processes into the familiar Microsoft Outlook interface. These business processes included Time Management, Leave Management, Team Management, and Budget Monitoring. Later, Duet was extended to include Purchasing Management, Recruiting, Travel Management, Sales Management, and Demand Planning.

The original Duet exposed or delivered an organization's SAP data into Microsoft Outlook. For the "occasional" SAP end user, there was no longer a need to log on to SAP at all. Imagine coming into the office in the morning and upon opening Microsoft Outlook finding your morning sales report. You might also find an email from one of your direct reports requesting vacation, along with another email from the HR department asking you to approve a one-time bonus for another employee. With Duet, you could review the report, reject the vacation request, and approve the bonus without ever leaving Outlook. Duet made people and processes more effective and efficient.

Introduction to Duet Enterprise

The release of Duet Enterprise in 2011 marked a new development effort between SAP and Microsoft. Whereas Duet 1.0 and 1.5 were products that integrated SAP with Microsoft Exchange and Office, Duet Enterprise integrates with *Microsoft Office SharePoint Server* (MOSS) 2010. Thus, the two product lines are actually nothing like one another; the only points of commonality are the name and the fact that Duet has always been a joint development effort between Microsoft and SAP.

The original Duet offerings focused on predelivered content such as Time and Leave Management (outlined earlier). Duet Enterprise, on the other hand, was developed to deliver a platform enabling easy integration between SAP and SharePoint. Duet Enterprise can still integrate with Microsoft Exchange, but it accomplishes that bit of functionality through SharePoint integration with Exchange rather than SAP integration. Duet Enterprise is focused on five keys areas of integration:

▶ Enterprise Collaboration

▶ Contextual Workflow

▶ Duet Profile

▶ Federated Search

▶ Duet Reporting

Each of these is briefly outlined next.

Enterprise Collaboration

Enterprise Collaboration provides a framework for automated creation of SharePoint sires and it tracks the link between an entity and that site. This allows SAP to present business information within a SharePoint site and then allow the consumers of that data to collaborate and manage that data with SharePoint. These sites can be created on-the-fly for business data instances. Duet Enterprise runs on SharePoint 2010, which provides end users access to the SharePoint Ribbon functionality. This functionality provides easy access to all the SharePoint user tools, such as easy linkage into Outlook through SharePoint.

Contextual Workflow

Duet Enterprise's Contextual Workflow functionality allows users to receive workflow approval requests within a SharePoint tasks folder. It may even be extended to an end user's Outlook email inbox. From SharePoint, you can monitor and manage your workflows just as you manage other work tasks. You can also customize or extend SAP workflow functionality by initializing follow-on SharePoint workflows. Finally, workflow requests may be delegated to another user.

Duet Profile

Using MOSS 2.0 Enterprise services, you can search for and collaborate with people based on their SAP and SharePoint profiles. For instance, an end user could search for sales representatives inside the company who have been tasked with supporting a particular set of sales accounts. When you pull out an individual's profile, it would include information related to current availability, a list of specific accounts for which the salesperson is responsible, and more. In this way, you could easily determine who your "extended team" is and begin working together.

Federated Search

Federated Search enables you to initiate a search for information from within SharePoint. The search would not only search information that is available in SharePoint but it would also search within SAP and then present the results jointly within SharePoint. When you click the link, the data displays within SharePoint, regardless of the actual location of the data.

Duet Reporting

Duet Reporting, based on SAP Security, allows you to create and run an SAP ad hoc report from SharePoint. You can schedule the report to run daily and then subscribe to the report within Outlook so it automatically appears in your email inbox as soon as it has been executed every day. You may select reports from a report catalog and personalize them as needed. Duet Reporting also enables you to distribute reports to a group of users based on rules. For instance, you could run a series of sales reports and then automatically deliver them to the appropriate users based on their sales area, specialty, geography, or other criteria.

In summary, Duet Enterprise may be viewed as a platform that enables certain capabilities out of the box. This platform provides a secure pipeline between SAP and SharePoint. After the SAP data is exposed through SharePoint, it can then be accessed and manipulated by other tools, including Microsoft Outlook.

Using OpenText with SAP

OpenText Corporation, an Enterprise Content Management company, created a solution specifically tailored for SAP. Called OpenText ECM Suite for SAP Solutions, it consists of four components:

▶ OpenText Data Archiving for SAP Solutions

▶ OpenText Archiving for SAP Solutions

▶ OpenText Document Access for SAP Solutions

▶ OpenText Extended ECM for SAP Solutions

Each solution is briefly outlined next.

OpenText Data Archiving for SAP Solutions

The OpenText data archiving solution provides the ability to archive data from SAP, reducing not only the size of your SAP database but also helping you meet federal and other regulatory requirements regarding data storage and retention. This solution moves data from SAP to optical disk storage where it may be secured for years. This data can still be accessed directly within SAP, but it will take a few seconds to retrieve it from the optical media. Many times, products such as these are used to meet compliancy regulations. You might keep two or more years of data in the local SAP database, for example, but you move the rest of the data offline, where it still remains retrievable. By reducing the size of your SAP database, system performance can be held steady, and you can put off or avoid altogether costly disk subsystem and other infrastructure upgrades.

OpenText Archiving for SAP Solutions

The OpenText Archiving solution is not to be confused with the Data Archiving solution. The former is sold by SAP as "SAP Archiving by OpenText," and it links document content to SAP business content. For example, a company might seek to link native or faxed incoming and outgoing invoices, orders, HR employee documents, and other documents to the business processes these documents facilitate. All of these documents are moved out of SAP (to save storage space and preserve system performance) and placed on less-expensive but still readily accessible storage.

OpenText Document Access for SAP Solutions

OpenText's Document Access for SAP Solutions is also directly available from SAP and is called the SAP Document Access by OpenText product. It is a system-independent

SAP module. OpenText Document Access adds a process-oriented view to all your business documents and data. Whether the business document is in SAP or another application, this solution allows you to bring everything together in one location so that users need to peruse only one location for all business data. OpenText Document Access is embedded in standard SAP interfaces like the SAPGUI and SAP NetWeaver Portal, making it a powerful and intuitive addition to an SAP system.

OpenText Extended ECM for SAP Solutions

This product, sold by SAP as SAP Extended ECM by OpenText, extends your transactional process management capability with classic content management capabilities such as document management, records management, and collaboration. It provides access to enterprise-wide data spread across multiple applications using SAP's standard user interfaces. Considering all of the documents a company needs to track and maintain for each of its customers—emails, contracts, electronic forms, various reports and spreadsheets, and so on—this solution's ability to capture, manage, store, preserve, and deliver data on behalf of one or more customer owners within SAP makes is tremendously useful.

Using SAP Interactive Forms by Adobe

Adobe entered the SAP forms business years ago. Its latest offering, SAP Interactive Forms by Adobe, provides intelligent forms that can be used to enable business processes. These forms are easy and intuitive to use, streamlining how end users manage and complete their daily work. The forms integrate with SAP and support two-way data communication. This allows prepopulation of the form from data that already resides within SAP. It also allows the information that an end user provides to be placed within SAP via a web service (discussed earlier this hour).

Adobe's interactive forms also provide the ability to apply business logic to a process. For example, let's consider a customer request for a life insurance request. The end user accesses your system and clicks Life Insurance Quote (or something similar), which in turn commences your life insurance business process. The initial request would be routed to SAP, where all the customer's information is gathered. For existing customers, this information could prepopulate an interactive quote form. All the user would have to do is complete the remaining information on the form. Based on that information, such as a recent reported illness requiring a hospital stay, you might require additional information. This logic can be built in to the form so that the end user would automatically be prompted to provide additional required information. After all the necessary information is gathered, an SAP Workflow could then be invoked to route the form for processing. At this point, based on your business process, the form could be sent to a particular person to contact the end user to discuss a quote, or the form could invoke the online quote process, where additional business rules might be applied. In this life insurance example, the completed application would then run through the company's rules engine within SAP, automatically generating a quote for the end user. Carrying the business process through to the end, the person seeking life insurance could review the quote, decide to purchase the life insurance, and submit the application form electronically. Other interactive forms might be triggered to address billing, shipping, and so on. SAP Interactive Forms by Adobe also features the ability to gather electronic signatures and apply them to the appropriate documents.

The real value of SAP Interactive Forms by Adobe is twofold: its rich end-user experience and its ability to facilitate business processes. The intuitive and familiar forms are simple for the user to complete. By applying business logic to the forms and coupling them with SAP Workflow, companies can quickly deploy new business processes.

Integrating Microsoft Directory with SAP

Before we close this hour, we need to touch on one final SAP/Microsoft infrastructure integration feature: *Active Directory* (AD) integration. Although this functionality is enabled at a technical and administrative level and therefore does not align to the "business user" nature of this hour, AD integration is remarkably useful to SAP's customers and business users. Microsoft AD is at the heart of every Microsoft infrastructure; it provides a single security context for all users and servers. Through this mechanism, SAP servers register as objects into the directory, which in turn are search-enabled. It's through this feature that SAPGUI users can automatically populate their SAP Logon Pads and quickly connect to SAP systems. AD also plays a key role in facilitating SSO. All told, AD integration makes an SAP end user's life remarkably easier. Work with your SAP Basis team and Windows AD team to encourage this fundamental level of SAP and Microsoft integration.

Summary

With the integration naturally afforded by SAP for Microsoft's core suite of products, much of an organization's reporting can be handled by Microsoft products or natively through SAP. This hour provided insight into how Microsoft Excel, Word, Access, and SharePoint are used for such reporting purposes. Additional easy-to-use functionality was also outlined. And the joint effort between SAP and Microsoft culminating in Duet and Duet Enterprise highlighted several advanced features associated with integrating SAP and Microsoft. A quick look at OpenText's solutions for SAP, Adobe's Interactive Forms, and the intrinsic value of integrating Microsoft Active Directory with SAP concluded this hour.

Case Study: Hour 14

Consider this case study and the questions that follow. You can find the answers posed by the questions related to this case study in Appendix A, "Case Study Answers."

Situation

MNC runs SAP Enterprise Resource Planning (ERP) on Microsoft Windows with SQL Server. The implementation is new, and currently only limited business functionality has been enabled. Two of the modules implemented by MNC are Time Management and Budget Monitoring. The IT budget for further SAP enhancements is limited, but automation and ease of use have been communicated as the project's keys to implementation success.

Questions

1. How can MNC's end users quickly download data using only the SAPGUI and no special software tools?

2. In the context of this hour, what is a web service?

3. What replaced the iView Web Part in SharePoint 2010?

4. What technology or capability enables SharePoint 2010 to support bidirectional communications (both ways between SAP and SharePoint)?

5. Though many differences exist, what is the primary way in which Duet Enterprise differs from its predecessors?

6. What four components make up the OpenText ECM Suite for SAP Solutions?

A Project Manager's Perspective on Implementing SAP

What You'll Learn in This Hour:

▶ The role of the project management roadmap

▶ A deeper look at SAP's ASAP methodology

▶ Other contemporary SAP methods and tools

▶ The role and makeup of the SAP project team

▶ Various SAP leadership bodies

As we found in Hour 2, "SAP Business Basics," Hour 3, "SAP Technology Basics," and Hour 4, "SAP Project Basics," there are business, technical, and project management perspectives to implementing SAP. The project management perspective is important because it wraps up the business and technology perspectives into a single overarching plan intended to help a company ultimately realize SAP's value. In this hour, we explore the project management perspective in more depth.

SAP and the ASAP Methodology

SAP AG found long ago that without a sound implementation roadmap, its customers would typically underachieve or outright fail to realize their SAP-derived business process reengineering goals. To explain their failure, they would often blame SAP's complex software. Truth be told, SAP's software is indeed complex and surely time-consuming to implement. But the reasons for this complexity are largely beyond SAP's control. SAP is difficult to implement because

▶ Running a business is innately complex.

▶ Global economics only further complicate matters.

▶ Business users are typically uninterested in changing how they do things.

▶ Executives and other business leaders are not inclined to naturally endorse the kinds of changes and therefore business risks embodied by introducing such a comprehensive change-enabler as SAP (or its competitor's enterprise products, for that matter).

▶ Calculating an SAP project's *return of investment* (ROI) can be subjective at best, and nearly impossible in many cases.

▶ Until recently, IT computing platforms have artificially limited innovation or failed to provide the necessary technical agility needed by an organization's business applications to in turn enable greater business agility.

▶ SAP implementation teams have historically lacked the fundamental project management, change management, or business transformation skills necessary to pull off a successful project.

▶ The *enterprise resource planning* (ERP) implementation process itself is cumbersome, subject to iterations, and therefore inordinately expensive—often double what was original budgeted!

To help ensure its software lived up to its customers' expectations, SAP had to provide a predictable methodology. As you learned in Hour 2, that methodology was *Accelerated SAP* (ASAP).

> Did you know that SAP projects have a significantly greater chance of failure under weak change management processes? To remedy this, initiate your project with strong alignment and commitment among all stakeholders as to how changes will be controlled, managed, and enforced throughout the project. This not only facilitates project success, but also helps maintain focus on the project's value and the business problems the project was initiated to resolve.

Introduction to ASAP

Originally envisioned for smaller SAP projects, ASAP eventually became the de facto standard for describing an SAP implementation roadmap from a project management perspective. It helped organizations get their arms around what it meant to reengineer their current operating environments, structures, systems, and processes (from both business and IT perspectives).

Close to 15 years after it was developed, ASAP continues to be used by systems integrators to help firms design their SAP implementation roadmap in a manner that's both efficient and comprehensive. ASAP helps steer a project team to optimize the time, people, and other resources necessary to implement SAP. Throughout its five phases, ASAP focuses on leveraging reusable templates, tools, and training:

▶ Phase 1: Project preparation

▶ Phase 2: Business blueprint

▶ Phase 3: Realization

▶ Phase 4: Final preparation

▶ Phase 5: Go-live and support

▶ Phase 6: Run (also called Run SAP)

Figure 15.1 provides a view into the ASAP roadmap and the time typically spent executing each phase (although, of course, the idea of running SAP post-go-live actually represents years and years). Each phase is outlined next.

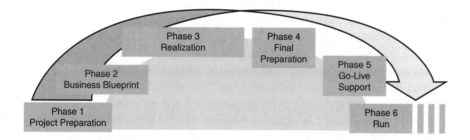

FIGURE 15.1
SAP's ASAP roadmap continues to provide a simple framework for organizing new SAP implementations.

Phase 1: Project Preparation

Phase 1 comprises many of the steps necessary to start an SAP implementation on the right foot. During this phase, the project management team is initially structured and assembled. This team then begins the process of identifying, collecting, developing, and managing all the resources and tools necessary to manage the implementation. Several important milestones occur in phase 1:

▶ Obtaining senior-level management/stakeholder support

▶ Identifying clear project objectives

▶ Developing an efficient decision-making process

▶ Creating a working environment suitable for change and reengineering

▶ Building a qualified and capable project team

The next phase, business blueprinting, was briefly mentioned in earlier hours and is detailed next.

Phase 2: Business Blueprint

The intent of the business blueprinting phase is to help extract pertinent information about the firm seeking to implement SAP and then map the existing organization's business processes into those that reflect industry best practices. The blueprinting information is collected via templates, which are essentially questionnaires designed to probe for business-specific data describing how a company currently (or should be) conducting business. As such, these questionnaires also serve to document the essence of the implementation. Each business blueprint document outlines business requirements and thus the groundwork for future reengineered business processes. The kinds of questions asked are germane to many different business functions and reflect data points such as the specific information necessary to complete a purchase requisition or pull together information for a particular financial report.

Tools such as the *Question and Answer Database* (QAdb) were originally used to facilitate business blueprint creation and maintenance; it housed all the data and thus acted as the heart of the blueprint. Systems integrators have married their own methodologies and tools to supplant the QAdb, but the process and ideas remain the same. The same holds true for the SAP Issues Database, another one-time tool used in the blueprinting process. This database and its successors store open concerns and pending issues that relate to the implementation. Centrally storing this information assists in gathering and then managing issues to resolution, so that important matters do not fall through the cracks. The idea of a database makes it possible to easily search through, assign, and update tasks. Today's SAP implementation teams use SAP *Solution Manager* (SolMan). Much more robust and capable, SolMan provides better visibility and support to contemporary implementations.

Phase 3: Realization

> It's not too early to start thinking about knowledge transfer. As the realization phase progresses toward a close, be sure that all data and rationale regarding business process configurations are indeed captured; don't let all your business process knowledge walk out the door when the lead systems integrator and other partners conclude their work. This is also a good time to start thinking about how and when the company's end users tasked with actually using the system for day-to-day business purposes will be trained.

As mentioned in Hour 4, it's the realization phase where most of a project's resources and time are consumed. After the business blueprint has been wrapped up, business function ("functional") experts can begin prototyping and configuring SAP, essentially modeling the business processes outlined during blueprinting. The realization phase is divided into two parts:

- ▶ **Baseline configuration**—The SAP consulting team configures a basic functioning system, which acts as a baseline system to later be refined.

- ▶ **Fine-tuning configuration**—After a baseline system has been established, the implementation project team fine-tunes the system to meet the blueprint's specific business process requirements.

The initial configuration completed during the baseline configuration is based on the information provided in the blueprinting documents. This configuration represents something like 80% of the system's ultimate capabilities. The remaining 20% of the configuration not tackled during the baseline configuration is completed during the fine-tuning configuration. Fine-tuning takes care of the exceptions and final tweaking necessary to meet the business's needs. As phase 3 transitions to phase 4, you should find yourself not only in the midst of SAP training, but also at the tail end of what should have been rigorous functional testing, integration testing, and computing platform-specific stress testing.

Phase 4: Final Preparation

Phase 4 comprises the necessary final preparation and fine-tuning of the computing platforms and SAP applications prior to go-live. Phase 4 also includes migrating the last of your data from the old legacy system or systems to SAP. Be sure to complete the remaining functional, integration, and stress testing. The teams are under tremendous pressure as last-minute issues are uncovered and functionality is discovered lacking. Save any real rework for after go-live; there will be plenty of time to introduce new functionality in subsequent releases or change waves. Now is the time to ensure that the SAP system delivers the core business functionality needed to run the business.

Also take this time to perform any final preventative maintenance on the platform. Validate that the overall system performs adequately if not optimally; the system's online response time performance and the performance of critical batch jobs and reports are critical to end-user perceptions as to whether the project has succeeded or failed.

Finally, give yourself plenty of time to plan and document your go-live support strategy. Outside of typical computer operations and IT maintenance tasks, preparing for go-live needs to include preparing for your end users' inevitable questions as they start to actively work on the new SAP system. Be sure that the SAP help desk is properly staffed and adequately trained to support the new system, for example.

Phase 5: Go-Live and Support

The go-live milestone itself looks straightforward to achieve on paper—with a flip of a switch, everyone has access to the new system. Orchestrating a smooth and uneventful go-live is another matter altogether, though. Preparation is the key, including attention to what-if scenarios related not only to the individual business processes deployed but also to how the technology underpinning these business processes performs. Business processes need to be proactively monitored for performance. Similarly, the technology stack layers need to be monitored relative to how well each layer and the computing platform overall enables the SAP application to meet the business's *service level agreements* (SLAs).

Don't forget to nail down maintenance contracts, post-go-live consulting agreements and to document all operational processes and procedures. Fortunately, with literally thousands of successful go-live "nonevents" to their name, the support professionals at SAP and in the SAP partner community have a wealth of information to share. Additional resources are available, too, ranging from blogs, wikis, and whitepapers, to conferences, SAP publications, SAP's own online support site, and more. Turn to Hour 24, "Other Resources and Closing Thoughts," for all the details.

Phase 6: Run

The run phase is the final and most recent addition to the ASAP methodology. Also called Run SAP, the goal of this phase is to ensure the system continues to operate and perform well post-go-live. SAP helps IT organizations deliver a highly available and well-performing system through several tools, the most important of which is SAP SolMan. For more information, see Hour 20, "SAP System Administration and Management."

The Project Management Office

An organizational structure with executive power and extensive business/IT relationships needs to provide the overall SAP implementation's project management.. Often labeled the project management office (PMO), this team is responsible for developing and coordinating a cooperative environment among all the different team members, so that together the team may succeed. The PMO's leader typically reports to an executive steering committee or perhaps the company's chief operating officer (COO) and is intimately familiar with the inner workings and politics of the firm for which SAP is being implemented. The PMO leader might designate a senior project manager over the triumvirate of PMs responsible for the SAP project (representing the company, the primary SAP systems integration partner, and SAP itself), or might fulfill that role personally. Key PMO tasks include the following:

▶ Managing scope and resource planning, and validating and aligning resources and budgets to the project's goals and objectives

▶ Developing and maintaining the overall project plan and scheduling tasks

▶ Maximizing project quality, which might include escalating issues to the stakeholder committee or project board as necessary

▶ Managing communications, including monitoring and improving upon the project's progress via regular reporting and stage-wise or phase-specific scheduled meetings

▶ Managing risks and contingencies, and providing direction to the project team when priorities and leaders conflict

Each of these responsibilities is explored next. In the end, the PMO provides the resources and methods necessary to help ensure a successful SAP implementation.

Scope Management

Managing scope is particularly important for the PMO. Allowing a "sky is the limit" mentality neither serves well the company introducing SAP nor the IT delivery team. Without an agreed-on scope, there's just no hope that anyone will walk away happy at the conclusion of the project (if indeed a conclusion can be arrived at, given the ongoing scope creep implied by "the sky is the limit").

Scheduling

Effective and efficient projects are founded on accurate task duration estimates, balanced by controls, and steered by active (rather than passive) management. Schedules created at the project's onset will change. Therefore, it's imperative that stakeholders from across the project team meet regularly to discuss what-ifs and potential schedule issues. Maintaining a well-thought-out and regularly updated schedule gives stakeholders an idea of what to expect throughout the project's execution.

The schedule communicates milestones, critical path activities, and the relative importance of resource commitments. The affects of project constraints and other potential issues give further weight to scheduling's importance. Remember that effective time scheduling requires risk assessment; buffer time needs to be allocated to tasks, for example, where the risk of an overrun significantly impacts the project's cost, schedule, or quality. A daily review of the schedule is therefore probably warranted.

Quality Planning

Planning for (rather than hoping for) quality helps ensure that various project tasks and the overall project achieve their intended results. Note the difference between *quality assurance* (QA) and *quality control* (QC). QA speaks to the processes used by the PMO to ensure that the project's tasks are wrapped in quality planning and systematic evaluation activities. Conversely, QC determines how well the project's results align to known quality standards. This alignment is accomplished through regular process-monitoring activities. Together, QA and QC help ensure that problems with quality may be addressed early on by the project's leaders.

Communications Planning

In any project, the PM needs to regularly communicate the project's progress and activities to a set of stakeholders. In the same way, every member of the team needs to communicate in some form or fashion to other members and to external stakeholders, partners, and so on. Especially in the case of complex, multiphased, and collaborative projects like SAP, good communications planning and processes are critical.

Risk and Contingency Planning

Risks are inherent in every project. Any number of activities or resource losses will affect the project's schedule, dependencies, costs, quality, task completion, and so on. Therefore, it's incumbent upon the PM to identify key risks as soon as possible. In this way, contingencies may be weighed and developed prior to any real emergencies. All of these what-if items are then placed in the project's contingency plan.

Assembling the Project Team

With the high-level project methodology and PMO details behind us, let's turn our attention to the SAP project team. The design, makeup, and skill sets embodied in the SAP project team are critical to an implementation's success. Team buy-in and participation needs to encompass executive management support, underlying IT support, and especially all the firm's various business units transitioning to SAP. When structuring the project team, consider the following:

▶ Assess all the business areas that will be affected by the SAP installation (such as the finance department, accounting team, warehousing group, plant maintenance organization, an executive decision making body, and so on).

▶ Identify the skills required of each team member, from managerial and leadership to professional and technical skills.

► Assess the members of the company's IT organization specifically tasked with supporting SAP (sometimes called the SAP *support team* or *SAP virtual team*).

The company's project team needs to comprise key individuals from the business groups who will be impacted by the SAP implementation and IT organizations who will support the implementation prior to and after go-live. Executive-level management support is absolutely required. Throughout the project team, members must be focused on day-to-day tactical even as they keep central the company's long-term vision. Figure 15.2 illustrates a sample project team structure.

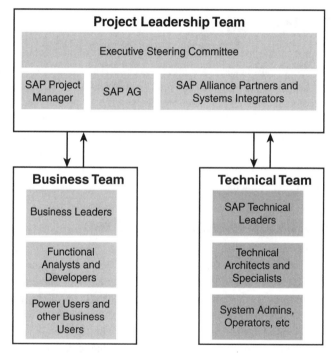

FIGURE 15.2
The SAP project team's structure should reflect a similar design where business teams and technical teams report to a central leadership body.

Regardless of the specific role a member in the project team might hold, there are five key characteristics the team overall (and individuals where it makes sense) should embody:

► The aptitude to assess how the new system will enable or affect individual and collective business processes companywide

► The ability to identify the impact on current business processes

► The ability to comprehend the requirements for reengineering identified business processes hosted by SAP

▶ The knowledge to design and complete the integration of the SAP structure, hierarchies, and business process configuration across the enterprise

▶ The ability to efficiently share their knowledge throughout the implementation and serve as a willing and available body of knowledge well after go-live

With the team assembled and ready to go, the overall SAP project leader is finally positioned to manage the project's execution. Before we cover that key position, however, a quick discussion of the SAP project leadership bodies is in order.

SAP Project Leadership

A typical project structure for SAP implementation consists of an executive steering committee or project board headed by a project sponsor. The overall SAP project leader (also called the *SAP cross-bundle project leader*) is answerable to this committee. In turn, the core project team itself is headed by the overall SAP project leader. This PM is supported by a number of "bundle" or project leads. Reporting to each project lead are leads for the different SAP "rows." Examples of common SAP rows include the Order Management row, Purchasing row, and Warehouse Inventory row. As you might have noticed, rows equate to functional business areas; they form the core functional deliverable team for each SAP implementation.

The Executive Steering Committee

The executive steering committee (sometimes called the *project board*) consists of the SAP project's key stakeholders, executive decision makers, senior business and IT leaders, and other stakeholders with a keen interest in seeing the SAP implementation through to completion. It is this committee's ability to steer the project, given the inevitable changes both inside and external to the project, that makes it vital. The project sponsor is a key member of the committee who, along with the overall SAP project manager, provides the bulk of the project's leadership. Other committee members include the following:

▶ The committee chair, who if not the project's sponsor is probably a senior executive with a vested interest in making SAP a reality.

▶ The chair or lead of the firm's PMO.

▶ Key functional area or *workstream* leaders, each of whom is a high-level representative of his or her respective business areas (such as finance, manufacturing, logistics, worldwide sales, and so on).

▶ The firm's chief information officer (CIO) or another senior IT representative who has the final say in IT-related matters.

▶ The director of enterprise computing (or someone holding similar responsibility and authority). This person is usually responsible for the systems currently in place, systems that will be retired when SAP is introduced.

▶ An executive-level chief architect (who may also be SAP AG's appointed project manager). This person acts as the SAP technical liaison to the steering committee and is responsible for setting strategic technical direction and to some extent driving IT-related decisions.

The steering committee meets daily in many cases to review status, to quickly work through issues, and to publish decisions, recommendations, and overall opinions. Tasks crucial to the executive steering committee include the following:

▶ Identifying and approving the scope of the project

▶ Prioritizing the project among all corporate projects

▶ Providing the necessary funding and resources from the business to ensure project success

▶ Setting priorities

▶ Settling disputes

▶ Committing resources to the project

▶ Monitoring the progress and impact of the implementation

▶ Empowering the team to make decisions

The importance of upper management's buy-in and other influence cannot be underestimated; they have a direct impact on the success of the implementation. Not surprising, the SAP implementation projects that have the most problems are often the ones where upper-management support is unclear or divided.

Project Sponsor

At this point, certain senior-level executives have already been convinced that implementing SAP is right for the company and its stakeholders. Others executive might still be on the fence, unconvinced that the business units are on the right track or that the investment in SAP is warranted and in the organization's long-term best interests. The project sponsor plays a key role in getting everyone on the same page. The project sponsor builds momentum, gains buy-in, and socializes the project throughout the company. In their role, the project sponsor has the following responsibilities:

▶ Providing the business leadership required for ensuring the project is carried through

▶ Leading the project board in resolving issues

▶ Acting as the champion of the board, linking end-user organizations and their functional areas to the SAP project and linking the SAP project to the firm's executive management team

▶ Helping drive much of the initial decision making regarding who the firm will partner with to implement and oversee SAP

The project sponsor is also typically involved in selecting the candidate within the firm who will lead the SAP implementation on behalf of the firm—the cross-bundle (or company-internal) project leader, discussed next.

The Overall SAP Project Manager

One of the most absolutely critical roles in an SAP implementation is held by the overall SAP project manager or cross-bundle project leader (so called because this person manages and leads the various functional area workstreams or bundles them together to make the project what it is—a complex collection of people, teams, and other resources). Because this position is almost exclusively held by an employee of the firm implementing SAP, the position is sometimes generically referred to as the *SAP project manager*. Regardless of title, this leader's role is critical:

▶ Chairs and manages the project within the company's PMO structure

▶ Acts as a single point of accountability and contact into the project board

▶ Controls and oversees the project from a resource synchronization and staffing perspective, ensuring high-level project activities fall in place within the larger scope of the project

▶ Manages costs, schedule, quality, and other key issues across the various functional areas and teams

▶ Acts as the point of escalation when business needs and IT limitations fail to mesh

▶ Maintains and communicates the pulse of the project with regard to risk management, escalating quality issues, and communicating overall project milestones and status

During project execution, the cross-bundle project leader also spends a great amount of time managing others who are responsible for blueprinting, test plans and testing, training plans and delivery, production support, and developing the cut-over plan (used to methodically transition from the legacy system to the new SAP system).

Contemporary Tools and Methodologies

Because ASAP has proven itself effective, most SAP implementation partners continue to use the ASAP framework or a customized version of it, if not the tools. Many years ago, ASAP evolved into GlobalSAP and later ValueSAP. ASAP was intended to be limited in terms of rigid phases; the fact that implementation phases in the real world often overlapped, or that businesses found themselves in the midst of multiple ASAP phases as a result of a geographically phased rollout, was contrary to ASAP. The new SAP deployment methodologies therefore added *evaluation and continuous business improvement* to their core focus on implementation. These changes helped overcome some of the previous shortfalls. At one point in time, the roadmap changed a bit, as well, shrinking from five to four phases (although we generally speak of five again).

SAP AG released an improved delivery vehicle—SAP Solution Manager, or SolMan—many years after ASAP was introduced. Today SolMan has matured considerably, offering not only multiple roadmaps to implementation but also improved content. This content includes sample documents, new templates, a repository for canned business processes, and excellent project management tools.

SAP SolMan has built upon ASAP's groundwork. Robust project monitoring and reporting capabilities have been recently augmented with Learning Maps, which are role-specific Internet-enabled training tools featuring online tutoring and virtual classrooms. In this way, the project team can more quickly get up to speed. With training and related support of the ASAP and ValueSAP methodologies replaced by SolMan, project teams do well to transition from ASAP-based and other methodologies to those facilitated by SAP SolMan.

It's important to remember, though, that at the end of the day these approaches all amount to little more than frameworks or methodologies with supporting templates. Even SolMan facilitates only an implementation; much real work still needs to be done. However, if you are seeking to deploy well-known and mature SAP functionality, and are focused on avoiding too much custom development, SolMan is a wonderful tool in your implementation arsenal.

Project Closeout

Eventually, every SAP project comes to a conclusion (hopefully a positive one), where the new system is turned on, the old one shut down, and the work of the project team is gracefully halted. After production cut-over and go-live, it is important for the overall

PM to clearly indicate that the project has been completed. Review the following to capture lessons learned and document the SAP project's closeout:

- ▶ Project objectives versus what was achieved

- ▶ Actual delivered quality of the project versus the level of quality requested

- ▶ The status of project issues

Ensure the following questions can be answered affirmatively:

- ▶ **Project documentation**—Have all project documents been accepted and signed off by the responsible customer party?

- ▶ **Financial health of the project**—Have all payments been made or negotiated?

- ▶ **Financial outcome**—Has a final report been developed and shared with the stakeholder committee regarding the project's budget and financials?

- ▶ **Project team evaluation**—Has an evaluation for each project team member been written and delivered?

It is also important to capture what the team learned as the project progressed. Project issues and resolutions, the status of change orders, installation and configuration check lists, and so on constitute useful insight and knowledge. In addition, be sure to track and return all assets used by the project team, to file or dispose of confidential or restricted materials, and to close out other remaining housekeeping matters.

Summary

In this hour, we covered SAP's project implementation methodology ASAP, developed by SAP in response to the need to consistently manage SAP implementations and do so in a repeatable manner. We also outlined the structure and development of key leadership positions, contemporary SAP-specific project management tools, and more. Matters of project execution and control, followed by the project closeout process, concluded the hour.

Case Study: Hour 15

Read the case study situation and address the questions that follow. You can find the answers posed by the questions related to this case study in Appendix A, "Case Study Answers."

Situation

MNC is seeking to transition its aging human resources management system with SAP ERP HCM. Given your 20 years of project management and business experience, combined with your excellent network of business and IT relationships across MNC, you have been selected as the overall SAP PM. You need to make a brief presentation to the steering committee regarding the immediate viability of this project. A quick assessment before your presentation reveals the following:

▶ The project must be completed in less than a year from today.

▶ MNC has a strong and proactive PMO.

▶ MNC has no available senior technical leaders or architects.

▶ The vice president of human resources has personal history with a failed SAP implementation and openly shares his distaste for SAP in general.

Questions

1. Given the timeframe, is SAP's ASAP methodology a good starting point for going live in less than a year?

2. With your IT team's lack of technical leadership regarding SAP, where should you turn for help?

3. How will MNC's PMO work toward the project's advantage?

4. What challenges do you face given the VP of HR's past history with SAP?

5. Considering the whole situation, what initial recommendation should you make to the steering committee regarding this project?

A Basis Professional's Perspective on SAP

What You'll Learn in This Hour:

▶ Mapping business priories to technical implementation

▶ Key installation planning tasks

▶ Technical preparation tasks

▶ SAP technology stack considerations

▶ SAP Basis team staffing and working considerations

With the project manager's SAP perspective behind us, it makes sense to now look at the SAP Basis professional's perspective. After all, it's the SAP Basis team that will make the most impactful contributions near term, setting the stage for the developers and configurators to ultimately create an SAP business solution. These company-internal SAP Basis professionals and their hired-gun consulting counterparts are responsible for planning, delivering, and maintaining the technical infrastructure necessary to run SAP. From strategic technical architecture to tactical decisions such as how to operate the system, the Basis professional's job is as broad as it is essential.

Shifting Focus: From Business to Technology

After the business blueprinting and project management tasks have been addressed, as outlined earlier, the next phase in conducting an SAP deployment involves the technical infrastructure underpinning SAP's components and products. SAP Basis professionals take care of this, starting with identifying and deploying the actual SAP components to be deployed based on the business requirements outlined earlier in the project. The SAP Basis team temporarily changes the SAP project's attention from a business focus to a technology focus. Blueprinting and design work give way to questions of how to integrate the various SAP and third-party applications, the specific development and testing methodology to be put into place, and finally the evaluation and selection of the SAP computing platform—a combination of hardware, one or more operating systems, and database software. These steps are covered well by SAP's Master Guides, as discussed next.

Installation Master Guides and SAP Notes

Even for long-time SAP specialist, preparing to install SAP—not to mention the actual installation process—is confusing. The best place to start is SAP's Master Guides. They are component-specific and worth their weight in gold. Use them. For example, if you are tasked with installing SAP ERP 6.0, just download the latest "SAP ERP 6.0 Powered by SAP NetWeaver" Master Guide to get a quick handle on what this particular installation entails. The Master Guide points you to where to go for the actual electronic media required for your installation, and they walk you through the installation scenario. Different installation scenarios are typically covered, in fact, guiding you through installing the different combinations of software components necessary to create the foundation for a specific SAP solution. Your high-level roadmap, following the Master Guide, makes it difficult to go wrong.

You need more than a Master Guide, though. You also need to download the many installation-specific notes (SAP Notes) related to the technical scenario you're implementing. Obtaining the guides and notes is easy. Point your browser to http://service.sap.com/instguides and then to http://service.sap.com/notes (the latter of which requires an SAP Service Marketplace user ID). To install an Oracle-based SAP system on the Linux operating system, for example, the first step might be to download the following resources (keeping in mind that some of these resources are only available internally, requiring a valid SAP Service Marketplace ID):

- ▶ Part I, "Planning and Preparation"

- ▶ Part II, "Installation and Post-Installation"

- ▶ Note 171356, "SAP Software on Linux: Essential Information"

- ▶ Note 958253, "SUSE LINUX Enterprise Server 10: Installation Notes"

Before SAP is technically deployed, it only makes sense to outline exactly *what* is being deployed and under what circumstances and scenarios. An ABAP+Java implementation of SAP Enterprise Portal front-ending *Enterprise Resource Planning* (ERP), *Customer Relationship Management* (CRM), and *Supplier Relationship Management* (SRM) is a much different technical solution than a classic ABAP-derived SAP ERP implementation, after all. So again, take the time to read through the guides to determine whether you're indeed ready to continue. Are you missing a particular piece of software? Do you have all the latest patches and updates recommended by the installation guides? Are your server and disk platform standards up to the task? These and other questions need to be addressed before moving on.

Setting the Stage: The SAP Landscape

A typical SAP environment consists of multiple SAP instances (or installations) in a landscape. A three-system landscape is historically the most common approach and comprises a development system, a quality assurance or test system, and a production system. IT organizations interested in doing technical training or having a safe place to try new installations will add a user training system and technical sandbox to this list. In the same way, instances for testing new components and functionality, dedicated business training systems, and production break/fix or "staging" systems are also common in many environments.

Realistically, business and IT support requirements could drive you to deploy a seven- or eight-system landscape for some of the most complex SAP components, such as SAP ERP. Other components, such as SAP SCM or SAP *Product Lifecycle Management* (PLM) might dictate a leaner landscape. Regardless, determine what your system landscape is going to look like before you actually start doing any installations. Once the breadth of the landscape for each component is defined, take a critical look at how each of these various systems are architected or "sized," which is discussed next.

Architecture and Sizing Considerations

Before an SAP installation is ever performed, someone must plan for, or "architect," the SAP environment. This process gives way to designing the system, a process called *sizing*. Decisions have to be made as to which SAP components are going to be deployed and how they will be deployed. For example, the number of application servers must be taken into consideration given the workload expected to be hosted by SAP. Also the size of the database server—the most critical component of all, given that it hosts all the company's data—must be determined. Other metrics or sizing dimensions must be taken into account. How scalable does the system need to be? What kind of availability or disaster recoverability is necessary to meet the business's needs without breaking the IT bank? What kind of online response time performance is acceptable, particularly under changing workloads such as those associated with month-end financial closings?

To answer these questions, the customer IT department works with SAP, their prime integrator (big 4), and their hardware partner. Combined, all these partners lend their expertise and knowledge of real-world SAP deployments to help the customer design a system that truly meets the business's needs. Sizing is a balancing act between what the business thinks its new system needs to do and how it needs to perform. Sizing is also an art; there are literally hundreds of unique technology solutions capable of hosting a 1,000-user SAP ERP workload, for example. Our recommendation is to start the architecture and sizing process early. Engage the business as quickly as possible. Listen to their business application, performance, and availability requirements, and then help the prime integrator and hardware partners translate these requirements into robust and properly architected and sized SAP solutions.

ABAP and Java Stack Considerations

Before sizing, it's necessary to determine the technical stack that will eventually be deployed. Business requirements will drive some of this decision for you. The SAP NetWeaver platform supports both ABAP and Java stacks, either alone or in conjunction with one another. Typically, the decision as to which platform to use is dictated by the SAP components being deployed. For example, *Employee Self-Service* (ESS) requires Java, whereas ERP 6.0 requires ABAP.

How do you find out which technology stack you need to install? Turn to your Master Guide, which outlines the required components for a scenario and the underlying technology stack (ABAP or Java). The SAP enterprise architecture needs to specify the number and function of the underlying servers for each component, too, and whether they require Java or ABAP. Look to your functional team leadership to help determine which might be most appropriate when you have a choice.

Infrastructure Architecture

With the technology stack noted, the SAP Basis professional needs to turn the list of all the required SAP components and products into an infrastructure architecture. Beyond the list of software components (such as SAP ERP 6.0), the modules being deployed and the number of users for each module are important; the number and their "weight" (heavy, medium, or low) will help the hardware partners make the right choices in terms of memory and processing power required for each server.

All SAP-certified partners maintain one or more SAP Competency Centers (perhaps based on geography or specialization). The output of these typically time-consuming and detailed sizing efforts is a physical infrastructure architecture model (diagram or figure) and bill of materials reflecting the SAP software components and the associated servers (including number of CPUs and RAM required) for each landscape and component. The architecture needs to account for what it means to provide acceptable performance, availability, scalability, disaster recoverability, and so on.

For larger systems or systems where the workload might be less understood, the SAP Basis professional works to design systems to run on a mix of separate physical and virtualized servers. Virtualization and cloud computing should be employed where they make sense. For example, it's common to virtualize many of the nonproduction systems that typically require only a fraction of the horsepower capable of being delivered by today's hardware solutions. In the end, many of these systems are probably excellent candidates for cloud computing, as well. It's recommended that you take a conservative approach at first and then let your budget and datacenter constraints drive any final tuning and tweaking to your SAP architecture.

To read more about the role cloud computing can play to help you deliver your SAP solutions, start with Hour 3, "SAP Technology Basics," and then check out Hour 19, "SAP and the Cloud."

High Availability

Arguably, availability is probably the most important consideration in your SAP architecture. There are many high-availability options for SAP installations, each of which depends on the hardware platform, operating system, and integration requirements. Options such as hardware-based clustering and replicated SAP enqueue provide protection for the database and central instance against unplanned downtime. SAP applications servers are normally made highly available through a combination of redundancy in the form of multiple application servers and the use of SAP logon groups. Other *high-availability* (HA) offerings can prove useful, as well, extending HA capabilities to include disaster recoverability. For example, look to Microsoft SQL Server database mirroring as a solution to approximate disaster recovery.

Disaster Recoverability

After SAP is deployed, it is likely the business will depend on the new system's availability for the firm's very existence. With all the firm's revenue flowing through the system and all the books of record maintained in one place, it's simply not acceptable to just have some kind of plan in case of a disaster. In conjunction with business interruption or business continuity planning, a *disaster recovery* (DR) plan is necessary—it marries the business side of DR with technical requirements.

SAP and its hardware and software partners support many different DR approaches and solutions. Some of these are hardware-specific and therefore demand attention during the sizing and architecture phases. Other "bolt-on" DR solutions can be incorporated into an SAP architecture later. Common DR solutions include

- ▶ Basic backup/restore from tape or disk (an essential part of any disaster recovery plan, which may or may not include the options that follow)
- ▶ Database log shipping (configured at the database layer)

▶ Solutions involving storage replication technologies (for example, via your EMC, HP, or IBM storage systems, or directly through a database such as SQL Server, or through a special utility specifically designed to provide this capability)

Well before you ever think about purchasing a DR system, spend your time talking with colleagues or peers at other firms who have already implemented a similar solution. You will probably be surprised at how complex a DR solution can become once all the business requirements and technology constraints are brought to light. And turn to your technology partners for real-world lessons learned and other takeaways.

SAP Technical Readiness and Security Considerations

The SAP Basis professional's perspective on SAP goes well beyond SAP itself. Up to this point, much of our discussions have focused on SAP rather than the technologies that enable SAP to run. Let's turn our attention to these more foundational technical matters, from client access strategies to network and deeper SAP technical considerations, including how security weaves its way through all these matters.

Building and Hosting Site Readiness

Like many other project stakeholders, the SAP Basis team influences where and how the SAP system's physical assets will be located and managed. Perhaps a company-internal datacenter is ideal for security or secure access considerations, or maybe a hosting partner is more cost-effective or strategically equipped to support a particular geography. Today, it's easy to install and monitor systems remotely regardless of computing platform. For organizations concerned with controlling site access and managing their data's location, however, these kinds of hosting facility choices are important.

Network Considerations

Back in Sun Microsystems's most impactful days, the company had an interesting motto: The Network Is the Computer. Today, that motto is more relevant than ever. Cloud computing, global hosting providers, and end users working around the world have created an environment where business applications like SAP depend on the network more than ever. Network security has become the most important facet of easy network access. From *Secure Network Communication* (SNC), to *Public Key Infrastructure* (PKI, enabling users to securely move data across unsecured networks), to *Single Sign On* (SSO; which brings multiple applications together, at least from a logon perspective), access to SAP is becoming easier.

The easier this front-end or end-user access, though, the more complex the back end becomes. Shared routers and switches need to be physically protected; dedicated network links connecting SAP application, web, database, and other servers together need to be secured; and the entire end-to-end network infrastructure needs to be monitored for unauthorized intrusion and managed in terms of capacity and performance. The SAP Basis team needs to work closely with an organization's IT network architecture and support teams to ensure access, security, provisioning, and a host of other network services are performed. Fortunately, the bulk of IT organizations tasked with supporting an SAP implementation are well aware of these requirements simply because of all the other mission-critical applications they are likely already supporting.

The availability of SAP components through the Internet (if applicable) must also be addressed. The goal of all this is to provide a secure environment for the SAP servers without impacting the application's ultimate functionality. Depending on the specific situation, the network might need special firewalls or proxy servers or other such devices targeted to provide a more secure environment for SAP. Within each system of an SAP system landscape, it is further possible—and often desired—to create separate network segments. Some of these might be dedicated to end-user access, whereas others might serve only the intense database-to-application server traffic, or traffic dedicated to network-based server backups. A fourth network segment might even be designated for systems management and monitoring traffic.

Server, Disk Subsystem, and OS Considerations

SAP systems require compute, disk, and *operating system* (OS) resources. We covered SAP systems from these perspectives earlier this hour and also in Hour 3, "SAP Technology Basics." Suffice it to say here that the SAP systems require infrastructure designed for outstanding availability, excellent performance, and tight security. The SAP Basis team works through the SAP project lifecycle to nail down these matters and more. If a SAP service runs on it, through it, before it, or because of it, the SAP team needs to be involved in designing, integrating, managing, and hardening it. Such activities might include general tasks like hardening an OS to repel viruses, Trojans, and similar threats. Or it might include SAP-specific activities such as implementing SNC to interface with an external security provider tasked with increasing application layer security. Finally, the Basis team needs to be involved in safeguarding the system's physical servers and disk infrastructure from internal *and* external attacks. With all this is mind, take the time to establish an excellent working relationship with the organization's IT security team.

Data and Database Layer

Securely installing and managing the databases and other data stores supporting SAP are important to the SAP system's overall availability, performance, and security. Setting up and enforcing database-specific roles (such as who can access and back up the data, update database executables or binaries, or act as a database operator) are also important. Databases need to be hardened from worms and other threats, just like the OS. It is important to develop a backup/recovery strategy prior to go-live. The backup/recovery strategy doesn't affect the SAP installation process; it generally involves something such as loading a backup agent on the database server. Be sure to test the backup/recovery strategy not only before go-live but afterward on a regular basis. Perhaps most important, data needs to be protected from unauthorized access via utilities such as those that use table-level auditing to verify by whom and when data may have been read, changed, or created.

SAP Basis and Application Security Considerations

Maybe it should go without saying, but the SAP Basis professional will spend a good amount of time working to ensure the SAP application layer itself performs well, is secured, and is available, starting with performing a secure SAP Basis installation. Once installed, the application needs to be secured via security administration and basic risk mitigation practices. For example, ensure that SAP Basis professionals, computer operators, and database administrators practice the same kind of segregation of duties used to minimize end-user-derived fraud. Good checks and balances help keep honest people honest (and secured systems secure).

Beyond basic tasks like maximizing the performance of and controlling access to SAP's executables and binaries, pay attention to matters such as SAP archiving and backup/restore. These processes are mission critical when it comes to availability and system governance. If misconfigured, however, the infrastructure necessary to perform these functions can be used to improperly access data. And work with the SAP security team (described in Hour 11, "SAP User Roles and Authorizations") to help that team support role and authorizations management, user provisioning, power user monitoring, and user-centric segregation of duties.

Third-Party Application Considerations

Many other applications outside of SAP play a role in enabling SAP's business scenarios. We've identified several, ranging from tax calculation programs to enterprise faxing and printing solutions, user portals, back-end data marts and data warehouses, and so on. Utility-like applications from Oracle, IBM, and Microsoft might be employed to connect systems together. Companies might use other software vendors to supply their *customer relationship management* (CRM), *supply chain management* (SCM), or business analytics systems. In the end, these third-party applications need to be made highly available, safeguarded, and integrated consistent with the SAP system's availability, security, and performance targets.

End-User Access Strategy

End users can access SAP in many ways. From WebGUI and portal access to using the traditional SAP *graphical user interface* (GUI), the BEx Explorer, or an easily developed

SharePoint web part, the SAP Basis team needs to be involved in managing this access. Developing a "client access" strategy addresses how the SAP application's end-user community will access its system, including how to access the system when the primary access method is unavailable.

Different access strategies have their own advantages and disadvantages. Regardless of method, each strategy requires some kind of network connection between the SAP user and the datacenter housing the SAP servers and data. Users at headquarters may leverage their fast access over the *local area network* (LAN), whereas remote office users might connect over slower *wide area network* (WAN) links. Occasional users might be granted access to easy-to-use SharePoint sites. Meanwhile, home-based users might dial in via a phone line to a Citrix server farm, whereas a company's suppliers and vendors might be given ubiquitous access over the Internet. The key to determining the best access strategy falls back to balancing the level of functionality required by the user against what constitutes acceptable performance delivered in a secure and cost-effective manner.

Staffing and Operational Considerations

Beyond helping to architect the technical systems and deploy the components that make up an SAP system, the SAP Basis professional has another perspective: how their team should be staffed to operate and maintain the systems once they're in place.

SAP Basis Staffing

One of the most valuable resources behind an SAP implementation, the SAP Basis team directly impacts how well the SAP production system will perform its intended function: to support the company's business processes. A good team needs to have the experience and ability to do everything from correctly installing the system to maintaining steady-state operations, minimizing downtime via smartly applied change management practices, calculating the impact of growing workloads down the road, spearheading business-aligned IT projects, planning for and completing SAP functional enhancements and upgrades, and more.

Many SAP Basis teams are composed of two subteams: a project team and a run (or steady-state or "base load" team). Further, it's common for SAP Basis teams to be made up of a mix of company employees, hosting partner resources, and contractors possessing specialized skills or experience.

Although the SAP Basis team often takes the lead in matters related to SAP, they cannot do so alone. In the end, many other IT "sister" teams are employed part-time (that is, as a shared service) by the SAP Basis team:

▶ The IT *project management office* (PMO) team, consisting of project management professionals experienced in managing large-scale and complex IT/business projects.

▶ A datacenter team tasked with deploying and managing the server and *storage area network* (SAN) infrastructure, the network infrastructure, and the racks, cooling equipment, and overall facilities making up an enterprise datacenter site.

> Only a well-structured and completely staffed SAP Basis organization can pull off a new implementation, much less maintain an SAP production system over many years. Although the list of teams provided here might seem extensive, this is only the beginning. Work with the project's prime systems integrator, hardware and hosting partners, SAP, and your IT department to determine the best mix of teams and people given your unique SAP system landscape and project constraints.

▶ A server infrastructure team tasked with racking and building out servers, loading operating systems, and generally preparing and maintaining the various database, application, Internet, and other servers for the specific roles they will play in the SAP landscape.

▶ A SAN/disk subsystem team responsible for SAN design, deployment, performance, and maintenance oversight. The SAN/disk team plays a critical role given that the lifeblood of the system—the data—sits squarely within its area of responsibility.

▶ One or more security teams tasked with managing physical security and SAP-specific end-user roles and authorizations.

▶ The database team responsible for deployment and ongoing administration.

▶ The computer operations team tasked with ensuring that backup and restore, systems monitoring, and basic availability tasks are regularly and proactively addressed (covered in more detail in the next section).

Beyond properly staffing the SAP Basis team and working with other teams, there's another broad collection of tasks that consume the SAP Basis professional's time: proactively performing the necessary operations, administration, and management tasks necessary to keep the SAP system running well. Several of these tasks are outlined next.

Operations, Administration, and Management

Among others, an organization's Computer Operations team will assist the SAP Basis team in taking care of SAP after go-live. This is a really big job, though, spanning not only the entire SAP technology stack, but also multiple business applications perhaps serving several different end-user communities. Because maintaining SAP is so complex, we gave it a full hour. Check out Hour 20, "SAP System Administration and Management," for more information about how to

▶ Proactively monitor SAP's business processes

▶ Review the SAP system's logs

▶ Manage the system's computing platform and other infrastructure

▶ Verify and fine-tune workload distribution

▶ Perform database administration

▶ Manage printed output

▶ Manage batch jobs (also called *background processing*)

▶ Conduct performance management

▶ Address day-to-day operations

With your foundation in the SAP Basis professional's perspective, we're ready to shift gears and take a closer look at the final critical cog in an SAP IT implementation: the SAP developer. Afterward, we look at the real technical matters related to installing, maintaining, and enhancing SAP.

Summary

In this hour, we reviewed the priorities and perspectives of the SAP Basis professional. We covered what it means to mesh business requirements with the various technologies and technical considerations underpinning an SAP implementation. From addressing which components to plan for, along with architecture and sizing, we also reviewed basic network, storage, server, application, and end-user access matters that need to be addressed well before SAP is installed. A brief introduction to the SAP-related IT teams necessary to deploy and maintain SAP concluded this hour.

Case Study: Hour 16

Consider this SAP Basis professional case study and questions that follow. You can find the answers posed by the questions related to this case study in Appendix A, "Case Study Answers."

Situation

As a new senior Basis lead for MNC's upcoming SAP *Enterprise Resource Planning* (ERP) implementation, you have been asked to review the current state of affairs and make recommendations. In your review, you note that MNC has excellent computer operations, server, and database administration teams but that there seems to be poor alignment between the company's current mainframe computing standards and the proposed SAP ERP *Human Capital Management* (HCM) environment (which is being built atop a Windows/SQL Server platform). The company is also used to supporting mission-critical computing applications with development, test, and pre-production staging environments, although (surprisingly) the company has no formal experience with disaster recovery.

Questions

1. *What are your thoughts on the current technical teams in terms of their readiness for helping you support SAP?*

2. *As outlined in this hour's introduction, what are the three broad areas that the SAP Basis team is responsible for performing?*

3. *Where will you point the team to begin preparing for installation planning?*

4. *Would you recommend MNC maintain its current system landscape strategy?*

5. *From a disaster recovery perspective, MNC is quite familiar and comfortable with performing regular tape backups and restores. What are two other types of DR solutions you might look into, though?*

A Developer's Perspective on SAP

What You'll Learn in This Hour:

▶ Roles and differences between a developer and configurer

▶ Overview of programming tools

▶ Reviewing your implementation options

▶ How Solution Manager facilitates development

▶ Viewing the SAP procedure model

▶ Tracking tasks in the IMG

This hour looks at SAP implementation and support from a developer's perspective. Like end users, IT project managers, and SAP Basis professionals, SAP developers have a unique perspective when it comes to SAP business applications. The term *development tool* is often used generically to refer to any number of utilities provided by SAP to create or enhance SAP systems, code, and configuration. These can be categorized into two specific groups: programming tools and configuration tools. A review of several developer tools and methodologies used to create or customize SAP functionality concludes this hour.

Programming Tools

SAP programming tools were introduced in Hour 6, "SAP NetWeaver: The Foundation for SAP." A broad label, these tools can be further divided into three major areas based on the underlying SAP platform: ABAP, Java, and the SAP NetWeaver Composition Environment. Programming tools make it possible for systems to be customized beyond a system's basic capabilities, filling in gaps in an SAP application's standard functionality. Customizing might be necessary to

▶ Develop enhancements (new functionality) unavailable in the standard SAP programs

▶ Create special reports requested by business leaders to help run the business

▶ Create special forms needed to bring new data into the system (in such a way that most of the risks related to human data entry errors are avoided)

▶ Connect or *interface* SAP with a nonSAP system

▶ Develop special conversion programs capable of transferring data from one system into another (typically from a legacy system to a new SAP system)

Several of the tools used to carry out customization are covered next.

ABAP and SE80

Advanced Business Application Programming (ABAP, best pronounced "ah bop") programming dates back to the 1980s. Despite newer alternatives, ABAP remains the primary tool used for SAP programming. At the heart of ABAP programming is the ABAP Development Workbench, available via transaction SE80. This workbench offers a rich set of functions developers can use to create and modify SAP programs. Its primary functions include the following:

▶ Object Navigator

▶ Package Builder

▶ Object Navigator

▶ Web Application Builder for ITS (*Internet Transaction Server*) Services

▶ Web Application Builder for BSPs (*Business Server Pages*)

▶ Web Services

▶ ABAP Dictionary

▶ ABAP Editor

▶ Class Builder and Function Builder

▶ Screen Painter and Menu Painter

▶ Web Dynpro

The last tool in the list, Web Dynpro for ABAP, is probably the most important. SAP has described this as the future of SAP ABAP development. It has largely replaced the older SAPGUI-based screen painter development tools. In addition to Web Dynpro, the ABAP

Workbench includes test tools such as the ABAP Debugger, Runtime Analysis, a Transport Organizer, and more. If you intend to develop in SAP, learn Web Dynpro for ABAP.

Java and NWDS

Java development for SAP's NetWeaver application server is based on the current Java EE 5 standard. Java was adopted by SAP as a platform-independent open source development framework to allow customers to leverage existing nonSAP development resources. At one point in time, it was thought that ABAP development would be replaced by Java development. With arch-enemy Oracle's acquisition of Sun Microsystems (and therefore Java) back in 2010, however, SAP's priorities have likely changed; if anything, expect to see Java's role diminish.

To develop in Java, SAP provides the *SAP NetWeaver Developer Studio* (NWDS). Often shortened to *Developer Studio*, this tool is based on the open source Eclipse software development framework and includes the following features:

- ▶ Built-in Java EE 5 design-time support

- ▶ Web services support

- ▶ On-the-fly application debugging

- ▶ Hot deployment

- ▶ Wizards and graphical tools to speed up development

SAP offers several options for distributing Java changes through the SAP landscape. Although Java objects can still be deployed locally via manual processes, SAP's *NetWeaver Development Infrastructure* (NWDI) allows customers to manage Java development with a capable change management tool modeled after SAP's ABAP-oriented *Transport Management System* (TMS).

Composition Environment

The SAP NetWeaver *Composition Environment* (CE) provides a service-oriented and standards-based development environment where SAP developers can model and develop composite applications called *composites*. These composites are nothing more than solutions developed by combining readily available functions, data sets, or existing solutions. Using "reusable" SAP and third-party components in this way accelerates business process innovation.

The ABAP Development Workbench, Java NWDS, and the SAP CE provide the core toolsets for SAP development. However, the real work of creating a usable SAP application is accomplished through SAP's various configuration tools, covered later this hour. For now, let's turn our attention to methodologies used by SAP developers.

Developer and SAP Methodologies

The latest ASAP methodology and Solution Manager tools include sample documents, new templates, a repository for canned business processes, and better project-management tools than their predecessors. How these assets align with the latest ASAP 7.x methodology is outlined next.

Implementation Development Phases

As shown in Figure 17.1, the core implementation development phases include a four-phased approach, which is essentially a shortened version of the original ASAP methodology.

FIGURE 17.1
The four core implementation phases.

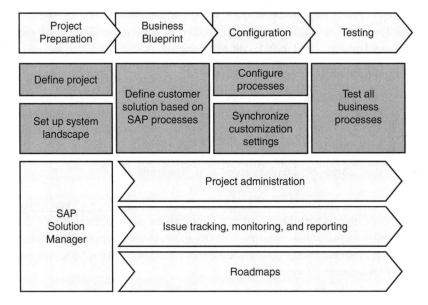

Project Preparation

Project preparation starts by retrieving information and resources. It is an important time to assemble the necessary components for the implementation. Some important milestones that need to be accomplished during this time include the following:

▶ Obtain senior-level management/stakeholder support.

▶ Identify clear project objectives.

▶ Architect an efficient decision-making process.

▶ Create an environment suitable for change and re-engineering.

▶ Build a qualified and capable project team.

Business Blueprint

SAP has defined a business blueprint phase to help extract pertinent information about your company that is necessary for the implementation. As such, business blueprinting also essentially documents the implementation, outlining your future business processes and business requirements.

To further assist with this process, SAP offers implementation content on a variety of products and scenarios, which can be pulled in to Solution Manager from the *Business Process Repository* (BPR). This content from the BSR provides predelivered documentation, transactions, and configuration support to assist customers with specific relevance to the business scenario being implemented.

Configuration

With the completion of the business blueprint, the "functional" experts may begin configuring SAP. The configuration phase is broken into two underlying phases:

1. The SAP consulting team configures the baseline system (baseline configuration).

2. The implementation project team fine-tunes the baseline system to meet the SAP project's specific business and process requirements (fine-tuning).

The initial configuration completed during the baseline configuration is based on the information you provided in your blueprint document. The remaining approximately 20% of your configuration that was not tackled during the baseline configuration is completed during the fine-tuning configuration. Fine-tuning usually deals with the exceptions that are not covered in baseline configuration. This final bit of tweaking represents the work necessary to fit your special needs. During this phase, you also work through configuring the SAP *Implementation Guide* (IMG), the tool used to actually configure SAP in a step-by-step manner.

Testing, Final Preparation, and Go-Live

From a tool's perspective, final preparation and go-live equates to testing. Workload testing (including peak volume, daily load, and other forms of stress testing) and integration or functional testing should be performed to ensure the accuracy of your data and the stability of your SAP system. Now is an important time to also perform preventive maintenance checks to ensure optimal performance of your SAP system. Preparing for go-live means preparing for the inevitable end-user questions, for example, as they start actively working on the new SAP system.

By the Way

The screens depicted in this hour might not appear exactly as the screens appear on your system. The SAP components and modules being implemented, your SAP version number, the progress in the implementation, and your specific user/authorization access all affect the appearance of the screens.

Preparation is the key to a successful go-live, including attention to what-if scenarios related not only to the individual business processes deployed but also to the functioning of the technology underpinning these business processes. And preparation for ongoing support, including maintenance contracts and documented processes and procedures, is essential. Fortunately, a wealth of information and additional resources are available.

Run SAP and Other Roadmaps

The Run SAP roadmaps provide a methodology to help organizations achieve operational efficiencies. These include "how-to" and best practice documentation for management and administration tasks. SAP continues to grow its number of product-specific roadmaps as new applications and components are developed. A few of the Run SAP roadmaps available today include

- ASAP Implementation Roadmap for SAP NetWeaver Enterprise Portal
- Solution Management Roadmap
- Global Template Roadmap
- Upgrade Roadmap
- Methodology for Accelerated Transformation to Enterprise SOA

It is important to remember that at the end of the day these approaches all amount to little more than frameworks or methods or organizing development work through supporting templates. Even Solution Manager only facilitates an SAP implementation. The real work still needs to be done, in most cases through the SAP Implementation Guide, which is outlined next.

Configuration and the SAP IMG

If you return to the configuration phase, you will remember that the *Implementation Guide* (IMG) plays a central role in assisting you with configuring SAP. The IMG is essentially a large tree structure diagram that lists all actions required for implementing SAP, guiding you through each of the steps in all the different SAP areas that require configuration. For each business application, the SAP IMG

▶ Explains all the steps in the implementation process

▶ Communicates the SAP standard (default) settings

▶ Describes system configuration work (tasks or activities)

The guide begins with basic settings such as "What country are you in?" It ultimately drills down into specific matters such as "What number do you want your purchase orders to begin with?" It is nearly impossible to complete an SAP implementation without SAP IMG familiarity. To begin, execute transaction code /nSPRO or follow the menu path **Tools, Customizing, IMG, Execute Project**. The main screen appears, which is similar to Figure 17.2.

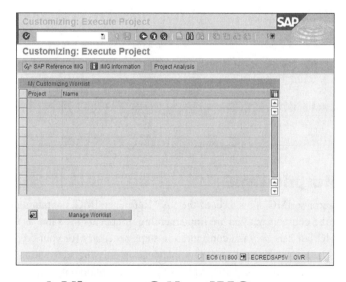

FIGURE 17.2
The Implementation Guide main screen varies in appearance depending on your SAP component, installation, and the amount of configuration that has been completed.

Different Views of the IMG

Developers use the SAP IMG in several different ways, taking advantage of different *views*. Different views provide different information and priorities. You can also create your own custom views of the IMG. Note that there are four levels of the SAP IMG, each explored next:

▶ SAP Reference IMG

▶ SAP Enterprise IMG

▶ SAP Project IMGs

▶ SAP Upgrade Customizing IMGs

SAP Reference IMG

The SAP Reference IMG (click the button by the same name illustrated in Figure 17.2) contains documentation on all the SAP business application components supplied by SAP. It serves as a single source for all configuration data (see Figure 17.3).

FIGURE 17.3
Using the SAP Reference IMG, you can customize your entire SAP implementation from a single console.

SAP Enterprise IMG

The SAP Enterprise IMG is a subset of the SAP Reference IMG, containing documentation only for the components you are implementing. It appears the same as the Reference IMG but lists only the configuration steps necessary for your company's implementation. For example, if you are implementing only logistics within SAP *Enterprise Resource Planning* (ERP), your IMG would contain only logistics-related information; other information related to configuring HR payroll, for example, would not be present.

SAP Project IMGs

SAP Project IMGs are Enterprise IMG subsets that contain only the documentation for the Enterprise IMG components you are implementing (such as a Customizing project). For example, if you are implementing SAP ECC Logistics exclusively but have divided the implementation into two projects—one for Sales and Distribution and a second for Materials Management—you can set up two different projects. This can make the projects easier to manage and configure.

SAP Upgrade Customizing IMGs

SAP Upgrade Customizing IMGs are based either on the Enterprise IMG or on a particular Project IMG. This particular IMG view shows all the documents linked to a Release Note for a given release upgrade (see Figure 17.4). To read a Release Note for a particular functional component, click its respective square icon.

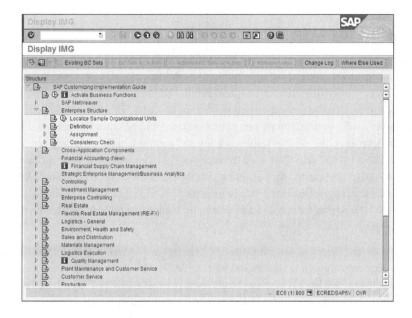

FIGURE 17.4
An SAP Upgrade Customizing IMG enables you to specify a configuration based on specific SAP releases.

Integration with Solution Manager

With the latest features of SAP *Solution Manager* (SolMan), you can now create projects within SolMan and link them to one or multiple IMG projects in component systems. This enables you to navigate configuration for one or more projects from a central location and provide a single configuration repository within SAP Solution Manager.

Additional IMG Fundamentals

With the transaction code SPRO, the initial view of an IMG structure is always a tree diagram with symbols shown to the left. You can use the plus (+) sign to the left of each item (for older SAP releases) or the triangle (for newer SAP releases) in the tree structure to expand a branch of the tree to view its substructure. You can also expand a branch by placing your cursor on a line item and then following the menu path **Edit**,

Expand/Collapse or by placing your cursor on a line item and pressing the **F5** key on your keyboard. To expand all possible branches, place your cursor on the highest level and select **Edit**, **All Subnodes**.

Viewing an IMG screen with its subnodes expanded gives you a good idea of the IMG's purpose—to configure basic settings for SAP. Looking at each of the line items, it is easy to see how this tool facilitates implementation.

Help in the IMG

The first thing you should learn about the IMG is how to retrieve help for any individual line item. Just by looking at the description of each line item, it is not always clear exactly what the configuration of that item entails. You can access selection-specific help by double-clicking any activity (line item) in the IMG. This brings you detailed help on the configuration activity you have selected. In some cases, it launches a small window describing the reasons for the activity and what it entails, including actual examples of what the activity is used to configure. In other instances, it might launch your SAP Help application, thus enabling you to search for more information. Help is also available after you execute a line item in the IMG. Most activities in the IMG bring you to a screen where you need to add or modify values in a table to configure your SAP system.

The field descriptions and selection-specific help might not have provided all the information necessary for you to understand what to do. Placing your cursor in any field and then pressing the **F1** key on your keyboard from any IMG activity screen launches field-level selection-specific help. The Help file is presented as a small window describing the possible values for entry in that field. Using Help in the IMG is essential to obtaining additional information about the activities required to configure your SAP system.

Documentation in the IMG

The IMG is typically your main source for configuration. That is essentially why, along with Solution Manager, it is the ideal location for documenting your configuration. Use the **Status Information** icon to navigate to the **Memo** tab of the Status Information screen. From there, record your comments, notes, or configuration information about the appropriate configuration step provided in the IMG. Alternatively, use your cursor to select the documentation symbol, and your screen launches into a screen like the one shown in Figure 17.5.

For each line item in the IMG, you can enter text in this way and, in doing so, document the system as you go along. This is therefore a very helpful tool, not to mention a great reference to use after your implementation is complete or during SAP upgrades and changes. You can type configuration notes into the space provided in the Memo tab and save them with that line item in the IMG. You can then use the Read Note symbol to review any of these notes at a later time.

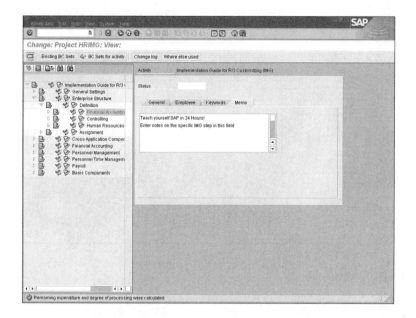

FIGURE 17.5
Use the IMG's Memo feature to write configuration notes documenting particular activities.

Status Information

Selecting the **Status Information** symbol brings you to the General tab, as shown in Figure 17.6. This tab allows you to record the status and progress of your configuration for a particular line item, including planned versus actual start and end dates and more.

Status

One purpose of the Status Information screen is to maintain a record of your configuration to date and to track your implementation progress. It is also a good place to see who is working on what. One of the first things you need to assign on this screen is the Status field. Status types include the following:

▶ In Process

▶ In Q/A Testing

▶ Complete

You set up the different status levels, as determined by your company's specifications. This status designation segregates your configuration tasks into different completion categories.

FIGURE 17.6
The Status
Information
screen records
the status of
the item,
planned versus
actual start and
stop dates, the
percentage
completed, and
much more.

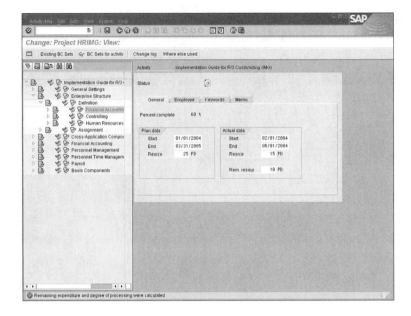

Percent Complete

The Percent Complete field is used to display a processing status for an activity expressed as a percentage. Sample percent completed values include 25%, 50%, 75%, 100%, and so on. At one time, these values were up to the individual to maintain. In newer releases of SAP, though, the percent complete is actually calculated by SAP.

Plan Start and End Dates

The Plan Start Date field is where you record the initial projected date on which this particular activity should commence. Click the **Possible Entries Help** button on this field to display a calendar that enables you to select the date (so that you do not have to enter it directly). The date is selected using the calendar control by selecting the month, date, and year and then double-clicking or by selecting the green check mark. The Plan End Date field is where you record the projected completion date for this particular activity. The SAP calendar is also available on this field.

Plan Work Days

The Plan Work Days field records the planned duration of an activity in days. The planned expenditure can be maintained manually. If neither actual expenditure nor processing status is maintained, the remaining expenditure is calculated.

Actual Start and End Dates

In the real world, things do not always go as planned. The Actual Start Date field records the actual date that an activity was started. Similarly, the Actual End Date field records the actual date that an activity was completed. These fields are maintained when the planned start date and the actual start date differ.

Actual Work Days

The Actual Work Days field records the actual duration in days of an activity. This field is usually maintained only when the planned start and end dates conflict with the actual start and end dates.

Remaining Work Days

The Remaining Work Days field records the remaining expenditure for an activity in days. The remaining expenditure is calculated from the actual expenditure and the processing status, or from the planned expenditure, if these fields are not maintained. You can also set the remaining expenditure manually.

Employee Tab for Resource Assignments

For each particular task in the IMG, you can assign resources (or people) responsible for that task. Use the **Employee** tab in the Status Information screen to denote these resource assignments. By using the **Possible Entries Help** button in the resource field, you can select the resources responsible for performing an activity. As the multiple resources boxes depict, you can assign multiple resources to a single task.

Release Notes

Release Notes contain specific relevant information about changes to the SAP system since the last release. They contain functionality and screen changes, as well as menu path and table structure changes. Release Notes are helpful when developers are supporting an upgrade from one SAP version to another. They are also a good tool for retrieving additional information explaining how something a particular piece of functionality works in the SAP system. To see whether Release Notes are available in your case, turn on an indicator in your IMG that displays a marker next to each activity.

Summary

Decisions concerning the development tools and implementation strategy affect the time, cost, and path you follow in your SAP implementation. SAP rapid deployment options are effective and efficient solutions that might not be the best fit for your company. Because no two companies are alike, you should discuss your company's individual needs with your SAP representative before deciding what tools and methodologies you should employ, and take it from there. When an "empty" shell of SAP is installed, the IMG is the tool used to assist you in customizing and implementing your SAP system. The IMG is designed to pinpoint the configuration activities you are required to perform for your SAP implementation to be a success. It also enables you to tweak your SAP system to ideally suit your company's individual needs through custom configuration.

Case Study: Hour 17

Consider this developer-related case study and the questions that follow. You can find the answers posed by the questions related to this case study in Appendix A, "Case Study Answers."

Situation

You recently attended a team meeting hosted by MNC's developers and configurers. Upon your return to your business unit, you were asked several questions from junior colleagues anxious to understand more.

Questions

1. *What is the transaction code to launch the ABAP Development Workbench?*

2. *What is the name of the development environment for creating SAP Java applications?*

3. *What are the three primary toolsets used for SAP development?*

4. *The ASAP Implementation Roadmap for SAP NetWeaver Enterprise Portal is an example of what?*

5. *Which view of the IMG contains only the relevant documentation for the SAP components your company is implementing?*

6. *What is the transaction code to launch the IMG?*

HOUR 18

SAP Technical Installation

What You'll Learn in This Hour:

- ▶ The SAP technical installation phases
- ▶ The planning and preplanning phases of an installation
- ▶ The basic steps of a real SAP installation
- ▶ How to acquire and install the trial version of SAP
- ▶ How to set up Single Sign-On

We've come a long way on our path toward implementing SAP, and we've finally reached the point of the actual technical installation. To make this hour more relevant to all the readers who do not actually have access to SAP software, we walk through installing the trial version of SAP as well as a real (though abbreviated) SAP installation.

GO TO ▶
Go to Hour 15, "A Project Manager's Perspective on Implementing SAP," to review a more detailed version of the same installation we walk through here (SAP Solution Manager installed in a central system configuration, on Linux with an Oracle database).

Installation Overview

The idea of our installation is to create a simple one-user technical sandbox. In the case of the trial version of SAP, we really have it easy; no other software components are necessary outside of what is included in the trial version's two compressed downloadable files. The trial version runs on many different flavors of Windows, and it includes SAP's own MaxDB database software. And we do not need any high-powered servers or a tremendous amount of disk space either.

To put the trial version installation process into perspective, let's first review an actual installation. In the case of our "real" installation walkthrough, our assumption is that you probably will not actually use the process to install SAP. After all, it's not a trivial task to obtain all the necessary hardware, software, and system/resource access. Instead, we assume you just want to understand the steps and complexity involved. To this end, we walk through performing a simple central system installation using an Oracle database on the SuSE Linux operating system.

Installing SAP can be organized into four phases: planning, pre-installation, the actual installation itself, and post-installation. Careful attention to planning and all the pre-installation tasks results in a smooth installation. Careful attention to the post-installation tasks ensures the SAP system is actually usable.

SAP Installation Planning

The first phase in an SAP installation is planning, much of which amounts to research and reading. For starters, obtain the SAP installation guides and associated SAP Notes. The installation guides are available from the SAP service marketplace via http://service.sap.com/instguides. Similarly, obtain the latest SAP Notes via http://service.sap.com/notes. You need an SAP Service Marketplace ID to access this system.

To install SAP Solution Manager 4.0, download the SAP Solution Manager 4.0 Master Guide. The master guide provides a wealth of valuable information, including notation of the media required for your installation. It also covers scenarios, which are basically the different ways you can use an SAP software component. For example, you might be asked to implement Employee and Manager Self-Services. The master guide explains the installation sequence for these specific scenarios and details the requirements.

> In most every new SAP implementation, the first SAP technical installation is some kind of technical sandbox or "crash and burn" system. The idea is to become accustomed to the installation procedure before installing a system that will actually be used as a development, test, training, production, or other system.

We also want to make sure we obtain the related installation and configuration guides. In our case, we need SAP ERP 2005 SR2 ABAP on Linux: Oracle, and we need SAP Web Application Server ABAP 7.0 on Linux: Oracle, Parts I and II ("Planning and Preparation" and "Installation and Post-Installation," respectively). Finally, we need to download and review the notes associated with our installation. There will almost always be a note associated with the installation from an OS perspective (Linux, in our case) and from a combined platform/database perspective (in this case Linux and Oracle). We cannot overstate the importance of planning; in our experience, following the procedures in the installation guides along with the associated notes is the most critical step to a smooth installation. To put these steps in perspective, consider the following list of downloads (keeping in mind that updates are regularly published by SAP; this list can change monthly if not weekly):

- ▶ SAP Solution Manager on Linux: Oracle—Installation Guide

- ▶ SAP Web Application Server ABAP on Linux: Oracle Part I—Planning and Preparation Manual

- ▶ SAP Web Application Server ABAP on Linux: Oracle Part II—Installation and Post-Installation Manual

- ▶ SAP Note 171356—SAP Software on Linux: Essentials

- ▶ 958253—SuSE Linux Enterprise Server: Installation Notes

- ▶ 980426—Oracle Software Installation on New Operating Systems

- ▶ 861215—Recommended Settings for the Linux on AMD64/EM64T JVM

- ▶ 1090932—IBM Download Site for Special JDK Builds—iFix

Infrastructure Readiness

To install SAP, we first need to have the corresponding infrastructure in place. This includes

- ▶ Storage infrastructure:Space requirements need to be determined; *storage-area network* (SAN), *network-attached storage* (NAS), *Infrastructure as a Service* (IaaS)-based assets, or other disk infrastructure needs to be in place; and disk space must be allocated for SAP's various file systems.

- ▶ Network infrastructure:Network requirements need to be determined, and the network infrastructure must be put in place.

- ▶ Server infrastructure:Servers have been sized, acquired, racked (or allocated, in the case of IaaS-based assets), and connected to the network and storage infrastructure.

Believe it or not, from a technical perspective, getting the infrastructure in place and optimized for the actual installation can be a significant part of the project—the SAP installation itself might be relatively easy after all the infrastructure is finally in place.

SAP Infrastructure Review

With the infrastructure in place, we need to validate and document our SAP standards and conventions. Creating a single spreadsheet with all the pertinent information grouped onto different worksheets (Network, Disk, Operating System, Database, SAP, and so on) makes it easier to quickly walk through an installation. (Having all the information in a central location makes installation a snap.) Let's spend a few minutes further reviewing the infrastructure requirements.

Network

For the SAP install, all we need are the server to be on the network and an IP address. But for the network team, things are not quite this simple—a network architecture has to be developed before this happens. One of the major considerations in a network design for SAP is whether each environment (production, quality assurance, and development) will have its own network segment. It is also possible for customers to create separate network segments for user access and data (database access and backups). The availability of SAP components through the Internet (if applicable) must also be addressed. The goal of all this is to provide a secure environment for the SAP servers without impacting the functionality. Depending on the company, the network team usually cables up the server and assigns the IP address, leaving the SAP installer oblivious to all this behind-the-scenes complexity.

Disk Subsystem Requirements

For capacity and performance reasons, SAP databases require high-performance storage (another task typically handled behind the scenes). For the SAP installation to proceed, the storage team needs to allocate storage for all the SAP file systems: database data files, log files, sort files, space for the operating system and database binaries (executables), and so on. Behind the scenes, many considerations come into play. For example, disk groups and *redundant array of independent disks* (RAID) levels might need to be configured, *logical units* (LUNs) and stripe sets created and assigned to hosts, performance and availability validated, and so on.

DVD and Downloadable Media

You normally receive the installation DVDs as part of the installation package from SAP. However, it is more typical to download the latest and greatest required media from SAP at http://service.sap.com/swdc. In most cases, you want to copy the media to a central location. (You need the same media to install your technical sandbox, development, test, quality assurance, training, and production installations, for example.) Based on the master guide, to install SAP Solution Manager 4.0 for our simple example, we need the following media:

- ▶ 51032955: SAP Solution Manager Support Release 3 Installation Master

- ▶ 51032956_2: SAP Solution Manager Support Release 3 Installation Export

- ▶ 51031676_1: Oracle 10.2 64-Bit RDBMS Linux on x86_64 64bit

- ▶ 51033032: SAP NetWeaver 2004S SR2 Kernel 7.00 Linux on x86_64 64bit

- ▶ 51033272: Oracle 10.2 Client Location: /dvd/ORACLE 10.2 Client

- ▶ 51031811: Oracle 10.2 RDBMS Patch 10.2.0.2 Linux_X86_64

- ▶ 51032958: SAP Solution Manager 4.0 Support Release 3 Java Components

- ▶ JCE policy files (available at https://www6.software.ibm.com/dl/jcesdk/ jcesdk-p; you must register with the site to download these files)

Imagine all the media required to install the entire SAP Business Suite and set of NetWeaver components!

Performing a Real-World SAP Installation

From a solution stack perspective, installing the SAP central server can be viewed as a four-step process:

1. Install and configure the operating system.

2. Address a number of prerequisites.

3. Install and configure the database software.

4. Perform the actual SAP software installation.

Operating System Installation

Many company IT departments maintain separate teams for Linux, Windows, UNIX, and mainframe server builds. These teams are typically provided network IP addresses by the network team, the necessary disk storage from the storage team, and so on.

The operating system installation for SAP systems is similar to that of any other application. Basic OS recommendations include using standard drive mount points or letters and using standard file allocation unit sizes. For Linux systems, swap file and package requirements are found in the installation guide. For Windows systems, SAP makes some recommendations for the page file size and a few settings to optimize performance in the install guide. The customer is always responsible for licensing and obtaining the OS media. The final step in the operating system installation should be going through a prerequisite checklist, as detailed next for a SuSE Linux/Oracle installation.

A Linux RPM actually refers to several different entities. It may refer to the RPM Package Manager, the rpm program (used to manage installed software), or the file format used for such files (the rpm file format). In the last case, the rpm file format is used for distributing software in a "packaged" format, either as a pre-compiled binary or in its source code format.

Prerequisite Checklist

In this case, we have developed a list of prerequisites for a Linux-based system. A similar checklist can be developed for other operating environments:

- ▶ Check network teaming and other network interface properties.
- ▶ Install the *Java Runtime Environment* (JRE).
- ▶ Verify the appropriate Linux rpms have been installed.
- ▶ Select *message digest 5* (MD5) algorithm password encryption as the default encryption method used.
- ▶ Verify enough swap space is available. (Check your SAP Notes for minimum requirements.)
- ▶ Verify the file system is laid out as described in the master guide.
- ▶ Verify that you have downloaded the updated RUNINSTALLER. (Refer to SAP Note 980426 for specifics relative to an Oracle-based installation.)

Creating such a prerequisite checklist is a great way to ensure that the operating system is properly configured and ready for SAP to be installed.

Database Server Software Installation

The installation process for the database depends on the SAP software release and the database software. While SAP supports several database platforms including its own MaxDB, the two most popular options are explored next.

Microsoft SQL Server

Microsoft SQL Server is always installed "outside" of the SAP installation procedure. SAP provides installation instructions for SQL Server, too, although for the most part the installation process reflects a standard SQL Server database installation. Like nearly all of Microsoft's software installation processes, it's also quick and fairly pain-free. SAP supports Enterprise and Datacenter editions of SQL Server. With its high-availability features and outstanding real-world performance, SQL Server has been increasing not only its market share for SAP, but also the average size of SAP systems that rely on it for business-critical and mission-critical computing. Finally, because Microsoft licenses SQL Server by the processor and not by the processor core, it is generally one quarter to one eighth the cost of Oracle, outlined next.

Oracle

Although its market share has declined over the years, Oracle databases are still commonly found in SAP environments. After all, despite its expense, Oracle is a capable and mature database product. The installation of the database software is normally accomplished by running a batch file provided by SAP that contains answers to all the configuration questions asked by the Oracle installer. In more recent releases of SAP, the Oracle Server software comes in SAR files, which are unzipped during the SAP installation process. Interestingly, the SAP installation process still stops and requires the installer to complete the Oracle install before proceeding by running RUNIN-STALLER. After the Oracle installation completes, the current Oracle patch set must be installed. Oracle Enterprise Edition is required.

SAP Software Installation

The following needs to be done before commencing the SAP software installation:

- ▶ Choose your basic system variants.
- ▶ Identify basic SAP system parameters.

We have reached the point where we need to choose the basic system variants and identify the basic SAP system parameters.

System Variants: Different Installation Types

SAP can be installed in several different ways or variants, depending on the system's end-user requirements (which in turn affect the system's workload), gathered long beforehand in the ASAP blueprinting phase. These installation types include

- ▶ Central Services Instance for ABAP (ASCS)
- ▶ Central Services Instance (SCS)
- ▶ Database Instance
- ▶ Central Instance
- ▶ Dialog Instance

The SAP installation is started from the master installation media using the SAP installation utility, *sapinst*.

SAP Central Services Instance for ABAP (ASCS) Installation

Perform the following steps to install SAP Central Services for ABAP (ASCS):

1. As user root, log on to server linux-test1.

2. Start SAPINST.

3. In the SAP Installation Master window, select **SAP Installation Master**, **SAP Solution Manager 4.0 Support Release 3**, **SAP Systems**, **Oracle**, **High Availability System**, **Based on AS ABAP and AS Java**, **Central Services Instance for ABAP (ASCS)**, and then click **Next**.

4. In the SAP System, General Parameters window, enter the SID (that is, **TST**) and the SAP System Mount Directory (that is, **/sapmnt**), and then click **Next**.

5. In the SAP System, Administrator Password window, enter the SAP System Administrator password, confirm the password, and then click **Next**.

6. For the SAP System, ASCS Instance Number, enter **02**, and then click **Next**.

7. In the SAP System, ASCS Instance Number window, enter the necessary port numbers (that is, **3602** and **3902**) and then click **Continue**.

8. In the Media Browser, Software Package Request window, enter the location of the kernel DVD and then click **Next**.

9. In the SAP System, Unpack Archives window, check **Unpack Box for Archive "DBINDEP/SAPEXE.SAR"** and then click **Next**.

10. In the Parameter Summary window, review the choices to ensure they are correct and then click **Start**.

11. In the Task Progress window, click **OK** when you see the message "Execution of Service has been completed successfully."

Now we can turn our attention to installing the SAP SCS.

SAP Central Services Instance (SCS) Installation

Perform the following steps to install SAP Central Services (SCS):

1. In the SAP Installation Master window, select **SAP Installation Master**, **SAP Solution Manager 4.0 Support Release 3**, **SAP Systems**, **Oracle**, **High Availability System**, **Based on AS ABAP and AS Java**, **Central Services Instance (SCS)** and then click **Next**.

2. In the SAP System, General Parameters window, enter the same SAP SID and SAP mount directory entered previously and then click **Next**.

3. In the SAP System, SCS Instance window, enter the SCS Instance number (**02**) and then click **Next**.

4. In the SAP System, SCS Instance window, enter port number **3902** and then click **Next**.

5. In the Parameter Summary window, verify the parameters and then click **Start**.

6. If a "Your system does not meet some prerequisites" message displays, ignore it.

7. When you see the message "Execution of service has been completed successfully" in the Task Progress window, click **OK**. You're done!

Now we can walk through installing the database for SAP.

SAP Database Instance Installation

Perform the following steps to install the SAP Database Instance:

1. In the SAP Installation Master window, select **SAP Installation Master**, **SAP Solution Manager 4.0 Support Release 3**, **SAP Systems**, **Oracle**, **High Availability System**, **Based on AS ABAP and AS**, **Database Instance** and then click **Next**.

2. In the Media Browser, Software Package Request window, select the proper media and click **Next**.

3. In the SAP System, Java Development Kit window, enter the path to the JDK directory and click **Next**.

4. In the SAP System, JCE Unlimited Strength Jurisdiction Policy Archive window, enter the appropriate path and click **Next**.

5. In the SAP System, General Parameters window, check the **Profiles Are Available** check box, enter a profile directory (that is, **/sapmnt/TST/profile**) and then click **Next**.

6. In the SAP System, Master Password window, enter and confirm the password for all users of this SAP system and then click **Next**.

7. In the SAP System, Database Parameters window, enter the database ID (DBSID) and database host (that is, **TST** and **linux-test1**) and then click **Next**.

8. The SAP System, Database Administrator Password window should be filled in already. Click **Next**.

9. In the Media Browser, Software Package Check window, enter the locations of the installation export DVD media and click **Next**.

10. In the Oracle, Database System window, enter the instance memory, ABAP schema, Java schema, and related passwords and then click **Next**.

11. In the Oracle, Database System window, select **Database Advanced Options** and specify MaxDatafilesize of **10000**. Then check the **Advanced DB** configuration option and click **Next**.

12. In the Oracle, Standard Database Users window, confirm passwords and then click **Next**.

13. In the Media Browser, Software Package Check window, enter the path to the Oracle RDBMS software and then click **Next**.

14. In the Oracle, Listener Configuration window, configure the Oracle Listener and click **Next**.

15. In the Oracle, Advanced Configuration window, select the appropriate settings and click **Next**.

16. In the Oracle, Database System window, highlight **sapdata2** through **sapdata19** and then click **Remove**. Only sapdata1 should remain. Click **Next**.

17. In the Oracle, Database Instance File System window, enter the $ORACLE_HOME Directory, Oracle Stage Directory, and the Sapdata Home Directory and then click **Next**.

18. In the Oracle, Tablespace Extensions window, make sure all options are set to **Autoextend** and then click **Next**.

19. Click **Next** in the Oracle, General Tablespace Storage window.

20. In the SAP System, Database import window, enter the SAP codepage of **4103** and **8** for the number of parallel jobs and then click **Next**.

21. In the Secure Store Settings window, enter the key phrase and confirm it.

22. In the ABAP System, Create Database Statistics window, click the **Create Statistics at the End of Import** option, and then click **Next**.

23. In the SAP System, Unpack Archive window, check the appropriate SAR files (ORA/SAPEXEDB.SAR, ORA/DBATOOLS.SAR, and OCL10264.SAR) and click **Next**.

24. Review your choices on the Parameter Summary window and then click **Next**.

25. Enter the parameters of the SAP database system in the Oracle, Database System window. Change the sapdata path for all instances of SAPDATA listed to **SAPDATA1** and then click **Next**.

26. Sapinst now stops the installation. Install the Oracle database by

    a. Logging in as **oratst**

    b. Setting the **DISPLAY** variable

    c. Changing to directory **/oracle/stage/102_64/database/SAP**

    d. Starting **./RUNINSTALLER**

27. Verify the full path of the inventory directory (/oracle/oraInventory), specify the operating system group name (dba) and then click **Next**.

28. In the Available Product Components window, click **Next**.

29. In the Product-Specific Prerequisite Checks window, change the status of Warnings and Not Executed to **User Verified**.

30. Click **Install** in the Summary window.

31. Open a terminal window and log in as root.

32. Run orainstRoot.sh and root.sh.

33. Click **OK** in the Execute Configuration Scripts window.

34. On the End of Installation screen, click **Exit**.

35. Install the Oracle patches.

36. Click **OK** in the "SAPinst now stops the installation" message box.

37. When you see the message "Execution of service has been completed successfully" in the Task Progress window, click **OK**.

Next, let's walk through installing the SAP Central Instance.

SAP Central Instance Installation

Perform the following steps to install an SAP Central Instance:

1. In the SAP Installation Master window, select **SAP Installation Master, SAP Solution Manager 4.0 Support Release 3, SAP Systems, Oracle, High Availability System, Based on AS ABAP and AS Java, Central Instance** and then click **Next**.

2. In the Media, Software Package Request window, enter the location of the Java component and then click **Next**.

3. In the SAP System, Java Development Kit window, enter the location of the JDK directory and then click **Next**.

4. In the SAP System, General Parameters window, enter the profile directory location and then click **Next**.

5. In the SAP System, Master Password window, enter and confirm the master password for all users of this SAP system and then click **Next**.

6. In the Oracle, Listener Configuration window, enter a listener name of **LISTENER** and a listener port of **1527**.

7. In the SAP System, Central Instance window, enter a Central Instance number of **00** and then click **Next**.

8. In the SAP System, ABAP UME window, enter the J2EE engine and communication usernames and passwords and then click **Next**.

9. Click **Next** in the SAP System, DDIC Users window.

10. In the Media, Software Package Request window, enter the location of the kernel and Oracle client media and click **Next**.

11. In the SAP System, Unpack Archives window, check the **Unpack** box for DBINDEP/IGSEXE and DBINDEP/IGSHEL and then click **Next**.

12. Click **Next** in the SAP System, NWDI Landscape window.

13. In the SAP System, System Landscape Directory window, check **Configure a Local SLD** and then click **Next**.

14. In the SAP System, Local SLD window, enter the object server name and other requested inputs and then click **Next**.

15. In the SAP System, ADS Users window, enter and confirm the passwords for ADSUSER and ADS_AGENT and click **Next**.

16. Review your choices in the Parameter Summary window and then click **Next**.

17. When you see the message "Execution of service has been completed successfully" in the Task Progress window, click **OK**.

This concludes the sapinst portion of the SAP Solution Manager 4.0 install. Given all the steps involved, you certainly by now appreciate the complexity an SAP installation entails.

Post-Installation Tasks

The installation of SAP is almost complete, but you still need to carry out the following tasks before the system is ready to use:

▶ Stop and start the system using stopsap and startsap, respectively.

▶ Log on to the system (user SAP* or DDIC in client 000, 001, or 066 [the latter of which can only be accessed by user SAP*]). The default passwords for

SAP* and DDIC are no longer 19920706 and 06071992 as in days past. For new systems, use the passwords you provided during the installation.

▶ Install the permanent SAP license. The temporary license key, which is valid for weeks, is created during the install. You can obtain a permanent license key for the installation from http://service.sap.com/licensekeys.

▶ Apply the latest kernel and support packages. After the installation, apply the most current support package stack available for download from the SAP Software Distribution Center (http://service.sap.com/swdc).

▶ Create a client copy (just in case you need to fall back later to a pristine client or create a new pristine client to be modified by the development team).

▶ Modify the SAP profiles based on recommendations from SAP Notes and from recommendations from your Basis team. For example, you'll want to change the default number and mix of SAP work processes, memory configuration and buffer parameters, and so on.

This concludes our successful installation of an SAP Solution Manager 4.0 system. With all the complexity of a real-world SAP installation behind us, let's turn our attention to the much simpler process of installing the trial version of SAP.

Installing the SAP Trial Version

Though it's much less complex than a real-world SAP installation, there are still several steps involved in installing the trial version of SAP. The underlying system must be prepared, and then the software must be acquired, downloaded, extracted, and installed.

Preparing for Installation

Before you download the SAP trial version, you need to take care of several prerequisites. System requirements for the desktop or laptop (or server or cloud hosting platform) on which you will install the SAP NetWeaver 7.01 ABAP trial version include

▶ A 32-bit operating system is required. (Windows XP Professional SP2, Windows Vista, and Windows Server 2003 are officially supported, but other versions may work as well.)

▶ The machine's hostname must not exceed 13 characters. (Open a command prompt and run the command `hostname` to confirm this.)

▶ The NTFS file system is required. (FAT and FAT32 are not supported.)

▶ Internet Explorer 5.5 or later, or Firefox 1.0 or later must be present. (Newer versions might yield an error message indicating they are not supported.)

▶ At least 1GB RAM is required. (4GB or more of RAM is highly desirable.)

▶ Intel Pentium III/1.1GHz or higher (or similarly powered AMD platform) is necessary.

▶ A minimum of 25GB of hard disk space is necessary during the installation (and 12GB will be consumed permanently after the installation is complete).

▶ A 10GB pagefile is suggested. (Pagefiles larger than the 1GB minimum noted in the installation documentation have been known to greatly speed up the installation process.)

▶ A monitor that supports 1024x768 or higher resolution and 256 colors is recommended.

▶ The trial version cannot coexist on an operating system where other SAP systems have been installed (including older trial versions, mini SAP versions, or fully licensed official SAP systems).

▶ The SAP system requires several ports for communication services. Specifically, the %WINDIR%\system32\drivers\etc\services file must not include an entry for the ports 3200, 3600, or 8000.

▶ To avoid many common problems associated with permissions (including the ability to update the hosts and services files), perform the installation as an administrator or as a user with "Full Control" privileges.

▶ If no *Dynamic Host Control Protocol* (DHCP) server is available on your network (a DHCP server dynamically provides IP addresses), or your machine is not connected to a network, install the Microsoft Loopback Adapter (a virtual network interface adapter). The procedure to install this adapter can be found in the extracted download files.

Acquiring, Downloading, and Extracting

As soon as your machine is prepared, you can locate and download the SAP NetWeaver 7.01 ABAP trial version from SAP's Solution Developer Network. As of this writing, we used www.sdn.sap.com/irj/scn/downloads?rid=/library/uuid/80fd9a0a-e306-2a10-c896-b84c77c13ed2. Click the **Click Here for Download** link on this web page.

On the next screen (illustrated in Figure 18.1), select the radio button to download the first of two compressed rar files and then click the **I Agree—Download Selected File** button. Note that the license agreement specifies that the SAP NetWeaver 7.01 ABAP trial license is valid for four weeks.

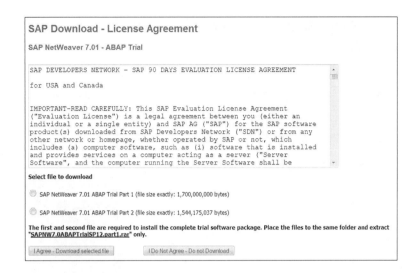

FIGURE 18.1
After reviewing
the SAP trial
license agree-
ment, select
the first file to
download, and
after success-
fully download-
ing it, select
the second file.

Download the first file (1.6GB) into a local directory on your machine and then download the second file (1.5GB). We suggest creating a "temp" folder off the root of C: and
downloading both files into C:\temp, as illustrated in Figure 18.2. Combined, the two
compressed rar files consume just over 3GB of disk space.

FIGURE 18.2
Save the two
compressed rar
files to a direc-
tory on your
local machine.

Extract only the first rar file into the C:\temp directory, using a common tool like
WinRAR or 7-zip. A collection of 3.3GB worth of files will be extracted into a folder
called SAPNW7.01ABAPTrial. Do not extract the second file; it's done automatically
when the first file is extracted. Many rar extraction tools are available at no cost. If you
need to download one of these tools, take care to ensure your malware and virus protection are up-to-date on your machine; "freeware" websites are notorious for malware.

Step-by-Step SAP Trial Version Installation

When the contents are extracted, start the SAP installation by doing the following:

1. Click **start.bat**. A web page opens similar to the one illustrated in Figure 18.3.

FIGURE 18.3
A web page
walks you
through the
overall Trial
Version installa-
tion process.

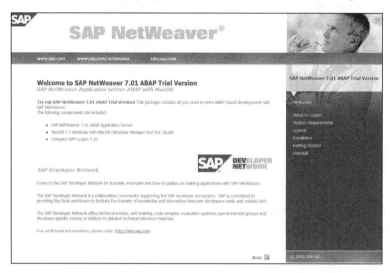

2. Read through the Welcome screen and then click **Next**.

3. Review the What to Expect screen and click **Next**.

4. The System Requirements screen is displayed next. Confirm that your system meets the minimum requirements make changes as necessary, and click **Next**.

5. Review the License screen and click **Next**.

6. Read through the steps outlined on the Installation screen. Ensure you are logged on to your machine with administrator privileges.

7. Make sure the SAP Management Console is installed. If it's not, install it by executing sapmmcX86u.msi from the C:\temp\sapmmc folder.

8. Click the **Installer** hyperlink to start the Installer and choose **Run** in the follow-on pop-up window (or just run setup.exe from C:\temp\image).

Depending on your specific configuration, the screen shown in Figure 18.4 might display. (Again, it is highly recommended to install the SAP trial version on one of the supported Windows operating systems noted previously.)

At this point, the InstallShield Wizard takes us through the next part of the installation. Complete the following steps:

1. Click **Next**, and the Welcome screen in Figure 18.5 appears.

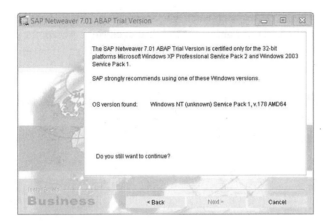

FIGURE 18.4
If you vary from the recommended Windows operating systems, you will receive a warning message.

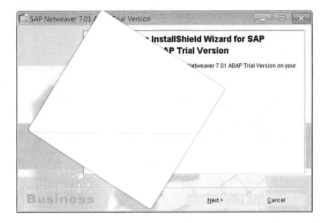

FIGURE 18.5
The Welcome screen is displayed.

2. Click **Next** to review the SAP evaluation license agreement (see Figure 18.6).

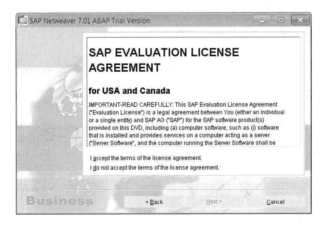

FIGURE 18.6
The SAP trial version license agreement is displayed.

3. Read the license agreement, and if you agree, click the statement **I Accept the Terms of the License Agreement** and then click **Next**. Accept the default SAP installation directory of C:\SAP (recommended) or change if necessary (see Figure 18.7).

FIGURE 18.7
Accept or change the SAP trial version's installation path.

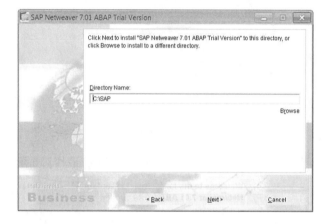

4. Define a master password (enter one of your liking), confirm the password, and then click **Next**. A screen displaying the summary information shared in Figure 18.8 is displayed. Click **Install**.

FIGURE 18.8
Accept or change the SAP trial version's installation path for the MaxDB database.

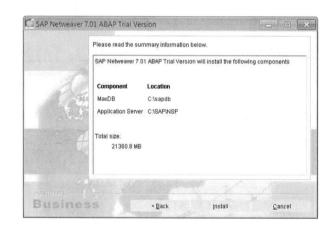

The remainder of the installation process takes hours, as many as six or more depending on the machine. Be patient! Ours took three hours. The SAP installation process is disk-intensive and therefore pretty slow when installed on a desktop or laptop. If your machine's hard disk light is furiously flashing away, you are probably in good shape. If you run into trouble, read through the installation troubleshooting guide included in the SAPNW7.01ABAPTrial folder. SAP recommends that you restart your machine after completing the SAP trial system installation. Afterward, start SAP by clicking **Start Application Server**.

Using the SAP Trial Version

To log on to SAP, install the SAPGUI. After the SAP trial version is extracted, an SAPGUI directory is created. Inside the directory is a file, SapGuiSetup.exe. We suggest you remove other SAPGUI installations before you install the trial version of the SAPGUI (and run the included tool to clean the OS Registry). When you're ready, run the SapGuiSetup.exe program and follow the prompts. Alternatively, access the trial version by pointing your browser to http://localhost:8000/sap/bc/gui/sap/its/webgui?sap-client=000 and logging on with user **bcuser** and its default password **minisap**.

Introducing SAP Single Sign-On

It's time to leave the trial version of SAP behind and cover one more important installation step. Once a real-world SAP system has been installed, and assuming a basic level of Microsoft Active Directory integration has been performed, *Single Sign-On* (SSO) should probably be enabled. SAP SSO allows a user's Windows-based user account (assigned in Active Directory) to be mapped to the same user's respective SAP user account. This makes it possible for users to enter their user IDs and passwords only once (when they log on to their Windows workstation, for example); they do not have to enter logon information again when they want to log on to SAP. And if the user has accounts in multiple SAP clients on an SAP system, it is only necessary to click once on the desired client.

Basic SSO integration is rather simple. It requires only a Generic Security Service API v2 *dynamic link library* (DLL) (which is free of charge from SAP) to be distributed to each server and end-user computer participating in SSO. This technology uses the Microsoft NTLM (*NT LAN Manager*, itself comprised of the legacy acronyms *New Technology* and *local-area network*) Security Service Provider or Kerberos, and SAP's SNC (*Secure Network Communications*). Unfortunately, this SSO technology is available only in a pure Microsoft environment; mixed environments cannot take advantage of this simple integration method. For SSO installation and configuration instructions, refer to one of SAP's installation guides for Windows (http://service.sap.com/instguides).

Enabling SSO Using SPNego

An alternative way to enable SAP SSO is by using SPNego (best pronounced ess-pea-nay-go). The name SPNego is derived from the security mechanism used: the *simple and protected GSS API negotiation mechanism*. SPNego is used to authenticate a client application with a remote server. This capability was first introduced by Microsoft in Internet Explorer 5.1 and was called Integrated Windows Authentication. Today, SPNego is integrated with the most popular web browsers including Firefox and Google Chrome. The authentication is handled through Kerberos, which allows systems to communicate securely to one another.

SPNego is configured both on Microsoft Windows and SAP. On the Microsoft side, Kerberos is used by Active Directory to validate the user. On the SAP side, Kerberos communicates with SAP to validate an end user and determine that user's ability to access SAP. Within Windows Server, a service user account (Windows user account) must be created and then some configuration is done to relate the SAP system with this service account. Then within SAP, the SPNego Wizard is executed to define the Windows Server and the service account. The user mapping within SAP must also be defined.

When everything is configured, the logon process is actually quite elegant. When users log on to their computers using their network accounts through Active Directory, they receive *ticket-generating tickets* (TGT). When a user attempts to retrieve data from SAP, SAP sends a request to the user's system to negotiate security. The user's system retrieves its TGT and then sends the ticket to SAP (see Figure 18.9). This ticket contains

FIGURE 18.9
The core work behind the SPNego negotiation process is quite elegant in its simplicity.

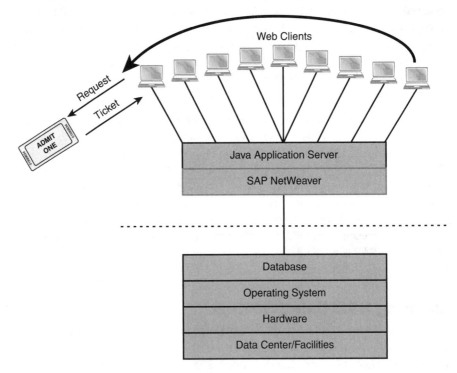

the user's account information and other data. SAP then takes that ticket and determines whether the user is mapped to an SAP account. If so, the user's access is further validated to ensure permission exists to access the requested data.

SPNego is often used to link SAP and *Microsoft Office SharePoint Server* (MOSS) 2007. It can also be used with MOSS 2010. In addition to SPNego, however, MOSS 2010 can use yet another SSO method: Security Assertion Markup Language, covered next.

Enabling SSO Through SAML

Security Assertion Markup Language (SAML, pronounced sam-el) is an open and powerful standard for exchanging authentication and authorization data between different security domains. This means that a user with Company A may request and obtain data from an application running within Company B. Because it is an open standard, SAML is not tied to a particular technology. SAML was created by the OASIS Security Services Technical Committee for the purpose of resolving web browser SSO issues in complex, real-world business scenarios.

SAML is new to both SAP and Microsoft. Microsoft has begun to roll out SAML support with its Active Directory products, but where you will see the most impact of SAML is between SAP and Microsoft Office SharePoint Server 2010. SAML is also used for authentication and authorization within Duet Enterprise.

SAML relies on an identity provider to authenticate users. MOSS 2010 and other trusted resources can act as SAML identity providers. If the authentication proves successful, the user is issued a token. This token is then used when the user tries to access another system; it presents its token containing the user's assertions. Assertions contain information describing and validating a user (essentially consisting of a packet of security data). If a target system "recognizes" a user, the user is granted access.

Summary

This hour outlined the steps necessary for a successful technical installation. With careful planning and preparation, we walked through the steps necessary to install an actual installation of SAP on the Linux/Oracle platform. Finishing the post-installation phase marks the end of the technical implementation; the functional team may step in next. Afterward, we walked through obtaining and installing SAP's trial version. The hour concluded with a discussion of SAP's technical integration with Microsoft's Active Directory and SSO, including the roles of SPNego and SAML.

Case Study: Hour 18

Consider this SAP installation case study and the questions that follow. You can find the answers posed by the questions related to this case study in Appendix A, "Case Study Answers."

Situation

MNC has standardized on Windows/SQL Server and has decided to implement SAP Solution Manager. You have been tasked by MNC's SAP Basis team leader with installing a technical sandbox for the team. You have worked with your implementation partners to architect and size the solution, and the infrastructure is in place. With all necessary planning behind you, you are ready to begin the installation process.

Questions

1. What should you do first?

2. What is the name of the media from where you start the SAP installation process (sapinst)?

3. After the installation, through which two methods might you implement Single Sign-On?

4. In case you cannot find one of the DVDs, where can you go to download SAP media?

5. MNC is looking for ways to cut IT support costs. Currently, MNC's IT help desk spends an inordinate amount of time changing and resetting passwords. What low-cost technology can be implemented that will immediately provide relief to the IT help desk?

SAP and the Cloud

What You'll Learn in This Hour:

▶ The three cloud consumer perspectives

▶ The four cloud provider perspectives

▶ First-mover cloud applications

▶ How SOA facilitates cloud computing

▶ A brief history of cloud and other computing delivery models

▶ How SAP can use the cloud today and how SAP may use it tomorrow

This hour introduces cloud computing, including how different clouds appeal to different types of consumers and providers. It then outlines several classes of cloud providers. An evolution of computing platforms from legacy to client/server, web-based, *service-oriented architecture* (SOA), and finally the cloud helps set the stage for a closer look at how SAP is already using (and can further use) the cloud today. This hour closes by reviewing how SAP and its cloud story might evolve over the next few years.

Introduction to the Cloud

Although there's a lot more to it, the simplest way to define "the cloud" is this: somebody else's computers used to deliver a "service" to a consumer. That consumer may be a business application end user, an application developer, or an IT professional. Cloud computing is a *style* of computing in the same way that client/server and mainframe (monolithic or vertically integrated) were styles of computing in their own day. With several exceptions, cloud computing can generally be described by the following attributes or principles:

▶ Resiliency or the ability to "self-heal"

▶ Elasticity or the ability to grow and shrink based on workload demands

▶ The perception of infinite scalability

▶ Self-service or automatic provisioning capabilities

▶ Consumption-based or "pay-as-you-go" (PAYG) pricing models

▶ Shared infrastructure and other resources (often enabled through the use of virtualization, although this is not required)

Such attributes drive a host of benefits related to how, where, and who adopts this style of computing, outlined next.

Benefits of the Cloud

Using the cloud, IT organizations can more quickly provision IT resources based on rapidly evolving business demands. This is especially true for short-term IT resource needs where the ability to quickly meet new business needs might enable first-mover or some other kind of competitive advantage to the business. Such increased IT agility not only equates to business agility but also sets the stage for more efficient resource management and faster *return on investment* (ROI).

The whole idea behind pay as you go also equates to faster ROI. IT organizations that only pay for the IT services they need and use—when they need and use it—minimize resource consumption and the need to track and manage resources. Such IT organizations also simplify IT budgeting and forecasting. In some cases, IT organizations can potentially eliminate entire data centers or colocation facilities earmarked for disaster recovery and business continuity.

With less infrastructure, platform, and similar matters to tend to, IT organizations that use cloud-based resources need fewer of their own IT professionals. Costs related to hiring, training, and retaining people with these skillsets are naturally reduced, as well.

The ability to change how business users get their work done is another great unexplored area of cloud computing. The cloud can provide a mobile workforce with access to quickly evolving IT services and solutions, for example. That same workforce can also benefit from business intelligence systems hosted in the cloud and therefore easily and inexpensively updated real time. With more ubiquitous access from corporate and noncorporate sites and data sources alike, cloud-based systems open the door to round-the-clock access, just-in-time updates, and real-time business insight.

First-Mover Cloud Applications

Based on these benefits, there are many first-mover applications (SAP and non-SAP) that just "make sense" to be hosted in the cloud. These include

▶ Blogs, wikis, social networks, and similar communications vehicles

▶ Consumer and (in many cases) corporate email systems

▶ A company's customer relationship management system, marketing and promotions systems, or other systems

▶ End-user productivity applications (particularly low-frills desktop applications like basic word processing and collaboration systems)

▶ An organization's training systems or "technical sandboxes" (used to teach a new application to end users or a new technology to technical teams)

▶ Business demonstration and prototyping systems (where the ability to quickly stand up new infrastructure, for example, can help the business in turn react more quickly to new business opportunities)

▶ Web-based systems that must naturally accommodate spikes or seasonal peaks in workload (school registration sites, a company's annual benefits registration system, other HR functions, and so on)

▶ Test or quality assurance systems (and to a lesser extent, development systems) supporting a production system that itself might or might not be ready for the cloud

▶ Data storage or "filing" systems for photos, email archives, system backups, and other electronic data (particularly if it's easily encrypted or not considered sensitive)

▶ Self-contained (rather than highly integrated with other systems) business intelligence repositories

▶ Disaster-recovery and business continuity systems (with many exceptions based on technical constraints, business-continuity requirements, and more)

With some thought, you could quickly add to this list. Think about all the applications you use at work and those that you personally access after the workday is over. The list is only growing.

On the other hand, there are still many applications today that might continue to benefit from traditional infrastructure, platform, and software delivery methods for the near future. These holdouts are discussed next.

Cloud Application Holdouts

Not every application is ready to be tossed into the cloud. The reasons are rather simple, if not obvious, and relate to enduring matters such as the following:

▶ Application and platform risk (mitigating and managing it)

▶ Application and platform maturity (which is really just another way to describe risk; mainframe and UNIX platforms have such a huge head start when it comes to hosting business-critical and mission-critical applications, for example)

▶ Application and platform architectures (specifically, supportability for the cloud by application and platform vendors)

▶ Application and platform security (securing and preserving access to data)

▶ Real-time system performance (especially important in high-volume transactional systems where online users need near-instant results)

▶ Overall system complexity (particularly related to integration with applications that might be physically hosted elsewhere, which incidentally affects performance, as well)

▶ Cost (For very large organizations, the economies of scale offered by cloud computing might not offer any real differentiation; further, internal IT organizations successful in adopting cloud-like principles in the way they procure, deploy, and support their own infrastructure might not believe that an external service provider could do so any better.)

▶ Federal compliance and other regulations (Many federal and international organizations may affect where data is housed and how applications are hosted.)

For the reasons noted here, companies are not yet flocking to cloud hosting providers, anxious to turn over their applications and computing platforms. The corporate *enterprise resource planning* (ERP) system, complex multisource data warehouses, real-time credit card processing services, company-sensitive research and development projects, and applications requiring specialized platforms might not make sense in the cloud. For everyone, that is. And certainly only for the time being; the day is quickly coming when IT and business professionals will start to ask, "Why should we *not* put our applications and platforms in the cloud?"

Cloud Consumer Perspective

Cloud computing is often divided into three broad service models or types based on the different consumers of each model and who provides or manages the assets. The three models are *Software as a Service* (SaaS), *Platform as a Service* (PaaS), and *Infrastructure as a Service* (IaaS). Figure 19.1 illustrates each service model in terms of its provider (as noted) and consumer orientation.

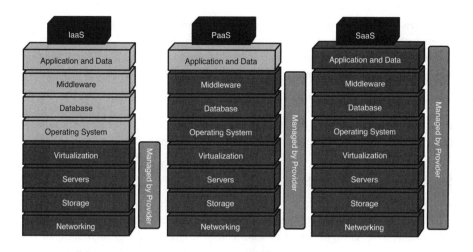

FIGURE 19.1
SaaS, PaaS, and IaaS cloud service models differ in terms of their provider and targeted "consumer."

SaaS: For Business End Users

Software that is delivered as a service is targeted at the software's business-oriented end users. SAP's Business ByDesign, for example, is software delivered in a pay-as-you-go way for SAP's end users. NetSuite offers a similarly delivered ERP solution, while Microsoft and Salesforce.com offer SaaS-based customer relationship management systems.

The simplest way to understand SaaS is to think of it as prebuilt applications in the cloud. The cloud provider hosts, develops, manages, and delivers the application to a business's end users; the business's IT department has absolutely nothing to do in this regard.

Software delivered as a service has actually existed since the late 1990s. *Application service providers* (ASPs) were the first to take advantage of the ubiquitous connectedness provided by the Internet. As communications technologies matured and network bandwidth between homes and businesses exploded, APSs offered a number of consumer applications to a growing base of users. Ranging from email systems to web conferencing, collaboration, and end-user productivity suites (like word processing), ASPs eventually extended their offerings to include departmental and other (less-than-business-critical) business applications.

PaaS: For Application Developers

Platforms delivered as a service are targeted at application developers. Externally managed application platforms are used by developers to build and operate a new class of applications, services, and solutions. PaaS environments remove all the complexity associated with lower-level cloud computing like IaaS (covered next) but unlike SaaS, give a developer control over how data and applications are controlled.

Typical PaaS offerings provide runtime and development frameworks along with the necessary agile development tools required to build an application. The underlying plumbing necessary to support world-class applications is also included. For example, services such as authentication, authorization management, session management, inter-system integration, and so on are provided. PasS also gives developers the mechanisms necessary to ensure transactional consistency and integrity, business process reliability, and more. Microsoft Windows Azure, Force.com, Google App Engine, and Amazon's latest offering, Elastic Beanstalk, are all examples of platforms delivered as a service.

IaaS: For IT Professionals

The fastest growing cloud service is infrastructure delivered as a service. In many respects, IaaS does little to transform what an IT department needs to manage day in and day out. Sure, IT doesn't have to acquire and manage servers and disk subsystems—and IasS's rapid provisioning ability goes a long way toward enabling IT agility. But IaaS is only a baby step into the cloud. The real headaches surrounding operating system patching and upgrades, database management, and managing systems integration still need to be performed by IT.

Regardless, IaaS should play a role in an organization's cloud strategy (if only to offer that initial baby step to "test" cloud computing and quickly realize some measurable benefit). Look to IaaS providers like Amazon, Rackspace, Verizon, AT&T, and GoGrid to provide highly virtualized physical hardware assets abstracted enough to be delivered as a cloud service. Amazon's many years of experience delivering its *Elastic Compute Cloud* (EC2) serves as the ideal role model for organization's seeking to stick a toe in the cloud.

Cloud Service Provider Perspective

Just as cloud computing can vary based on its targeted consumer or user community (business end users, application developers, and IT professionals), cloud computing also varies or can be differentiated based on the entity that hosts the actual computers and other resources employed to deliver the cloud services. This hosting entity is often referred to as a service provider. Where these computers are physically located represents still another dimension. The industry generally recognizes several variations of cloud service providers:

▶ Internal private cloud

▶ Hosted private cloud

▶ Public cloud

▶ Hybrid cloud

Each variation is briefly explored next.

Internal Private Cloud

Internal private clouds comprise compute, network, disk, and other resources specifically allocated for a single company at the company's very own location. For example, a company might want to run some of its applications in an environment that is nearly infinitely scalable, highly elastic, and above all resilient to underlying hardware and datacenter facility failures. However, for reasons related to risk, security, or government regulations, the company might want to keep all these resources under its own tight control. Therefore, an internal private cloud hosted in the company's very own data center might be most appropriate solution.

A private cloud can represent an excellent introduction to cloud-enabling a business. We recommend that an organization start using private cloud resources for training, functional testing, integration testing, demonstration systems, technical and business sandboxes, development systems, and even disaster-recovery solutions. Key characteristics of private clouds in general include

- ▶ High level of control and security

- ▶ Innovative first step toward cloud computing

- ▶ Ability to comply with regulatory requirements

- ▶ Fewer integration or performance issues than its public counterparts

- ▶ Lower cost than its traditional computing platform counterparts

Hosted Private Cloud

As opposed to an internal private cloud, a company might want to avoid the hassles and expense of installing, managing, and maintaining its own locally provisioned cloud computing assets. Such a company might instead sign up with a hosting provider that specializes in providing dedicated cloud resources to its customers. The provider would essentially "carve out" some of its own resources and earmark these specifically for its customer. This collection of resources is called a hosted private cloud.

Because the resources are not shared with other companies and are therefore "private," they are more secure than their public counterparts. However, there's also less opportunity to reduce the provider's overall resource costs (and therefore less opportunity to pass on any kind of savings to the end customer); such a private cloud would naturally cost more than its more broadly shared public cloud brethren. But the tradeoffs related to security and control nonetheless would appeal to a company interested in reaping many of the core benefits associated with cloud computing.

Public Cloud

Any cloud infrastructure, platforms, or software hosted outside the company and provided by another party is considered part of the public cloud. The public cloud is as diverse as it is broad; the vast majority of cloud offerings today are public. Because a company has little to no control over how public cloud assets are managed and maintained, the public cloud is perceived (accurately, we believe) as the most risky of all cloud service provider approaches.

This lack of control is precisely why the public cloud is so appealing, though. Think about it: If your application is delivered in a way that meets your service level, performance, and availability needs, do you really otherwise care how it's managed and maintained? The key is obviously related to how well the public cloud service indeed meets your needs. Good, well-negotiated, financially-incentivized *service level agreements* (SLAs) can mean the difference between an application that meets a business's needs and one that fails miserably.

With some of the most immature and poorly crafted SLAs known in the cloud community, though, many (but certainly not all) public cloud systems are simply not ready to handle the next wave of business-critical and mission-critical applications. Beyond service level issues, other risks or potential issues related to the public cloud include

- ▶ Little maturity and guidance and therefore few business-critical and mission-critical references.

- ▶ New administrative tools and operational processes might be necessary to marry public cloud systems with the company's existing applications and platforms.

- ▶ Questionable or non-existent support for international, national, or local regulations and other matters of governance related to ITAR, FDA, PCI, HIPAA, and so on.

- ▶ Lack of legacy application support in most cases (including the ability to natively support SAP application servers in all but the simplest and least beneficial cloud service models, for example).

Hybrid Cloud

By its very description, a hybrid cloud can be many things. Generally, we define a hybrid cloud service as any extended or "tiered" platform comprised of interconnected public and private or on-premises and cloud resources. Hybrids are most often employed to enable front-end scale and resiliency while safeguarding back-end resources like data, differentiating business processes, and other sensitive assets. Important attributes or characteristics of a hybrid cloud include

▶ The ability to enable best-of-breed innovation, both from a platform and application perspective (Hybrids enable you to weave together best-in-class hosted *customer relationship management* [CRM] systems with your own back-end proprietary systems, for example.)

▶ The potential to significantly reduce risk compared to a pure public cloud scenario

▶ Similarly, the ability to enable incremental transformation (by taking safe baby steps into the cloud)

▶ The ability to craft a custom cost model that better balances capital expenses with operational expenses, enables partial pay-as-you-go benefits, and so on

With fewer (or more manageable) risks than a pure public cloud counterpart and greater opportunities to introduce business-enabling innovation than its traditional computing counterpart, for many consumers the hybrid cloud represents the most reasonable and realistic first step into the cloud.

Brief History of Computing and the Cloud

The information technology industry has a funny way of reinventing itself every decade or two. We were doing virtualization back in the heyday of the IBM mainframe, and today we're all making a big deal of virtualization as if it's something new. We redistributed the power of IT from centralized mainframe computing to every desktop through client/server computing, and today we're busy recentralizing IT through the architectural equivalent of mainframe computing in the sky. After all, what are clouds but simply a new paradigm for delivering a service from some faraway computer? Today's cloud "mainframe" only differs in that it provides scalability, performance, and resiliency in a different manner and at a much lower cost per transaction than mainframes ever could.

But cloud computing isn't really all that new either. If you've ever used Microsoft's Live Hotmail product, you've been using the cloud. It is widely considered the first cloud computing application, and Hotmail was launched in 1996, well before people started labeling everything with "as-a-Service!"

Another great example of the cloud in use is the Salesforce.com CRM product. Founded in 1999, Salesforce.com is often described as the first successful example of a company delivering an application as a service, from a provider to a business consumer. Until just a few years ago, the Salesforce.com SaaS model was attacked as too rigid or inflexible. Today, CRM vendors who don't offer their products as a service are viewed as relics, has-beens—and a legacy provider that costs too much and innovates too little.

More mature IT providers like Microsoft created PaaS development platforms capable of being accessed through a "pay-per-use" billing model, featuring agile tools and the ability to support multiple development environments. And Amazon, interested in putting to use its vast collection of computing resources (otherwise sitting idly by until the occasional seasonal or viral purchasing peak put more of it to use) is probably the quintessential model of early cloud innovation.

That an online bookseller would all but define the IaaS computing model has got to give the big IT providers like CSC, HP, and IBM pause. Amazon pioneered the idea that inexpensive bare-boned servers could be tied together with a set of contemporary principles to create a computing fabric more resilient and cost-effective than ever possible through the industry's legacy computing paradigm—the *availability through redundancy* (ATR) model. In the same way Microsoft changed development economics with PaaS, Amazon was the first big IaaS cloud provider to offer hope to organizations constrained by ATR's high costs and complexity, subsequent inflexibility, and therefore IT's inability to help a company quickly react to changing business needs or new opportunities.

Today, Amazon owns and continues to innovate across much of the IaaS space, particularly with regard to storage and server resources. As of this writing, Amazon has been providing this style of cloud computing for eight years! Unsurprisingly, others have quickly jumped onto the IaaS bandwagon.

So again, cloud computing is really nothing entirely new. It's just the reinvention of a computing delivery model that (again!) makes sense to a group of consumers seeking a more complete set of services delivered more effectively. As the cloud matures through time and adoption, we expect to see more computing move to the cloud.

Client/Server Architectures

While it's just a matter of time until much more computing is performed in the private, public, or hybrid cloud, client/server solutions for SAP and its business-enabling enterprise application counterparts still prevail. After all, change isn't as easy for business-critical and mission-critical applications and their underlying computing platforms. To transition today from a proven solution that meets a client's core needs to a new architecture that promises greater rewards but may require significant retooling is simply not palatable to everyone. Besides, the ATR conundrum we outlined earlier makes change very costly and difficult. SAP and its partners can talk of increased business agility and flexibility that comes from the cloud and its predecessor of sorts, Enterprise SOA, but the pain of technical replatforming costs money, incurs downtime, and is generally disruptive for months.

Just look at SAP's previous legacy, its mainframe-based R/2 application platform—it has been decades, and still some companies do not believe that changing their core applications and platforms is worth the effort, cost, and risk. Add to this reality the need to retool and retrain both IT and the organization's business community, and it's no wonder that the transition to the cloud will remain slow and deliberate for the most risk-averse and change-averse organizations. In the meantime, those customers will be faced with how to modernize their existing client/server SAP applications.

SAP's Web Application Server

SAP didn't make the switch between client/server and more contemporary computing models in one great leap. Web-based computing platforms helped propel the SAP application platform's evolution. Although not originally envisioned as NetWeaver specific, SAP's *Web Application Server* (or WebAS, a more comprehensive Basis layer developed for mySAP at the turn of the century) was designed to simplify installation, integration, and ongoing maintenance. In addition, SAP wanted to give its developer community a choice, adding Java/J2EE support to SAP's ABAP/4 programming mainstay. Eventually, SAP integrated its web server (*Internet Transaction Server*, or ITS, first introduced in 1996) into this new powerful platform.

Within a few short years of its inception, SAP WebAS evolved into a formidable web-enabled and SOA-compliant technical platform. The new platform helped firms transform how they conducted business in a world that continued to demand greater nimbleness, more flexibility, and ever-increasing business agility and therefore underlying technology agility. WebAS provided enhanced support for *Extensible Markup Language* (XML) and web services technologies, including early support for *Simple Object Access Protocol* (SOAP) and *Web Services Description Language* (WSDL). With support for Unicode offered as of WebAS 6.30, the capability to standardize on a particular companywide technology platform relative to matters as diverse as language support also made a compelling argument for deploying what ultimately morphed into the platform undergirding NetWeaver—the same platform that also made Enterprise SOA possible (covered next).

The Advent of Service-Oriented Architectures

Service-oriented architecture (SOA) is nothing more than an approach to designing a more innovative computing platform that takes advantage of reusable services to build powerful business processes. As such, it's a distinct departure from systems that were custom-designed and developed from the ground up (sometimes called custom apps) and is just as much a departure from prepackaged client/server applications as SAP R/3 and its peers from the 1990s.

SOA provides for definitions and methods of building an IT infrastructure that makes it possible not only to exchange data between different systems and other data repositories, but to build and extend business processes. As such, SOA is necessarily tied to both the underlying operating systems and to the development/programming languages native to an application. But the link is a loosely coupled one. In this way, SOA makes it possible to support business processes spanning completely different operating environments, from traditional UNIX and Microsoft Windows offerings to Linux and even mainframe platforms.

If you're a programmer, you've known for years the value of modular programming, where chunks of code can be easily reused. This approach takes a bit more time up front but saves a huge amount of time in the long run, particularly with regard to ongoing maintenance when changes need to be made. SOA takes the same approach but from an architecture perspective. SOA segregates functionality into modular services, which in turn can be combined and reused to create and change business applications. Services communicate with one another by passing data or by coordinating interservice activities.

Thus, it is this idea of services, web services in particular, that make an SOA architecture actually useful. Services set the broader stage for cloud computing. A web service encompasses some kind of business function or application logic that may be accessed and used over and over again in support of a business process. SAP speaks of aggregating web services into business-enabling enterprise services.

Before we explore how web services enable automated enterprise-scale business scenarios and ultimately cloud computing, we need to step back and look more closely at SAP's adaptation of SOA, called Enterprise SOA.

Enterprise SOA

According to SAP, Enterprise SOA is like a blueprint used to create an adaptable, flexible, and open IT architecture, which in turn may be leveraged to create services-based business applications. To realize its own vision of such applications, SAP engineered NetWeaver to provide the required technical platform. The result is SAP's ability to create real-time enterprise applications that benefit from both rapid prototyping and deployment, and high-reusability/low-development costs.

SOA is more generic than Enterprise SOA; any computing architecture that allows for reusable services describes SOA. In the same way, any system that uses web services is SOA-compliant or -enabled. SOA's concept of creating composite complex business applications through bundling reusable services is fairly broad. Reusable services might include web services or might also encompass open services such as those described by WSDL, SOAP, and *Universal Description, Discovery, and Integration* (UDDI). Thus, SOA is just a set of technical specifications—an underlying architectural approach—rather than a methodology for creating business applications.

On the other hand, Enterprise SOA has a definite business focus; it's not simply a technical architectural approach. Built on SAP's *Enterprise Services Architecture* (ESA), Enterprise SOA is SAP's version of the more generic SOA. Enterprise SOA enables composite applications to be built by assembling enterprise services (a similar concept to web services, although more generic in nature), while SAP NetWeaver's *Enterprise Services Repository* (ESR) serves as the central building block for creating SAP Enterprise SOA applications.

For a detailed review of SOA and how SAP's technical architecture evolved pre-cloud, see Hour 14, "Extending SAP with Microsoft and Other Products," in the third edition of *Sams Teach Yourself SAP in 24 Hours*.

By the Way

It is actually these enterprise services that really differentiate SAP's Enterprise SOA from SOA. SAP has engaged not only its internal development team but countless partners as well to develop a robust collection of enterprise services. SAP calls this its "inventory of enterprise services," more formally described as SAP's *Enterprise Services Inventory* (ESI). As Enterprise SOA's foundation, these enterprise services occupy the ESR and do the job of fulfilling a specific business need. Further, each enterprise service in turn passes data and then triggers another enterprise service.

Not surprisingly, SAP continues to engage its development teams and partners to build new services, engaging its customers in the process to help identify or initiate and then vet out new potential enterprise services. SAP created the *Enterprise Services Community* (ESC) to give credence to its concept of enterprise services; the ESC also busies itself with defining and refining enterprise services. Another SAP tool, the ES Workplace, provides initial access to SAP's customers and partners to newly published enterprise services. SAP also published business maps that essentially map services to business processes and solutions. In this way, SAP effectively promulgates its concept of Enterprise SOA while simultaneously giving its approach the legs it needs to prove effective in the real world.

Open services require structure and description. WSDL describes a SOAP message in terms of encoding and transport. SOAP, in turn, is essentially an HTTP-capable XML carrier protocol. Combined with the API for interacting with web service registries, UDDI, these three components make up the *Web Service Interoperability* profile, or WS-I.

By the Way

Principles of Enterprise SOA: Journey to the Cloud

SAP describes five principles of Enterprise SOA. In doing so, SAP created a loosely controlled set of development precepts for its enterprise services, including the enablers to support cloud computing. These principles include

- ▶ Abstraction—Served to mask unnecessary or otherwise puzzling details.

- ▶ Modularity—Enabled the development of reusable components or building blocks by breaking down services into fundamental units.

▶ Standardized connectivity—Used to describe and enable data sharing and trig-
gering, which in turn were used to build and combine flexible services into
full-fledged enterprise business processes, scenarios, and solutions.

▶ Loose coupling—Another necessary property that enabled individual services
to grow and evolve without requiring a rewrite. Loose coupling preserved
reusability and integration and connectivity between services.

▶ Incremental design—The ability to enable changes to a service's composition
and configuration without requiring a rebuild.

Through these five principles, SAP AG became an early market leader in enterprise
application software built atop service-oriented architectures. These principles made it
possible for SAP to continue developing world-class enterprise services that ultimately
began the work of incentivizing SAP's hordes of legacy R/3 customers to finally move
away from their trusted though increasingly inflexible client/server architecture.
Enterprise SOA's flexible and standardized architecture supported business better than
its older architectural counterparts because it simplified a firm's ability to innovate, connect to partners and vendors, and improve its customer connections. Enterprise SOA
unified business processes and simplified their deployment and maintenance by structuring complex business applications as merely ad hoc collections of enterprise services.

With the roadmap from legacy computing through client/server, web-enabled, SOA, and
Enterprise SOA behind us, let's turn our attention to where the cloud dovetails into
SAP's strategy today and in the near future.

Bringing Together SAP and the Cloud

Like many other software providers that can point to long-time cloud attributes, SAP is
no exception. SAP's core transactional systems, even dating back to R/2, have long supported the idea of multi-tenancy. SAP's client model—where company A can run alongside company B on the same application instance using the same underlying computing
platform—is one of the earliest examples of multi-tenant software. Similarly, SAP has
long provided its customers with subscription-based pricing. These are both examples of
"cloud computing." In the next few pages, we explore other real-world intersections
between SAP and cloud computing. Along the way, we also identify how the cloud can
be leveraged outside of SAP's native capabilities to reduce costs, increase flexibility,
and enable business agility of applications like those found in the SAP Business Suite.

SAP and SaaS

To be clear, we need to set the stage appropriately: SAP's only production-ready SaaS-
based cloud solution is its midmarket offering *Business ByDesign* (BBD). None of

SAP's other applications can be delivered in this way simply because they haven't been architected from the ground up as SaaS applications. SAP's CRM-on-demand is pretty close, and you could argue it supports the basic tenets of a SaaS model. But it isn't a by-the-book SaaS implementation. Therefore, SAP's SaaS story is pretty short. And given the tremendous effort and expense necessary to rearchitect and retool SAP Business Suite and NetWeaver, the list of SAP's fully SaaS-enabled applications is expected to remain limited for some time.

One could argue that SAP's focus has really been to move its existing customers to the latest version of SAP ERP. Once there, SAP could presumably rest in the fact that most organizations (because they infrequently upgrade their mission-critical applications) would be happy to stay another 5 to 10 years on that release, buying SAP more time to transform its software delivery model. If true, we might have quite a ways to go before we see a groundswell of native cloud-enabled SAP applications.

SAP and PaaS

With regard to SAP and PaaS, SAP's composition environment could be PaaS-enabled. More specifically, it could be hosted in such a way that the hardware, virtualization layer, operating system, database, and middleware layers are managed by a "cloud" provider. Other dimensions of the SAP development process could be similarly deployed and managed using PaaS. This aligns with the idea that PaaS offerings support developers as their primary consumers.

But what about using a PaaS platform to support existing SAP systems? Is there a scenario where PaaS might make sense? Perhaps, but SAP's vision is unclear. Not long ago, SAP purchased a PaaS provider, Coghead, that layered an Adobe development environment atop Amazon's IaaS offering, EC2. So in this respect, SAP not only supports PaaS but has the ability to provide its own take on what it means to quickly develop web-based SAP applications.

In parallel, SAP and Microsoft have been working together for several years to learn what it means to rearchitect SAP to run natively on Windows Azure and SQL Azure. And by way of example, Microsoft successfully installed the most current release of SAP ERP on Windows Azure. So yes, it can be done. But this engineering feat is better characterized for now as more of a learning exercise than mastery of what it takes to fully support current SAP applications on Azure (or any other platform offered as a service). And in truth this latest accomplishment was more of an IaaS experiment than a native PaaS victory because Azure's *virtual machine* (VM) role was used. Regardless, the exercise helped proved a point: Most any application can *in some way* be deployed in a cloud scenario or take advantage of cloud resources.

SAP and IaaS

In terms of using IaaS to support SAP business applications, the opportunities to marry SAP with cloud infrastructure are very real and very prevalent. We covered several scenarios in Hour 3, "SAP Technology Basics," related to server and disk or storage opportunities. Public cloud resources, such as Amazon's S3 and EC2 offerings, respectively, are natural fits. Keep in mind, however, that as of this writing, few vendors are SAP cloud certified providers; most cloud providers are relegated to hosting nonproduction systems only.

On the other hand, the growing number of private cloud solutions supported for SAP are not only growing but becoming widely available by a breadth of IT providers. Microsoft's Hyper-V cloud platforms offered by Dell, HP, Fujitsu, IBM, and others are one example. VMware's private cloud offering in conjunction with EMC and Cisco represents another private cloud opportunity. Other dynamically provisioned and managed cloud infrastructures are being regularly introduced by vendors such as Rackspace, AppNexus, GoGrid, Virtustream, and many others.

Virtualization Is Not Cloud Computing

Keep in mind that although virtualization might help enable cloud computing, the terms are not interchangeable, despite how the virtualization vendors might choose to advertise. In fact, virtualization is not even a necessary ingredient to the cloud; elasticity, flexibility, automated provisioning, and pay-as-you-go pricing models can all be accommodated by software-enabled bare metal (physical hardware), too. This is actually good news because so many client/server applications were never designed with virtualization in mind. Some applications work quite well virtualized, whereas others might require or perform best only through direct access to server and disk hardware. Fortunately, the benefits of cloud computing can be harnessed in either scenario.

SAP as a Service?

There is a growing mindset in the SAP customer ecosystem that SAP may be run or accessed "as a service." What does this statement mean? To potential customers looking for an SAP-as-a-Service offering, they probably envision a pay-as-you-go model for accessing SAP business applications. Many hosting providers could presumably host both the SAP application and the underlying virtualized SAP infrastructure; own and manage the IT operations and administration staff; and work out the back-end OS, database, and SAP licensing details for each business application's technology stack. A well-staffed hosting provider might even own the development and customization resources necessary to keep the application's capabilities and the customer's changing business needs in sync. In the end, the customer would ideally cut a monthly check based on the number of SAP end-users who accessed the system. Isn't this cloud computing?

Close, but no! Is it a compelling way to deliver SAP nonetheless? Perhaps. But this scenario has simply been shoe-horned into a description that at first glance *sounds* like cloud computing. In reality, it's an interesting single-customer outsourcing model at best. The scenario provides no automated provisioning, no resource elasticity based on changing workloads, nothing akin to support for multi-tenancy, and no automated patch management or platform maintenance. Everything seemingly "cloud-like" is actually handled in a manual fashion, and with these manual processes come the requisite downtime windows, inability to dynamically scale up and back down, and so on. SAP's architectural limitations combined with traditional technology platform architectures preclude creating a true SAP-as-a-Service model. The private cloud IaaS solutions outlined previously will move us closer to such a model. Despite the limitations of this kind of service delivery, however, it's again worth noting that such an approach might be desirable to a growing subset of SAP's customer base.

Today: SAP and the Cloud

Back in 2009, SAP announced a cloud strategy based on four pillars. Today, we can see what materialized from that strategy and what still remains of these four pillars as work-in-progress.

Pillar 1: Scalability

SAP spoke of immense scalability as its first building block for cloud computing. SAP has always been amazingly scalable given its tiered architecture (where the database, application server, and Internet services may be broken out into their own horizontally scalable service delivery platforms). And SAP supports customers running workloads as intense as eight million transactions an hour. So yes, the underlying platform is scalable. And that scalability will only increase as SAP pursues in-memory database technologies. But that scalability is being delivered by a platform constrained by old-world architectural paradigms rooted in client/server technologies and ATR principles.

Pillar 2: Cloud Services

Second, SAP spoke of providing its own cloud services, citing examples such as talent management and salesforce automation. This kind of approach makes sense and helps extend or modernize what can be characterized as a legacy backend SAP platform. Critics argue this is like putting paint on a crumbling building, but we disagree—it's precisely the kind of incremental innovation that's both palatable and requested by SAP's customers. And with more of these services in the works, this kind of modernization effort makes good sense.

Pillar 3: SAP Business ByDesign

The third pillar in SAP's cloud strategy is its Business ByDesign solution. Unlike its more limited competitors, SAP explains that BBD offers the only truly broad-based, fully comprehensive ERP solution on the market. As you learned in Hour 8, "The SAP Business Suite and Other SAP Applications," BBD enables a company to run its financials, manufacturing, and procurement processes, execute necessary CRM and analytics, and more—everything an SME customer needs to run the business. SAP has learned a tremendous amount about what it takes to deliver enterprise-class mission-critical business services in a true SaaS model and will presumably apply this knowledge as it updates its broader portfolio of applications.

Pillar 4: Bridging the Old and New Worlds

The fourth and arguably most transformational pillar of SAP's cloud strategy is related to tying together public cloud capabilities like those available through Amazon web services with an SAP application platform's native capabilities. This idea of bridging traditional on-premises datacenter resources with cloud resources, or marrying private cloud with public cloud, holds tremendous promise. And we can see this in action today. SAP has done a great amount of internal work with Amazon to ensure the two work together. One of SAP's cloud management projects and related toolset has also been based on this foundation. And the results are impressive, if unfortunately not ready to be shared with the world just yet.

Real-World Cloud Scenarios

So with many of today's realities in mind, let's take a closer look at several real-world cloud scenarios and how SAP may realistically take advantage of cloud computing *now*. General rules of thumb indicating that the cloud might make sense in a particular situation include the following:

- ▶ Where speed of deployment related to new systems, new functionality, or new prototyping and demonstration systems is critical

- ▶ Where the increased risks and immaturity associated with newer platforms and service providers are balanced by opportunities to significantly decrease costs or increase the promise of business agility

- ▶ When existing applications or functions are loosely coupled and therefore where a certain amount of latency is acceptable (that is, where real-time performance isn't necessary or where business processes don't span multiple applications and bolt-ons)

- ▶ Conversely, where the SAP ecosystem of infrastructure and services can be co-located in the same physical cloud-enabled data center

▶ Where applications are horizontally scalable, which naturally includes SAP but more to the point may include SAP bolt-ons

▶ Where external complexity is minimal (for example, where standard web protocols are employed, few interfaces are required, or a low level of integration is necessary)

▶ When it comes to hosting nonproduction and other supporting systems

This final point holds the most promise for enabling SAP *today* through the use of cloud computing and is explored in more detail next.

Hosting Nonproduction Systems in the Cloud

When you consider the one to five physical servers and related OS licenses, disk space, and so on required *for every single one* of your nonproduction SAP business systems, and then factor in the benefits related to rapid deployment and the ability to spin up new and wind down unnecessary assets, the potential cost savings related to hosting nonproduction systems in the cloud are tremendous. We've seen infrastructure costs drop to one-third to one-tenth the costs of traditionally hosted and internally managed systems. True, an organization might not actually want to lose the tax deductions associated with depreciating capital expenses. But the increased flexibility and employee bandwidth associated with cloud-enabling nonproduction resources can be a real asset as the economy recovers and business teams begin pushing their IT organizations to dust off all those projects shelved in the past few years.

To put the potential cost savings and other impact into perspective, consider a typical "Global 2000" company running three production SAP ERP systems (one per major geography, for example). They probably run three different *customer relationship management* (CRM) systems, a global SAP *Product Lifecycle Management* (PLM) system, and a global SAP *Software Relationship Management* (SRM) system, too. Several SAP and Microsoft data warehouses and analytics solutions are probably deployed to round out the business's reporting needs, and for historical reporting, the company probably maintains several reference systems (reflecting retired SAP or other legacy systems that need to be kept around for legal or *governance, risk management, and compliance* [GRC] reasons). All told, we could easily be looking at 12 SAP production systems.

A fantastic opportunity to reduce costs sits behind each of these 12 production systems. We might hear a lot about three-system SAP landscapes in books and at conferences, but in the real world of SAP many more systems are typically deployed over time. We tend to see anywhere from one to six of these "behind-the-scenes" nonproduction systems deployed for every production system. Common ones include staging (or preproduction) systems, multi-tiered quality-assurance systems (to better support parallel functional integration and regression testing) and development systems, several training systems (supporting different end user communities), and specialized technical sandboxes (to help the IT team work through quarterly enhancement cycles). Other technical sandboxes might be in place, too, to learn the latest products or pilot a pending functional upgrade. And the business teams might ask for any number of last minute business sandboxes to pilot new SAP solutions as they seek to develop new business capabilities. Even when we remove the various development and test/QA systems from this list (which can complicate matters related to the promote-to-production process), we are conservatively counting up a total of 30 nonproduction systems that could more flexibly and less expensively be hosted in an IaaS cloud.

Along these same lines, systems described as "standalone" may be easily transitioned to IaaS clouds, too. Reference systems maintained for historical purposes (and seldom used in reality) are excellent candidates. Pilot and *proof-of-concept* (POC) systems are too. Adding these standalone systems to the 30 already identified gives us probably 40 systems that are good candidates for the cloud. Many of these systems are small and need minimal computing resources. Many are transitional or short-lived in nature (here today, gone tomorrow). Still others support highly flexible user communities with low utilization and less-than-critical availability expectations. In other words, these systems are excellent candidates for the cloud! Hosting these systems in the cloud—whether private, public, or hybrid—can enable better levels of service, flexibility, and business agility than most of the older hosting paradigms could ever hope to deliver. And with even a marginally improved resource deployment and consumption model, combined with a pay-as-you-go pricing model, moving these nonproduction systems into the cloud can significantly reduce deployment and management costs over a 3-year to 5-year SAP lifecycle.

Tomorrow: Completely Cloudy, No Chance for Sun

What does the future hold for SAP cloud computing? To be clear, we have no proprietary knowledge beyond what SAP has publicized and what many of its customers are clamoring for. So it's hard to pinpoint much besides the fact that the cloud will continue to change how SAP systems and platforms are delivered and managed. We expect, however, that many of the changes over the next few years will be driven by SAP's mission-critical *customers*. SAP's customers will continue to demand both a new round of innovation-enabling platforms and applications and the same or better levels of platform and application maturity necessary to move their businesses to the next level. And they'll require that this innovation and maturity be delivered at minimal risk if any. For example

▶ Based on individual customer-unique risk profiles, or their appetite for risk, the maturing base of an intentional collection of well-known cloud providers will begin to be perceived by more and more companies as finally ready to host an organization's mission-critical and business-critical systems.

▶ Customers will continue to demand from cloud providers the kind of stringent SLAs that align with mission-critical systems—high reliability, great availability, markedly less planned downtime, and greater resiliency in the wake of inevitable platform and data failures.

▶ Security, safeguards, and control of critical corporate data in the cloud, as well as how privacy issues are managed and enforced, will continue to drive cloud maturity.

▶ A renewed focus by cloud providers intent on helping their customers avoid vendor lock-in will actually encourage *more* customers to move to the cloud (comfortable in the knowledge that if their decision doesn't pan out as well as they like, they could presumably pick up their data, business processes, and portable applications and drop them into another SAP-supported cloud).

▶ The most forward-thinking cloud vendors will create policy engines that allow customers to specify where data can and cannot reside, spell out their key performance indicators, and precisely address their real-time performance needs, critical batch processing do-not-exceed windows, availability requirements, workload bursting policies, service management requirements, tiered storage policies, data backup/retention policies, disaster recovery and business continuity considerations, operational priorities, and so on. In this way, a company hosted on such a cloud could be sure that its GRC mandates (such as those associated with ITAR, FDA, HIPAA, and so many others), end-user issues, and strategic concerns are properly and proactively addressed.

The key areas SAP should and will likely focus on are related to their cloud strategy and in particular pillars three and four. With greater application maturity and support for cloud-enabled workloads, combined with the ability to burst workloads into the public cloud (to address unplanned peaks or seasonal workloads), SAP will be better positioned to keep its cash cow customers happy. So expect to see SAP's relationship with the big IaaS and PaaS providers continue to grow, SAP's Adaptive Computing Controller and cloud management products to mature, and its application architecture to slowly evolve until talk of a full-blown rewrite is actually unnecessary. As mentioned several times already, the cloud groundswell is coming. A combination of economics and increased business agility make it inevitable. It's only a matter of time and maturity.

Summary

This hour commenced with an introduction to cloud computing, including information about the ideas of cloud consumers and providers. We reviewed the evolution of the cloud, looked at SOA and SAP's Enterprise SOA, in particular, as a precursor to the cloud and then investigated how SAP's current applications reflect cloud principles and can use the cloud today. A look at how SAP might continue to evolve from a cloud-enablement perspective concluded this hour.

Case Study: Hour 19

Consider this SAP cloud case study and the questions that follow. You can find the answers posed by the questions related to this case study in Appendix A, "Case Study Answers."

Situation

With pressures to reduce costs and increase business agility, MNC's entire IT organization has been tasked with reviewing opportunities to leverage cloud computing. Your SAP technical team has been scheduled to work with the CIO's new cloud steering committee, and you have been tasked with building awareness regarding the cloud and what it really means in the context of SAP. Assist the committee by answering their questions.

Questions

1. *Who are the consumers of SaaS, PaaS, and IaaS?*

2. *Of the four outlined cloud provider models, which represents the most reasonable or realistic first step toward cloud computing?*

3. *Which of SAP's applications are delivered through SaaS?*

4. *Of the first-mover cloud applications and systems outlined this hour, which ones might be most applicable to the SAP team today or soon?*

5. *What are the five SOA-inspired principles that will continue to enable SAP's journey to the cloud?*

HOUR 20

SAP System Administration and Management

What You'll Learn in This Hour:

▶ Proactive system monitoring

▶ Introduction to SAP CCMS

▶ Introduction to the SAP system logs

▶ Managing an SAP system day-to-day

Administration, maintenance, and ongoing operations of your SAP systems are crucial. Administration includes monitoring for availability, performing user administration and basic authorizations, and addressing other fundamental technical administrative functions. Management, on the other hand, is akin to controlling the system. This hour finds us covering both SAP administration and management.

Administering SAP

Administering your SAP systems is essential for good performance and to avoid surprises. SAP provides a number of easy-to-use administration tools available through the SAP *Computing Center Management System* (CCMS). These tools allow SAP administrators to monitor and manage SAP's overall health, application server performance, the database server, user and batch job performance, print jobs, and more.

System Status (SICK)

As part of your daily routine, run /nSICK to verify the overall system remains healthy. Although it's an exceedingly simple "system status" transaction, it's equally useful to validate that SAP's foundation remains sound (see Figure 20.1).

FIGURE 20.1
SICK verifies
the SAP founda-
tion is sound.

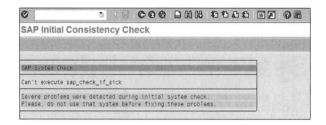

Monitoring Application Servers (SM51)

System monitoring designed to ensure the availability of SAP to its end users is a primary function of the system administrator. In the course of system monitoring, the system administrator watches over the running (active) SAP instances and their services,
looking to ensure that these resources are indeed "up" and available (see Figure 20.2).

FIGURE 20.2
SM51 monitor-
ing needs to be
performed regu-
larly by an SAP
system admin-
istrator.

You can view the SAP Servers System Monitoring screen following the menu path
Tools, **Administration**, **Monitor**, **System Monitoring**, **Servers** or by running transaction code /nSM51. This screen displays all available instances in your SAP system,
including the core services (hosted by specialized work processes) provided by each
instance—services earmarked for online users, batch jobs, performing database updates,
and so on.

By the
Way

> Remember that SAP provides three different SAP NetWeaver application servers:
> ABAP, Java, and ABAP + Java. If the J2EE service is running alongside the tradi-
> tional ABAP services (as shown in Figure 20.2), the application server reflects a
> dual-stack environment running both ABAP and Java.

Workload Distribution (SM50 and SM66)

You can use SM50 to view the status of all work processes of a specific application server. For example, many administrators review the following:

▶ The number of active work processes versus the number configured (particularly dialog, batch, and update work processes).

▶ How many dialog work processes indicate they've never been used (one or
more work processes reflecting zero time used indicates that the application

server has available bandwidth). Several "never-used" work processes is a good rule-of-thumb metric.

▶ Similarly, ensure that your batch, update, and print work processes have available bandwidth too.

▶ Review what the active work processes are doing by scrolling to the right and reviewing each work process's status. For example, a work process that displays "load report" might indicate that the application server's program buffer is fragmented.

Unlike SM50, SM66 displays a real-time snapshot of only active work processes. Further, SM66 displays system-wide work processes rather than just the work processes associated with a single application server. Administrators often compare the number of active work process "lines" or "screens" to get a sense of the system's work load. For example, your system might average 20 or so active work processes (each of which are displayed as a line in SM66) during the middle of a typical day. Anything less could be construed as a quiet day, whereas a whole lot more might be seen as a really busy day.

Reviewing SAP System Logs (SM21)

SAP maintains system logs that record important events that occur in your SAP system. Which system log and which tool to use to display the events depends on whether the SAP NetWeaver application server consists of the ABAP, Java, or ABAP + Java stack.

System Log for ABAP Stack

You can view the SAP System Log screen by executing transaction /nSM21. The selection screen that appears—similar to the one shown in Figure 20.3—enables the system administrator to sift through and select certain criteria from what can ultimately be a very large and complex log of events and occurrences.

After identifying key search criteria such as dates, user IDs, and so on, the administrator then clicks the **Reread System Log** button to generate the specified subset of the entire log. Figure 20.4 illustrates an abbreviated log.

System Log for Java Stack

SAP provides several different Log Viewers to display events. The Visual Administrator, for example, offers the Integrated Log Viewer. Logs written from the J2EE engine and all applications running on that particular J2EE engine are automatically registered in the Integrated Log Viewer and can be displayed by following the menu path **Cluster**, **Server**, **Services**, **Log Viewer**.

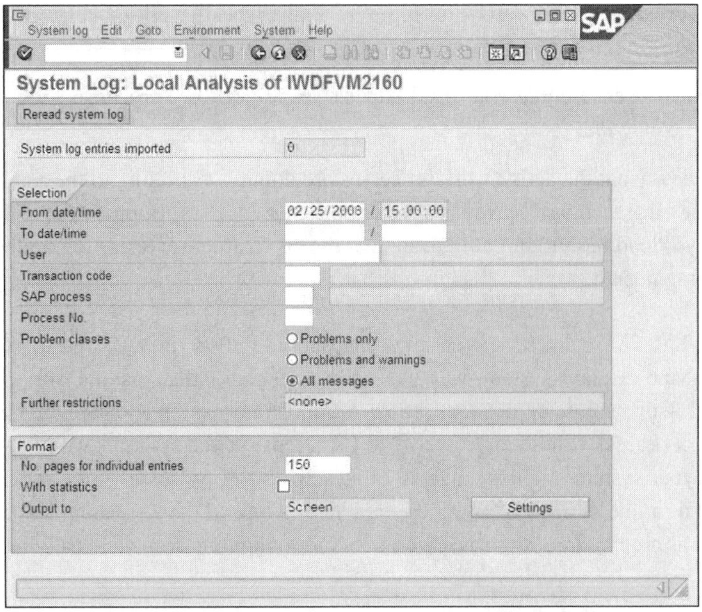

FIGURE 20.3
You can specify
certain system
criteria to be
displayed on
your system log
by using the
System Log:
Local Analysis
screen.

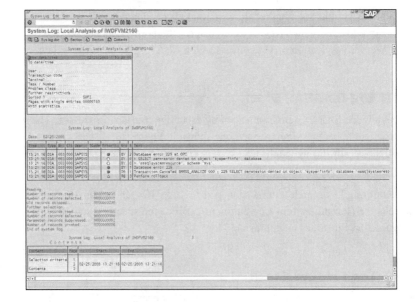

FIGURE 20.4
After specifying
specific selec-
tion criteria, you
can display a
subset of the
SAP system
log.

Displaying Logs and Traces

Another tool to display events is the SAP NetWeaver Administrator. This Web Dynpro-
based tool offers, among other administration and monitoring capabilities, a central

access point for logs and traces generated from local SAP systems and the entire SAP NetWeaver system landscape. The Logs and Traces component of the SAP NetWeaver Administrator can be easily accessed following the menu path **System Management, Monitoring, Logs and Traces** (see Figure 20.5).

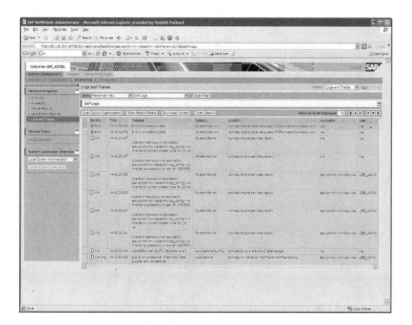

FIGURE 20.5
The SAP NetWeaver Administrator provides several predefined views or filters for displaying logs and traces. Here, the chosen view is SAP Logs.

Reviewing the Alert Monitor (RZ20)

One of the CCMS tools is SAP's Alert Monitor. It provides an entry point to the CCMS system repository, the database that stores data about your SAP system. A capable and customizable tool, SAP's Alert Monitor features the following:

▶ Comprehensive, detailed status of any number of SAP systems, host interfaces, underlying database and OS layers, and more.

▶ Easy-to-read color-coded status indicators (green, yellow, and red) for all your SAP components, interfaces, and so on.

▶ Proactive alerts, based on whether the threshold of a particular status indicator has been exceeded.

▶ Analysis and autoreaction methods can be assigned to alerts such as reports, SAP transactions, function modules, and more.

▶ Monitor sets, monitors, thresholds, and more can be customized to your needs.

By the Way

It might make sense to declare one CCMS environment as the *central monitoring system* (CEN) for all SAP system landscapes in your firm. The monitoring architecture of the CEN allows you to gather and, with the Alert Monitor, display all available alerts of SAP ABAP, Java, dual-stack, standalone components, and non-SAP components in one CCMS environment.

Spend time getting comfortable with the Alert Monitor—it is powerful, capable, and free (in the sense that it's paid for with the purchase of the SAP license). To use this tool, follow the menu path **Tools, CCMS, Control/Monitoring, CCMS Monitor Sets**, or execute transaction /nRZ20. Figure 20.6 shows an example of an Alert Monitor screen.

FIGURE 20.6
The RZ20 Alert Monitor can display and monitor the status of multiple SAP functions and parameters.

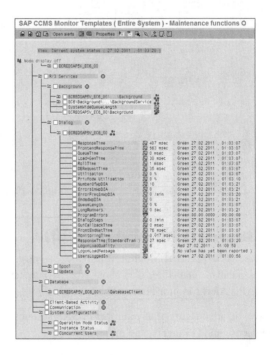

Managing the SAP System

In addition to the SAP CCMS transactions used to administer or monitor the system, CCMS includes several transactions geared toward managing or controlling the system. Several of the most common are outlined next.

Database Management (DBA Cockpit, DB02, SM12, SM13)

Formerly accessed through ST04 and several other database-related SAP CCMS transactions, the DBA Cockpit (run /nDBACockpit) lets you review the database's most critical attributes and performance statistics (see Figure 20.7):

▶ Data cache:Ensure this is 95% or greater.

▶ Procedure cache:Ensure this is 95% or greater.

▶ Physical reads and physical writes:Reads should be 15 to 20x greater than writes (a change in mix might help explain the system's performance); typically 94% or more of all I/Os will be reads.

▶ The ratio of direct to sequential reads:This is also valuable in that different reads affect the disk subsystem differently.

▶ Busy waits:Indicates when an Oracle block is being read into the buffer cache by a session which in turn is waiting on another session.

▶ Ratio of user calls to recursive calls:A 10 to 1 ratio is good, and 3 to 1 is sometimes considered "worst case."

▶ Expensive SQL:Buffer gets should not exceed 5% of total reads. (Click **Detail Analysis**, **SQL Requests**, **Buffer Gets**.)

▶ Review the database's error logs (underneath the Diagnostics tab):

    ▶ Database Calls (those that hit the DB directly; a "bad" number)

    ▶ Database Requests (those that hit DB buffers; a "good" number)

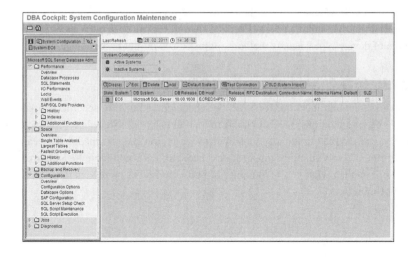

FIGURE 20.7
The DBA Cockpit provides insight into the database's performance, space statistics, configuration, and more.

In addition, run /nDB02 on occasion to review the database in real time. For example, you can review the total space actually used by the database (versus the space allocated for the database), the mix of tables to indexes, and the number of missing tables or indexes. Reviewing DB02 over time lets you perform an apples-to-apples DB-specific comparison to watch over the growth of high-use tables like MSEG, GLPCA, COPA, and MARA.

Finally, run /nSM12 on a regular basis to review the database's lock entries and /nSM13 to display real-time database update activity. Understanding how quickly database updates are committed to the database (and whether lock entries are holding things up) helps a database administrator explain overall database and disk subsystem performance.

Print Management (SPAD)

Verify the SAP print management function works by running /nSPAD (see Figure 20.8). This enables you to execute an SAP spool installation check.

FIGURE 20.8
Use SPAD to view the print spool adminis-tration screen.

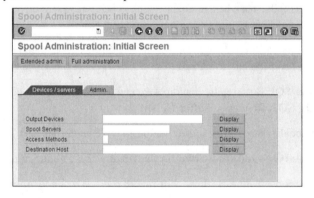

From the main SPAD menu, click the **Configuration** drop-down, click the **Check Installation** button, and then press **F8**. As shown in Figure 20.9, each spool is checked in terms of device types, access methods, unprocessed output requests, and more.

Batch Job Management (SM37)

The SAP system administrator (or SAP job scheduler, or function-specific job special-ists in large organizations) needs to confirm that all batch jobs have been completed suc-cessfully. Run /nSM37 to identify jobs by name, user, job status (scheduled, released, ready to run, actively running, finished, or cancelled), date, and more (see Figure 20.10). After you establish what you're looking for, press the **F8** button to generate and review the list of jobs.

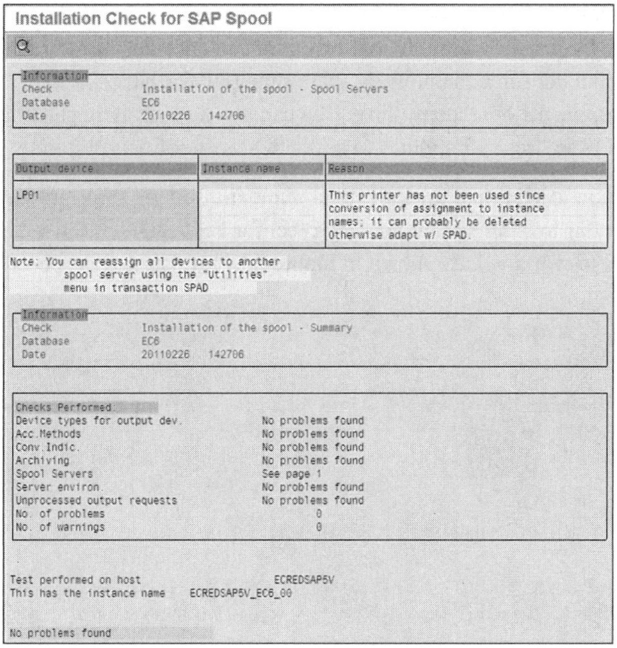

FIGURE 20.9
SPAD can verify the spool system is problem-free.

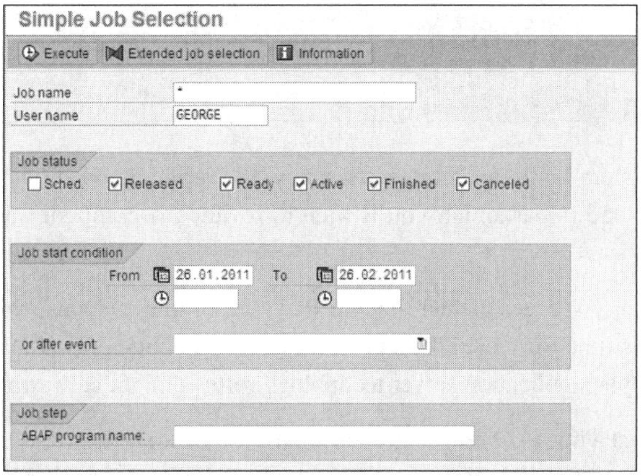

FIGURE 20.10
Manage jobs using SM37.

SAP Workload/Performance Management (ST03)

The SAP Workload Monitor (also called the SAP Transaction Monitor) is a long-time favorite of SAP Basis teams. Reviewing a system's unique workload is one of the most important components of performance management. Execute the Workload Monitor by running /nST03 or /nST03N. This enables you to display your SAP workload in total or organized by dialog, batch, update, and other work process types.

Select the work process type and then click the **Transaction Profile** button. From here, sort the results by response time. In this way, you can analyze your top transactions— the programs that consume the most database time (DB Request Time), CPU time, and other core components of response time. You can also look at aggregate totals over various periods of time, from 15 minutes to a month's worth of data at a time.

It's also common to view and track the total number of dialog steps processed each day, broken down hour by hour so that you get a feel for how each hour in a day holds up when it comes to workload. As shown in Figure 20.11, this proves especially useful

FIGURE 20.11
Among other functions, use ST03 to review online user workload and response-time metrics.

Instance	Dialog steps	Av.resp. time(ms)	Avg CPU time(ms)	Avg wait time(ms)	Avg load time(ms)	Av.DB rq time(ms)	Avg DB requests	Av. phys DB calls	Avg Kbyte requested
TOTAL	3,262,673	1,244	78	362	4	478	822.3	48.7	83.8
prams_PRA_02	66,587	1,071	235	4	18	588	317.6	39.7	312.8
pr1ap009_PRA_10	326,655	744	56	170	3	349	369.3	31.2	53.3
pr1ap010_PRA_10	236,635	1,009	114	82	6	493	410.4	50.0	71.6
pr1ap011_PRA_10	257,683	1,230	96	358	4	501	448.6	50.0	71.4
pr1ap012_PRA_10	208,576	847	99	28	2	457	417.5	68.2	85.2
pr1ap013_PRA_10	255,080	1,365	100	370	6	523	462.6	75.1	91.4
pr1ap015_PRA_10	125,189	1,087	23	27	0	424	118.3	30.1	101.7
pr1ap016_PRA_10	29,989	1,299	50	434	3	497	279.6	41.4	68.8
pr1ap017_PRA_10	21,763	1,323	52	307	4	696	367.2	37.6	71.2
pr1ap018_PRA_10	32,767	1,353	55	451	5	514	284.6	35.4	37.8
pr1ap019_PRA_10	32,711	1,265	67	262	3	640	343.0	61.9	86.0
pr1ap020_PRA_10	24,219	1,633	83	197	7	894	435.5	73.4	141.3
pr1ap021_PRA_10	31,491	1,070	51	155	11	562	307.0	30.5	62.4
pr1ap022_PRA_10	31,177	1,220	59	298	5	426	290.6	50.2	143.5
pr1ap023_PRA_10	38,817	1,145	88	141	4	598	481.4	54.8	141.0
pr1ap024_PRA_10	31,598	2,159	57	1,342	4	411	272.7	47.9	102.6
pr1ap025_PRA_10	26,589	1,696	91	694	5	580	520.8	69.8	104.3
pr1ap026_PRA_10	25,583	3,549	61	2,299	16	500	321.5	45.0	112.9
pr1ap027_PRA_10	27,432	1,250	58	313	11	477	332.8	36.9	34.1
pr1ap028_PRA_10	29,305	1,164	71	275	5	608	401.5	82.0	102.9
pr1ap029_PRA_10	20,337	2,664	63	1,431	5	577	328.8	42.0	156.4
pr1ap030_PRA_10	20,930	2,367	57	1,229	5	620	337.9	49.6	66.1
pr1ap031_PRA_10	27,672	1,161	50	138	6	577	324.6	39.9	90.9
pr1ap032_PRA_10	28,563	1,413	58	488	12	598	345.1	44.7	57.8
pr1ap033_PRA_10	28,389	1,962	50	956	3	398	297.5	31.9	113.9

Selected task type is   DIALOG
Summary of average workload

when an SAP system landscape comprises many SAP application servers. For dialog user-based workload in particular, you'll want to review the components of online user response time:

▶ CPU Time—Averages greater than 30% to 40% of total response time might indicate it's time for more CPUs or faster CPUs. Adding application servers or performing an application server technology refresh might be warranted as well.

▶ DB Request Time—Averages greater than 40% of total response time can indicate it's time to redo indexes, redistribute the workload, or consider upgrading the disk subsystem.

▶ Wait Time—Anything over 20ms is high. A high wait time can indicate there's not enough work processes to process the workload.

▶ Load Time—When load time exceeds 10% of total response time, it could indicate that the SAP application server's buffers are too small or fragmented, that the database is missing indices, or simply that the system load is unusually heavy.

▶ Network/Missing Time—Monitor the remaining missing time to ensure it doesn't grow over time. Such a situation might indicate a poorly performing network or increasingly inefficient SAP roll/lock mechanism, for example.

▶ Front-End (SAPGUI) Time—If more than 100ms, the front-end client devices might benefit from a technology refresh or component upgrade.

Beyond pure response time metrics, the Time Profile and Transaction Profile buttons available from ST03 enable you to quantify a system's load over a particular time period, or based on a particular work load. The top transactions responsible for placing the most load on a certain hardware component are easily identified in this way, too, as discussed in previous chapters. And with the ability to aggregate data at an "application" level, you can validate after a test run that the run indeed emulated the correct mix of functional workload desired from the beginning (something akin to a "historical" ST07).

Run /nST03G to view and analyze the load associated with external systems such as J2EE engines, older Internet Transaction Servers, and more. ST03G also provides the ability to analyze the performance of systems underpinning business processes that span multiple systems. For SAP IT organizations responsible for managing multiple systems, ST03G is a good tool to add to the SAP Basis team's toolbox.

SAP Computing Platform (ST06)

ST06, the Operating System Monitor, is ideal for analyzing the performance of the entire SAP technology stack. Much of this analysis occurs server by server because there's no real-time roll-up mechanism within SAP CCMS. Use ST06 to review the following on a regular basis, keeping in mind that you can glean all this information from the operating system's statistics, as well:

▶ CPU User Utilization—Add to CPU system utilization to get a sense of overall CPU utilization.

▶ CPU System Utilization—Add to CPU user utilization to get a sense of overall CPU utilization.

▶ CPU Idle—Time spent doing nothing.

▶ Load Average—The number of processes waiting for CPU time should be an average of three or lower.

▶ Physical Memory Available versus Physical Memory Free—Self-explanatory.

▶ Pages in/second—For Windows systems, this number should be relatively low, preferably zero.

▶ Pages out/second—For Unix systems, this number should be zero.

As you see in Figure 20.12, ST06 displays real-time performance data: CPU utilization broken down by user, system, and idle, the CPU load count at 1-, 5-, and 15-minute intervals, current-state memory/swap metrics, and so on. However, ST06 is special in that you can access historical data, too. Click the **Detail Analysis Menu** button to view a breakdown of historical data across all major hardware subsystems. This includes not only detailed data encompassing the last 24 hours (under the section "Previous Hours"), but also longer-term data housed in the SAP Performance database.

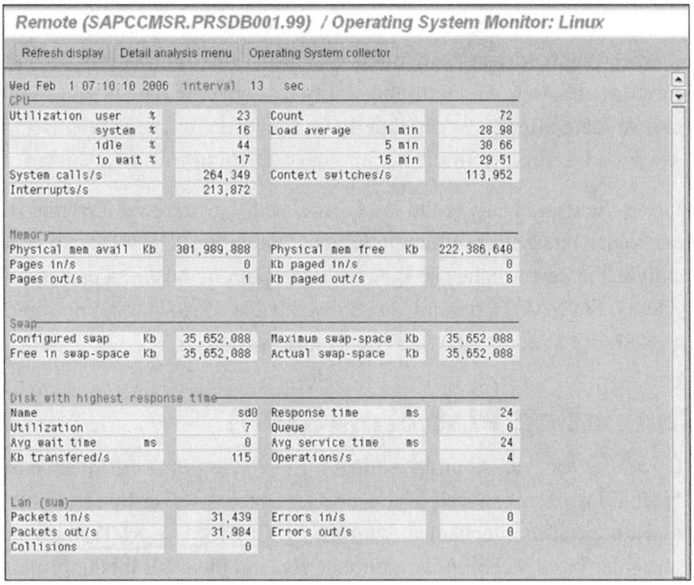

FIGURE 20.12
The ST06 Operating System Monitor details real-time SAP application server performance.

```
Remote (SAPCCMSR.PRSDB001.99) / Operating System Monitor: Linux

 Refresh display   Detail analysis menu   Operating System collector

Wed Feb  1 07:10:10 2006  interval  13  sec
CPU
Utilization  user    %          23    Count                          72
             system  %          16    Load average    1 min       28.98
             idle    %          44                    5 min       30.66
             io wait %          17                   15 min       29.51
System calls/s             264,349    Context switches/s        113,952
Interrupts/s               213,872

Memory
Physical mem avail  Kb  301,989,888   Physical mem free  Kb  222,386,640
Pages in/s                        0   Kb paged in/s                    0
Pages out/s                       1   Kb paged out/s                   8

Swap
Configured swap     Kb   35,652,088   Maximum swap-space  Kb   35,652,088
Free in swap-space  Kb   35,652,088   Actual swap-space   Kb   35,652,088

Disk with highest response time
Name                           sd0    Response time      ms           24
Utilization                      7    Queue                           0
Avg wait time      ms            0    Avg service time   ms           24
Kb transfered/s                115    Operations/s                     4

Lan (sum)
Packets in/s                31,439    Errors in/s                      0
Packets out/s               31,984    Errors out/s                     0
Collisions                       0
```

Application Server Load (SMLG, AL08, and ST07)

SMLG monitors how many users are logged on to each application server and how well SAP's logon load-balancing mechanism is working. SAP uses a "quality" metric to indicate how well the application server is performing. Press **F5** to drill down into logon group-specific performance data (see Figure 20.13).

You use SMLG to change logon groups, too. For example, if the SAP *Enterprise Resource Planning* (ERP) Finance logon group seems to be constantly saturated with so many users that the group's overall performance suffers, the SAP administrator can work with the server infrastructure team to deploy a new application server and add it to the Finance group. In this way, the users could be distributed over a greater number of servers and work processes.

Several other SAP transactions are used to monitor application server user load. Run /nAL08 to review a real-time summary of end users (called interact users, meaning interactive users) organized by application server. RFC users are also included (see Figure 20.14). By paging down the list, you may also view the details associated with each application user. For example, AL08 displays every end user logged on to SAP, along with the transactions he or she is currently executing.

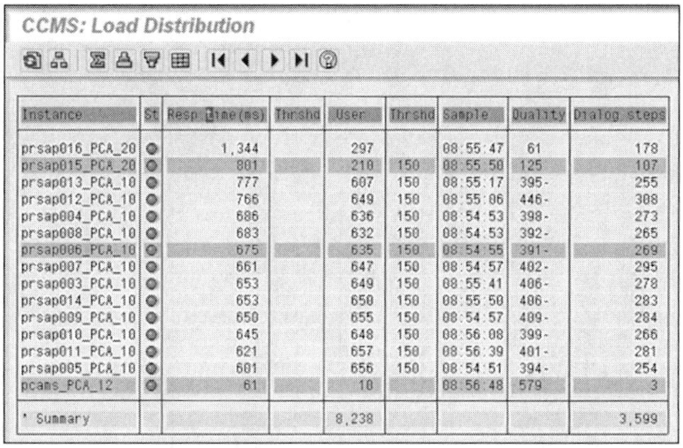

FIGURE 20.13
Use SMLG to review how well the system is performing online user logon load balancing.

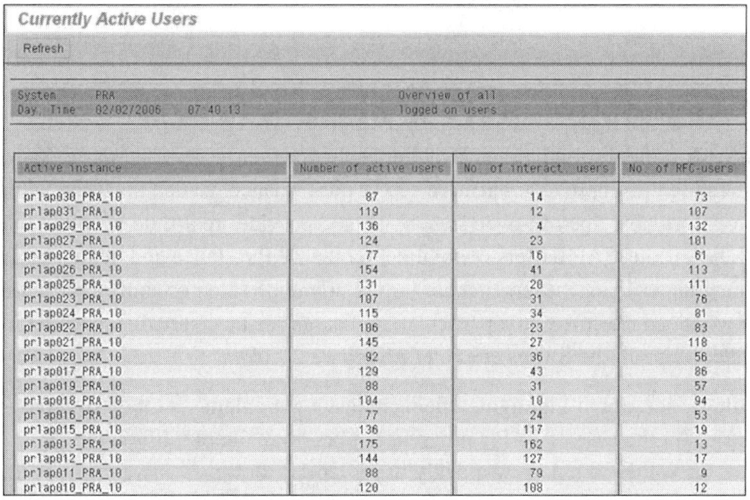

```
CCMS: Load Distribution
```

Instance	St	Resp.time(ms)	Thrshd	User	Thrshd	Sample	Quality	Dialog steps
prsap016_PCA_20	◉	1,344		297		08:55:47	61	178
prsap015_PCA_20	◉	801		210	150	08:55:50	125	107
prsap013_PCA_10	◉	777		607	150	08:55:17	395-	255
prsap012_PCA_10	◉	766		649	150	08:55:06	446-	308
prsap004_PCA_10	◉	686		636	150	08:54:53	398-	273
prsap008_PCA_10	◉	683		632	150	08:54:53	392-	265
prsap006_PCA_10	◉	675		635	150	08:54:55	391-	269
prsap007_PCA_10	◉	661		647	150	08:54:57	402-	295
prsap003_PCA_10	◉	653		649	150	08:55:41	406-	278
prsap014_PCA_10	◉	653		650	150	08:55:50	406-	283
prsap009_PCA_10	◉	650		655	150	08:54:57	409-	284
prsap010_PCA_10	◉	645		648	150	08:56:08	399-	266
prsap011_PCA_10	◉	621		657	150	08:56:39	401-	281
prsap005_PCA_10	◉	601		656	150	08:54:51	394-	254
pcams_PCA_12	◉	61		10		08:56:48	579	3
* Summary				8,238				3,599

FIGURE 20.14
Use AL08 to review specific users and transactions running on specific application servers.

```
Currently Active Users
Refresh
```

System   PRA
Day, Time   02/02/2006   07:40:13

Overview of all
logged on users

Active instance	Number of active users	No. of interact. users	No. of RFC-users
prlap030_PRA_10	87	14	73
prlap031_PRA_10	119	12	107
prlap029_PRA_10	136	4	132
prlap027_PRA_10	124	23	101
prlap028_PRA_10	77	16	61
prlap026_PRA_10	154	41	113
prlap025_PRA_10	131	20	111
prlap023_PRA_10	107	31	76
prlap024_PRA_10	115	34	81
prlap022_PRA_10	106	23	83
prlap021_PRA_10	145	27	118
prlap020_PRA_10	92	36	56
prlap017_PRA_10	129	43	86
prlap019_PRA_10	88	31	57
prlap018_PRA_10	104	10	94
prlap016_PRA_10	77	24	53
prlap015_PRA_10	136	117	19
prlap013_PRA_10	175	162	13
prlap012_PRA_10	144	127	17
prlap011_PRA_10	88	79	9
prlap010_PRA_10	120	108	12

A similar transaction is also useful for reviewing end users logged on to the system. ST07 also displays the total number of dialog steps processed. ST07 sorts users by SAP functional areas (such as SAP ERP FI, MM, PM, PS, SD, and so on), though, rather than by application servers as AL08 does.

Unlike AL08, an SAP administrator can also run /nST07 to drill down into historical data. For example, use ST07 to review the number of dialog steps processed every day, week, or month divided by functional area, the average response times associated with each area's transactions, and so on (see Figure 20.15).

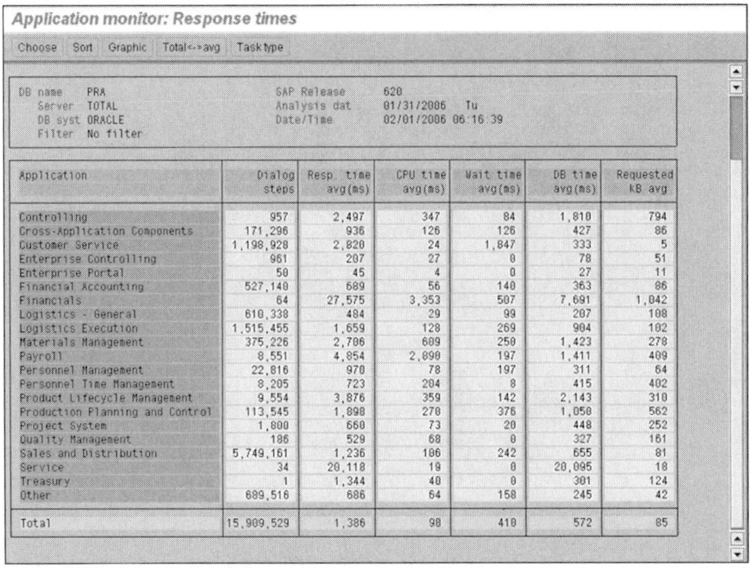

Application	Dialog steps	Resp. time avg(ms)	CPU time avg(ms)	Wait time avg(ms)	DB time avg(ms)	Requested kB avg
Controlling	957	2,497	347	84	1,810	794
Cross-Application Components	171,296	936	126	126	427	86
Customer Service	1,198,928	2,820	24	1,847	333	5
Enterprise Controlling	961	207	27	0	78	51
Enterprise Portal	50	45	4	0	27	11
Financial Accounting	527,140	689	56	140	363	86
Financials	64	27,575	3,353	507	7,691	1,042
Logistics - General	610,338	484	29	99	207	108
Logistics Execution	1,515,455	1,659	128	269	904	102
Materials Management	375,226	2,706	609	250	1,423	278
Payroll	8,551	4,854	2,890	197	1,411	409
Personnel Management	22,816	970	78	197	311	64
Personnel Time Management	8,205	723	204	8	415	402
Product Lifecycle Management	9,554	3,876	359	142	2,143	310
Production Planning and Control	113,545	1,898	270	376	1,050	562
Project System	1,800	660	73	20	448	252
Quality Management	186	529	68	0	327	161
Sales and Distribution	5,749,161	1,236	106	242	655	81
Service	34	20,118	19	0	20,095	18
Treasury	1	1,344	40	0	301	124
Other	689,516	686	64	158	245	42
Total	15,909,529	1,386	98	410	572	85

FIGURE 20.15
The ST07 Application Monitor breaks down workload by application or functional area.

SAP Application Server Buffers (ST02)

Run /nST02 to monitor individual SAP application server buffers and more. Various buffers are used to improve application server performance. Called the Tune Summary (or more informally "the red swap screen"), ST02 provides real-time visibility into how well all the various SAP buffers configured via the SAP instance and default profiles are performing under load. Buffers that are improperly configured or simply not optimal for a given workload executed on a particular application instance are displayed with a red-highlighted value in the Swaps column (see Figure 20.16).

Interestingly, not all red-highlighted fields indicate a problem—a bit of swapping is quite normal in the case of SAP's program buffers, for example. If you tend to see a lot of red, or the values in red grow quickly day after day, however, increasing specific SAP buffer sizes could increase overall system performance. Check historical trends using the Detail Analysis Menu button from the ST02 main screen.

Beyond buffers, use ST02 to also track the size and utilization of each SAP application server's roll area, paging area, extended memory, and heap memory (the latter of which needs to be as small as possible). By bringing together the data shown in ST02 with ST06, ST03, and other data, it's possible to conduct application server-specific capacity planning.

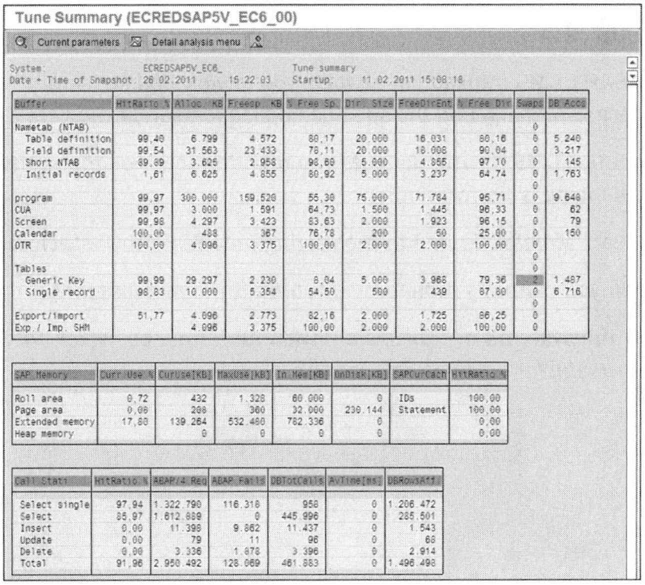

FIGURE 20.16
The ST02 Tune Summary enables you to view real-time and historical SAP buffer statistics.

Summary

Proactive SAP system administration and management are key to maintaining a highly available and well-performing system. Therefore, system administration in the broadest sense cannot exist in a vacuum; it must be tied to tools and approaches that facilitate proactive maintenance and management by exception. SAP's very own CCMS represents an ideal starting point for such system administration and management tasks. This hour provided insight into only a few of the many tools and techniques used by SAP IT professionals to administrator and manage SAP.

Case Study: Hour 20

Consider this SAP system administration and management case study and the questions that follow. You can find the answers posed by the questions related to this case study in Appendix A, "Case Study Answers."

Situation

MNC's SAP environment has been growing and consists now of about 50 different SAP instances. Part of your team's responsibilities is to monitor proactively the entire SAP environment, particularly the SAP ERP ECC 6.0 dual-stack environment along with MNC's latest addition, an Enterprise Portal (Java only) system landscape.

Questions

1. Which SAP CCMS transaction enables you to view online users, the transactions they're running, and the specific application server they are logged on to?

2. Which SAP CCMS transaction lets you monitor how well the system's logon load balancing is performing?

3. Is the Alert Monitor limited to monitoring only SAP ABAP stack instances?

4. How can you centrally monitor your entire SAP environment?

5. To view the system's overall system-wide performance, which RZ transaction is most useful?

HOUR 21

SAP Enhancements, Upgrades, and More

What You'll Learn in This Hour:

- ▶ The three most common types of SAP system updates
- ▶ The significance of enhancements
- ▶ Upgrade and enhancement terminology
- ▶ Differences between technical and functional upgrades
- ▶ Avoiding confusing upgrades and migrations
- ▶ Upgrade project requirements

Despite how well an SAP system might be running, it'll eventually need to be updated. Keeping up with minimally required technology changes and "inevitable, if only minor" business functionality requests make updating SAP mandatory. Most SAP systems after they've finally gone "live" are updated monthly or quarterly in one way or another. These updates come in the form of what SAP terms *enhancements*, *upgrades*, and *technology stack updates*, topics we cover this hour.

Setting the Stage: Making Changes to SAP

In the world of SAP, systems are changed or *updated* fairly regularly. The nature of these updates can vary tremendously, though. The SAP and infrastructure technical teams update the technology stack on a fairly regular basis, for example:

- ▶ Server system boards and disk controllers require firmware updates every now and then to fix bugs or support new hardware options.

▶ New and faster network cards, disk controllers, disk drives, and so on are updated every few years.

▶ Operating systems and database software require patches and other updates in response to bug fixes or to protect against virus and other potential threats.

Beyond technology updates, the various business teams put in requests to change or add business functionality:

▶ The finance team might need updates made in SAP *Enterprise Resource Planning's* (ERP's) Finance module to adhere to a new accounting principle or to help close the monthly books faster.

▶ In response to new federal and state regulations, the logistics team might request updates in how international trade is conducted or accounted for.

▶ A power user in the warehouse group might seek to make several updates in a transaction's screen layout to make it easier for new hires to manage inventory and storage locations.

The word *update* is used in other specific ways, making its generic use earlier pretty confusing. To make matters worse, people toss around many other words that also imply changing SAP. In the case of non-ERP SAP components and applications, major business updates come in the form of upgrades, for example. In the case of SAP *Enterprise Resource Planning* (ERP), business updates are delivered more incrementally through SAP's *enhancement packages* (EHP). And in other cases, systems and data are migrated. How to correctly use these terms and what they mean are the subjects of this hour.

Enhancement and Upgrade Terminology

A discussion of terminology is in order before we go further. There are many similar and therefore confusing terms when it comes to making changes to a live SAP environment, especially when it comes to changing SAP. The terms *migration* and *upgrade* are misused quite often, while the general term *enhancement* is simply misunderstood. Let's turn to enhancements first.

Enhancements Explained

In general, SAP enhancements are modifications or updates to existing SAP systems; they modify or extend current functionality. After your organization has "gone live" with SAP, you might be inclined to think all the real work in terms of developing and maintaining functionality has been done and little follow-on work remains. To some extent, this is true for the IT team; the stress of implementation and late-into-the-night testing will be replaced with steady-state maintenance, occasional technology stack patches, and so on.

For the business analysts and development teams tasked with representing the business and its needs, however, much work remains to be done well after go-live. After all, the business will continue to evolve, and new functional needs will come to light in the wake of these changes. Even more common, bug fixes and other updates to existing business processes need to be tested and introduced, as well. This is where enhancement planning pays great dividends for the organization.

Enhancements can be SAP-driven (such as those done through SAP support packages) or customer-driven (meaning they are developed in-house and transported through the SAP landscape). Enhancements in many cases can represent a combination of updates, too. For instance, to enhance a current financial business process, an organization might need to update the technical system's Basis layer to a required support package level and then make subsequent custom modifications to adapt the new functionality to an SAP system's specific business process.

Enhancements can also be delivered through specific SAP EHPs. EHPs are prepackaged collections of business functionality that act as a "mini upgrade" to the core SAP system's functionality. EHPs differ from support packages in that they add functionality on top of the SAP application stack instead of providing it through modifying existing functionality. Surprisingly, SAP makes it possible to install EHPs without impacting the system; no downtime is required to actually implement them. However, to actually make the enhancements or changes to the system, they must be activated in the SAP *Implementation Guide* (IMG; see Hour 17, "A Developer's Perspective on SAP," for a discussion of the IMG). In this way, through EHPs, SAP customers have the ability to modularly upgrade functionality. Although EHPs can extend the product lifecycle for a season (for SAP ERP systems), there will come a time when an upgrade will indeed be necessary, which leads us to our next discussion.

Upgrade Terminology

The term *upgrade* is confusing only because the term is so general. The key is to ask what is actually being changed or "upgraded." Are we talking about an SAP server hardware upgrade, an *operating system* (OS) upgrade, an Oracle or SQL Server database upgrade, an SAP kernel upgrade, an SAP support pack upgrade, or a full-blown SAP functional release or version upgrade? As you learned earlier, most of these examples fall under the realm of "technology updates" and have nothing to do with upgrading SAP. When using the term *upgrade*, be as specific and detailed as possible to avoid confusion. When upgrading non-SAP components in the SAP landscape, it is okay to say, "We are upgrading our SAP servers," or "We are upgrading the database to SQL Server 2008 R2." However, it's preferable to talk of updating rather than upgrading these technology stack components.

Talk of doing an SAP upgrade really means upgrading SAP itself. This might mean you're upgrading the functionality of the SAP system—performing an SAP functional upgrade. Such a change is a major undertaking, nearly akin to doing a new implementation. On the other hand, the technical team might speak of performing an SAP *technical* upgrade. As mentioned, this is an upgrade to the Basis layer underpinning the SAP application; no functionality is changed or even touched in an SAP technical upgrade. Technical upgrades equate to updating the SAP kernel (replacing old files with new ones) along with perhaps some other updates to the technology stack (necessary for support reasons because not every SAP Basis release is supported by every operating system version or hardware platform, for example). Suffice it to say here, therefore, that it is important to communicate properly about the scope and magnitude of an SAP upgrade, if only to keep everyone on the same page.

Upgrades Are Not Migrations

Because the term *migration* is often thrown about interchangeably with the term *upgrade* (they mean completely different things in the world of SAP), it's necessary to differentiate between the two. Figure 21.1 properly aligns these terms. Even longtime SAP customers talk inaccurately about "migrating" their SAP ERP systems to SAP ERP 6.0 or "migrating" SAP *Customer Relationship Management* (CRM) to the latest functional release. These statements are incorrect.

FIGURE 21.1
In the world of SAP, the terms upgrade, migration, and update are not interchangeable.

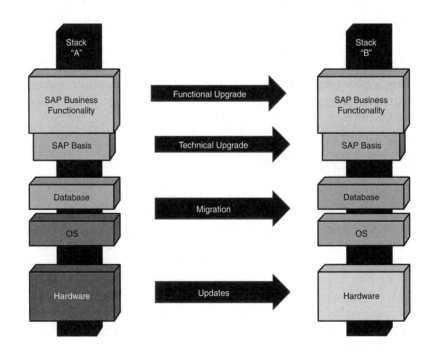

What's more, SAP has released a tool called *Test Data Migration Server* (TDMS), which has nothing to do with traditional migrations but rather is more aligned with copy functionality. (Specifically, TDMS allows SAP customers to essentially copy a portion of an SAP database and build a new system around the smaller, condensed database, thus enabling rapid prototyping for new projects.) With TDMS, the term *migration* takes on yet another new meaning. TDMS enables data migration, such as helping to move data from a non-SAP system, such as Oracle PeopleSoft, into an SAP system. TDMS also facilitates moving data *between* SAP systems in the form of partial or full client copies. These types of projects are labeled a SAP data migration.

Again, it is for all these reasons that we find it necessary to differentiate between different types of migrations. In SAP vernacular, *migration* is most correctly associated with technology platform changes. These are properly labeled as *OS/DB migrations* (operating system/database migrations). An OS/DB migration is required when a customer's IT department decides to move the SAP computing platform from one operating system or database platform to a different operating system or database platform. Such a move is a complex endeavor that requires the services of a properly certified OS/DB migration specialist. And such migrations have nothing to do with upgrades. In fact, in a migration, the functional release level remains static; it's not even an option to perform an upgrade concurrently with an OS/DB migration.

SAP OS/DB Migrations

An SAP OS/DB migration may be conducted to change platforms between different flavors of UNIX, Linux, and Windows. It is also conducted to move between different database platforms, such as from Oracle to DB2 or SQL Server. The problem an OS/DB migration solves is that operating systems are not "binary compatible" with one another (meaning the SAP system's database data files cannot just be copied from one platform to a new platform). Similarly, a change of database vendors requires reloading the SAP data into the new database—you can't move data files recognized by IBM DB2 to a system running Microsoft SQL Server without unloading the data into a generic format and then reloading it into the new database's format.

Sometimes you'll hear the term *heterogeneous system copy* also used to describe an OS/DB migration, as opposed to its cousin the *homogenous system copy* (where the OS or DB platform does not change). Regardless, customers execute OS/DB migrations for a few different reasons. One of the primary reasons is cost. The cost of running SAP on an older version of one of the big UNIX platforms can be tremendous. When these big UNIX boxes are out of support, a customer is required to pay handsome support costs. Another big cost factor tends to be outsourcing. For some customers, it can make sense to outsource their SAP environment to one of the many hosting providers. However, other shops are better suited to support SAP in-house. Very infrequently, an IT organization might determine that the platform underpinning SAP requires a fundamental computing platform change, particularly if the potential for greater business application innovation or reduced cost is desired (reasons often cited for moving to the Microsoft Windows platform). Perhaps the database on which SAP runs is being retired. Maybe the operating system itself is being retired, too (as was the case with DEC UNIX, later Tru64, when HP unceremoniously dumped it). In these cases, it makes a lot of sense to step back and reassess the SAP technical landscape while simultaneously looking ahead at where the business might be in the next three to five years. For instance, perhaps a higher level of performance or availability beyond the current platform's capabilities will be in order soon, given the growth expected in user counts, *mergers and acquisitions* (M&A) activity, or other business acquisitions. In such cases, IT may be asked to perform an OS/DB migration. An OS/DB migration is the method used to move to that lower-TCO (*total cost of ownership*), more-innovative, or more-viable platform.

> SAP OS/DB migrations are beyond scope of this current edition of *Teach Yourself SAP in 24 Hours*. For a broader review of OS/DB migrations, turn to Hour 19, "After Go-Live: SAP Technical Platform Migrations," in the third edition of this book.

More on SAP Upgrades

Stated previously, *upgrade* refers to installing a major version change of SAP, such as moving from SAP R/3 Enterprise to SAP ERP 6.0. In a technical upgrade, the upgrade project is about changing the SAP Basis layer's version and not about moving in the added functionality of that new version. In a functional upgrade, on the other hand, the goal is to move to the new functionality provided by the new SAP system.

There are many reasons why an existing SAP customer might want to upgrade an old R/3 system to SAP ERP 6.0, for example. The best one is simply that the company needs the new functionality offered in the newest release. Another reason customers upgrade, though, is because SAP eventually ceases to support its older releases (although an organization might determine that the incremental cost of extended support fees is acceptable).

Many times, adding functionality requires individual components of the SAP system to be upgraded. For instance, an SAP add-on or a number of support packages might need to be installed in the system (using either the SAP transaction SPAM or SAINT). And the SAP Basis layer typically needs to be upgraded, as well. Upgrade projects are complex and confusing, with different project team member requirements depending on what is being upgraded or changed. The entire process is planning-intensive, which brings us to the topic of the next section: high-level planning for upgrades and enhancements.

High-Level Project Planning

Planning for upgrades and enhancements is critical due to the magnitude of change and therefore the magnitude of risk! Remember, SAP systems are used to run the company business; when the system is down, the business is down. So the idea of managing and minimizing the risk of this downtime is nearly always the most important matter surrounding any kind of pending change, whether it's a hardware update, OS/DB migration, or functional upgrade. Said another way, changes of such great consequence to mission-critical SAP systems deserve nothing less than careful planning. In return, the IT team should see its planning work help them avoid unplanned outages and unsatisfied unproductive users.

Project Planning for Enhancements

Enhancements are often implemented in quarterly "waves" or phases comprising multiple SAP user groups and therefore multiple functional areas and business processes. Complicating matters further, each wave typically takes one to two quarters to plan for and test. And beyond the functional updates, technology changes might be required to support the new functionality. Quarterly enhancements might also include one or even all of the following updates, as well:

▶ Server, disk subsystem, or other infrastructure refreshes

▶ Database patches updates and "upgrades"

▶ Operating system updates, security patches, and "upgrades"

▶ SAP kernel updates

▶ SAP support package stack (ABAP and Java) updates

▶ SAP modification transports

▶ Customer transports

As you can imagine, this scope of changes can require significant team coordination and project management expertise. In some cases, the better part of an IT department can be absorbed while implementing a wave of SAP enhancements, especially when you consider that these changes have to be moved through multiple environments as part of the SAP landscape (development, quality assurance, production, and so on).

After these changes have been implemented, one or more testing cycles have to be performed to ensure that all the changes do not break any existing processes and to ensure that the changes are ready for the move to production. This is usually performed by a combination of SAP experts and business users who (either manually or via automated scripts) test at minimum the core pieces of changed SAP functionality to ensure they still work properly. As errors are encountered in testing, fixes have to be developed that are then applied after the enhancements to subsequent environments. For example, it might be discovered in testing that an SAP support package caused a particular SAP business transaction to abort, also called a *short dump* (because an SAP short dump is created in the process of aborting). During the troubleshooting process, the tester might find a relevant SAP *Online Service System* (OSS) note that has been released by SAP that resolves the problem. This note is then downloaded into the development environment, and a corresponding transport is created. In the next phase of testing, it is confirmed that this fix indeed resolves the problem with the SAP transaction. This transport is then added to the post-enhancement transport list scheduled for production and eventually moved into production.

Project Planning for SAP Upgrades

Technical upgrades are more common than functional upgrades and certainly more common than migrations. Nonetheless, they are still pretty infrequent, occurring every six months to perhaps two years. Interestingly, an SAP technical upgrade is similar in nature and duration to a migration; they take three to six months of planning and require the same SAP infrastructure support folks and SAP Basis professionals. It is also necessary to add ABAP programmers, SAP functional analysts, and power users (to do the necessary business process testing after each test wave) to the list of project resources. A functional upgrade takes this complexity one step further because it requires functional (business) specialists, as well.

During the planning stages of an SAP upgrade, it is wise to evaluate whether the existing database should be converted to Unicode. SAP recommends all customers convert to Unicode because it supports more-complex languages, like Chinese (Mandarin). For reasons like Unicode support, most SAP upgrade projects require new hardware and therefore a new underlying infrastructure on which to implement. In fact, it's becoming more common to find combination OS/DB migration and SAP technical upgrade projects where the migration and upgrade are performed sequentially (not concurrently, but one after the other) over a very long weekend. In the recent past, SAP AG would not support a combined migration and upgrade performed as one project with a go-live in a single weekend. Customer pressure on SAP has made such complex projects "supported," however, despite the obvious risks of making so many changes all at once.

Getting Started

When the new SAP infrastructure is in place, a system copy must occur from one of the source SAP systems to the new environment. Typically, a copy of production is used as the source for the first test upgrade. It's the biggest system, after all, and naturally represents all the current system's functionality that will eventually be upgraded (and then need to be tested). Some customers prefer to start with an upgrade of the development environment, but this choice complicates things. Why? Because any changes put into the real development and promoted through the system to production on the source environment must also be pushed and promoted through the upgraded environment. This "dual path to production" keeps the environments functionally synchronized but adds a lot of work. Smart IT organizations will forgo upgrading development as long as they can.

Upgrade Tools and Options

The Basis team will use two SAP tools—*PREPARE* and the *Upgrade Assistant*—to perform the technical upgrade. The PREPARE tool performs a thorough evaluation of the SAP system and recommends changes, fixes, and service packs that must be applied to the system before the upgrade can actually begin (preparing the system for upgrade). After the changes have made and running PREPARE shows no more preparation steps are required, the upgrade can begin.

One critical prepare phase allows the Basis team to bind support packages and add-ins to the upgrade process. In many cases, a certain support package level is required to be bound to the upgrade. In most cases, it makes sense to put in all the latest support packages during the upgrade, instead of waiting until the upgrade completes to apply them. The reason a certain support package level may be required is due to the level of the support packs on the source system. If the source system is at a support package level that introduced functionality that was not included in the base target system but was included for the target version as a support package, the upgrade must apply the same level of functionality through support packages. Otherwise, data will be lost.

The Upgrade Assistant tool graphically displays the upgrade process. It is menu-driven, allowing the Basis team to choose one of several options as to how to proceed with the upgrade. Options such as *Downtime Minimized* and *Resource Minimized* help determine how long the upgrade will take and at what point in the upgrade the system must be shut down. The Downtime Minimized option enables the team to do much of the upgrade work while the system is still up and running, thus reducing the overall system outage (downtime) required to finish the upgrade. The Resource Minimized option forces the system to go offline at an earlier phase. However, it reduces the overall time it takes to actually execute the upgrade process.

Upgrade Testing and Remediation

After the first development upgrade, the system needs to be handed over to the functional and ABAP teams for remediation and testing. SAP tracks problems to upgraded objects with transactions /nSPAU and /nSPDD. SPAU tracks repository objects, whereas SPDD tracks dictionary objects. SPAU and SPDD enable the developer to look at objects affected by the upgrade and gives options on how to proceed with remediation. Once the objects are repaired, the changes are saved to a transport and can be used to quickly repair the problems as they appear in the upgrades to the quality and production systems. Optionally, the Reset to Original option with SPAU or SPDD allows a developer to revert to the standard SAP code applied by the last upgrade or support pack. Version control is handled in SPAU and SPDD so that the developer can call up previous versions of the object in question.

ABAP code remediation efforts depend on the amount of customization done to an SAP system. Most customers spend about 30% of an upgrade project testing and fixing their custom code. Many IT consulting companies have developed tools that analyze an SAP system before an upgrade to accurately estimate the effort required for code remediation. Such an investment is an excellent idea for all but the most vanilla of installations.

Summary

SAP enhancements, migrations, and upgrades are significant project undertakings, requiring specialized skill sets. With your understanding of the correct definitions and terminologies for each, in conjunction with knowledge of how each project is pursued to completion, you should be well prepared to consider these options as they naturally arise in the SAP deployment and maintenance lifecycle.

Case Study: Hour 21

Review and address the enhancement case study questions posed here. You can find the answers posed by the questions related to this case study in Appendix A, "Case Study Answers."

Situation

Today, MNC runs SAP R/3 Enterprise as its core ERP application for Financials and Human Resources. The system is hosted by a provider, and ongoing support costs are astronomical. In addition, the SAP system runs on an out-of-support version of UNIX and Oracle. MNC is planning an upgrade to the latest release of SAP ERP 6.0.

Questions

1. *What is the most important factor that needs to be managed and minimized regarding this very critical change?*

2. *MNC Global has employed a recruiter to help hire a project manager for the project. The online advertisement reads, "Project Manager with migration skills, requires experience migrating from R/3 to SAP ERP2005." Is this ad technically accurate? How should it read?*

3. *From a platform perspective, how can MNC Global potentially lower the ongoing support costs for the SAP system, or increase the ability to innovate, after the upgrade project?*

4. *In general, what's the difference between updates, upgrades, and migrations?*

5. *If support for new languages like Mandarin will be required by the business soon, what other technical change should MNC consider along with the upgrade project?*

SAP Careers for the Business Professional

What You'll Learn in This Hour:

▶ Where to find SAP business professional career opportunities

▶ Various job roles available in the SAP market

▶ How to position yourself for a business-oriented career in SAP

Now that you have learned so much about SAP and its products, technologies, direction, and how to use it, you may be thinking about how you can pursue a career in the SAP market. SAP, its partners, and its customers create an ecosystem of literally thousands of jobs worldwide in a variety of disciplines. Working with SAP can prove to be a challenging and rewarding career path, but finding the right opportunity can be a daunting task, especially if you have little direction. In this hour, we provide much-needed direction as we attempt to shed some light on the art of finding and developing a business-oriented career in SAP. For those of you interested in developing a technical career, turn your attention to Hour 23, "SAP Careers for the IT Professional."

What Exactly Is an SAP Business Professional?

SAP business professionals and the business-oriented careers they hold vary tremendously. A decade ago, such a career might have been narrowly defined as an end user or super user working at a customer site. Even more so, a business configurator or project manager working on behalf of SAP or one of SAP's partners has long been considered a business professional.

Today, though, the term *business professional* is more broadly applied. SAP business professionals (business process/scenario experts and functional or business area experts) still work in the positions mentioned, but they also work in areas such as:

- Presales, assisting prospective customer understand SAP's business functionality and various components and products from a business perspective

- Business development, inside sales, account management, and similar "sales" roles

- Quality and risk management, as experts in one of these domains

- Education roles, ranging from selling to actually developing and delivering end-user or other functional/business-related training

- Quasi business/technical roles such as workflow and security (each of which has a business component and a technology component)

- Project management, which consists of project and program managers (at many levels of seniority, with many different skill sets and backgrounds), project specialists, resource management specialists, and so on

- Recruiting, including recruiters and other HR/career development specialists

Let's turn our attention to where these jobs might be available.

Where Do I Look?

The first question you might ask yourself when seeking a career in SAP is, "Where do I look?" The Internet is a valuable resource, to be sure, and we outline popular SAP resources and job websites in Hour 24, "Other Resources and Closing Thoughts." However, such resources give only a glimpse into where SAP career opportunities actually exist. In this section, let's take a closer look at some of those in detail.

Right Where You Are

The first obvious choice when searching for a career in SAP is to look right at home at your current employer. Search your employer's job boards and (as funny as it might sound) search popular websites using your company's name as your search criteria. If your company is an SAP customer or has plans to become an SAP customer soon, the potential advantage you have as a current employee can make this an ideal method for uncovering an SAP opportunity.

By the Way

Be sure to do some due diligence before assuming that your company does not use SAP. At large companies, certain divisions might have implemented SAP, whereas others have not, especially if mergers or acquisitions have occurred. Also if your company is a supplier or vendor of an SAP customer, you might be interfacing with an SAP system and not even know it, missing an opportunity to pick up valuable SAP experience in the process.

Of course, your "opportunity" depends on a number of factors. Are you well-regarded? Do you work well across organizational boundaries and with other teams and people? Do you get results? Can you be freed from your current assignment? When you are certain that no SAP opportunities exist available at your current company, it might be time to take a look outside. Let's review some of these options.

SAP

When looking for a business-user career in SAP, starting right at the source with SAP itself is not a bad idea. With thousands of employees around the globe, SAP AG and its worldwide subsidiaries represent a long list of job prospects on their own. As of this writing, a quick search on SAP's career site (see Figure 22.1, or navigate to www.careersatsap.com) reveals more than 1,400 job openings around the world. If you narrow this down to strictly business-related (by removing technical, administrative, and similar such jobs), the total is still well over 700.

FIGURE 22.1
Use SAP's career site to identify available positions around the world.

Business-oriented jobs include areas as diverse as the following:

▶ Business-user specialists and consultants (with an emphasis on different industries and languages)

▶ Solution and product managers and directors

- ▶ Presales managers and directors

- ▶ Business development managers

- ▶ Inside sales specialists

- ▶ Channel development managers

- ▶ Account executives

- ▶ Industry advisors and other specialists

- ▶ Various line-of-business (LOB) specialists

- ▶ Various business process, functional, and SAP component specialists (from interns to entry-level college graduates to senior specialists)

- ▶ Quality management experts

- ▶ Functional education and training delivery and sales specialists

- ▶ Project management analysts

- ▶ Risk specialists

- ▶ Recruiters and other HR/career development specialists

With so many opportunities across such a breadth of careers, it should be easy to identify several prospective opportunities.

SAP Partners

Beyond working at SAP, your next option may be to pursue an SAP job at one of the many SAP partners that provide software and services for SAP and SAP customers. These partners include the full gambit, from large multibillion-dollar corporations such as SAP that employ thousands of workers, to outsourcing providers like Accenture, CSC, EDS, HP, and IBM, to small specialty companies that provide more discrete services. SAP has broadened its partner categories into the following:

- ▶ Integration partners

- ▶ SME channel partners (broken down by SAP's offerings)

- ▶ Content partners

- ▶ Education partners

- ▶ Hosting partners

- ▶ SAP BusinessObjects partners (further divided into several specialties)

- ▶ RunSAP Operations partners

- ▶ Services partners

- ▶ Technology partners

- ▶ Software solution partners

These different partners, along with SAP and the SAP customer base, form what SAP calls its *ecosystem*. To get an idea of the SAP partners available, execute a partner search at www.sap.com/ecosystem/customers/directories/SearchPartner.epx. Note that you will have to enter one set of criteria, such as name, country, or category, to return a set of results.

Within this partner network are also the elite groups of global services partners that provide SAP consulting opportunities across business sectors. Combined, these companies employ thousands of SAP professionals worldwide and help support the growing SAP customer base. The current list of global services partners has changed significantly in the last few years and includes the following:

- ▶ Accenture

- ▶ Atos Origin

- ▶ Capgemini

- ▶ Cognizant

- ▶ CSC

- ▶ Deloitte

- ▶ Fujitsu

- ▶ HCL AXON (SAP Services Division of HCL)

- ▶ Hitachi, Ltd.

- ▶ HP

- ▶ IBM Global Business Services

- ▶ Infosys Technologies Ltd.

- ▶ itelligence

- ▶ L&T Infotech

- ▶ Logica

- ▶ Mahindra Satyam

- ▶ Siemens IT Solutions and Services

▶ Tata Consultancy Services

▶ T-Systems

See www.sap.com/ecosystem/customers/directories/services.epx to browse this list and read more. As you can see, these global partners are SAP's "Who's Who?" for global SAP openings. They offer prime career opportunities for the serious SAP professional. Whether you are looking for a position in business process management at one of the global services partners such as Capgemini or IBM or seeking an SAP financial auditing position (a great way to learn a lot about SAP, by the way) at Deloitte or Accenture, these partners can offer a well-developed SAP career path.

SAP Customers

Although many SAP career settings have been presented, another likely alternative is that you will find an opportunity working with one of SAP's many customers. Located around the globe, they offer a similar breadth of opportunities as SAP and its partners. The key may be to find an employer that aligns with your industry expertise.

More Details

As you've seen by now, SAP opportunities for the business professional are everywhere. Whether a company is planning an SAP implementation or maintaining an existing SAP landscape, a team of business professionals is required to keep the systems in a state where the requirements of the business may be met. In this section, we review several types of opportunities in more detail.

Business and Functional Positions

On any SAP implementation or in any SAP environment, individuals are needed who can bridge the gap between an organization's business requirements and business processes and the technology necessary to support the business. From functional analysts, super users, and more, there are a variety of positions for the prospective business professional. Although the actual job title for these positions can vary greatly, we discuss a few of them here.

On the business side of the house, every SAP implementation needs personnel who can champion SAP business solutions for their team. For this reason, and rightly so, they are often called super users. They are usually the IT-savvy business-knowledgeable folks within their respective departments who can communicate well and have the ability to bring along those who are challenged by new technology. Super users are often the first trained on a given SAP project, and they work most closely with their SAP functional configuration counterparts to resolve issues. This puts super users in a prime position to gain priceless SAP knowledge.

In the SAP technology arena, we have functional analysts, often called configuration leads, business analysts, or business process owners. We also have technical analysts, who can be referred to as functional developers or configuration experts. All of these roles are generally aligned with a particular SAP module or modules, such as FI, HR, MM, and so on. These individuals have to work with their business-side counterparts to make the company SAP vision a reality. This is important to note because the more SAP modules a company has implemented, the more people they will require to fill these areas of expertise.

For example, a functional analyst may work with a team leader or super user to gather business requirements for an enhancement to the SAP system. The functional analyst will then work with the technical analyst and potentially other members of the technical team to have SAP configuration activated or modified to meet the business requirements.

As you can see, business and functional roles can be very involved and require tremendous coordination and expertise. All of these roles are vital to an SAP implementation and require motivated, competent individuals to be successful.

Functional Project and Program Management

As you can imagine, bringing together all the functional and technical roles, tasks, and dependencies necessary to pull off a large-scale SAP project is challenging. Many companies and consulting organizations have established Project Management Offices (PMOs) to coordinate their project managers. And as you have read previously, it is not uncommon for an SAP project to require a number of project managers to direct a set of SAP initiatives or represent different stakeholder bodies. Again, this provides a prime opportunity for those looking to break into the SAP arena as a PM.

And project managers are in high demand. Certification from the Project Management Institute (PMI) and the right timing could land you just the SAP opportunity for which you are searching. As a PM, you can pick up multitudes of information about SAP functional design or technical architecture as you work with project team members, which can lead to a career change into a technical or functional role in the future if you so desire.

Functional Trainers and Testers

Although they do not receive the same recognition as other SAP positions, SAP trainers and testers are noteworthy and critical to the success of SAP implementations and projects. As companies learn to carry out their business processes on SAP, trainers take on the difficult challenge of carrying out the new vision to end users who may or may not be completely on board with the new changes. This takes talented trainers and training leads to develop training classes, organize students, and deliver a variety of training modules to an enterprise perhaps unwilling to change.

Likewise, the SAP testing process is a never-ending cycle. Whether it is project-related enhancements to the system or quarterly patches and updates, SAP systems have to be tested to ensure changes are ready for production. This requires people who can create and exercise test scripts either manually or via automated testing tools. Although a tester might not always be the most high profile of positions, you can gain valuable experience on SAP configuration and SAP business processes that can lead to other rewarding positions.

Preparing for a Business Career in SAP

Now that you know where SAP positions are available and have an idea what types of jobs are out there, how do you get one? The key is to *drive your own career*. Don't be passive and assume others will do this for you. Your manager may be helpful, for example, but then again your manager might not. Think about how often your managers have failed to make it through the latest round of layoffs, have retired, have moved on to other positions, or have simply done a less-than-stellar job thinking about people other than themselves. In this section, we look at how to prepare for a business-oriented career in SAP.

Right Where You Are

As discussed in the first section this hour, if your current employer is planning an SAP implementation or currently runs SAP, there is probably no better place to look than right where you are. Generally, companies that commence a new SAP project are looking for volunteers from the business willing to take on the new challenge and champion the project. If your company does have an SAP initiative planned, there is no time like the present to put your name in the hat as an interested party. New projects are also ideal because there are a variety of positions needed and very little in-house expertise. This means a motivated individual can take advantage of the situation and take the opportunity to develop a new career path.

Although it can be more challenging to move from a non-SAP job to an SAP role at a company already running SAP, you should pursue it as diligently as you possibly can. Leverage your current experience and knowledge of your company to put your potential move in a positive light. Also if your dream SAP career position is not yet available, do not be afraid to tackle less-appealing SAP positions. They can serve as stepping-stones to a more rewarding position later.

Of course, if your current company does not use SAP, has no plans to use SAP, or refuses to give you an opportunity, you need to search elsewhere.

Leverage Existing Business Experience

As mentioned in the preceding section, SAP creates many positions built around business modules and business processes. Just as it is important to know how to configure business processes in SAP, it is equally important to understand the detailed inner workings of the business process itself. If you have that kind of knowledge, you can be a valuable asset to the SAP team. In fact, it is very common for business process experts to become SAP configuration experts and vice versa.

If you have significant experience in a particular business area but your company does not use SAP, do not be discouraged. This kind of expertise often translates within your industry. For instance, if you worked in the materials management area in the chemicals industry for 15 years, you might be able to leverage that experience to find a job at another chemicals company with a similar business model that uses SAP. This concept applies to all SAP modules across industry segments. Simply identify your role, find a company using SAP, and then pursue that role at the new company!

Similarly, if you pick up new business solutions or applications quickly, think about becoming an SAP super user or taking on stretch assignments to become the "go-to" person in your business area for all things SAP. Alternatively, consider using your in-depth knowledge to become a trainer! Use your business experience to quickly learn how your business processes run on SAP. Then teach others in your department or elsewhere to become proficient end users of the system. With a bit of luck and a good measure of positive feedback from your students, one of these interim training roles can open the doors to other SAP career opportunities, perhaps one you *really* want down the road.

Look for Work on the Fringe

There are many other "fringe" business functions you may use to break into the SAP market. As discussed earlier, SAP integrates with almost every area of IT, so you have the prospect of working your way into SAP over time. The whole area of workflow management is a good example; it requires a special combination of business and technical skills to plan, build, and maintain workflows.

Change management is another example. One of our peers started out as an IT change management analyst and handled change management documentation for her company's SAP team. She eventually took on the job of managing and sending SAP transports throughout the system landscapes and today works as an SAP Basis technician (yes, she chose technology over a business career!) at a large corporation. Just by being a team player, making the most of her opportunities, and taking advantage of her experiences, she advanced her skill set and career.

Similar prospects exist in other areas where business and IT functions converge. An SAP bolt-on or complementary product may end up integrating with your business area of expertise and open a window of opportunity. So pay attention and be ready to take advantage of your skills and experience when the opportunity presents itself. Better yet, *pursue* those opportunities while carefully and purposefully building your skills and experience.

Work on the Intangibles

Although skill sets and expertise are necessary in your pursuit of an SAP career, do not underestimate the multitude of soft skills and other intangibles that make the difference between getting hired and forever being an interview candidate. As we wrap up with this hour, let's focus on several of the little things that make a big difference.

Your Ability to Network

Despite all of your business acumen, experience, and know-how, candidates who cannot show how they've successfully networked to get the job done are in trouble. Today's business world is complex, and the days of the Lone Ranger are behind us. Getting things done really amounts to working well with others, especially with those you cannot directly influence (such as co-workers and peers, not your direct subordinates).

So be prepared to help your prospective employers understand how you worked in a team to make things happen. Be sure to highlight your individual contributions (including personal leadership and your focus on delivery excellence), but give credit to the team for making its deadlines. Show off your professional network and describe how you will extend that network in your new environment if you're given the chance to work there. By covering this base in an interview, you are telling prospective employers that you understand you can't do it all by yourself. They will not only appreciate your selfless perspective, but gain some real insight into how you'll fit into their team.

Get Educated!

SAP professionals are just that—professionals—and as such, SAP jobs reflect minimum qualifications similar to other professional positions. Many of the positions you see posted at SAP, its partners, and customers require at least a Bachelor's degree. Often, an MBA or other Master's degree is desirable if not mandatory. That is not to say that a certain number of years of experience will not get you the job, but advanced education certainly helps plant you at the head of the pack (or nearer to the top of a resumé stack).

Likewise, SAP certification can give you a great advantage as you search for your SAP career. Although it is expensive and might not be as accessible as some certifications, for these same reasons it offers you more exclusivity and regard in the SAP industry. SAP currently has three levels of proficiency: Associate, Professional, and Master. (Find out more about SAP certification at www.sap.com/services/education/certification/index.

epx). Any of these certifications can put you well on your way to an SAP career, and the Professional and Master certifications really put you in another class of demand. Take care to take training classes that reinforce or augment your experience, however; careening off into a completely different industry or functional specialty can backfire for those seeking initial SAP employment.

If you are not in a financial position to advance your degree or pay for SAP training classes, keep striving. In Hour 24, "Other Resources and Closing Thoughts," you learn about a host of helpful sources. Most of these are available on the Internet, where you can pick up a wealth of information on SAP and its products. Though you still have to find the right opportunity, do not miss out because you are not prepared and knowledgeable. Terminology, architecture, and standards available to you in easy-to-consume presentations, PDFs, YouTube, and other video-based training, and so on, are just a click away. Use these resources to fill in as many gaps as you can in your education and knowledge and trust you will be given the opportunity to put to good use the time you invested in learning on your own. In the right interviewing circumstances, this kind of proactive self-education can help differentiate you from your less self-motivated colleagues, too.

Professional Presentation

As we discuss the intangibles, it is worth mentioning that how you present yourself is as important as ever. You may have heard the line, "Dress for the job you want, not the job you have." Sure, much of the world is becoming more casual—especially in light of work-at-home and other remote-office accommodations.

But when you're interviewing, and later when you actually show up at company meetings and other get-togethers, consider your wardrobe. In most corporations using SAP, especially the more conservative brands, this idea of business professionalism is very much alive. After all, these are companies that can *afford* SAP. They are generally not running the business on a shoestring, and they expect their people to properly reflect the company's success.

Besides, SAP business-oriented positions invariably interact at all levels of management and with all manner of business and IT professionals. As a senior SAP Financials expert or SAP upgrade project manager, you may be called upon to give a presentation to a group of business leaders, the CIO or COO, or another group of stakeholders. The last thing you want to do is walk in looking unprofessional and have people naturally wonder if a mistake was made in the hiring process.

So if you are serious about advancing your career, invest in your wardrobe, consider minimizing all the piercings that make you special to your significant other, and essentially separate yourself in terms of professional appearance from your peers. Meanwhile, we seasoned professionals will keep wearing our shorts and flip-flops (because we *can*, but that's another matter you don't need to worry about just yet).

Also as part of your own "presentation layer" (a play on SAP's use of that term to describe its front-end GUI, forgive us), you need to improve your communication skills. Study the culture and primary language reflected by your employer and work not only to fit in but to excel in communication. Your communication skills ultimately reflect who you are more than anything else, including your wardrobe. Many senior-level SAP professionals are not where they are necessarily because they are the most knowledgeable business process expert or masterful business development leader, but rather because they are able to communicate well across business and technology departments. Simply broadening your vocabulary, improving your pronunciation, and clearly articulating your words is a big help.

Thinking before speaking is an even bigger help. Live by the mantra "only the facts." Speak the truth and avoid anything outside the truth. If you're not 100% sure what you are saying is accurate, keep your mouth shut. Don't be the person quick with an answer that turns out to be incorrect. When you open your mouth to speak, you want people to edge in a little closer to you because they know what you're going to say is accurate, truthful, and worth their time. This little tip alone can boost your career advancement quickly and continuously.

Don't stop at verbal skills, though. Make sure you're a consummate professional when it comes to email and other written communications. You may also want to think about familiarizing yourself with how to create an *effective* Microsoft PowerPoint. There are plenty of poor examples in the world. Don't create another one. Know your audience and know your material. Stick with three or four bullet points per slide and use graphs and figures to communicate data trends and complex relationships, respectively. The ability to deliver a succinct and effective presentation says a lot on its own because it shows upper management that you are capable of communicating well. The ability to share business matters in this way, with accuracy and confidence, is a skill as rare as it is sought after.

A Word on Ethics

In an effort to run their businesses with accuracy and transparency, SAP customers spend millions of dollars on their SAP systems. Themes such as system availability, compliance, and data integrity are paramount in these organizations. In the same way, these attributes need to be reflected by the *people* tasked with managing and supporting these systems.

Make no mistake, companies know more than ever today that they can train the right candidates. If you are a bit weak in a particular technology, business concept, application, or soft skill, a good hiring manager knows those specific gaps can be filled through training and a certain amount of mentoring. Instead of waiting to find the absolute perfect fit, these people are instead often looking for the right *kind* of people to hire. The basic experience, talent, and education prerequisites need to be in place, sure. But companies know they can't really teach ethics and responsibility (despite all the time many of us spend annually in corporate compliance training and similar initiatives, which are fine in themselves as a way to educate but certainly do little to change innate behavior)—and it is precisely this kind of ethical and responsible behavior that smart companies are seeking more than ever today. So in whatever you do, strive for integrity. Showcase your strong character and ethical foundation during the interview process. And at work, make every decision as if it will be publicly broadcast around the world. People notice the choices you make, and one day those good choices will pay off, maybe with just the career change you are hoping for. We believe it happens quite frequently, actually.

Summary

Now that we have looked at the what, the where, and the how of discovering a career in SAP, the rest is up to you. There are a slew of challenging and rewarding opportunities available to the willing and able. If you are serious about making a career change to an SAP business professional, follow the simple advice in this hour and get to work. Make every effort to achieve your goal by managing your own career rather than letting others drive for you. Markets change, and companies rise and fall, but SAP professionals are generally in high demand regardless of the economy. Work on your skills—business, technical, and soft skills—while you continue to pursue the avenues outlined this hour. We wish you all the best in your endeavors and hope to call you an esteemed SAP colleague and peer someday soon.

Case Study: Hour 22

Consider this business-user career development case study and the questions that follow. You can find the answers posed by the questions related to this case study in Appendix A, "Case Study Answers."

Situation

After 10 years in various banking-related business roles at DeadEnd, Inc., you are ready for a change. You heard about the new SAP ERP implementation down the road at MNC's banking affiliate, and through several job boards you are aware that the firm is actively hiring. Answer the following questions as you research what opportunities are available and how you might work your way into a new SAP business career at MNC.

Questions

1. *You have heard that MNC is relying on a number of consulting firms to assist with its implementation. Where might you be able to find information about these SAP partners?*

2. *As a banking conglomerate, which one of the three major industry categories might MNC fall into, and why might that prove insightful in your job search?*

3. *With a background in accounting and your ability to pick up technology quickly, what might be a good fit for you in the business/functional arena?*

4. *In your time at your current employer, you managed a number of high-profile projects. What type of certification might you pursue to enhance your education and improve your chances of obtaining an SAP project management position at MNC?*

5. *You have shown a strong ability to act as a liaison between the business teams and the IT organization at your current employer. What intangible soft skills do you think you might possess that you could highlight in your interviews at MNC?*

SAP Careers for the IT Professional

What You'll Learn in This Hour:

- ▶ Where to find technical SAP career opportunities
- ▶ The breadth of technical roles in the SAP market
- ▶ Important attributes of a technical professional
- ▶ Ways to prepare for a technical career in SAP

In the same way that SAP has created an ecosystem of opportunities for business professionals, an amazing variety of opportunities for technical professionals exists, as well. In this hour, we walk through these opportunities. As in the previous hour, in your reading, keep one thought central: It's *your* career. Manage it proactively and intentionally.

SAP, Its Partners, and Its Customers

Like developing a business career in SAP, if you're interested in developing a technical career, you'll probably follow a similar path and work for SAP, one of its partners, or one of SAP's customers. Each of these potential avenues is covered next.

SAP

SAP itself offers outstanding opportunities to develop a technical career in SAP consulting and support. Point your browser to SAP's home page at www.sap.com, and click the **Careers** link (or navigate directly to www.careersatsap.com).

From the Careers page, you can search for open jobs posted in SAP's Online Career Center. Choose your language (only four options are offered, but that's probably enough), and you're presented with SAP's Job Search screen. As of this writing, nearly

800 technical jobs were available around the world. Some of the more interesting ones included

▶ System Landscape Optimization (SLO) Consultant

▶ Technical Quality Manager (TQM)

▶ Technical Training Specialist

▶ Engagement Architect

▶ Enterprise Information Management Consultant

▶ SAP Utilities Consultant (along with hundreds of other SAP industry-specific and component-specific technical positions)

▶ Ph.D. students for SAP research positions

▶ Technical interns (specifically for positions developing iPad/iPhone applications, Flash applications, and various database projects probably related to SAP's in-memory work)

▶ SAP Technology/Basis Consultant

Other attractive technical positions abounded. Several reported into SAP Labs, some into various SAP Centers of Excellence (CoEs) around the world, and many more into different consulting and customer support organizations.

SAP Partners

Beyond working at SAP, your next option might be to pursue an SAP job at one of the many SAP partners that provide software and services for SAP and SAP customers. These partners include the full gambit, from large multibillion-dollar corporations such as SAP that employ thousands of workers, to outsourcing and consulting providers such as Accenture, CSC, Deloitte, Freudenberg IT, and IBM, to software partners such as BMC, Microsoft, Open Text Corporation, Winshuttle, and nearly 600 others, to small specialty firms that provide discrete consulting or support services. Check out Hour 22, "SAP Careers for the Business Professional," for a complete list of SAP's largest partners. Combined with SAP and its customer base, these partners form what is called the *SAP ecosystem*.

SAP Customers

Although many SAP career settings have been presented, perhaps the most likely alternative is that you will find an opportunity with one of SAP's thousands of customers. What types of customers, you may ask? The SAP customer base spans numerous industry segments as outlined in Hour 1, "SAP Explained." As a refresher, remember that SAP breaks these industry segments into several major categories, each of which comprises many specific industries ranging from banking, healthcare, and public sector to automotive, chemicals, oil and gas, media, retail, utilities, and so on.

Moreover, these are just a small subset of the industry segments available. Chances are, no matter where you live, you are not very far from a company that runs SAP. In the next hour, "Other Resources and Closing Thoughts," you find information on popular job search engines where SAP's customers and recruiting partners post thousands of employment opportunities at a given time.

What Types of Opportunities Are Available?

As you may recall, SAP projects create a variety of roles and job functions both in the technical and business arenas. Whether a company is planning an SAP implementation or maintaining an existing SAP landscape, a support network is required to keep the systems technically running, functioning well, and in a state where the requirements of the business are met. In this section, we look at the types of opportunities available in more detail.

Technical Positions

Similar to the business and functional positions, there are wide varieties of technical positions required to keep an SAP landscape running effectively. Hour 6, "SAP NetWeaver: The Foundation for SAP," outlined Basis or NetWeaver expert roles serving as SAP system administrators. Experienced or senior Basis personnel often take on team lead or architect roles and are responsible for designing the overall SAP technical strategy for their enterprise. SAP security, which is also a Basis component, has become specialized enough that it now stands as its own job function in the majority of companies. SAP security experts work closely with the functional teams to make sure end users can do their job while at the same time maintaining the system's business process integrity.

In addition to system administration roles, a team of developers and programmers are required to manage SAP configuration and code. At one time, these individuals were known as ABAPers (pronounced *ah-bop-ers*) when there was only a simple Basis layer with which to contend. Today, with so many other development platforms, this term has broadened. Development can now include ABAP, Java, SAP NetWeaver Composition Environment, .NET, and many other development niches in or around the core SAP Enterprise Resource Planning (ERP) environment.

With the array of SAP products available, technical positions are becoming more and more specialized. SAP basis "jack of all trade" system administrators can grow into SAP Process Integration or SAP NetWeaver Portal experts, for example. Similarly, ABAP programmers are adding Web Dynpro and other skills to keep up with changing technology. All of these role-expanding trends bode well for those looking to find not just a job in SAP, but a career.

Technical Project Management

Good technical project and program managers (technical PMs), especially those with experience on SAP projects, are in high demand. With new SAP product releases, upgrades, migrations, hosting alternatives, hardware refreshes, and other technology projects occurring every day, the demand for capable project managers continues to grow. Many companies and consulting organizations have established Project Management Offices (PMOs) to coordinate groups of project managers working across disciplines. And as you have read previously, it is not uncommon for an SAP project to require a number of project managers—technical, functional, and so on—to direct a set of SAP initiatives or represent different stakeholder bodies.

This need for seasoned project managers provides a prime opportunity for those looking to break into the SAP arena as a technical PM. Certification from the Project Management Institute (PMI) and the right timing could land you just the SAP opportunity for which you are searching. As a technical PM, you are exposed to several dimensions of an SAP project, from functional design to technical architecture, sizing, development, testing processes, and more. As you work with your project team members, any number of doors might be opened, leading to a potential career change if so desired.

Technical Trainers

Like their business counterparts, technical trainers play an essential if unrecognized role in SAP implementations, upgrades, and similarly complex projects. Technical trainers help ensure that technical teams are educated to perform their roles. Many trainers work for small SAP-authorized training companies delivering SAP's training classes. Others work for SAP itself, delivering training on behalf of the company. Still others work for or contract on behalf of SAP to develop these training materials. Finally, large companies that have deployed SAP sometimes create their own training organizations as part of a larger SAP Center of Excellence or company-wide training organization.

SAP Testers

Similar to training, the SAP testing process is a never-ending cycle. Whether it is to test project-related enhancements to the system or confirm that quarterly patches and updates have not broken any existing functionality, SAP systems have to be tested to ensure changes are ready for production. This requires people who can create and exercise test scripts either manually or via automated testing tools. Although testers may not always hold the highest-profile positions, they can gain valuable experience on SAP configuration, SAP business processes, and the important area of technical change management—any of which might lead to other rewarding positions.

Preparing for a Career in SAP

Now that you know where SAP positions are available and have an idea what types of jobs are out there, how do you get one? This section focuses on just that, as we explore how to develop a career in SAP.

Again, Right Where You Are

As discussed in the first section this hour, if your current employer is planning an SAP implementation or currently runs SAP, there is probably no better place to look than right where you are. Generally, companies that kick off a new SAP project are looking for volunteers from the business willing to take on the new challenge and champion the project. If your company does have an SAP initiative planned, there is no time like the present to put your name in the hat as an interested party. New projects are also ideal because there are a variety of positions needed and very little in-house expertise. This means a motivated individual can take advantage of the situation and take the opportunity to develop a new career path.

Although it can be more challenging to move from a non-SAP role to an SAP role at a company already running SAP, you should still pursue it as diligently as you would any good opportunity. Leverage your current experience and knowledge of your company to paint your potential move in a positive light. Also if your dream SAP career position is not available yet, do not be afraid to tackle less-appealing SAP positions. They can serve as stepping-stones to a more rewarding position later. Of course, if your current company does not use SAP, has no plans to use SAP, or refuses to give you an opportunity, you need to search elsewhere.

Leverage Existing Business Experience

As mentioned in the preceding section, SAP creates many positions built around business modules and business processes. Just as it is important to know how to configure business processes in SAP, it is equally important to understand the detailed inner workings of the business process itself. If you have that kind of knowledge, you can be a valuable asset to the SAP team. In fact, it is common for business process experts to become SAP configuration experts and vice versa.

If you have significant experience in a particular business area but your company does not use SAP, do not be discouraged. This kind of expertise often translates within your industry. For instance, if you worked in the materials management area in the chemicals industry for 15 years, you might be able to leverage that experience to find a job at another chemicals company with a similar business model that uses SAP. This concept applies to all SAP modules and functional areas across industry segments. Simply identify your role, find a company using SAP, and then pursue that role at the new company.

Similarly, if you pick up new technologies or business solutions quickly, think about becoming an SAP super user or taking on stretch assignments to become the "go-to" person in your technical group for all things SAP. Alternatively, as outlined in Hour 22, "SAP Careers for the Business Professional," consider using your specialized knowledge and excellent communications skills to become a trainer! Leverage your technical savvy and a desire to share what you know with others and teach your junior or SAP-aspiring colleagues how to install, upgrade, maintain, or in some other way support the technical underpinnings of an SAP system.

Leverage Existing Technical Expertise

If you are an IT professional but SAP technology is all "Greek" to you, do not worry. SAP technology touches almost every facet of the IT industry. In the past, many technical SAP professionals got their starts in another area of IT and eventually transitioned over to a more SAP-focused role. There is hope for everyone, regardless of where you might be employed today. We have seen computer operators, self-taught programmers, SAN specialists, network administrators, and desktop support specialists work their way into senior architecture, project management, IT director, and other valuable positions. Years and many SAP projects later, these people are seasoned SAP professionals with impressive careers. With this in mind, let us now look at various IT positions and how they line up with potential careers in SAP.

Hardware/Infrastructure Specialists

If you currently support server hardware and understand enterprise computing topics such as storage area networks, high availability and clustering, or virtualization, you might be in a good position to add SAP experience to that foundation. Hardware architecture and sizing are critical to the performance of SAP systems, and as such, SAP NetWeaver and Basis professionals have to work closely with their hardware expert counterparts to design and implement SAP systems. As part of this collaboration effort, valuable SAP experience can be gained and leveraged for a career in SAP.

In addition, if you have specific hardware experience for a certain vendor, you might want to consider talking to them about an in-house position. Both HP and IBM, for example, are SAP technology partners that can provide server, storage, and systems management platform experts specifically to their respective SAP customers. Staffed by literally thousands of IT professionals worldwide, such an opportunity makes a great stepping-stone for seasoned technology infrastructure experts.

Platform Administrators

Hour 3, "SAP Technology Basics," discussed operating systems (OSs) and databases (DBs) and the platform combinations available for SAP. If you are already an administrator on one of these platforms, you might be able to leverage that experience as well. Microsoft Windows Server, UNIX, or Linux administrators and Microsoft SQL, IBM DB2, or Oracle database administrators can have an advantage over the rest of the competition. If your company or another company runs SAP on the platform with which you are an expert, it might present just the right opportunity at the right time. If not, consider a position somewhere such as Microsoft or Oracle, for instance, where the company may be looking for individuals with existing skill sets on their products to work on their SAP (internal or services) teams.

In addition, network with your SAP NetWeaver peers whenever possible. Ask questions about how SAP runs on your OS or DB and what aspects affect performance. Find out why your company selected this specific platform to meet its business needs; computing platforms differ in terms of innovations, for example, that can minimize downtime, increase flexibility, and ultimately increase business agility. These types of questions can be the source of priceless knowledge and can also show interest on your part, which can be equally valuable if the right person is listening.

Developers and Programmers

As mentioned in an earlier section, SAP development and programming has gone from the more one-dimensional fourth-generation language of ABAP to a suite of options with object-oriented languages, Java, and Web Services among others. This shift to provide more web-based open access to SAP development could play right into your strengths, for instance, if you are an experienced Java or .NET developer. As outlined in Hour 6, "SAP NetWeaver: The Foundation for SAP," many of the IT scenarios now call for the Java stack as a required component. Likewise, Microsoft and SAP continue to collaborate on tools such as the .NET connector for SAP, the .NET platform development kit (PDK) for SAP Enterprise Portal, and Microsoft Duet Enterprise. These changes present an assortment of opportunities for those willing to put in the time to adapt their programming knowledge to SAP.

Content management is also a popular topic in today's SAP environments. If you are a web developer, consider picking up SAP NetWeaver Portal and applying your web development and design expertise to the SAP world. SAP NetWeaver Portal integrates with existing company portal strategies and products such as Microsoft Office SharePoint Server (MOSS) and IBM WebSphere. Experience in one or more of these technologies can make you a valuable resource and put you in a position to broaden your skill set with SAP.

SAP NetWeaver Business Warehouse (BW) also presents a host of development opportunities. It brings the best of both the technical and functional worlds, as it is somewhat of a hybrid. SAP NetWeaver BW developers become the information management experts in a given enterprise. For this reason, technical experience in data mining, database administration, and so on and functional experience in specific business processes such as FI, HR, and MM are equally important. Therefore, experience in either of these facets may have you well-positioned to pick up some SAP NetWeaver BW experience and enhance your career in the process.

Working on the Intangibles

In Hour 22, we reviewed four broad areas benefitting both business and technology professionals that you should review before reading further:

▶ The ability to network between teams and organizations

▶ The need for further education

▶ The need to present yourself professionally

▶ The need to conduct yourself responsibly and ethically

One final word is in order for the technology professional. Although it might seem a little cliché, there is a lot of truth to the statement a friend shared long ago: "There is no substitute for a little hustle." Often the only distinction between those who achieve their goals and those who complain about how they cannot get out of their current situation is simply a lot of hard work. Many SAP professionals have done just that—*worked* their way into their positions. There is nothing in this hour that says you are guaranteed an SAP position if you follow these directions. However, there are some great tips and ideas to follow. And if you take advantage of what you have learned and apply a little hustle, you will be well-positioned to one day also work *your* way into an SAP technical career.

Summary

This hour covered many of the same themes outlined in the previous hour, but from a technology perspective. Put what you've read here into practice and begin further developing the skills you have. Meanwhile, through an honest self-assessment, build new skills—technical, soft skills, and business skills alike—while you continue to pursue the avenues outlined this hour. And above all else, manage your own career!

Case Study: Hour 23

Consider this career development case study and the questions that follow. You can find the answers posed by the questions related to this case study in Appendix A, "Case Study Answers."

Situation

With MNC's new SAP-on-Windows implementation scheduled to start in three months, you've heard about several new opportunities on the SAP technical team. You are ready for a change but unsure what to do first; your manager seems uninterested in your ideas, much less your career, but you don't want to burn any bridges. You enjoy a broad and fantastically diverse background in infrastructure implementation, SQL Server administration, technical training, and a bit of project management. Answer the following questions as you consider your next move.

Questions

1. *Reviewing your background again yields a thought about better managing your career. What's the rule you should follow?*

2. *Your experience could be useful to the new SAP project. How should you frame this experience?*

3. *If you eventually land a job in the SAP Basis team as a generalist or "jack of all trades," how might you develop your career down the road?*

4. *A phone screen with the hiring manager indicated the SAP technical team could use some testers after the system is physically implemented. What do technical testers do, and how do they do it?*

5. *During your interviews, a member of the SAP technical team asked what you thought about the SAP platform MNC had chosen. He alluded to the platform's innovative capabilities. How might you further this conversation?*

Other Resources and Closing Thoughts

What You'll Learn in This Hour:

▶ Overview of professional resources

▶ Important user groups, journals, and more

▶ A review of helpful websites

▶ An introduction to select SAP career resources

▶ A review of additional SAP resources, including SAP-sponsored and other SAP-focused conferences and events

As it is one of the largest software vendors in the world, it's not surprising to find a wealth of widely available and often free support and similar resources for SAP. What's really surprising is that many of these resources have only become available in the past few years. There are also many low-cost resources such as magazines and books dedicated to SAP (many of which are often provided online at no cost). And there are numerous websites outside of SAP's own web-based resources, and certainly hordes of consulting companies teeming with billable resources anxious to answer all your questions for a fee. But if you just have a few questions and little money to spend, where should you go? To answer this question, this hour outlines SAP resources available to users, developers, Basis engineers, and other SAP business and IT professionals.

Professional Resources

Professional resources for SAP span the gamut, from SAP's very own online resources to inexpensive books, magazine subscriptions, membership in professional user-based organizations, and more. Part of the reason for this diversity is SAP's size—beyond its installed base and the hundreds of thousands of users who depend on SAP day in and day out, there's a supporting cast of another hundred thousand consultants, contractors, developers, engineers, and other support personnel. Some of the more prominent and useful professional resources are outlined in the following sections.

SAP's Service and Support Resources

Before going elsewhere, turn to SAP's own online resources. From sites focused on serving the development and technical communities to those targeted at partners, SAP provides a wealth of readily accessible information. The following list is by no means exhaustive but should give you several excellent places to start:

▶ SAP Service Marketplace—Accessed via service.sap.com, this is your primary portal into other SAP sites and resources. This portal is subdivided into Customer, Partner, and General Visitor sections, each of which provides links to relevant resources. For example, the General Visitor portal affords access to the SAP Community Network, SAP Help Portal, and SAP Education.

▶ SAP Developer Network—Accessed via www.sdn.sap.com, this site is touted as the "social network for SAP professionals." Use it to join and participate in numerous technical, business-oriented, and product-specific communities; access wikis and blogs; subscribe to newsletters; learn of upcoming events; and much more.

▶ SAP Ecosystem—Accessed via www.sap.com/ecosystem, this site provides broad access to partner, co-innovation, and community sites, most of which do not require any special access or user IDs. The community site, for example, offers links to the SAP Community Network, SAP Developer Network, SAP Business Analytics Community, SAP Business Process Expert (SAP BPX) Community, and the SAP Idea Place (a site focused on innovation). The SAP ecosystem also enables connections with fellow academics via the SAP University Alliances Community or fellow colleagues via the SAP Ecosystem for SAP TechEd.

▶ SAP Help Portal—Accessed via help.sap.com, this site provides documentation and other library support materials spanning SAP Enterprise Resource Planning (ERP), SAP NetWeaver, SAP Business Suite, SAP R/3 and R/3 Enterprise, SAP for Industries, Composite Applications, SAP Solution Manager, and more.

▶ SAP Partner Portal—Accessed via partner.sap.com, this is the ideal site for partners interested in connecting with SAP's ecosystem, joining SAP's partner program, pursuing certifications, and obtaining access to partner-only SAP software and other materials.

▶ SAP Support Portal—Accessed via service.sap.com/support, use this site for software downloads, license keys, release and upgrade information, and to use SAP's extensive knowledge base (also referred to as SAP Notes).

SAP support professionals might even consider setting the SAP Service Marketplace as their browsers' home pages. Keep in mind you need an SAP Service Marketplace ID (often called an OSS ID) to access many of these sites, however.

Americas' SAP Users' Group

In almost every facet of business, it is helpful to network with people who are using the same products and solutions you are. SAP is no exception. The Americas' SAP Users' Group (ASUG) is an independent, not-for-profit organization composed of SAP customers and eligible third-party vendors, consulting houses, hardware vendors, and others. Visit ASUG's website at www.asug.com (see Figure 24.1). Although decidedly North American in make-up, the site offers a wonderful breadth of insight offered through its CIO council, events calendar, diverse community and special interest groups, industry-specific benchmarking capabilities, and best practices.

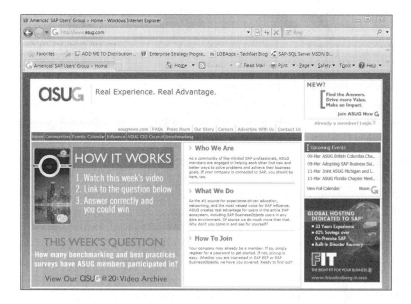

FIGURE 24.1
Look to ASUG for an independent view into SAP based on customer experiences.

ASUG's goals of educating members, facilitating networking among colleagues and SAP representatives, and influencing SAP's global product and service direction form the foundation of all that ASUG does. ASUG provides a forum for members to communicate mutual concerns to SAP, influence software development, exchange ideas and best practices, and establish future priorities.

Brief History of ASUG

Founded in 1990, ASUG followed the SAPPHIRE conference (today called SAP-PHIRE NOW) in Orlando, Florida. A year later, ASUG was officially incorporated. Starting with a group of 15 participants, by the end of 1996 the organization had grown to more than 450 member companies, representing both R/2 and R/3 installations in North, Central, and South America. In the same year, ASUG expanded its customer-only membership to include third parties (vendors and consultants) under a new Associate Membership category. By the close of 1998, the organization was 950 corporate memberships strong, with more than 12,000 participants. ASUG today boasts more than 85,000 members.

The two types of ASUG membership are Installation Member and Associate Member. The former reflects membership at a corporate level of those companies that have installed and run SAP. Fees range from $500 for SAP Business One customers up to $5,000 for large customers with more than $5 billion in revenue. This membership gives all employees of the company benefits from ASUG. Each company designates a "champion" (the single point of contact for the company), along with a primary contact, executive contact, and up to six secondary contacts.

Associate Members include licensed vendors (that is, entities that are licensed Logo, Platform, Alliance, or Implementation Partners) along with certified Complementary Software Program (CSP) participants. Noncertified partners such as small consulting firms can qualify for Associate Member privileges, too.

With ASUG membership comes access to the members-only site within the parent ASUG website. This provides access to a discussion forum, the Member Network, various ASUG-sponsored webcasts, and past presentations and other materials. ASUG members also enjoy discounted rates to attend the annual ASUG conference, access to local and regional chapter meetings, webinars, teleconferences, group meetings, symposiums, and more. Joining ASUG enables a member company to learn from the shared experiences of other users, forging solutions to common user challenges and influencing and shaping SAP's product development over the next few years. And with Installation Membership, the special opportunity to influence SAP AG makes for probably the most compelling reason to "join the club." For more information about ASUG, email the group at memberservices@ASUG.com.

SAP Professional Journal

A bimonthly publication, the *SAP Professional Journal* targets a wide cross-section of SAP professionals, from developers to systems administrators to infrastructure/basis support personnel and more. But the journal also targets the business professionals who rely on SAP to keep their respective companies running. Within the pages of the *SAP Professional Journal*, you'll find technology tutorials, reviews of new products and options, coding and other technical tips, case studies, integration and systems management advice, migration and upgrade guidance, and a wealth of installation and support best practices. And these are not cursory articles or short abstracts; many are quite detailed articles that are immediately useful.

Perhaps even better than the printed journal is access to the online version. Take a look at www.sappro.com for a list of articles in the latest issue (plus abstracts). Even better, use this resource as a search engine, helping you to find some of the best technical materials and SAP best practices available anywhere. With more than 8,000 pages of published articles and other documents, this investment will pay big dividends for the entire SAP support department.

SAPinsider

SAPinsider is published by the same organization that publishes the *SAP Professional Journal*: Wellesley Information Services (WIS). Its format is decidedly different, though, in that it's a quarterly publication, it's free to qualified subscribers (typically anyone supporting or using SAP), and it's sponsored directly by SAP AG. In fact, *SAPinsider* is a joint venture between WIS and SAP. To this last point, the Editorial Board of Directors responsible for publishing valuable real-world SAPinsider content reflects a cross-section of some of SAP's most well-known executive and technical names. This helps ensure leading-edge insight. Important lessons learned are imparted every quarter, making *SAPinsider* an excellent addition to any SAP professional's reading.

In addition to solid technical advice, *SAPinsider* provides product walkthroughs and reviews, up-to-date news from SAP developers, and a number of useful regular columns—NetWeaver, Under Development, Recommended Reading (book reviews, slanted naturally toward SAP Press), and a New and Noteworthy section used by partners and SAP product organizations alike to share important findings. This variety of resources and information can help you stay well-rounded and abreast of the most current developments in the SAP community. It's no wonder that more than 125,000 professionals who develop, implement, support, and use SAP applications depend on *SAPinsider*. For information, visit www.sapinsideronline.com.

InsiderPROFILES Magazine

The newest addition to the small circle of SAP-focused magazines on the market today is *InsiderPROFILES Magazine* (formerly *SAP NetWeaver Magazine*). Founded in 2005, its purpose is to share innovations and insight related to SAP NetWeaver, BusinessObjects, and SAP in general. You will find that this is one of those magazines that does a good job aligning the business and IT sides of SAP. Managers will find the analysts' coverage, thoughts from industry experts, and real-world anecdotes and high-level case studies just what they need to build a business case for moving in a particular direction. Technologists and architects will find the best practices, detailed case studies, and independent insight proffered by SAP experts indispensable, as well, enabling them to make better and bolder decisions while mitigating the risk of deploying products without the benefit of long histories (a nicer way of saying "less-mature products"). The magazine is free and delivered online. Go to insiderprofiles.wispubs.com/issue.aspx to learn more about why this might be the magazine you need.

Books

Close to 1,000 books are available on the market today for SAP. Using online bookstores such as barnesandnoble.com (www.bn.com) and www.amazon.com, you can easily search for and uncover the latest SAP-related books. It's also worth your time looking at www.sap-press.com, which, unsurprisingly, offers a wealth of SAP books covering topics as diverse as SAP BusinessObjects, Solution Manager, Enterprise SOA, SAP Business One, performance optimization, ABAP and Java programming and performance tuning, SAP NetWeaver system administration, Workflow, SAP Customer Relationship Management (CRM) customizing and development, SAP Business Warehouse (BW), security and authorizations, SAP query reporting, and most every other product or capability related to SAP. Many other sites offer lists of popular books. These lists get stale pretty quickly but can offer good insight into what's proven useful to other readers around the world.

Technical Newsletters

WIS Publications, the same entity that publishes the *SAP Professional Journal*, offers a number of well-received technical newsletters. Each newsletter is laser-focused on a particular topic, such as the following:

▶ Financials Expert—Geared toward finance and IT teams that use or support FI, CO, or SAP ERP Financials. It covers quite a bit of reporting options, ranging from ERP and BW Reporting, to SEM, Financial Accounting, Profitability Analysis, G/L, Treasury, A/P, A/R, Controlling, and more. See www.ficoexpertonline.com for details.

▶ BW Expert—If you are tasked with deploying, upgrading, optimizing, or supporting SAP BW (or in a broader sense, business intelligence), this newsletter, focused on deploying and tuning BW for use as the central hub in a sea of transactional systems, is what you are looking for. For more information, check out www.bwexpertonline.com.

▶ SCM Expert—If your SAP team is tasked with optimizing your company's supply chain, this is your newsletter. All the usual supply chain functions are covered, including procurement, warehousing, manufacturing schedules, sales, and distribution. But more than SAP Advanced Planner and Optimizer (APO) is targeted; SCM Expert targets core SAP ERP modules as well, including Sales and Distribution (SD), Production Planning (PP), Materials Management

(MM), Quality Management (QM), and Project System (PS). Refer to www.scmexpertonline.com for details.

▶ HR Expert—For teams responsible for HR, look to this newsletter. From tutorials and case studies to real-world best practices and troubleshooting guidance, HR Expert provides the just-in-time advice an HR team needs to manage and optimize Employee Self-Service (ESS), Manager Self-Service (MSS), personnel administration, payroll, and more. See www.hrexpertonline.com for more information.

▶ CRM Expert—If your team is responsible for unlocking critical CRM functionality, such as marketing, sales, service, and analytics, including the various CRM user interfaces (three different ones exist), CRM Expert is just the ticket for you. Check out www.crmexpertonline.com.

Internet Resources

Many SAP Internet resources are available for you to communicate, learn, and share your own ideas and findings about your SAP system with SAP professionals, vendors, and the entire virtual user community. Always on and always available, the Internet is an ideal source for obtaining troubleshooting information in a pinch. It is always a good idea to search the Net every now and then for new SAP resources—an amazing wealth of new material is made available practically every day. The best of these resources and their content are covered next.

SAP ITtoolbox

One of the most popular and useful sites you can turn to is the SAP ITtoolbox. It's been helping those of us in the SAP field for years and continually proves its worth. With more than 700 active discussion groups and a history of serving its community with facts and integrity, the ITtoolbox portal is a must-have subscription for nearly everyone. ITtoolbox takes care not to inundate you with weekly trash; instead, you choose cafeteria-style the topics that most interest you, and ITtoolbox works to provide you with updated topic-specific content as it becomes available. Interested in SAP careers, training, or certification? Want to review knowledge bases focused on SCM, ERP project management, or hardware platforms for SAP? The SAP ITtoolbox has it all. Register at the main site at www.ITtoolbox.com.

For its SAP community members, the SAP Knowledgebase link at the bottom of the main site takes you directly to the SAP ITtoolbox site, an online service providing wonderful tools and information geared toward assisting SAP practitioners in making informed decisions and completing their daily activities. Like its sister sites, the SAP ITtoolbox combines a functionally organized database of information with the benefits of global communication capabilities to quickly bring useful information to your fingertips. Just check out the weekly SAP decision makers and SAP-doers newsletters (delivered through email), and the SAP ITtoolbox will soon become one of your essential resources if not a favorite site.

SAP Fans

SAP Fans, located on the Internet at www.sapfans.com, continues to be an excellent source of unbiased SAP information (the site is not affiliated with SAP AG). SAP Fans is designed as a forum to exchange ideas with other SAP customers working with SAP R/3, R/2, and other SAP systems. This website includes user-based, technical, and other "discussion" forums that provide you with the opportunity to post questions, comments, and experiences about your SAP system and retrieve responses from other SAP professionals. These forums are grouped into a number of areas. Arguably the most useful is the Technical area. There's also a Non-Technical forum area too, intended to host general discussions, share job postings and resumes, and focus on educational services, list training courses, and address certification questions. Finally, the Knowledge Corner, which is moderated in real time, lets you pose functional, technical, and ABAP-related questions. Using these discussion forums, you can easily post a question or problem that you are having with your SAP system. Other SAP Fans users will see your posting and (hopefully!) respond with possible solutions.

The network of contacts you gain as you discuss and share similar experiences can prove invaluable. As of this writing, SAP Fans boasts more than 108,000 registered users and nearly a million posts. And because it's an ideal source for SAP news, events, products, books, and employment opportunities, you should bookmark SAP Fans as one of your favorites. Yes, some of the material is outdated. But much of it is extremely current, making it one of the most useful (and very free!) resources available to aspiring and experienced SAP "fans" alike.

SAP FAQ

The SAP FAQ originated in 1994 as a web-based adjunct to the de.alt.sap-r3 Usenet discussion forum from Germany's University of Oldenburg, a pioneering SAP academic installation site. As a longstanding, not-for-profit, technology-specific resource, the SAP FAQ has earned and maintained a position of global credibility and respect. Its objective is to serve as a comprehensive point of information about SAP for those who work with SAP, companies that are implementing SAP, students, and those who are looking into SAP as a potential ERP solution or career option.

TechTarget and SearchSAP.com

What used to be termed the SAP FAQ's "by-subscription" discussion forum, ask-the-experts forum, and other similar resources are now accessed through TechTarget, the parent to SearchSAP.com. In fact, when you type www.sapfaq.com, you are rerouted to itknowledgeexchange.techtarget.com/itanswers, a wonderful portal into a wealth of materials, moderated discussions, salary surveys, events and conferences, great tips, useful newsletters, and so much more. It's a great way to exchange ideas while staying on top of new trends and products. An awesome SAP product directory covers much more than the usual ERP, CRM, and supply chain topics. You can access hard-to-find information pertaining to disaster recovery and capacity planning, for example. You'll also find much to review if you're interested in trying to understand what kind of products are available in the hot areas of business process management (BPM) or reporting. From general, core FI and HR module-related discussions, to industry-specific dialogue, subscribers can select a customized combination of discussions that fit very specifically into their areas of interest and expertise. And given the no-cost approach to subscription, SearchSAP.com and TechTarget in general are no-brainers for SAP professionals on a budget. For more information or to subscribe, visit searchsap.techtarget.com.

SAP Conferences

In addition to the ASUG conference and regular ASUG-sponsored events, a growing number of specialized SAP conferences are available to SAP professionals, users, and others. Some of these, such as SAP TechEd, are geared toward technologists and developers, whereas others, such as SAPPHIRE NOW, are geared toward executives and other decision makers. There's also a wealth of product-specific conferences and events hosted throughout the year by the same folks who publish the *SAP Professional Journal* and *SAPinsider* (WIS Publications, discussed in more detail earlier this hour).

Worried about the costs of attending a conference? Considering presenting a session or, better yet, co-presenting with a colleague or customer. Conference providers love bringing together practitioners and customers together to share real-world experiences. Sharing your experiences and lessons learned is also a great way to contribute to the SAP community. The networking opportunities are fantastic, too, not to mention hearing from your peers on the latest and greatest on everything SAP. In turn, nearly all the conference providers cover your airfare, hotel costs, and of course the conference fee for attending. They might even throw in a bit of a stipend for incidentals.

SAPPHIRE NOW

If you are seeking a high-level or executive-level perspective on SAP's current priorities and change-enabling initiatives, or just seeking an executive-level networking opportunity, consider attending the annual SAPPHIRE NOW conference. Also simply called SAPPHIRE, one is held every year in the United States, Europe, and usually other venues like Asia and India. A certain amount of technical sessions are offered, but SAPPHIRE NOW is better known for touting a who's who of keynotes, customer case studies and success stories, and a great number of business-oriented presentation sessions.

Review www.sapphirenow.com for information regarding the most recent or upcoming SAPPHIRE NOW event.

SAP TechEd

There is no better way to get the inside SAP scoop on everything out there and everything coming around the corner than SAP TechEd. Because this event is not interested in hosting marketing sessions, you actually learn things that are immediately useful in your day-to-day life, whether optimizing your current system or planning for your next functional upgrade. Finally, SAP TechEd consistently provides you the opportunity to easily, quickly, and cheaply take certification exams—this alone can save your travel and expense budget thousands, because you can combine multiple training and certification trips into a single 4- or 5-day jaunt to great destinations such as Orlando, Las Vegas, Bangalore, Madrid, and Beijing. Bring your family along and start off your family vacation with SAP!

Managing Your SAP Projects Conference

If you're on a team tasked with planning and deploying SAP, consider attending one of the proven SAP conferences out there, WIS's Managing Your SAP Projects. By offering real-world advice focused on resolving issues and duplicating successes, Managing SAP Projects gives you the chance to drill down into what makes or breaks a successful implementation or upgrade, to walk through customer case studies, and to hear about high-level strategies and leadership tactics used by SAP project leaders and their teams. Such practical guidance learned in the trenches is worth the nominal conference fee.

Because of the decidedly project management focus of this annual conference, certified Project Management Professionals (via the Project Management Institute [PMI]) will be glad to know that they can also earn Professional Development Unit (PDU) credits by attending many of the more than 90 sessions. This is helpful in maintaining PMP certification. And because this is very much a vendor-neutral conference—SAP AG does not sponsor it, although many of the speakers hail from various SAP organizations—those interested in perhaps a less-biased view of SAP will find the sessions refreshingly straightforward.

Other WIS-Sponsored Seminars and Conferences

Wellesley Information Services offers a host of other content-specific and product-specific conference venues. In recent years, WIS has delivered more than 50 conferences and seminars to a variety of North American and European cities. Topics ranged from SAP ERP for Managers to technology-focused SCM, PLM, HR, BW, CRM, IT, and other conferences. And the new SAP Solution Manager conference has received high marks from many SAP professionals. Like all of WIS's conferences, the SAP-neutral stance makes this a great conference for absorbing great real-world information in just a few days. See www.wispubs.com/eventCalendar_SAP.cfm for a list of upcoming SAP-focused conferences near you.

Employment and Career Opportunities

Even today, one of the first things you will notice when you begin an SAP project is that you're suddenly in demand from others. Your email inbox and voicemail box will be bombarded with messages from recruiters offering to outdo your present salary, reduce your travel, increase your opportunities for advancement, and so on. It's not a bad deal, actually, but it can catch you off-guard. Therefore, you need to be prepared.

SAP knowledge is a hot commodity today; a wealth of positions are available and growing for people with the right skills. This includes functional as well as technical skills, development as well as configuration expertise. Possessing in-depth knowledge on how to configure and set up a module in SAP ERP 6.0 is just as valuable as being able to write ABAP or Java code for SAP, or navigate an SAP system through a complex functional upgrade or OS/DB migration. And people with program management and project management skills gleaned through an SAP project are also in great demand. Unsurprisingly, a great number of websites are devoted to making their employment opportunities available to you. A sample of these websites is provided next.

SAP-Resources.com

Touting itself as the "independent home of SAP-only jobs since 1998," SAP-Resources still provides sound value ten years later. It provides a web-based recruitment service focused solely on the SAP marketplace. SAP-Resources enables you to approach the task of finding an SAP career opportunity in a couple of ways through the following services:

▶ The Jobs Database, which is constantly being added to, includes details of some of the hottest SAP positions currently available. Just enter some relevant keywords to perform a search.

▶ The Skills Profile Service is aimed at professionals who know that some of the best opportunities are never advertised and want to make their skill details available to the widest audience possible. It's simple to create and activate your skills profile and to be contacted by recruiters handling the hottest SAP opportunities. All levels of experience are always in demand. Check out the full details at the Professionals Information page.

▶ The Jobs-by-Email service provides subscribers with a daily email message listing the latest jobs posted to SAP-Resources. For more information and to review employment opportunities, visit www.sap-resources.com.

One of the most exciting things about the site is the Top Recruiters box located off the main page. Navigate here to find who's placing the most people (based on job posting popularity). Click the **Company Names** link to review the actual postings in real time.

Softwarejobs.com

Another great venue for posting and reviewing SAP employment opportunities is www.softwarejobs.com. Its online career resources are free and useful, including consultation and resume-writing help, links to free industry-related magazines and similar materials, access to career events and continuing education, and even access to a free personality test, a free career test, and a cadre of career-boosting and similarly inspired articles.

The site also offers free email, inexpensive background checks (to make the decision to hire you over 500 other candidates weigh in your favor), and a full-blown Resource Center portal site to provide access to all this and more. Finally, softwarejobs.com's Job Seeker Tools section makes it easy to build a portfolio, manage and post your resumé, conduct advanced job searches, and distribute your resumé through a number of venues.

ITtoolbox for Careers

As discussed previously, the ITtoolbox website provides outstanding career and job assistance. From the home page, you can launch the Career Center, giving you rapid access to recently posted jobs, the capability to sign up for "job alerts," the capability to introduce yourself to the IT industry's top recruiters, and access to the career-specific ITtoolbox knowledge bases.

Need to hire a couple of contractors for one of your own projects? ITtoolbox also features a section for employers. Use it to post a job opening, review the site's online Resumé Database (access is fee-based; use your credit card), and you'll be knee-deep in thousands of resumés in no time. Be sure to bookmark this site as one of your favorites; one day, you may likely use it.

Up and Coming

As SAP opportunities continue to grow, a number of other sites have popped up offering job databases worth checking out. A few popular sites are www.simplysap.com, www.justsapjobs.com, and www.sapcareers.com. In addition to these, it is always wise to take a look at SAP job offerings on mainstream sites such as www.monster.com and www.careerbuilder.com and on IT job sites such as www.dice.com. These latter sites can be particularly helpful when looking for specific opportunities at firms in your region. With the wealth of jobs available, you are sure to find an opportunity worth pursuing. (Be sure to again review Hour 22, "SAP Careers for the Business Professional," and Hour 23, "SAP Careers for the IT Professional," prior to pursuing or changing jobs in the world of SAP.)

Summary

You made it—a whole book in 24 hours or so! In this final hour, we looked at several resources available to you. Many of these are free, and all of them help you get the most out of your goal to become more familiar with SAP. Look to these resources every few months, if not more often; there's a wealth of knowledge captured in the Internet resources, for example, that can benefit all of us from time to time.

Do you feel like you've matured from a "sapling" to someone more experienced? We hope so. And we hope you have enjoyed the past 24 hours. On behalf of all of us, it's been our pleasure. Perhaps we'll get to work together soon. In the meantime, don't hesitate to contact us with your questions, insights, and experiences.

Case Study: Hour 24

Consider this SAP resource-related case study and the questions that follow. You can find the answers posed by the questions related to this case study in Appendix A, "Case Study Answers."

Situation

As the newest but one of the least-experienced SAP Financials developers at MNC, you have been tasked with quickly coming up-to-speed as the SAP project team prepares for a pending SAP ERP upgrade. Fortunately, your vast expertise in managing financial projects for several previous customers should come in handy. Not unexpectedly, you have also been told there's very little budget available for training.

Questions

1. With what group could you get involved to find out what other SAP customers are doing in the SAP Financials arena?

2. The big SAP Financials conference is coming up, is chock full of sessions you need exposure to, and your schedule looks like you can squeeze it in. With no budget for conference fees or airfare, how should you pursue attending?

3. How can you quickly find the top 100 books focused on SAP development?

4. How can you keep up-to-date with the latest SAP information available on the Internet?

5. What SAP conference might make the most sense for you to attend?

APPENDIX A

Case Study Answers

Appendix A reflects the answers to the questions posed in each hour's case study. In some cases, note that other answers may also be correct.

Hour 1: Answers

1. Although there are many smaller niche players in the business application market, three companies own the bulk of market share and mindshare in this space: SAP, Oracle, and Microsoft. Others, like NetSuite, are making a mark as well. Given SAP's dominance and MNC's size, scope, and global reach, the board might simply start with the proposition "Why not SAP?"

2. MNC needs to investigate SAP ERP first and foremost as it seeks to connect all its end users to a single financial system of record. At the same time, though, the company also needs to investigate SAP Supply Chain Management (SCM) to address its supply chain issues and look at SAP Customer Relationship Management (CRM) to address lost sales and other market opportunities. Finally, the board might be interested in investigating SAP NetWeaver Portal as perhaps a first step toward unifying how its end users "go to work," along with the SAP NetWeaver Process Integration (PI) product to integrate the company's diverse present-day solutions into a more cohesive albeit probably short-term system.

3. SAP offers a mining industry solution that should be of great interest to MNC. By implementing the mining industry solution atop SAP ERP, MNC could immediately leverage mining-specific industry and business best practices.

4. With 100,000 employees, MNC faces several challenges. Questions related to the mix of front-end client devices need to be posed, along with details regarding network links between the 500 different sites and the company's primary datacenter that would eventually house SAP. Fortunately for MNC, the company's adoption of Microsoft Windows on its desktops and laptops will allow for several graphical user interfaces (including browsers).

5. Language and currency issues should be no problem for MNC, although the board needs to have the specific languages and dialects the company must support investigated to be sure.

Hour 2: Answers

1. SAP is one of many different ERP solutions on the market today; it is premature to decide on SAP at this point, let alone specific SAP products and applications. Instead of focusing on vendors, solutions, or technologies, at this stage it's much more important just to develop the business architecture and related business roadmap.

2. The business roadmap should connect business vision, strategy, and architecture to desired business functions and requirements (business blueprinting), which in turn become business processes or workstreams that ultimately are configured atop specific applications (SAP or otherwise).

3. MNC's lack of repeat customers speaks to a problem with the basic business tenet of how to increase revenue. Interestingly, the company might decide to fix this problem (a prudent move) or simply refocus its efforts on a new revenue opportunity (commodity goods direct sales).

4. The task force needs to look at MNC's situation from four perspectives: business, functional, technical, and project implementation.

5. The functional perspective addresses the "what" of a business solution. It answers the question: What will a particular business process do?

6. The technical perspective addresses the "how" part of a business solution. It makes the business and functional perspectives possible through the deployment of specific applications and technologies.

Hour 3: Answers

1. Doing nothing allows the combined company to pursue business as usual without risk of disruption; it's the least risky option.

2. Doing nothing is expensive in that many different server, operating system, and database products need to be managed and maintained. The SAP Basis teams will remain as disjointed as they were when they worked for two different companies. Little to no infrastructure standardization or consolidation is really possible either.

3. Consolidating servers, disk subsystem, network gear, and other assets into a common datacenter could help reduce the costs associated with managing and operating these infrastructure components, and it could allow MNC to retire one of its datacenters.

4. Standardizing computing platforms would decrease complexity, enable all systems to be managed by fewer people, and position MNC to eventually consolidate its like-for-like SAP instances.

5. Regardless of the number of instances associated with each SAP component, AMI currently supports three production systems.

6. One method of converting capital expenditures to regularly recurring operational expenditures is to purchase Infrastructure (and other assets for that matter) as a Service (IaaS). The team might investigate hosting one or more of their systems in the cloud, particularly any sandbox, training, or demonstration systems outside of the promote-to-production process. The team might also consider cloud-based storage in some cases.

Hour 4: Answers

1. In MNC's case, only SAP Enterprise Resource Management (ERP) and Supply Chain Management (SCM) seem to currently be in scope.

2. For the realization phase, the teams will probably be organized around functions and tasks. This might include teams focused on the business and teams focused on technology. For example, MNC might organize by Business and Configuration, Integration, Development, Test/QA, Data, Security, and a host of various technical teams.

3. With regard to access strategies, explain the differences between the traditional SAPGUI fat client and web browser-based access. It's a good idea to avoid committing to one strategy or the other, however, because the blueprinting phase (where such matters are analyzed) has not yet been completed.

4. The most popular user interface for SAP, the Windows-based WinGUI (the classic SAPGUI or "fat client"), is actually the fastest access method; perhaps surprisingly, it's much leaner from a network bandwidth perspective than any of the available web browsers.

5. While the blueprinting phase definitely takes time and resources, the realization phase will consume much more time and consume much more budget.

6. The finance user's job will certainly be impacted by the SAP implementation. He will be trained in the new system, however, and likely find the SAP ERP application a powerful and more capable replacement to his current system.

Hour 5: Answers

1. SAP All-in-One is the best solution if the business processes are very complex and the system needs to support up to 2,500 users.

2. SAP Business One is the ideal solution for a small company with straightforward business processes and a requirement for the system to be fully deployed in eight weeks or less.

3. SAP Business ByDesign is a good solution for companies who prefer to have their own employees customize the system's business functionality.

4. For subsidiaries of 2,500 or more employees, SAP's ERP application is probably most appropriate.

5. SAP Business ByDesign is a good fit for a company without an IT staff or with no plans to develop such an organization because it is hosted by SAP and can be configured directly by the system's business users.

Hour 6: Answers

1. Strategic benefits that MNC may realize by implementing new NetWeaver functionality include reduced total cost of ownership (TCO) and greater potential for innovation. The end users who need the Business Warehouse (BW) reports may then receive their reports via push technology (information broadcasting) instead of by logging on to the SAPGUI and manually searching for them. This reduces time spent on this task, and it allows the users to focus on other business challenges, which ultimately creates cost savings and a more efficient workforce for MNC.

2. Of the six SAP NetWeaver components areas or themes, the Composition and Business Process Management areas are most focused on solution development.

3. SAP provides several resources useful for planning and implementing information broadcasting on its SAP BW system. These include the SAP NetWeaver 7.3 Master Guide as well as the installations guides for NW 7.3 systems, standalone engines, and clients, which are broken out by OS and DB platform combinations (all available at http://service.sap.com/instguidesNW73; keep in mind you must have a valid SAP Service Marketplace user ID to access these resources).

4. SAP changed its use of SAP BW and SAP BI several times over the past few years. They're generally interchangeable in much of SAP's documentation, with exceptions.

5. MNC could connect the chemical systems using the business-to-business Chemical electronic data interchange (EDI) adapter. Alternatively, the legacy system might be supported by one of the application-specific adapters or technology standards, as well.

Hour 7: Answers

1. SAP ERP Human Capital Management (HCM) comprises a number of features. It is a compelling solution for many reasons, including its integration with SAP ERP Financials, Manufacturing, and other SAP solutions; its world-class talent management functionality; its ability to enable and empower global teams and ability to connect a firm's workforce to a single system of record and accountability; its built-in business intelligence capabilities; its ability to be run as an outsourced business process, SAP's extensive SAP ERP Human Capital Management (HCM) partner network, the solution's open and extensible technology platform; and generally its reputation as a "safe choice" for HR organizations.

2. The components of plant maintenance include preventative maintenance, service management, maintenance order management, maintenance projects, equipment and technical objects, and plant maintenance information system.

3. SAP ERP Operations is an aging label for SAP's logistics offerings composed of Procurement and Logistics Execution, Product Development and Manufacturing, and Sales and Service. Within these offerings are found business processes related to purchasing, plant maintenance, sales and distribution, manufacturing, materials management, warehousing, engineering, and construction. The umbrella solution SAP Manufacturing comprises SAP ERP Operations.

4. SAP purposely engineers overlap between particular solutions and modules to enable companies to customize a business solution reflecting the specific business modules and processes necessary to meet their needs.

5. An important component of SAP ERP is the Analytics solution offering, a targeted solution consisting of financials, operations, and workforce analytics.

Hour 8: Answers

1. Three support-oriented features of SAP CRM are marketing support, sales support, and service support.

2. Innovations 2010 focused on three areas intended to help companies restore their financial health: facilitating a lean enterprise, growing the business, and improving business decision making.

3. SAP Manufacturing is an amalgamation of other SAP Business Suite components, products, and underlying technologies; it is assembled in the same way business scenarios are assembled, rather than purchased outright.

4. SRM's benefits are derived on four fronts: improved design collaboration (and therefore time to market); streamlined access to engineering documentation and other materials useful in optimizing product quality, manufacturing processes, and more; improved visibility into ERP back-end data; and the capability to mark up and "redline" computer-aided drawings.

5. In terms of maturity and years of availability, SAP SCM leads the pack of the other Business Suite components.

6. The three general components of a supply chain are supply, manufacturing, and distribution.

Hour 9: Answers

1. The technical team needs power user input in defining and reviewing how and to what extent SAP technologies and business applications will actually solve the firm's business problems. Without the perspective of its power users, MNC risks "solving" the wrong problems—or worse, inventing new ones.

2. The prime integrator knows SAP and knows specific functional or business areas but is missing the first-hand knowledge held by MNC's power users. The power users working in the various accounting teams will serve as internal consultants to the prime integrator's consultants, coaching the implementation team in terms of how business is currently conducted and therefore how the work flows through the organization today.

3. The four general types of testing supported by power users include unit or functional testing, systems integration testing, user acceptance testing, and load or stress testing.

4. With all the power users' knowledge of MNC's business processes and SAP's functional configuration, the biggest challenge faced by MNC after go-live might simply be retaining them.

5. The job of converting a firm's business requirements to functional specifications that may in turn be used to configure SAP appropriately is the responsibility of a special collection or matrix of people and teams—the functional business area or "row" leaders.

Hour 10: Answers

1. You need the hostname or IP address, the system ID, and the system number.

2. Drill down into the SAP menu path until you reach sales order entry (Logistics, Sales and Distribution, Sales, Order, Create).

3. SAP menus are good examples of the SAP tree structure.

4. No, the two-character language identifier is optional..

5. Highlight the text and press **Ctrl+C**. It is also possible to highlight the text, right-click, and then choose **Copy Text**.

Hour 11: Answers

1. A good way to decompose SAP infrastructure security is to subdivide it by SAP technology stack layer (hardware, operating system, database, the SAP application layer, the SAP client access layer, and various middleware layers related to integration points).

2. An SAP security process model is used to establish work flows; it ultimately identifies the various worker roles necessary to complete the work associated with a business scenario.

3. Run transaction /nPFCG to execute the SAP Profile Generator.

4. If a role reflects more than 15 discrete business transactions, it's probably too broad and therefore needs to be subdivided into two or more roles.

5. Instruct the user to run transaction /nSU53 to identify the specific authorizations the user is missing. Then the SAP security team can work to determine whether these authorizations need to be added to the user's profile.

Hour 12: Answers

1. To determine the instance to which your SAPGUI session is connected, view the Status field and click the instance icon. In this way, you may also determine the client to which you are connected.

2. The color setting for the WinGUI session can be changed under **Customize Local Layout** (or **Alt+F12**), **New Visual Design**, **Color Settings**. The changes can be saved under **Save As**.

3. Changes made through the Customizing button apply to any SAP system that you access via the front-end machine you customized, independent of the SAP server or SAP client in which you are processing. However, to make the color settings SAP systems-specific, you choose **Customize Local Layout** (or **Alt+F12**) and **Set Color to System**. The changes apply to all SAPGUI sessions of the SAP system you selected (old and new SAPGUI sessions).

4. The status bar at the bottom of the SAPGUI for Windows provides general information of the SAP system.

Hour 13: Answers

1. The Ad Hoc Query reporting mechanism is used to pose ad hoc queries to the database.

2. A variant is a group of selection criteria values (used to create a report) that has been saved and can then be used as a "shortcut" in the future. Instead of entering all the data fields again, just enter the variant name.

3. The transaction code to access the Create InfoSets screen is SQ02.

4. The transaction code to access the Create SAP Queries screen is SQ01.

5. A query area includes SAP Query elements, queries, InfoSets, and query groups.

6. The two query areas in SAP ERP are standard and global.

7. After creating or modifying an InfoSet, you must save and generate it.

8. The transaction code to access the QuickViewer is SQVI.

Hour 14: Answers

1. Leverage the OLE connectivity offered by the Microsoft desktop and use the %pc command to easily download data directly into Word and Excel.

2. A web service is nothing more than a program that in this case takes SAP data and formats it to be displayed within a web browser.

3. In SharePoint 2010, the older iView Web Part was replaced by the newer iFrame Web Part.

4. Business Connectivity Services (BCS) in SharePoint 2010 supports bidirectional communications between SAP and SharePoint.

5. The earliest versions of Duet were based on integrating SAP with Microsoft Outlook. Conversely, Duet Enterprise integrates SAP with SharePoint.

6. The four components making up the OpenText ECM Suite for SAP Solutions are OpenText Data Archiving for SAP Solutions, OpenText Archiving for SAP Solutions, OpenText Document Access for SAP Solutions, and OpenText Extended ECM for SAP Solutions

Hour 15: Answers

1. Given the timeframe, SAP's ASAP methodology might indeed be a good starting point. Go-live is less than a year away, and Human Resources (more precisely, Human Capital Management) is a common module of SAP. However, given ASAP's age, it will probably provide little value beyond simply organizing the initial project around a standard methodology.

2. MNC's lack of SAP technical skills and leadership mandates that a Senior Enterprise Architect familiar with the SAP solution being deployed (and MNC's industry) be contracted from SAP AG, MNC's prime systems integrator, or another third party.

3. Given that MNC has a mature Project Management Office (PMO), it should be assumed that the PMO is adept at creating project plans, contingency plans, communications plans, and escalation processes and is also well-versed in managing quality and risk.

4. The VP of HR's past history with SAP is a major warning sign. Without the VP's buy-in, leadership, and activities aimed at promoting the new solution, the project will almost certainly fail. The VP of HR will naturally be one of several key stakeholders (if not the project sponsor).

5. Considering the situation, you should tell the steering committee that the project needs to be put on hold until the issues outlined in this case study are addressed.

Hour 16: Answers

1. MNC's current IT teams will all need to be staffed and trained specifically for SAP. However, the data center team probably has the necessary knowledge to require only basic staff augmentation.

2. The SAP Basis team is responsible for planning, delivering, and maintaining the technical infrastructure necessary to run SAP.

3. Point the technical teams to SAP's Master Guides for detailed planning and preparation advice (see service.sap.com/instguides).

4. Though MNC's current use of a four-system landscape (development, test, pre-production staging, and production) is admirable, given the IT organization's technical gaps, the business's training gaps, and likely need for a business/functional sandbox as well as a DR solution, it's preferable to deploy a broader system landscape.

5. Two additional DR solutions outside of basic tape backup/restore capabilities include using database log shipping and implementing a DR solution involving hardware-based storage replication technologies.

Hour 17: Answers

1. The transaction code to launch the ABAP Development Workbench is SE80.

2. The name of the development environment for creating SAP Java applications is the SAP NetWeaver Developer Studio (NWDS).

3. The ABAP Development Workbench, Java NWDS, and the SAP Composition Environment represent the three primary toolsets used for SAP development.

4. The ASAP Implementation Roadmap for SAP NetWeaver Enterprise Portal is an example of a Run SAP roadmap.

5. The SAP Project Implementation Guide contains only the customizing steps necessary for the application components your company is implementing.

6. You use the transaction code SPRO to launch the initial screen of the IMG.

Hour 18: Answers

1. Download the installation guides, starting with the Master Guide. Following the installation guides and related notes is probably the most critical step toward a successful installation.

2. Installations are always started from the installation master DVD. From there, you select the software components and system variant.

3. Use SPNego or SAML to implement Single Sign-On.

4. The SAP Software Distribution Center houses all SAP media in downloadable format (http://service.sap.com/swdc).

5. In a pure Microsoft environment, Single Sign-On can be implemented with no extra infrastructure costs. This technology can eliminate many of the problems related to users calling the IT help desk to simply change their user IDs' passwords.

Hour 19: Answers

1. Generally speaking, a business's end users consume Software as a Service (SaaS), developers or programmers consume Platform as a Service (PaaS), and IT professionals consume Infrastructure as a Service (IaaS).

2. With less (or more manageable) risks than a pure public cloud counterpart and greater opportunity to introduce business-enabling innovation than its traditional computing counterpart, hybrid cloud models represent the most reasonable and realistic first step into the cloud (although a good argument may also be made for pursuing a private cloud hosting model).

3. Only one of SAP's applications, Business ByDesign, is delivered through SaaS. Other applications may be cloud-enabled, but this is accomplished primarily through IaaS and secondarily through PaaS.

4. Systems that might be good first movers into the cloud include CRM, end-user training systems, technical sandbox training systems, business demonstration and prototyping systems, any of the systems subject to seasonal spikes, the company's various test or quality assurance systems (and to a lesser extent, the development systems), systems used to maintain data or storage backups, and perhaps MNC's disaster recovery systems.

5. Abstraction, modularity, standardized connectivity, loose coupling, and incremental design are principles that will continue to enable SAP's journey into the cloud.

Hour 20: Answers

1. Use AL08 to view users by application server, including the transactions that each application server is executing.

2. Use SMLG to review real-time how well the system's logon load-balancing mechanism is performing.

3. The Alert Monitor enables you to monitor SAP and non-SAP components, including ABAP stack instances and more.

4. SAP's central monitoring system makes all alerts available in a central CCMS (Computing Center Management System) environment called CEN. CEN runs on every SAP NetWeaver application server and can monitor SAP ABAP, Java, dual-stack, standalone components, and non-SAP components.

5. Use RZ20 to review an entire system's configuration and performance, including color-coded warnings, error messages, and more.

Hour 21: Answers

1. The idea of managing and minimizing risk, particularly the risk of downtime, is usually the most important matter surrounding a major change like an upgrade.

2. No, this advertisement is not accurate. The ad should read, "Project Manager with SAP *upgrade* skills..." The fact that the SAP release is changing indicates this is a functional upgrade, whereas operating system or database changes constitute an OS/DB migration.

3. MNC can later pursue an SAP OS/DB migration to move SAP to a platform that offers a lower TCO or better opportunities to innovate.

4. Most changes to the computing platform are considered updates, changes to SAP functionality are considered upgrades, and completely changing the OS or database release constitutes a migration.

5. MNC should consider a Unicode conversion along with its upgrade.

Hour 22: Answers

1. To learn more about SAP's partners, review the partner search index at www. sap.com/ecosystem/customers/directories/SearchPartner.epx.

2. The banking industry is one of several specifically supported by SAP. With this knowledge, you can conduct your own research into the various business processes and functionality that will be required by MNC and therefore gain an advantage on several fronts—developing your resumé, honing your experience, and ultimately interviewing for a position.

3. With a background in accounting and the ability to pick up technology quickly, you might be a fit for an SAP super user role at MNC's banking affiliate.

4. You might want to pursue Project Management Professional (PMP) certification from the Project Management Institute (PMI).

5. With success as a liaison between the business and IT, you likely have strong communication and networking skills in addition to solid business and technical skills, a combination that will certainly prove to be a valuable asset in your interview with MNC. Ensure you highlight these sought-after qualities.

Hour 23: Answers

1. The number one rule is to manage your own career. Don't passively leave your career, your livelihood, in the hands of another—even your manager.

2. With such a broad background in infrastructure, database administration, training, and project management, you can offer the project four very different yet very useful skills. Frame this as the project's opportunity to fill in its most critical or pressing gaps.

3. Your SAP basis "jack of all trade" position could grow into a specialty focused on SAP Process Integration, SAP NetWeaver Portal, or a similar component.

4. Whether it is to test project-related enhancements to the system or quarterly patches and updates, SAP systems have to be tested to ensure changes are ready for production. This requires people who can create and exercise test scripts either manually or via automated testing tools.

5. The interviewer was likely interested in your thoughts regarding how computing platforms differ in terms of innovations. Further the conversation by discussing the platform's ability to minimize downtime, increase flexibility, and ultimately increase business agility.

Hour 24: Answers

1. It probably makes sense to join ASUG to find out what other SAP customers are doing in the SAP Financials arena.

2. If you had enough lead time, you could have worked with a colleague or customer to develop a session for the conference. With your background and expertise in managing financials projects and a compelling customer case study, your expertise would bode well for being selected to copresent a session. In turn, the conference provider would cover your airfare, hotel, the conference fee, and perhaps other costs.

3. You can find the top 100 or so books covering SAP development topics by searching through Amazon, Barnes and Noble, or similar online sites. Sort by date to find current titles or by best-selling status to find titles that other people are actually buying. Some of the popular SAP sites offer their perspectives on useful titles, as well.

4. It is a good idea to use an Internet search engine such as Bing, Google, or Yahoo! to search for new SAP sites on a periodic basis to keep up-to-date with the latest SAP information available. Be sure to visit SAP's SDN and main website page frequently, as well.

5. As a financial analyst, you will want to attend the Financials Conference hosted by WIS. SAPPHIRE NOW could also be useful to learn about the latest SAP products in the financials area. On the other hand, if your goal is networking, ASUG is ideal for connecting with other financials experts face to face.

APPENDIX B

SAP Acronyms and Common Terms

To help you navigate the world of SAP, this appendix includes acronyms and commonly used terms found in this book and throughout the SAP community. The goal is not to define these acronyms and terms, but to help you understand how and when to use them correctly and, therefore, credibly.

Acronyms

ABAP/4—Advanced Business Application Programming/4 (SAP)

ACL—Access Control List

ACC—Adaptive Computing Controller (SAP)

AD—Active Directory (Microsoft)

AFS—Apparel and Footwear Solution (SAP)

AIX—Advanced Interactive eXecutive (IBM OS)

ALE—Application Link Enabling (SAP)

AM—Asset Management (SAP ERP module)

API—Application Programming Interface

APO—Advanced Planner and Optimizer (SAP SCM component)

ASAP—Accelerated SAP (SAP methodology)

ASCS—ABAP Central Services (SAP)

ASUG—America's SAP Users' Group (SAP)

ATR—Availability Through Redundancy

B2B—Business to Business

B2C—Business to Consumer

BAPI—Business Application Programming Interface

BC—Basis (SAP ERP module)

BCS—Business Connectivity Services (Microsoft)

BDC—Batch Data Communication (SAP)

BDC—Business Data Connector (Microsoft)

BEx—Business Explorer (SAP BW user interface)

BOBJ—BusinessObjects (SAP)

BSP—Business Server Page (SAP)

BW—Business Warehouse (SAP)

C/S—Client/Server (three-tiered architecture)

CA—Cross Application (SAP products atop modules)

CAF—Composite Application Framework (SAP NetWeaver)

CATS—Cross Application Time Sheet (SAP)

CCMS—Computing Center Management System (SAP)

CE—Composition Environment (SAP NetWeaver)

CEN—CENtral monitoring system (SAP)

CI—Central Instance (SAP)

CO—Controlling (SAP ERP module)

CoE—Center of Excellence (or Expertise)

CPIC—Common Programming Interface Communication (SAP)

CRC—Content Repository Content (SAP)

CRM—Customer Relationship Management (SAP component)

CTO—Change and Transport Organizers (SAP)

CUA—Central User Administration (SAP)

DB—Database

DBA—Database Administrator

DBMS—Database Management System

DDIC—Data DICtionary

DEV—Development (SAP system landscape)

DIA—DIAlog (SAP work process)

DNS—Domain Name Server

DR—Disaster Recovery (or Recoverability)

EA—Enterprise Architecture

EAF—Enterprise Architecture Framework (SAP)

EBP—Enterprise Buyer Professional (SAP SRM component)

eCATT—Extended Computer Aided Test Tool (SAP)

ECC—ERP Central Component (SAP component)

EDI—Electronic Data Interchange

EP—Enterprise Portal (SAP; replaced by NetWeaver Portal)

ERP—Enterprise Resource Planning (SAP component)

ESA—Enterprise Services Architecture (SAP)

ESC—Enterprise Services Community (SAP)

ESI—Enterprise Services Inventory (SAP)

ESOA—Enterprise Service Oriented Architecture (SAP)

ESR—Enterprise Services Repository (SAP)

ESS—Employee Self Service (generic and SAP)

FDA—Food and Drug Administration (US)

GRC—Governance, Risk, and Compliance (generic and SAP)

GUI—Graphical User Interface (generic, and SAP)

HA—High Availability

HCM—Human Capital Management (SAP ERP module)

HIPPA—Health Insurance Portability and Accountability Act (US)

HTML—HyperText Markup Language

HTTP—Hypertext Transfer Protocol

IaaS—Infrastructure as a Service

IAC—Internet Application Component (SAP)

IASA—International Association of Software Architects

IC—Interaction Center (SAP)

ICM—Internet Communication Manager (SAP)

iDOC—Intermediate Document (SAP)

IE—Internet Explorer (Microsoft)

iFrame—Information Frame (SAP)

IIS—Internet Information Server (Microsoft)

IM—Investment Management (SAP ERP module)

IMG—Implementation Guide (SAP)

IP—Internet Protocol

IPC—Internet Pricing Configurator (SAP)

IS—Industry Solution (SAP add-ons to components)

ISV—Independent Software Vendor

IT—Information Technology

ITAR—International Traffic in Arms Regulations (US)

ITS—Internet Transaction Server (SAP)

iView—Information View (SAP)

J2EE—Java 2 Enterprise Edition

J2SDK—Java 2 Software Development Kit

JDK—Java Development Kit

JRE—Java Runtime Environment

JSP—Java Server Page

KM—Knowledge Management

KW—Knowledge Warehouse (SAP component)

LAN—Local Area Network

LO—Logistics (SAP ERP module)

LOB—Line of Business

LSMW—Legacy System Migration Workbench (SAP)

MDM—Master Data Management (SAP component)

MDMP—Multiple Display/Multiple Processing (SAP)

MI—Mobile Infrastructure (SAP)

MM—Materials Management (SAP ERP module)

MMC—Microsoft Management Console

MOF—Microsoft Operations Framework

MOSS—Microsoft Office SharePoint Server

MSCS—Microsoft Cluster Service (or Server)

MSS—Manager Self Service (generic and SAP)

MTBF—Mean Time Between Failure

NAS—Network Attached Storage

NIC—Network Interface Card

NLB—Network Load Balancing (Microsoft)

NWDS—NetWeaver Developer Studio (Java version for SAP)

ODBC—Open Database Connectivity

OLAP—Online Analytical Processing

OLE—Object Linking and Embedding

OLTP—Online Transaction Processing

OS—Operating System

OSS—Online Service System (SAP)

PaaS—Platform as a Service

PAM—Product Availability Matrix (SAP)

PAYG—Pay as You Go

PCI—Payment Card Industry

PDK—Platform Development Kit

PI—Process Integration (SAP NetWeaver component)

PLM—Product Lifecycle Management (SAP component)

PM—Plant Maintenance (SAP ERP module)

PMBOK—Project Management Body Of Knowledge

PMI—Project Management Institute

PMO—Project Management Office

PMP—Project Management Professional (certification)

PP—Production Planning (SAP ERP module)

PRD—Production (SAP system landscape)

PS—Project System (SAP ERP module)

QAS—Quality Assurance (SAP system landscape)

QM—Quality Management (SAP ERP module)

QoS—Quality of Service

R/2—Release 2 (SAP IBM Mainframe OLTP Product)

R/3—Release 3 (SAP Client/Server OLTP Product)

RAC—Real Application Clusters (Oracle)

RAID—Redundant Arrays of Independent (or Inexpensive) Disks

RAM—Random Access Memory

RDBMS—Relational Database Management System

RFC—Remote Function Call (SAP)

RICEFS—Reports, Interfaces, Conversions, Enhancements, Forms, and SAPscripts

ROI—Return on Investment

RPM—RPM Package Manager (a recursive Linux acronym)

RPO—Recovery Point Objective (disaster recovery term)

RTO—Recovery Time Objective (disaster recovery term)

SaaS—Software as a Service

SAML—Security Assertion Markup Language

SAN—Storage Area Network

SAP—*Systeme, Anwendungen und Produkte in der Datenverarbeitung*, or Systems, Applications, and Products in Data Processing (original American translation), or Systems, Applications, and Products (a later, simplified translation)

SAPGUI—SAP Graphical User Interface

SCM—Supply Chain Management (SAP component)

SD—Sales and Distribution (SAP ERP module)

SDK—Software Development Kit

SDM—Software Deployment Manager (SAP)

SDN—SAP Developer Network

SFA—Sales Force Automation

SID—System Identifier (SAP and Microsoft)

SIG—Special Interest Group

SLA—Service Level Agreement

SLD—System Landscape Directory (SAP)

SMB—Small and Medium Business (generic)

SM—Service Management

SME—Small/Medium Enterprise (SAP's equivalent of SMB)

SNC—Secure Network Communications (SAP)

SOA—Service Oriented Architecture

SOAP—Simple Object Access Protocol

SolMan—Solution Manager (SAP)

SPNego—Simple and Protected GSSAPI Negotiation Mechanism

SPO—SPOol (SAP work process)

SPOF—Single Point of Failure

SQL—Structured Query Language

SQL2K—SQL Server 2000 (Microsoft database)

SQL2K5—SQL Server 2005 (Microsoft database)

SQL2K8—SQL Server 2008 (Microsoft database)

SRM—Supplier Relationship Management (SAP component)

TCO—Total Cost of Ownership

TCP—Transmission Control Protocol

TOGAF—The Open Group Architecture Framework

TPC—Transaction processing Performance Council

TREX—Text Retrieval and EXtraction (SAP)

TSO—Technical Support Organization

TST—Test (SAP system landscape)

UDDI—Universal Description, Discovery, and Integration

UME—User Management Engine (SAP)

URL—Uniform Resource Locator (in Internet World Wide Web)

V1—Update (SAP work process)

V2—Update2 (SAP work process)

VLDB—Very Large Database

VM—Virtual Machine

VPN—Virtual Private Network

WAN—Wide Area Network

WebAS—Web Application Server (old SAP term, replaced by SAP NetWeaver Application Server)

WF—Workflow (generic and SAP)

WP—Work Process (SAP)

WSDL—Web Services Description Language

XaaS—Anything as a Service

XI—SAP Exchange Infrastructure (old component; replaced by SAP NetWeaver PI)

XML—eXtensible Markup Language

Common Terms

Accelerated Solutions

Adaptive Computing Controller

Authorization Concept

Cloud Services Model

Component

Enhancement Package

Go-Live

Guided Procedures

MaxAttention

Migration

Mobile Business—SAP Mobile Procurement

Mobile Business—SAP Solutions for Mobile Business

Mobile Sales

Module

SAP Aerospace and Defense

SAP Automotive

SAP Banking

SAP Basis

SAP Business All-in-One

SAP Business ByDesign

SAP Business Intelligence

SAP Business Maps

SAP BusinessObjects

SAP Business One

SAP Business Server Pages (BSPs)

SAP Business Suite

SAP BW ODS

SAP Chemicals

SAP Composite Application Framework

SAP EarlyWatch Alert

SAP Employee Self-Service

SAP Engineering, Construction & Operations

SAP Enterprise Resource Planning

SAP Enterprise Services Architecture

SAP ERP Corporate Services

SAP ERP Financials

SAP ERP Human Capital Management

SAP ERP Operations

SAP Event Manager

SAP Financials

SAP Global Trade Services

SAP GoingLive Check

SAP GTS

SAP Healthcare

SAP Higher Education & Research

SAP High Tech

SAP Industrial Machinery & Components

SAP Insurance

SAP Interaction Center

SAP Java Connector

SAP Knowledge Management

SAP Learning Solution

SAP Logistics Execution System

SAP Manufacturing

SAP Marketplace

SAP Master Data Management

SAP MaxAttention

SAP Media

SAP Mill Products

SAP Mobile Asset Management

SAP Mobile Direct Store Delivery

SAP Mobile Infrastructure

SAP Mobile Sales

SAP Mobile Service

SAP Mobile Time and Travel

SAP NetWeaver

SAP NetWeaver Application Server

SAP NetWeaver Business Intelligence

SAP NetWeaver Composite Application Framework

SAP NetWeaver Composition Environment

SAP NetWeaver Developer Studio

SAP NetWeaver Master Data Management

SAP NetWeaver Mobile

SAP NetWeaver Portal

SAP NetWeaver Process Integration

SAP NetWeaver Solution Manager

SAP Oil & Gas

SAP Pharmaceuticals

SAP Product Lifecycle Management

SAP Public Sector

SAP R/2

SAP R/3

SAP R/3 Enterprise

SAP Retail

SAP Service Marketplace

SAP Solution Manager

SAP Strategic Enterprise Management

SAP Supplier Relationship Management

SAP Supply Chain Management

SAP Support Package

SAP Telecommunications

SAP Utilities

SAP Warehouse Management

SAP Web Application Server

Single Sign-On

SPAM Update

Support Package Manager

Three-Tier Client/Server Architecture

Unicode

Upgrade

Upgrade Assistant

WebDAV

Web Dynpro

Web Service

Workflow

xApps

Index

REGISTER

THIS PRODUCT

informit.com/register

Register the Addison-Wesley, Exam Cram, Prentice Hall, Que, and Sams products you own to unlock great benefits.

To begin the registration process, simply go to **informit.com/register** to sign in or create an account. You will then be prompted to enter the 10- or 13-digit ISBN that appears on the back cover of your product.

Registering your products can unlock the following benefits:

- Access to supplemental content, including bonus chapters, source code, or project files.
- A coupon to be used on your next purchase.

Registration benefits vary by product. Benefits will be listed on your Account page under Registered Products.

About InformIT — THE TRUSTED TECHNOLOGY LEARNING SOURCE

INFORMIT IS HOME TO THE LEADING TECHNOLOGY PUBLISHING IMPRINTS Addison-Wesley Professional, Cisco Press, Exam Cram, IBM Press, Prentice Hall Professional, Que, and Sams. Here you will gain access to quality and trusted content and resources from the authors, creators, innovators, and leaders of technology. Whether you're looking for a book on a new technology, a helpful article, timely newsletters, or access to the Safari Books Online digital library, InformIT has a solution for you.

THE TRUSTED TECHNOLOGY LEARNING SOURCE

Addison-Wesley | Cisco Press | Exam Cram
IBM Press | Que | Prentice Hall | Sams

SAFARI BOOKS ONLINE

FREE Online Edition

Your purchase of **Sams Teach Yourself SAP in 24 Hours** includes access to a free online edition for 45 days through the Safari Books Online subscription service. Nearly every Smas book is available online through Safari Books Online, along with more than 5,000 other technical books and videos from publishers such as Addison-Wesley Professional, Cisco Press, Exam Cram, IBM Press, O'Reilly, Prentice Hall, and Que.

SAFARI BOOKS ONLINE allows you to search for a specific answer, cut and paste code, download chapters, and stay current with emerging technologies.

Activate your FREE Online Edition at
www.informit.com/safarifree

> **STEP 1:** Enter the coupon code: GEAJAZG

> **STEP 2:** New Safari users, complete the brief registration form.
> Safari subscribers, just log in.

If you have difficulty registering on Safari or accessing the online edition, please e-mail customer-service@safaribooksonline.com